Horses and Horse Sense

The Practical Science
of Horse Husbandry

Horses and Horse Sense

The Practical Science
of Horse Husbandry

James Blakely

Republic of Texas Press

DEDICATION

To the memory of James Perry "Hoss" Blakely, 1956-1979
semper fidelis

The following illustrations were drawn by Tom Stallman: Figures 1-1 through 1-15, 3-4, 3-5, 3-6, 3-7, and 4-1.

The following illustrations were drawn by George Taylor, Jr.: 1-16, 1-19, 1-20, 1-22, 1-23, 1-29, 1-32, 1-33, 3-3, 3-8, 3-9, 4-2, 6-7, 6-12, 7-1, 7-2, 7-6, 9-2, 9-3, 9-5, 9-10, 10-1, 11-1 through 11-6, 12-1 through 12-4.

Library of Congress Cataloging-in-Publication Data

Blakely, James, 1934-
 Horses and horse sense : the practical science of horse husbandry
/ James Blakely.
  p. cm.
 Originally published: Reston, Va. : Reston Pub. Co., c1981.
 Includes bibliographical references and index.
 ISBN 1-55622-483-4 (pbk.)
 1. Horses. I. Title.
SF285.B64 1996
636.1--dc20   96-13548
                                                               CIP

Printed in the United States of America

ISBN 1-55622-483-4
10 9 8 7 6 5 4 3 2 1
9610

All inquiries for volume purchases of this book should be addressed to Wordware Publishing, Inc. at 1506 Capital Ave., Plano, Texas 75074. Telephone inquiries may be made by calling (972) 423-0090.

Contents

Preface

This book was written for the student of horse husbandry. Its aim is to simplify the task of conveying essential, practical information to the expert or beginner in quest of knowledge. It is not written to impress other writers or animal scientists. Simplicity, both in style of writing and in the language of the horse world, is the cornerstone that supports the technical aspects of this endeavor. An attempt has not been made to write down to a lower level, but to express the world of husbandry in such a way that even the beginning horse enthusiast can understand and appreciate.

The basic information contained in this book can be used by the highly trained specialist as a foundation upon which can be built, with language as technical as he or she likes, an ever-expanding expertise. The value of this book is that it may be used as a self-study program of learning for a solid beginning, or, with the guiding hand of a knowledgeable instructor, it can be expanded as far as the instructor's capabilities will allow. Valuable time, in either case, will be saved through the use of the easily understood basics contained in these pages.

Much of the excitement of learning is often counteracted by the use of unnecessary technical terms and the lack of suitable illustrations. It is the intent of this text to provide a condensed, highly-illustrated, easy-to-read version of the wonders, as well as the technical aspects, of horse husbandry, while keeping in mind the needs of the instructor concerning visual aids. It is further recognized that the instructor is the cementing factor in welding together the body of knowledge which only he can assemble in the classroom. This text is intended to serve as a supply line, filling capable hands with raw materials for further refinement. The author's approach is simple and direct, aiming

- to provide teaching aids and resource materials for the *classroom teacher*.
- to provide a basic foundation of knowledge and appreciation of horse husbandry for the *general public*.
- to provide reference materials and illustrations for *the student*.

This book is the result of suggestions from active horse specialists who have urged the author to emphasize the practical aspects of horse science while still following the intent of technical advice.

James Blakely

1
Origin and History of the Horse

Man in his mysterious quest for knowledge has sought unceasingly to satisfy his curiosity about the origins of life. Most of earth's creatures are glimpsed in the past through a veil of secrecy. The horse is no exception.

For many, it is sufficient to know that the horse is a gift from the heavens and a blessed creator. A Bedouin legend states, "And God took a handful of southerly wind, blew his breath over it and created the horse."

The Koran says that Allah created the Arabian from a handful of south wind, saying, "Thy name shall be Arabian, and virtue bound into the hair of thy forelock. I have made thy master thy friend. I have given thee the power of flight without wings."

Christians would point to the scripture, "And God said, let the earth bring forth the living creature after his kind, cattle, and creeping thing and beast of the earth after his kind: and it was so."

The truth is that no mortal mind can know the exact beginning.

There are two theories of the origin of the horse, both backed by scientific evidence, both subject to a great deal of faith and speculation. Until recently only the theory of evolution proposed by Charles Darwin in 1859 was given credit for close, scientific scrutiny. More recently, the theory of Special Creation has also received wide attention and scientific compilation of impressive evidence. Actually three positions on the two theories are popularly taken on the origin of the horse:

1. Evolution—the horse simply evolved from previous, more primitive life forms, which originally sprang from nonliving substances.

2. Theistic Evolution—the Creator, or God, used an evolutionary process to develop the horse-like creature we know today.

3. Special Creation—this theory, which is gaining wide acceptance through scientific evaluations, holds that all life was created fully formed, with the ability for significant variation, but without the capacity to mutate into a completely different kind of animal.

Since Theistic Evolution is a combination of the views of the other two, only the twin theories of Evolution and Special Creation will be covered.

THE THEORY OF EVOLUTION

Fossil remains through the many, many centuries have given us some clue to how evolution may have taken place. Slowly the picture does begin to develop; and strangely enough, although horses were unknown to the American continent at the time of its discovery by Columbus, the horse, it is thought, had its origin somewhere in the central part of what is now the United States.

Basing their speculations on fossil remains found of a horselike animal with four functional toes and one splint on the front feet, and three functional toes and one splint on the hind feet, some scientists believe there is a five-toed, pre-horse fossil, remains of which have yet to be found. Using logic and scientific analysis, the horse "in the beginning" goes back to the Paleocene epoch, the "advent of mammals," which occurred about 71 million years ago. This pre-horse or original ancestor of modern day horses was a far cry from what we see today. The theory is that a curious little four-legged mammal (Fig. 1-1), standing seven or eight inches high at the shoulder, developed around the Rocky Mountain area of the United States. Its weight might have been that of our common house cat of today, its body covering was part fur, part hair, and it possessed three characteristics that would alter the course of history:

1. The bones in its legs were separate and capable of elongation.

2. Each of its feet had a pad and five toes with the middle toe being somewhat stronger.

3. Its forty-four teeth were arranged in an unusual manner: sharp teeth in front progressing back an open space, followed by grinding molars.

It lived in a marsh-like environment, browsing on leaves and marsh plants, and used the toes to distribute weight. Its teeth were not suitable for grazing on tough, coarse grass and few predators then existed

FIGURE 1-1. Artist's conception of the hypothetical pre-horse, fossil remains of which have not been found. Speculation has it that this earliest ancestor of the horse had five toes with claws, was covered by part fur and part hair, and stood 6 to 7 inches high at the shoulder.

to stimulate modification by the "survival of the fittest" process of natural selection. A natural selectivity favored those animals that were larger, stronger, faster, and genetically capable of modification of body design. Although no fossil remains have yet been found of this hypothetical creature, some think that it will one day be found. It could possibly be given the name Paleohippus (from the Paleocene epoch + hippus, greek for horse).

FIRST KNOWN HORSE— EOHIPPUS

Approximately 13 million years after the pre-horse existed, the first "known" ancestors of the horse evolved. Hundreds of skeletons of this small creature were laid down in rock so that its skeletal form is well known today although there is disagreement over its superficial appearance (Fig. 1-2). It was a small creature, no bigger than a fox, ranging from 10 to 18 inches tall at the shoulder and had four toes on its foreleg plus a splint (theory has it that this is a remnant of a toe from Paleohippus) and three toes plus a splint (Fig. 1-7) on its hind legs. This small mammal existed during the Eocene Epoch (58 million years ago) and has been given the name Eohippus or Dawnhorse (since the dawn of time). It lived in a damp, hot jungle of swamp, cyprus, and mammoth trees. Here it fed on leaves and roamed over boggy ground. Remains of this small sized, multi-toed horse have been found in such places as the Wasatch Range in Utah and in the Wind River Basin in Wyoming (as early as 1870).

FIGURE 1-2. (Left) Eohippus or the "Dawn Horse," originally called Hyracotherium when first discovered in Europe, is the first ancestor of which fossil remains have been found. It was no larger than a fox. Note the four toes on the front feet and three toes on the rear feet. (Right) The same fossil remains were the basis for this reconstruction of Hyracotherium which scientists opposed to evolutionary theories claim was not an ancestor of the horse.

FIGURE 1-4. Merychippus, with its erect mane, sleek three-toed arrangement, and greater size (40 inches at withers), appeared as a totally new adaptation.

limbs are the nearest approach to our present day horses. This horse also spread into South America as well as Asia, Europe, and Africa.

FINAL MODEL— EQUUS

Finally, about 2 million years ago, the horse as we know it today, Equus caballus, emerged as a rather large, magnificent creature (Fig. 1-6). About 8 thousand years ago, Equus became extinct in North America and was not to return until the Spanish brought horses to the new world in the 1400s.

Starting with the mysterious "undiscovered" five-toed ancestor, the horse showed great persistance and adaptability to changes on the earth, adhering to those mutations which proved to have the greatest chance for future survival (Fig. 1-7). Eohippus made its contribution to Merychippus, the first "horselike" in appearance, and Pliohippus contributed the single hoof. Dozens of variations died out because they

FIGURE 1-5. Pliohippus, the first truly one-toed horse, about 46 inches at the withers, was the nearest approach to modern day Equus.

did not contribute to the final form. But the horse, with its amazing adapability to changes in climate and predators, did survive. It was merely the beginning of a long and illustrious history.

The horse deserted its ancestral home in North America, or died out, or was driven out, for unknown reasons, perhaps because of climatic changes, famine, or a rampant disease. By the year 6000 B.C., it was extinct in the western hemisphere. Prior to that time, horses were magnetically pulled by some mysterious force westward in their subconscious quest for survival. Because of the development of the herding instinct and the mobility of horses who would sometimes cover 25 miles in a day, some herds gradually emerged from North America to travel across the Bering Straits to Asia. This was not as remarkable as it might seem in the light of current day geography. During this time the Bering Sea, which separated Asia from America, became nonexistant. Great glaciers used up so much ocean water during this era that the level of the sea dropped 300 feet, eliminating the sea altogether and in its place a massive land bridge emerged more than 1,000 miles

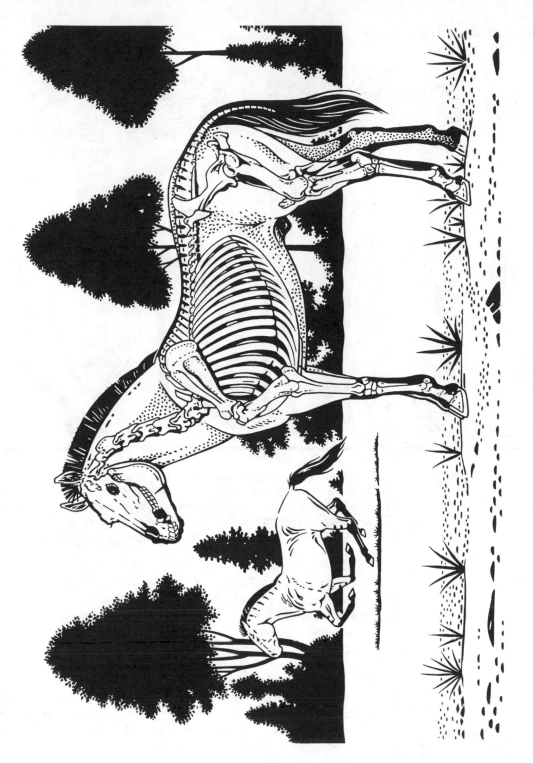

FIGURE 1-6. The skeleton of Equus is made up of some 210 bones.

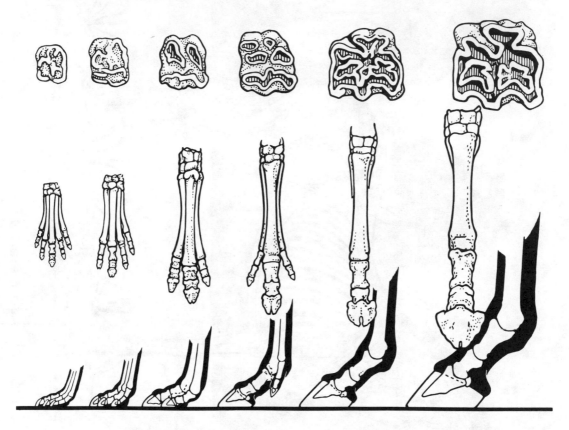

FIGURE 1-7. Feet and teeth adaptability was likely the key to evolutionary survival. As the horse changed from hypothetical Paleohippus, a forest browser, to a plains animal needing speed to escape predators, the number of toes was reduced. The change of diet from soft forest browse to abrasive grasses which needed grinding resulted in ridges of enamel on the teeth.

wide. It could acutally be referred to as an isthmus joining the two continents. Herds of horses could walk with security from Asia to America or the other way. We do not know why horses migrated into Asia but evolutionists think that this movement was the reason for survival of the species. Although they became extinct in North America under mysterious circumstances, the speculation is that they wandered into Mongolia to develop into wild horses that became ancestors of the modern animal. The Arabian, Percheron, Clydesdale, Appaloosa, Zebra, Ass, and all equines had their beginning in North America. These beginnings, however, were not without modification by man. And eventually, in countries like Spain, its very name would take on the meaning of gentleman. A caballero, gentleman, or "man of the horse," was taken from the designation Equus caballus.

CRITICISMS OF THE THEORY OF EVOLUTION

Critics of the evolutionary thesis point out that fossil remains are difficult, if not impossible, to use in proving that such an animal evolved from another organism. Subjective analysis of the data could be used to prove whatever theory one decided to accept. For instance, the evolutionists argue that a three-toed horse evolved over millions of years into a one-toed horse. Yet, there is evidence that both the three-toed and one-toed horses existed at the very same time, based on fossil findings. Opposition scientists do not doubt the existence of these animals, but argue that they were simply different kinds of beasts, some of which died out due to a variety of causes. Fig. 1-2 also illustrates how widely views can vary based on the same evidence. Using the same fossil remains evolutionists imagine reconstruction of the Eohippus to appear horse-like while the opposition imagines it to appear more rabbit-like and point to the hyrax, an animal living today, strikingly similar to ancient Hyracotherium, the name originally used in Europe for Eohippus. It is not difficult to see how both evolutionists and creationists have developed their theories from this original point of disagreement. Hyracotherium (and the living hyrax) and Eohippus are the same size. Both have four toes on the front feet and three on the hind limbs. Both have broad, heavy, hoof-like nails. Their tooth structure is the same. The behavior pattern of the living hyrax is the same as that proposed for Eohippus, a shy creature inhabiting the edge of open areas, easily frightened back to protective cover. Creationists feel that the Eohippus has little if any resemblance to the horse, but it is remarkably like the modern hyrax in so many ways that it might be a living variation of the extinct Hyracotherium.

Another strong criticism is the theory that the horse evolved from a five-, four-, three-toed individual into a one-toed horse. This theory is widely accepted and, until recent years, seldom doubted. However, fossil evidence in South America could be used as a guide to suppose that a one-toed, horse-like animal gave rise to a three-toed horse. This is the exact opposite of the supposed sequence of events that occurred in North American horses. However, evolutionists have never suggested that this even took place. Perhaps it is because the three-toed to one-toed sequence in North America had become so popularized that no one dared suggest the reverse procedure.

No transitional forms between the three-toed and one-toed horses are found in fossil remains, which some claim is convincing evidence that these animals were similar but unrelated.

A further point of confusion occurs in some geological formations which contain fossil remains of a primitive species that supposedly was the forerunner of a more advanced horse. The geological formations, according to specialists in that area, have been declared younger than formations containing advanced fossil findings. This presents a serious argument against the validity of linking different types of animals together.

Finally, even the theory of predators catching the slow, weak, or sickly animals, thus hastening evolution through survival of the fittest, has been disputed. Recent studies with predators indicate that wolves and lions have little trouble preying on any animal selected. In fact, the predators consistently avoided weak, sick, or slow prey, preferring the choicest of selections. One study concluded that predators select only from the top of their food sources and chance determined which animals of this group survived.

THE THEORY OF SPECIAL CREATION

The only other theory of origin which logically deals with the known laws of science, natural phenomena, and the geological record is the concept of special creation. This theory is the belief that all life forms were created by God and designed to reproduce according to their "kind." The biblical "kind" is not necessarily the same as genus and species. The determining factor of a "kind," mentioned in Old Testament writings, was not the physical appearance of the creature, but its reproductive capability. If two animals could breed and produce an offspring, they were of the same "kind." These creative "kinds" are not subject to unlimited change as required by Darwin's theory of evolution. That is, a fish cannot evolve into an amphibian, later a reptile, still later a mammal. Special Creation does not allow for the possibility of a small, multi-toed, rodent-like creature evolving into a horse. The fact of diversification, however, is recognized. Diversification means allowing for considerable variation in the outward characteristics of the offspring (Horses, Zebras, Asses, etc.). However, the "kind" of the offspring is not subject to change. An example is drawn from the cattle "kind." It is reasonably supposed that all cattle today came from a prehistoric ox, considerably different from cattle of today, but the hundreds of breeds of cattle have all been developed from this one "kind."

Special creation views the origin of the horse as follows. In the beginning, God created the original equid, referred to in this text as *Pro-equus*. This animal was the true horse in every sense of the word. As he reproduced according to his "kind," the principle of diversification began to work producing variations, as provided for and limited by his genetic boundaries in each generation. Because of the horse's tremendous capacity for variation within the fixed "kind," early horse was able to adapt quickly to various climates and conditions. This capacity for rapid adaption provided the animal with a tremendous survival advantage, and only superficial change in appearance.

Pro-equus lived before the great global catastrophy popularized through the story of Noah and the Ark. Evidence exists world-wide to indicate that a great flood did occur. All forms of nonaquatic life perished, including many of the variations of the horse that lived before the flood. The remains of these horses are found in fossil strata today and are recognized along with various nonhorse creatures like the four- and three-toed examples previously discussed. These extinct horses are erroneously used to demonstrate the evolution of the one-toed horse from the many-toed, nonhorse creatures.

Such a gigantic, prolonged flood aided by great global ocean currents could have resulted in the remains of these animals being distributed in sedimentary rocks the world over. Tremendous shifting of the sediment by the global waters could also explain why fossil remains are found at various depths. Unlike the theory of evolution, however, special creation suggests that all these fossil remains were laid down at approximately the same time. Further convincing evidence of the great flood theory is found in geological probes of the earth's surface. The Pre-Cambrian layer is a point beneath the earth's surface where all fossil remains abruptly end. No fossils have ever been found below this Pre-Cambrian layer. Creation scientists point to this fact as evidence of a living world "created" in a short time. They maintain that if evolution had taken place from nonliving matter, fossil remains would be laid down in gradually accumulating numbers proceeding upward from the Pre-Cambrian layer. Instead, fossils of many types of animals appear in large numbers as if they were suddenly made to predetermined specifications. The great flood destroyed all nonaquatic life forms except those chosen for salvation aboard Noah's Ark.

After the waters receded, the only horses to survive and repopulate the earth were those carried by Noah on the ark. They began their exodus into the post-world from the mountains of Arrarrat in Turkey where the ark came to rest. It is at this point that the evolutionary theory and special creation theory can merge without serious conflict. Fig. 1-8 illustrates the special creation theory and how this diversification continues into basic types of equines which have since developed into the various "kinds" we know today.

Special creation contends that the horses that disembarked from the ark gave rise to the asses and zebras. From the asses developed the donkey, burro, onager, kiang, kulan, and khar. The horses formed the basic primitive types from which our modern domestic breeds have been developed and it is here that the evolutionists and creationists come closer to agreement. Creationists generally agree that primitive types of horses such as those discussed in the Ewaldt theory following (Figures 1-12 to 1-15) are plausible decendants from Noah's ark's horses.

Despite the rich diversity of superficial changes between the ass, horse, and zebra, creationists insist that they are all of the same biblical

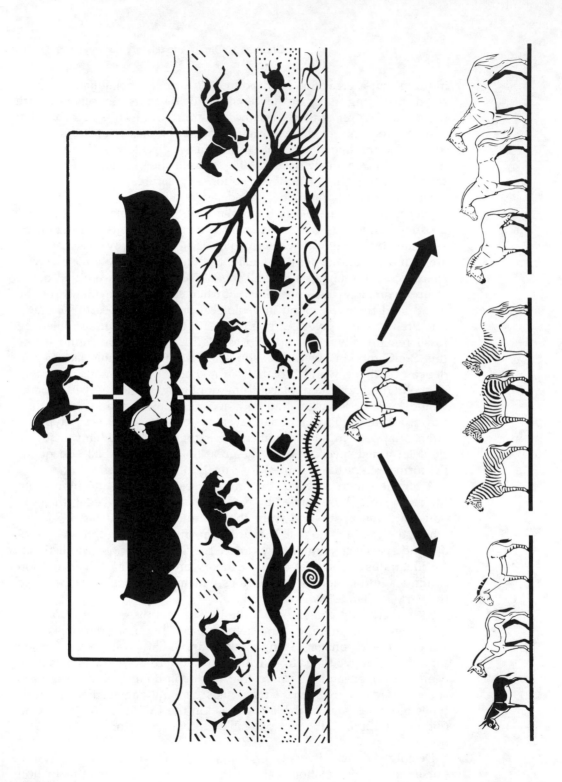

FIGURE 1-8. Special Creation scientists maintain that there is overwhelming evidence of a worldwide flood, proof enough to support the contention that a Supreme Being created original man and animals fully formed, including the horse, and preserved the chosen ones aboard Noah's Ark.

The silhouette at top center represents "pro-equus," the original created horse. Lateral arrows indicate different types of horses that developed from gene variations in "pro-equus." These horses perished in the great flood catastrophe and were deposited in flood sediments along with horse-like, unrelated creatures (note the 3-toed merychippus type, right of center just under the ark). The center line extending straight through the center of the Ark of Noah represents descendants of pro-equus carried aboard the ark that did survive the catastrophe and are ancestors of today's equines, including horse "kinds," from lower left to right, the Spanish-Jack Burro, Kiang, Somalia land Ass, Selous Zebra, Mountain Zebra, Quagga (recently extinct), Norse horse, Arab, and Turk. Today's horse breeds stem from further variations arising from the group in the lower right.

kind, each can cross with the other and are not evolving into other species. Thus, creation scientists hold that the Darwinian concept of evolution has not taken place.

CRITICISMS OF THE SPECIAL CREATION THEORY

Opposition scientists point to fossil findings of such striking resemblance to horses that the logical mind finds difficulty in rejecting the idea of evolution while data resulting from biblical scriptures is supposedly subject to mythical distortion and hardly a match for modern scientific evaluation.

The pendulum of public opinion periodically swings toward puritanical views on a variety of theories. It appears that the citizens and leaders of the world in general are currently shifting their values in the direction of theological teachings, which evolutionists may claim is emotional over-reaction.

Through the use of radioactive isotopes and half-life calculations, it has been determined that the earth is many millions of years old as opposed to the biblical theory that it is only thousands of years old. Sufficient statistical correlations between radioactive dating of excavated materials and documented time of occurrences has led opposing scientists to speculate a 95–99% probability of accuracy, while creationism heretofore has been a matter of faith.

For a theory to truly qualify as scientific, it must be supported by events that can be observed, it must be useful in predicting the outcome of future natural phenomena, and it must be subject to some experiment, the failure of which would disprove the theory. Special Creation fails to meet all three criteria, as does the theory of evolution.

While much argument can be generated regarding the exact origin of the horse, the most plausible theories have been set forth in this discussion. The horse has always carried men to conflict over differences of opinion. It cares not from whence it came or who is right, wishing merely to do the will of its master for some small reward. Perhaps the tale of two horsemen who experienced a difference of opinion will serve as a guideline to those who would argue with the twin theories used in this text based on archaeological excavations. Two brothers, General William R. Terrill, a graduate of West Point, declined to follow his state in secession during the Civil War and was killed at Perryville, Kentucky leading a federal brigade. General James B. Terrill, his brother, who remained loyal to confederate forces was killed at the Battle of Bethesda Church, Virginia. When the Civil War closed, their father brought their remains back to Virginia and buried them in a common grave. The monument erected explained his sorrow and bewilderment over the reason for the conflict. The inscription on the stone reads: "This monument erected by their father. God alone knows which was right."

**DEVELOP-
MENT OF
TYPES AND
BREEDS**

Whether it took the biblical "thousands" or the evolutionist's "millions" of years for the horse to evolve into Equus caballus, it took man little less than 3,000 years to improve dramatically upon the great scheme of the Author of Life. When or if the ancestors of horses came across the Bering Straits, they divided into four main groups: (1) the horse in Europe and Asia; (2) the wild Ass in North Africa (forerunners of today's donkey); (3) the Onager, Kiang and Chigetai (wild asses) of Asia (Fig. 1-9); and (4) the Zebra (Fig. 1-10) of Southeast Africa. Although the modern members of the horse family are zoologically so similar that they are often placed in the same genus (Equus), they can currently be grouped more clearly as zebras, asses, and true horses.

Opinions vary as to how the horse of modern day developed from these four groups but two schools of thought remain. Some authorities maintain that all horses descended from a type identical to Przewalskii's horse (Fig. 1-11), the oldest horse still in existence (Equus przewalskii). Ironically, this horse was discovered only in the last century. In 1879, the Russian captain Nikolai Mikailovoch Przewalskii sighted the horse as he traveled through the remote valleys of Mongolia. The modern Przewalskii (also known as the Taki, Tachi, or Tag) resembles many of the animals appearing in the cave paintings at Lascaux, France. It is believed by students of the Przewalskii school of thought to be a direct or collateral ancestor of all living breeds. The Przewalskii horse typically stands 12 to 14 hands high and has a dun (yellowish) coloring. It has a light colored muzzle and short upstanding mane, a dark streak along its back as well as dark legs. In its native Mongolia,

FIGURE 1-9. The Onager (left) and Kiang were offshoots of common ancestors.

FIGURE 1-10. Zebras are of several types, and are related to the horse. In addition to the mountain zebra (below), are Grevy's, Grant's, and Chapman's zebras.

it feeds on tamarisk, feather grass, and white roots of rhubarb. The Przewalskii horse was once threatened with extinction. Today the Soviet Union is establishing a refuge for the horse which will insure its continued existence and its freedom. Although held in captivity in many zoos around the world, the Przewalskii horse has never been effectively tamed and in fact can be vicious if threatened.

The other school believes that there existed perhaps as many as six distinct primitive races from which modern day horse evolved. These philosophers speculate that the tremendous variety of size and color found in horses today could not have been variations of a single race. They maintain that human intervention alone could not have produced the extreme variety existing in the horse kindgom today. The most recent speculation (The Ewaldt Theory) supports this view and separates genetic foundation material not into species but four separate types:

FIGURE 1-11. Przewalskii's horse, also known as Taki, Tachi, or Tag, is the last of the primitive forms of the wild horse. It is native to Mongolia and has never been effectively tamed. (Kentucky Horse Park, Lexington, Kentucky)

Type One (Fig. 1-12). A pony of Northwestern Europe (Ewart's Celtic pony or Atlantic pony), approximately 12.2 hands at the withers, bay or brown in color, straight head profile, small ears, wide nostrils, thick mane and tail. Descendants of this type are thought to be the Exmoor pony of Northwestern Europe.

Type Two (Fig. 1-13). A pony inhabiting northern Eurasia (Ewart's Norse horse), approximately 14.2 hands, full tail and erect mane. It had little or no fetlock, a heavy build as compared with type one, a coarser head, slightly convex facial profile and resembles the surviving Przewalskii's horse of today (Fig. 1-11). The modern breed most resembling it today is the Norwegian Fjord.

Type Three (Fig. 1-14). An inhabitant of central Asia, a horse, not a pony. This type stood 15 hands with a distinct convex profile, sparse mane and tail, long ears, long narrow head and neck, and a sloping croup. Thought to be the ancestor of the "Turks" and, therefore, to a certain extent, the Thoroughbreds.

Type Four (Fig. 1-15). A pony-sized horse of western Asia, approximately 12 hands, short head and back, flat croup, fine silky coat,

FIGURE 1-12. Type 1 of the Ewaldt theory of developing strains of horses probably originated in northwestern Europe.

FIGURE 1-13. Type 2 resembles the current day Norwegian Fjord horse.

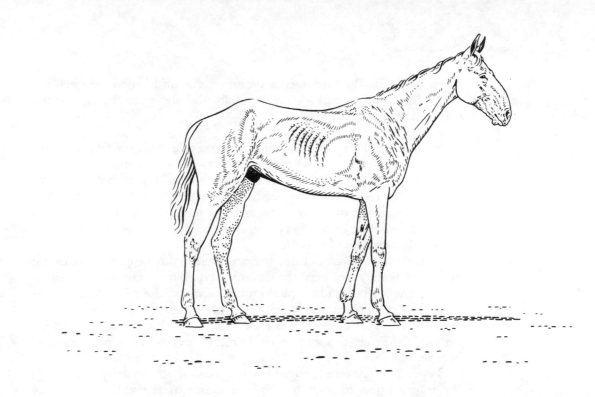

FIGURE 1-14.   Type 3 is the hypothetical ancestor of some hot-blooded strains.

FIGURE 1-15.   Type 4 probably gave rise to the Arabian horse.

mane and tail. The face is concave in profile and broad between the eyes. This type resembles the Arabian and the recently discovered Caspian pony of Iran.

Excluded is Przewalskii's horse because of a factor not known during the time of Ewaldt, who theorized it was a descendent of one of the other types. Since then, chromosome counting techniques have been discovered and evidence shows that Przewalskii's horse has a different number of chromosomes from any horses living today. It could conceivably be a fifth type and the sole surviving descendant of collateral ancestors of antiquity.

The theory is that natural barriers, mountain ranges, developing bodies of water, etc., kept the different types from crossing for thousands of years before the intervention of man. Their territories overlapped in certain instances, however, and crosses were bound to result. As man gradually domesticated the horse, he began to select for certain characteristics and to further the development of types and breeds.

Types 1 and 2 were thought to have crossed accidentally or through the intervention of man to produce many of the native ponies of Northern Europe.

Crosses of type 2 with type 3, adding feed and shelter, probably developed into the ancestor of the medieval war horse, forerunner of the draft breeds.

Crosses between types 3 and 4 are theorized to have lead to an increase in size and to have served as the basis for the modern light horse breeds.

As man began to use the horse increasingly for more specialized purposes, selections were inevitable that changed the type, size, and other characteristics of developing breeds. This process gradually signaled the emergence of specific breeds such as the Barbs and Arabians, which have had such a dominant influence on virtually every other breed of horse. Man is still manipulating, still combining genetic material, still developing new breeds from old races. The pattern changes constantly in response to new demands. The phrase "purebred" is a relative term. The history of the foundation sire of every pedigree remains cloaked in uncertainty and more often than not was mated to a nondescript mare of unrecorded ancestry to found a "purebred" type of horse.

The last wild species of horse (Equus przewalskii) exists today only on the Gobi desert of Mongolia. Another "wild" survivor, the Tarpan, was exterminated in the nineteenth century, the last one having died in the Ukraine in 1918. It has since been "reconstructed" from existing genetic material (see page 197).

Horses that evolved in colder climates were heavy and coarse. Descendants of these cold-climate horses are today referred to as "cold blooded" horses and include draft breeds as well as the Shetland Pony.

In contrast, hot and arid countries produced the small, light horse of the North African plains. These species became ancestors of the so-called "hot blooded" breeds, which include the Turk, Barb, and Arab. When breeders speak of infusing "hot blood," they are generally referring to the Arab and Barb; or Thoroughbred, which descended from Turks, Arabs, and Barbs.

DOMESTICATION AND EARLY USES

Strange as it may seem, the horse was not first used as a beast of burden or for transportation. The ass and ox served this purpose because they were more docile and easier to domesticate.

Man first learned to hunt and kill horses for food about 50,000 years ago, giving little thought to their agility, higher intellect, or specialized skills for transportation, hunting, warfare, etc. This oversight continued for a very long time as evidenced by skeletal remains of some 100,000 horses excavated at a historic campsite in Salutre, France. Horses were herded over a cliff at this site by Cro-Magnon hunters and butchered for meat, bone, and hide.

Archaeological evidence of the domestication of the horse dates back to about 4,000 B.C. on the western Persian desert. The horses weren't really much better off physically under domestication than they were in their wild state. Referred to as the "cow of the steppes," the horse was kept for meat and the mares were possibly milked by early farmers.

Horses undoubtedly were herded like sheep during this era and man probably learned to jump on and control a gentle animal in order to keep up with the herd. An agile man needed no saddle, but control was essential. This may have at first been only a rawhide rope around the jaw; but antler cheek pieces, which served as toggles to soft rope, rawhide, or sinew mouth pieces, have been found at sites of earliest domesticated horse on the steppes north of the Black Sea. It is thought that only casual and primitive riding of necessity occurred here because other evidence indicates very widespread use of the horse in harness. Control of the horse as with other equines was principally by nose ring developed in Mesopotamia about 2,000 B.C., probably because of its effectiveness as a control device on oxen and onagers. The driver held a rein to the ring in one hand and a whip in the other. This became the popular chariot method of transportation and was used by nations of the eastern Mediterranean from the Hittites to the Greeks. Because of its speed, the horse replaced the ox and onager. The Tarpan was the principal basis of the stock. At first horses were fitted with ox yokes which cut off the wind. Eventually, breast straps and collars were invented especially for draft horses.

The Mesopotamian nose ring continued in use as man, for convenience or economy, began riding the horse rather than driving it. A rein was held in one hand attached to the nose ring; a whip in the other hand added forward motivation. Directional control was achieved by leg, whip handle, voice command, or a shift in the rider's balance. Early horses were not popular for riding because of their small size— about 12 to 14 hands. Ancient art depicts riders mounted over the rump of a horse because this is the highest point on the back and prevented the rider's feet from dragging the ground. Selection for larger mounts became practical. This did not occur until the second millenium B.C.

The nose ring fell from favor when the all-metal snaffle bits were invented around 1500 B.C. by the Greeks. This greatly increased use of light chariot and cavalry warfare because of the more exact control of the animals, allowing for a rein on both sides of the neck. Two snaffle bits appeared almost simultaneously, the plain bar snaffle and the jointed bit. Both variants usually had studs on the inner surface of the cheek pieces to enforce directional control when one rein was pulled. Stirrups and saddle appear to have been unknown at this time.

The first recorded systematic plan for the training and caring of horses was devised about 1350 B.C. by a man named Kikkuli. A scribe recorded his ideas on clay tablets. Kikkuli was a Mittanian by birth but trained chariot horses for the Hittite King Supiluliumas. While some of Kikkuli's ideas, such as annointing a horse with butter, may seem bizarre today, his methods are remarkably detailed and sound, deserving recognition and serious attention. A complete scheme of feeds, feeding, and exercise indicated that several centuries of experience had accumulated to be passed on by word of mouth before Kikkuli took the initiative to record his findings.

The Scythians were masters of the art of war on horseback about 800 B.C. Scythian horses are also the first recorded geldings. Horses in the Near East, in antiquity (and largely today), were not castrated. Scythian wealth was counted in horses and a belief of the continuation of material possessions after death caused the wealthy to take quantities of the horses (in one case 400) to the grave with them. Trousers were also invented by the Scythians because of the horse. Other civilized warriors wore scanty or flowing garments at that time. We can thank the horse for this item of man's dress.

The year 700 B.C. roughly marked the turning point in the use of the horse. Chariotry declined rapidly as riding improved and mounted troops increased. The chariot retained its popularity only as a parade vehicle and for racing.

Xenophon (430–355 B.C.) is sometimes called "The father of classical equitation." A Greek, he wrote the first fully preserved manual on the riding horse. It is entitled "The Art of Horsemanship." Xenophon was a horseman for his entire life, first as a cavalryman and then as a country gentleman on an estate given to him by the King of Sparta. Xenophon differs from other ancient writers on the horse in that he urges his reader to know the horse's "physhe," its mentality. He knew that an animal that had confidence and the understanding and good will of his rider would more effectively respond to the command of the rider. Xenophon encouraged a mutual respect between horse and man.

Rodeos did not start in the American West. The oldest cowboys lived perhaps between 450–420 B.C. A coin from Larissa and northern Greece indicated that steer throwing was practiced at that time.

Alexander the Great was tutored by Aristotle in academic matters and studied horsemanship with his father, King Phillip of Macedonia. When he was 12 years old, Alexander found in his father's herd, a young horse that he admired for his great beauty. The boy named the horse Bucephalus, meaning a head that was broad like that of a bull. The horse would not allow anyone to ride him except the young Alexander. Having ridden the seemingly unbreakable Bucephalus, Alexander was inspired to conquer the world. In his attempt to do so, Bucephalus carried him from Greece to Egypt and India. When Bucephalus finally died, Alexander honored the horse by naming a city in central Asia after him.

All throughout the period of time before Christ, it should be noted that horses were not in favor with most civilizations. Few accounts of horses are written in the Old Testament because it was written by and for the people who had a taboo against horses. Horses were considered in the same class as dogs and pigs and it was not until after the time of King Solomon that horses gained any respect among Hebrews. To him, the horse was associated with foreign invaders, Assyrians, Egyptians, or Persians. The Old Testament tells us little about horses until approximately 900 B.C. at which time sufficient alternate information is available anyway.

The Egyptians, who had the most advanced civilization of its time, apparently were the first ones to find favor with the horse and are probably largely responsible for the spread of the domestication of horses to other countries. It is known that Greece had no horses during the time they were flourishing in Egypt but the Greeks certainly made use of the chariot and chariot racing at least a thousand years before Christ. The Egyptian theory of spreading the domestication of the horse is enforced by the Thessalians, colonists from Egypt, who settled in Greece. They became the first and most expert horsemen.

From Greece, horses spread to Rome and thence to other parts of

Europe. Of course, it is known that the Romans became superb horse-men and contributed the curb bit among other things to the science of horse control. As early as 55 B.C., historians recorded the use of horses being taken into foreign countries by Roman military.

Although many think the Arabs founded the science of horse hus-bandry, horses were not used in Arabia until after the time of Mo-hammed (570–632 A.D.). They depended almost totally on the camel and it was not until warring armies met the Arabs in battle and as-tounded them with their superior agility that the Arabs eventually re-placed camels with horses. This early rejection of horses would seem to indicate that Arabia was not the foundation for horse breeds, be-cause they had little use for them until half a century after the time of Christ.

As horses began to develop for specialized purposes, the various types and breeds from ponies to medieval war horses developed. By the time of the discovery of America, numerous breeds had been es-tablished throughout the old world. Although horses originated in America as previously discussed, they had been completely annihi-lated on the continent and were not to return until about 500 years ago. Columbus first brought horses to the new world—to what is now Haiti—on his second voyage in 1493. Breeding stations were set up in the Caribbean Islands to produce more horses for exploration of the new territory for the Spanish. Cortez brought some of these horses to Mexico in 1519 and thousands more were to follow in the conquest of Mexico. Introduction of horses directly to America can be traced to DeSoto in 1539 when 237 horses accompanied the expedition that ex-plored the interior of America. By 1600, the Spanish had begun to spread the use of horses throughout the new world through their sys-tem of establishing missions and accompanying them with livestock, which included horses. This stock and possibly some taken from other Spanish expeditions or outposts were the ancestors of the American Indian horse and the wild horse population later to become known as Mustangs.

During and shortly after the Indian wars of the nineteenth century, importations of light and draft horse breeds continued to improve the horse types of this nation. This has continued to this day and impor-tations still contribute to the building of a better pool of genes for im-proving existing types.

Great men and women mounted on the back of a horse have been perpetuated down through the years in marble and bronze. Perhaps no other animal has been so immortilized in art and legend. Horses of great leaders are known by many as well or better than their masters: Alexander the Great and Bucephalus, Napoleon and Marengo, the Duke of Wellington and Copenhagen, Washington and Nelson, Ulys-ses S. Grant and Jack, and Robert E. Lee and Traveler.

ANATOMY OF THE HORSE TODAY

Figure 1-16 illustrates the parts of the light horse, draft horse, or pony. Although equines come in different shapes, sizes, and types, the parts are the same. The interested horseman should become familiar with these terms because it improves the process of communication with other horsemen and experts. Parts terminology is especially important in judging and selection (covered more fully in Chapter 5).

Skeleton of the Horse

After millions of years, the horse has evolved into a distinct skeletal type represented by Fig. 1-17.

The skeletal system is divided into the *appendicular skeleton* (bones of the limbs), the *axial skeleton* (skull, vertebral column, ribs and sternum), and the *visceral skeleton* (bones that may be developed in soft tissue of some organs such as the heart). The appendicular and the axial skeleton are attached by means of two boney structures—the pectoral or shoulder girdle and the pelvic or hip girdle.

The pectoral limb (forelimb) functions mainly as a support for the horse; therefore, a strong bony attachment is not necessary. Because of the punishment that the pectoral limbs absorb in running, however, it is easy to understand why the horse has feet and leg problems in the forelimb. The angle of these bones is very important in selection because it gives a hint of the expected quality of the ride (discussed more fully in Chapter 5). Injury to these bones and joints can bring about serious foot disorders, discussed more fully in Chapter 6. Figs. 1-19 and 1-20 illustrate the proper leg set and common faults. Most of these defects are inherited disorders, some of which may be helped by corrective shoeing (see Chapter 10).

The hindlimb or pelvic limb provides the main propulsion for the horse and is more firmly attached to the skeleton by a ball and socket joint to the pelvis. (See Fig. 1-21.) The pelvis is firmly attached to the spinal column by a direct bony junction to the sacrum. This firm attachment is required to allow the powerful posterior muscles to give maximum propulsion. Figures 1-22 and 1-23 illustrate common defects in alignment of the hindlimb. These defects are much more serious and considered more difficult to correct. Selective breeding practices reduce the possibility of passing on such inherited defects as illustrated.

Figures 1-24 and 1-25 illustrate a more detailed view of the parts of the hoof of the horse. It may be divided into four basic parts: *wall, sole, frog,* and *periople.* The wall is that part visible when the foot is placed on the ground. It covers front and sides of the foot, bending sharply inward at the heel and upward to form the bars. Growth of the hoof begins at the *coronet,* the outer part of which is covered with a thin layer of horn called the *periople.* Looking at the foot from the bottom, the wall can be seen to unite to the sole by horn of lighter color and softer texture. This is the *white line,* marking the division between sen-

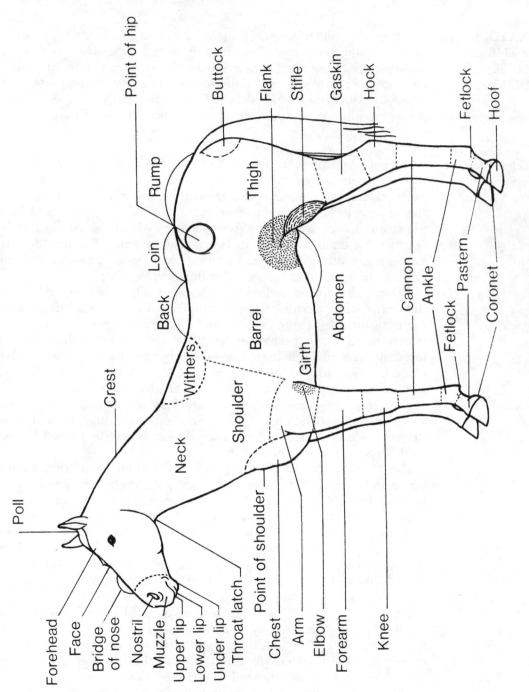

FIGURE 1-16. Parts of a horse.

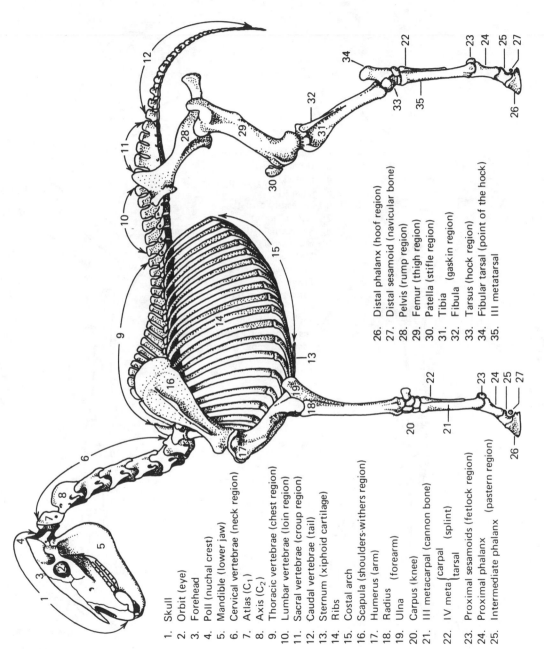

1. Skull
2. Orbit (eye)
3. Forehead
4. Poll (nuchal crest)
5. Mandible (lower jaw)
6. Cervical vertebrae (neck region)
7. Atlas (C_1)
8. Axis (C_2)
9. Thoracic vertebrae (chest region)
10. Lumbar vertebrae (loin region)
11. Sacral vertebrae (croup region)
12. Caudal vertebrae (tail)
13. Sternum (xiphoid cartilage)
14. Ribs
15. Costal arch
16. Scapula (shoulders-withers region)
17. Humerus (arm)
18. Radius   (forearm)
19. Ulna
20. Carpus (knee)
21. III metacarpal (cannon bone)
22. IV meta {carpal   (splint)
           {tarsal
23. Proximal sesamoids (fetlock region)
24. Proximal phalanx
25. Intermediate phalanx   (pastern region)

26. Distal phalanx (hoof region)
27. Distal sesamoid (navicular bone)
28. Pelvis (rump region)
29. Femur (thigh region)
30. Patella (stifle region)
31. Tibia   (gaskin region)
32. Fibula
33. Tarsus (hock region)
34. Fibular tarsal (point of the hock)
35. III metatarsal

FIGURE 1-17.   Skeleton of the horse. (From Bone, *Animal Anatomy and Physiology*, Reston Publishing Co., 1979)

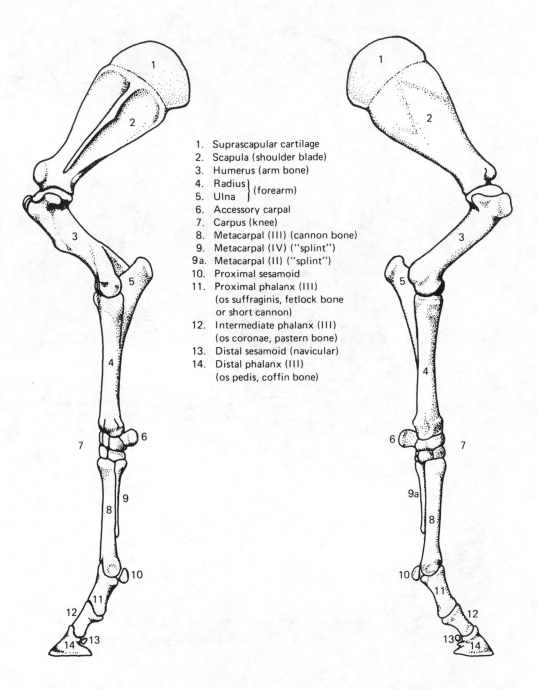

1. Suprascapular cartilage
2. Scapula (shoulder blade)
3. Humerus (arm bone)
4. Radius ⎫
5. Ulna ⎬ (forearm)
6. Accessory carpal
7. Carpus (knee)
8. Metacarpal (III) (cannon bone)
9. Metacarpal (IV) ("splint")
9a. Metacarpal (II) ("splint")
10. Proximal sesamoid
11. Proximal phalanx (III)
    (os suffraginis, fetlock bone
    or short cannon)
12. Intermediate phalanx (III)
    (os coronae, pastern bone)
13. Distal sesamoid (navicular)
14. Distal phalanx (III)
    (os pedis, coffin bone)

FIGURE 1-18. Bones of the pectoral limb of the horse. (From Bone, *Animal Anatomy and Physiology,* Reston Publishing Co., 1979)

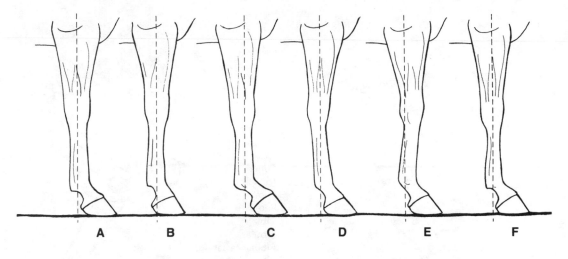

A. Correct, good bone.
B. Pastern too straight.
C. Pastern too long and flat, angle different from foot, "coon-footed."

D. Calf-kneed, short, straight pastern.
E. Buck-kneed or over on the knee.
F. "Tied in" or fine bone below the knee.

FIGURE 1-19. Forelimb structural norms and deviations, sideview. (U.S.D.A.)

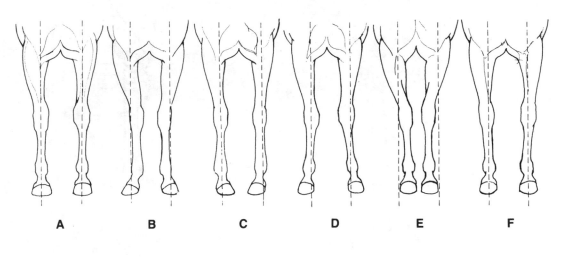

A. Straight legs, good front.
B. Splay-footed.
C. Pigeon-toed.

D. Knock-Kneed, narrow front, base wide.
E. Base-narrow.
F. Bow-kneed.

FIGURE 1-20. Forelimb structural norms and deviations, frontview. (U.S.D.A.)

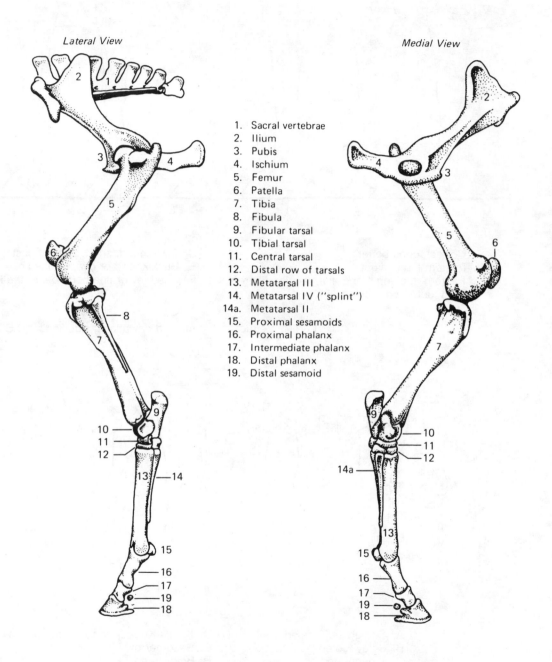

Lateral View

Medial View

1. Sacral vertebrae
2. Ilium
3. Pubis
4. Ischium
5. Femur
6. Patella
7. Tibia
8. Fibula
9. Fibular tarsal
10. Tibial tarsal
11. Central tarsal
12. Distal row of tarsals
13. Metatarsal III
14. Metatarsal IV ("splint")
14a. Metatarsal II
15. Proximal sesamoids
16. Proximal phalanx
17. Intermediate phalanx
18. Distal phalanx
19. Distal sesamoid

FIGURE 1-21. Pelvic limb of the horse. (From Bone, *Animal Anatomy and Physiology,* Reston Publishing Co., 1979)

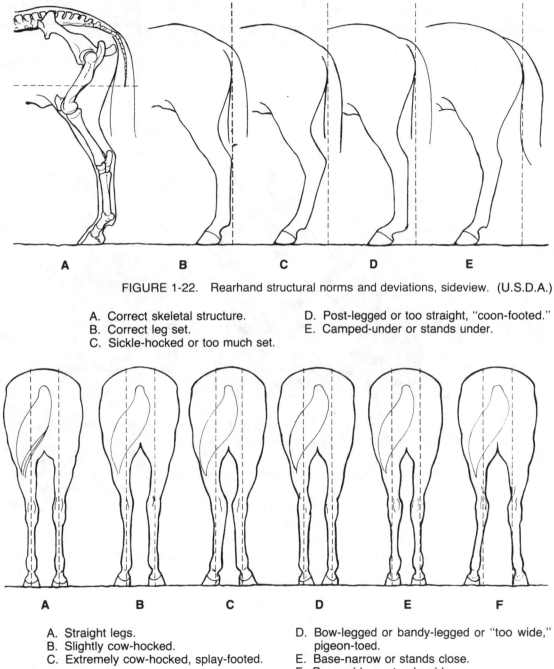

FIGURE 1-22. Rearhand structural norms and deviations, sideview. (U.S.D.A.)

A. Correct skeletal structure.
B. Correct leg set.
C. Sickle-hocked or too much set.

D. Post-legged or too straight, "coon-footed."
E. Camped-under or stands under.

A. Straight legs.
B. Slightly cow-hocked.
C. Extremely cow-hocked, splay-footed.

D. Bow-legged or bandy-legged or "too wide," pigeon-toed.
E. Base-narrow or stands close.
F. Base-wide or stands wide.

FIGURE 1-23. Rearhand structural norms and deviations, rearview. (U.S.D.A.)

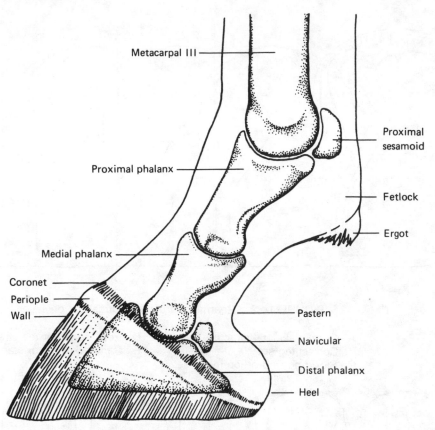

Metacarpal III

Proximal
sesamoid

Proximal phalanx

Fetlock

Ergot

Medial phalanx

Coronet
Periople
Wall

Pastern

Navicular

Distal phalanx

Heel

FIGURE 1-24. Parts of the hoof of the horse. (From Bone, *Animal Anatomy and Physiology*, Reston Publishing Co., 1979)

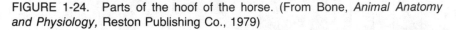

sitive and insensitive parts of the hoof. This is an important landmark for horseshoers (see Chapter 10) because a nail driven outside this white line will hold the shoe without injury to the horse but a nail driven inside this landmark can produce lameness.

A wedge-shaped mass of soft horn between the bars—the frog—acts as a cushion for the foot and also forms a kind of pump that is important in maintaining blood flow to the foot region. When the horse places weight on the foot, the frog expands into the bars, expanding the heel of the foot forcing blood outward. Lifting the foot releases the pressure and allows blood to flow back into the foot.

Another interesting feature of the foot are *chestnuts* and *ergots*. Chestnuts are found about half way between the carpus and elbow on the front leg, just below the hock on the hind leg. Ergots are found on all four legs embedded in the hair of the fetlock joint. Ergots are usually very small but chestnuts can be large and prominent. Speculation

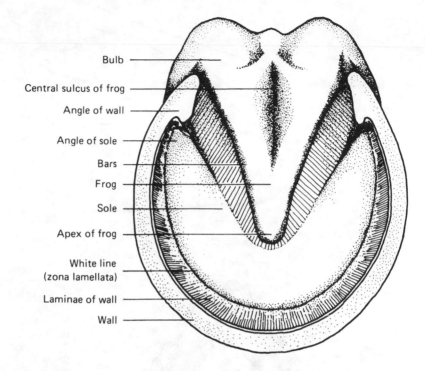

Bulb

Central sulcus of frog

Angle of wall

Angle of sole

Bars

Frog

Sole

Apex of frog

White line
(zona lamellata)

Laminae of wall

Wall

FIGURE 1-25. Plantar surface of the hoof. (From Bone, *Animal Anatomy and Physiology*, Reston Publishing Co., 1979)

has it that these horny structures are remnants of the first and fifth toes previously discussed, and thought to have long ago disappeared in the evolutionary process.

Fig. 1-26 illustrates the skull of the horse. Of important significance is the dental space between the incisors and the molars. This space has made possible the taming and control of the horse through the use of the bit. Also, the many sensitive bony structures (see Chapter 11) make numerous types of head gear effective in controlling the horse.

Figures 1-27 and 1-28 give a brief description of the eruption of the incisors, used to detect age in horses. Although an expert would look at more than just the incisors, the layman can get a fairly good idea of how age is determined by studying the illustrations. There are 12 incisors in the horse's mouth, 6 in the upper jaw and 6 in the lower. These erupt in pairs, the central pair being called *centrals* or *nippers;* the middle pair, *dividers;* and the outer pair, *corners.* A foal will have temporary incisors that will be complete at one year of age. At two and a half years of age (see Fig. 1-27), the centrals (nippers) begin to show. By three and a half years, they are complete. The next pair, as illustrated, are the dividers, then the corners. All permanent teeth in the

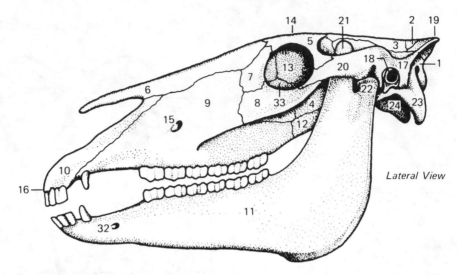

Lateral View

Dorsal View

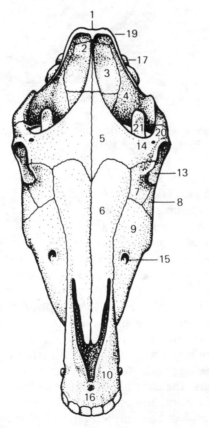

1. Occipital
2. Interparietal
3. Parietal
4. Squamous temporal
5. Frontal
6. Nasal
7. Lacrimal
8. Malar
9. Maxilla
10. Premaxilla
11. Mandible
12. Palatine
13. Orbit
14. Supraorbital foramen
15. Infraorbital foramen
16. Foramen Incisivum
17. Petrous temporal
18. External acoustic meatus
19. Nuchal crest
20. Zygomatic arch
21. Coronoid process of mandible
22. Condyle of mandible
23. Paramastoid process
24. Occipital condyle
32. Mental foramen
33. Lacrimal foramen

FIGURE 1-26.   Skull of the horse. (From Bone, *Animal Anatomy and Physiology,* Reston Publishing Co., 1979)

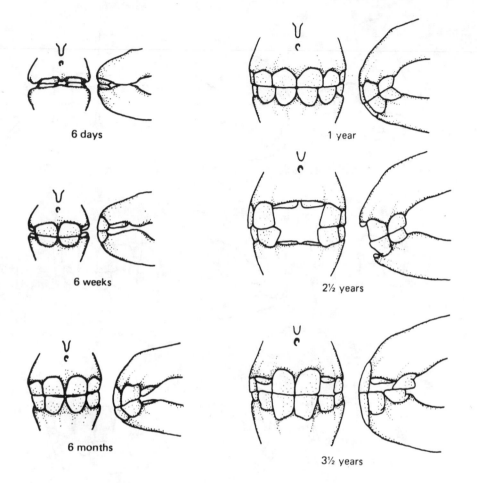

6 days

1 year

6 weeks

2½ years

6 months

3½ years

FIGURE 1-27.   Teeth of the horse—6 days to 3½ years. (From Bone, *Animal Anatomy and Physiology,* Reston Publishing Co., 1979, adapted from Huidekoper, *Age of the Domestic Animals*)

horse have erupted by five years of age. This explains why a five year old horse is said to have a "full mouth". Age determination in the horse is further illustrated with photographs in Chapter 5.

Muscular System

Figure 1-29 illustrates the muscular system of the modern horse. Although the scientific terms might be of little use to the layman, the illustrations of the specific muscles and attachments will orient the interested horseman to muscle anatomy and observation. Chapter 5 makes use of this information through the discussion of judging and selection based on common, practical muscle nomenclature.

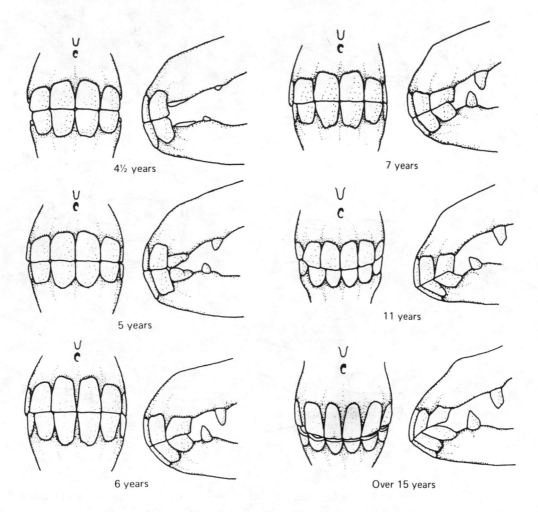

FIGURE 1-28. Teeth of the horse—4½ years through over 15 years. (From Bone, *Animal Anatomy and Physiology,* Reston Publishing Co., 1979, adapted from Huidekoper, *Age of the Domestic Animals*)

Circulatory System

Figures 1-30 and 1-31 illustrate the arterial system and the venous system of the horse. Arteries are responsible for pumping blood to the extremities and veins are responsible for the flow of blood back to the heart where it is pumped out again. Blood flowing through the various organs and tissues feeds body tissues of the horse. At least five factors are necessary in the production and maintenance of blood pressure to adequately perform the necessary biological functions within the scope of blood physiology. These are:

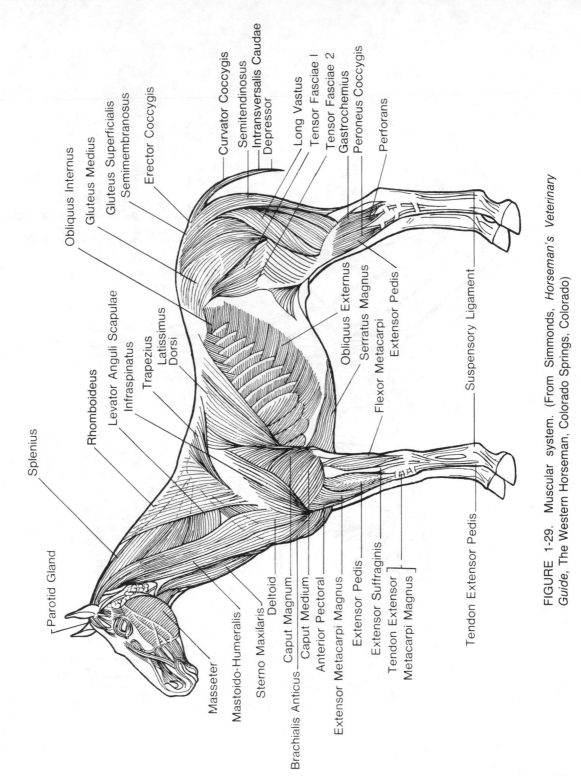

Parotid Gland

Splenius

Rhomboideus

Levator Anguli Scapulae

Infraspinatus

Trapezius

Latissimus Dorsi

Obliquus Internus

Gluteus Medius

Gluteus Superficialis

Semimembranosus

Erector Coccygis

Curvator Coccygis

Semitendinosus

Intransversalis Caudae

Depressor

Long Vastus

Tensor Fasciae I

Tensor Fasciae 2

Gastrochemius

Peroneus Coccygis

Perforans

Masseter

Mastoido-Humeralis

Sterno Maxilaris

Brachialis Anticus

Deltoid

Caput Magnum

Caput Medium

Anterior Pectoral

Extensor Metacarpi Magnus

Extensor Pedis

Extensor Suffraginis

Tendon Extensor Metacarpi Magnus

Obliquus Externus

Serratus Magnus

Flexor Metacarpi

Extensor Pedis

Tendon Extensor Pedis

Suspensory Ligament

FIGURE 1-29. Muscular system. (From Simmonds, *Horseman's Veterinary Guide*, The Western Horseman, Colorado Springs, Colorado)

39

FIGURE 1-30. Schematic drawing of the arterial system of the horse. (From Bone, *Animal Anatomy and Physiology*, Reston Publishing Co., 1979)

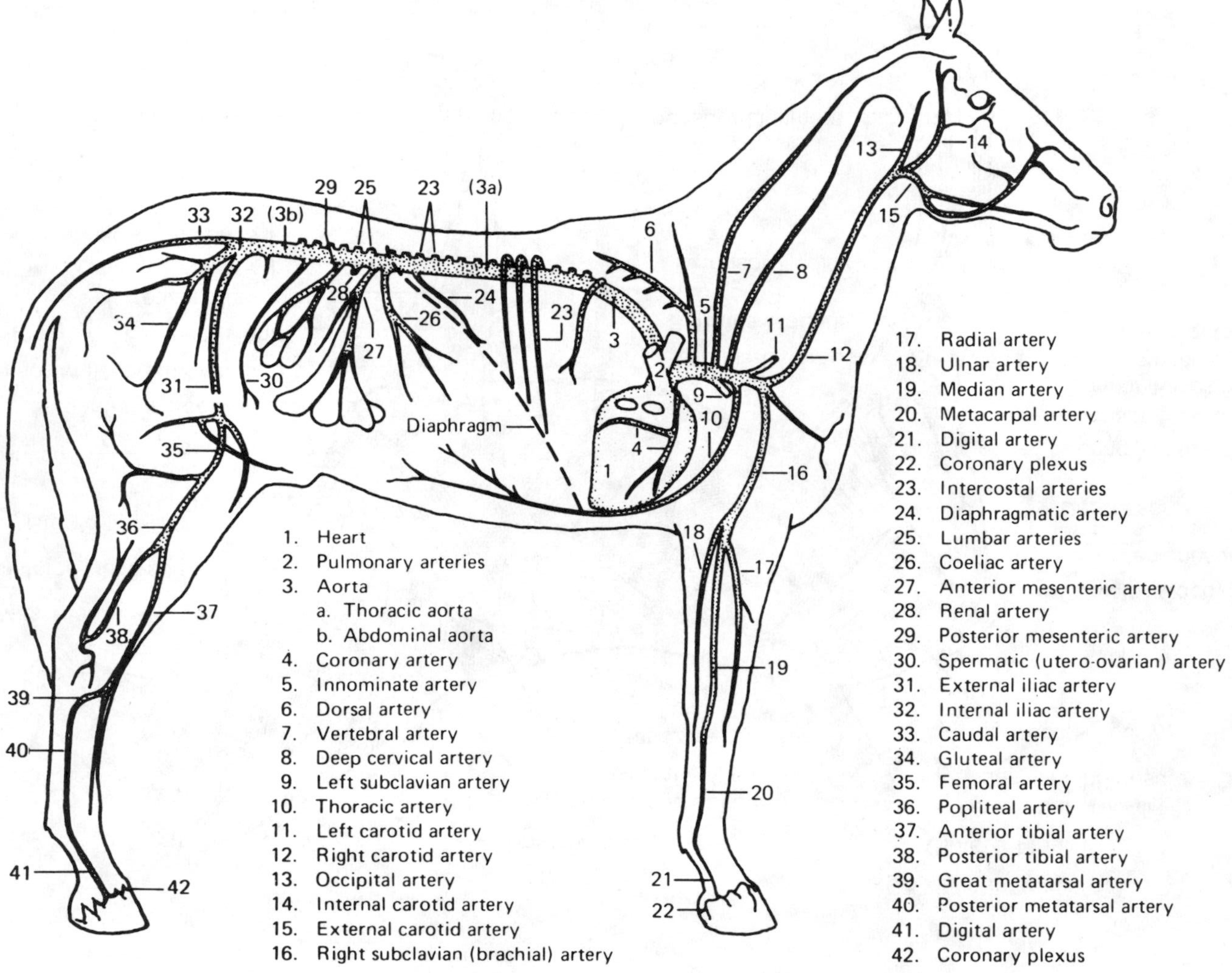

1. Heart
2. Pulmonary arteries
3. Aorta
   a. Thoracic aorta
   b. Abdominal aorta
4. Coronary artery
5. Innominate artery
6. Dorsal artery
7. Vertebral artery
8. Deep cervical artery
9. Left subclavian artery
10. Thoracic artery
11. Left carotid artery
12. Right carotid artery
13. Occipital artery
14. Internal carotid artery
15. External carotid artery
16. Right subclavian (brachial) artery

17. Radial artery
18. Ulnar artery
19. Median artery
20. Metacarpal artery
21. Digital artery
22. Coronary plexus
23. Intercostal arteries
24. Diaphragmatic artery
25. Lumbar arteries
26. Coeliac artery
27. Anterior mesenteric artery
28. Renal artery
29. Posterior mesenteric artery
30. Spermatic (utero-ovarian) artery
31. External iliac artery
32. Internal iliac artery
33. Caudal artery
34. Gluteal artery
35. Femoral artery
36. Popliteal artery
37. Anterior tibial artery
38. Posterior tibial artery
39. Great metatarsal artery
40. Posterior metatarsal artery
41. Digital artery
42. Coronary plexus

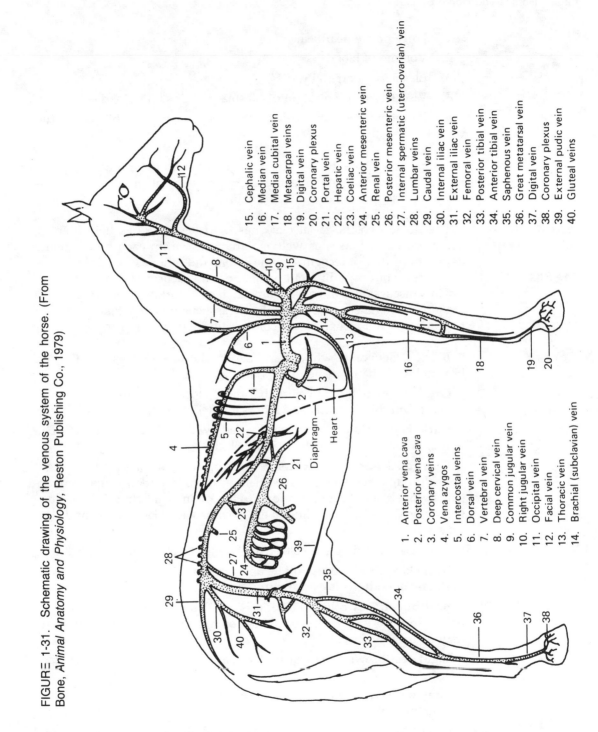

FIGURE 1-31. Schematic drawing of the venous system of the horse. (From Bone, *Animal Anatomy and Physiology*, Reston Publishing Co., 1979)

1. Anterior vena cava
2. Posterior vena cava
3. Coronary veins
4. Vena azygos
5. Intercostal veins
6. Dorsal vein
7. Vertebral vein
8. Deep cervical vein
9. Common jugular vein
10. Right jugular vein
11. Occipital vein
12. Facial vein
13. Thoracic vein
14. Brachial (subclavian) vein

15. Cephalic vein
16. Median vein
17. Medial cubital vein
18. Metacarpal veins
19. Digital vein
20. Coronary plexus
21. Portal vein
22. Hepatic vein
23. Coeliac vein
24. Anterior mesenteric vein
25. Renal vein
26. Posterior mesenteric vein
27. Internal spermatic (utero-ovarian) vein
28. Lumbar veins
29. Caudal vein
30. Internal iliac vein
31. External iliac vein
32. Femoral vein
33. Posterior tibial vein
34. Anterior tibial vein
35. Saphenous vein
36. Great metatarsal vein
37. Digital vein
38. Coronary plexus
39. External pudic vein
40. Gluteal veins

41

1. Force of the heartbeat
2. Volume of blood
3. Elasticity of arterial walls
4. Viscosity (concentration of plasma proteins and blood cells)
5. Peripheral resistance (friction between the moving blood and the vascular walls)

One practical application of this knowledge is to determine the pulse rate of a horse by palpating the appropriate point in order to determine if pulse rate is normal (see Chapter 6).

HAIRCOAT AND EXTERNAL MARKINGS

The horse's colors, facial markings, and leg markings help identify some breeds of horses as well as variations within each breed. Some associations do not recognize some colors and other associations recognize a color but by a different name. For all practical purposes, the following discussion will cover haircoat, facial markings, and leg markings in a general sense although breed associations may take exception to some and not recognize the color or terminology or both.

Colors

Black. Generally, white markings on the face or legs are allowed but no brown hairs are accepted on muzzle or flanks.

Grulla. A mixture of colors that more closely resembles steel gray. Usually with black points and a dorsal (back) stripe.

Dark bay. The body is usually red with dark brown parts. The mane, tail, and legs (points) may be black.

Dun (buckskin). These colors may be thought of as interchangeable although the Buckskin Association refers to darker duns as buckskins while scientific journals refer to buckskin as a light shade of dun. It may be described as a dingy yellow color with black points and dorsal stripe.

Light bay. A light red color usually with black mane, tail, and legs.

Buckskin (dun). Most often described as a clear, light yellow or dark cream body with black points, dorsal stripe.

Seal brown. A color so dark it is often mistaken for black. Brown hairs are most easily seen on flanks or muzzle. Legs, tail, and mane may actually be black.

Light seal brown. Similar to dark bay, but lacks reddish tint. Black points.

Gray on bay. A mottled color with progressive graying. It may occur on any color, not just bay.

Overo pattern. Occurs chiefly among Pinto and Paint type horses.

It may be described as white spots over any other color, most often bay (see Pinto, Chapter 2).

Roan. Roaning is seen from birth on horses. Best described as a speckled mixture of colors. Strawberry roan, for example, is a fine speckling mixture of white and red.

Appaloosa pattern. This is most characteristic of the Appaloosa breed and involves a less definite spotting, ill-defined edges often mixing in with other colors. The Appaloosa pattern is most often seen as a spotted, speckled, or splotching over the hindquarters but there are many other varieties (see Appaloosa, Chapter 2).

Dark red chestnut. Similar to dark bay but points are red instead of black.

Dark palomino. The "golden" horse color is familiar to most horsemen. It is similar to dun, usually with flaxen mane and tail but with no dorsal stripe or dark legs.

Red chestnut. A reddish colored horse with feet, tail, and mane of a chestnut (tan) color.

Palomino. Another golden horse, of lighter shade than the dark palomino, closer to dun but without black legs. Mane and tail are nearly white.

Red dun. A light colored reddish dun body, with darker red legs. Mane, tail, and dorsal stripe are usually red.

Light red dun. Similar to Palomino but with darker red legs, mane, tail, and dorsal stripe.

Black chestnut. Similar to black but usually shows brown hairs on muzzle, flanks, and legs.

Liver chestnut. A very dark brown color with brown chestnut colors evident on legs, flanks, and muzzle.

Sorrel. Similar to light chestnut but with more yellowish body showing little red pigment.

Perlino. A pearl colored off-white often with rust colored legs, tips of tail, muzzle, and mane. Not a true albino but often referred to as a type B albino.

Cremello. Similar to perlino, also not a true albino, with even lighter rust colored mane, tail, and body.

Other specific colors are pointed out in Chapter 2 under the discussion of each individual breed or type of horse.

Head Markings

Figure 1-32 illustrates the head markings recognized by the Arabian Horse Association. Although other breeds may vary somewhat from these markings, it should give the reader a general image of what is meant by star, snip, blaze, etc.

Leg Markings   Figure 1-33 illustrates a few of the leg markings encountered in the average solid colored horse. There is tremendous variation depending upon the breed of horse involved. Leg markings are usually some variation of a stocking, which normally involves white on some other color. As previously discussed in haircoat color, however, these points are not confined to any color. Further discussion of breed characteristics and peculiar color patterns are covered under individual breeds in Chapter 2.

FIGURE 1-32. Head markings. (Courtesy of the Arabian Horse Registry of America)
1. Faint star.
2. Star; snip.
3. Star and short connected strip; snip.
4. Wide star to left, connected strip and snip into both nostrils.
5. Tapering blaze flaring over nostrils and lips.
6. Star, connected strip, and connected snip.
7. Star, unconnected strip, separate snip.
8. Star; half blaze over nostrils, lips, and chin.
9. Blaze over nostrils, lips, and chin; dark mark in blaze over right eye.
10. Star; half strip with connected snip into left nostril.

FIGURE 1-33. Leg markings. (Courtesy of the Arabian Horse Registry of America)

1. Normal unmarked leg of Bay horse.
2. Some Bay foals are born with black points only faintly visible as shown here. Usually after shedding of the foal coat, the black points appear. The mane and tail of such foals will be black.
3. White mark outside left fore coronet band.
4. Coronet.
5. Pastern.
6. Fetlock.
7. High fetlock with dark marks at coronet band.
8. Sock.
9. Stocking.
10. High stocking above knee.
11. Heel.
12. Fetlock, higher in back.
13. Stocking.
14. Full stocking extending in front onto gaskin.

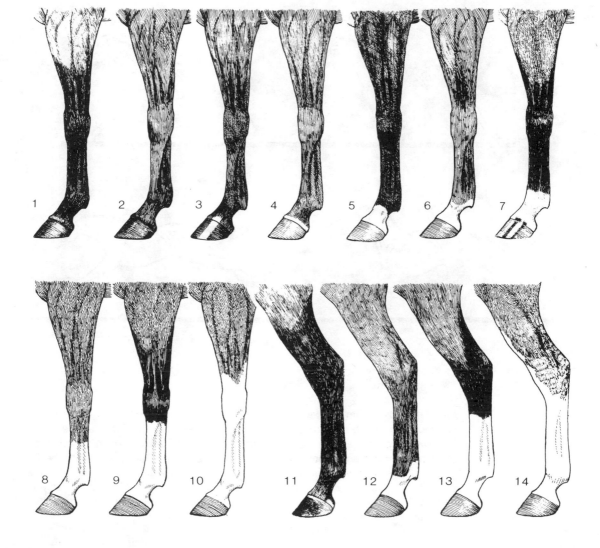

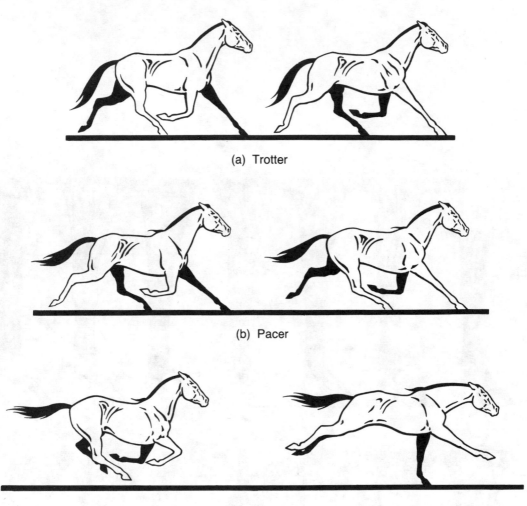

(a) Trotter

(b) Pacer

(c) Runner

FIGURE 1-34. The Trotter, Pacer, and Runner in action, representing further variations in the horse to add to the amazing variety of sizes, shapes, and colors. Notice the gaits so clearly shown in this illustration with each gaited horse showing its relative foot positions. The Trotter (a) strikes the ground with the forefoot of one side and the hind foot of the opposite side at approximately the same time. The Pacer (b) moves the forefoot and hind foot of the same side in unison. The Runner (c) moves legs in a rhythm unlike either, with rear feet often overstepping forelegs.

BIBLIOGRA-PHY

Blakely, J., & Bade, D. *The Science of Animal Husbandry*. Reston, VA: Reston Publishing Co., 1979.

Carter, W. H. *"The Story of the Horse."* Washington, DC: *The National Geographic Magazine*, November 1923.

Duggan, M. *Horses*. New York: The Ridge Press, Inc., 1972.

Edwards, E. H., et al. *Encyclopedia of the Horse*. London: Octopus Books, 1977.

Ensminger, M. E. *Horses and Horsemanship*. Danville, IL: The Interstate Printers and Publishers, 1964.

Gish, Duane T. *Evolution The Fossils Say No*. San Diego, CA: Creation-Life Publishers, 1973.

Kays, J. M. *The Horse*. New York: Arco, 1977.

Kidd, J., et al. *The Complete Horse Encyclopedia*. Secaucus, NJ: Chartwell Books, Books Sales, Inc., 1976.

Michener, J. A. *Centennial*. Greenwich, CT: Fawcett, 1975.

Reddick, K. *Horses*. New York: The Ridge Press, 1976.

2
Classes, Types, and Breeds of Horses

Three general separations of horses are used in organizing material in this chapter. Light horses, draft horses, and ponies make up the three major divisions. These divisions are further separated according to height, build, weight, use, or other variable. For purposes of clarity and discussion, the various equines covered in this chapter will be discussed according to classes, types, and, finally, individual types and breeds arranged in alphabetical order.

The total equine population in the United States was estimated to be 8,197,000 for 1980 according to estimates by the American Horse Council. The distribution of the equine population by states is illustrated in Table 2-1. Although all breed figures are not available, Table 2-2 gives the estimated figures for 14 registries. The 1994 estimate for registered horses in the United States was 238,279.

CLASSES

Although most authorities classify horses as anything over 14.2 hands at the withers and ponies as anything under 14.2 hands, many breed associations take exceptions to this philosophy. A typical defense is: "A horse is a horse regardless of size and a pony is a pony—not just an undersized horse." Equines, however, are usually divided into *light horse*, *draft*, and *pony* classes.

LIGHT HORSE

By far, the greatest number fall into the light horse class. Generally, this category is described as equines measuring 14.2 hands or more at the withers, weighing 900 to 1,400 pounds, used for riding, driving, racing, or general utility purposes, usually capable of more speed and mobility compared to *drafters* and *ponies*. Unfortunately, claim some associations, many small horses are referred to as ponies.

DRAFT HORSE

Draft horses generally range from 14.2 to 17.2 hands at the withers, weigh 1,400 pounds or over, are capable of less speed but much more strength, and are used primarily for drawing heavy loads.

PONIES

Ponies are actually just equines of smaller than average stature. Although most ponies are under 14.2 hands and range from 500 to 900 pounds, some small horses of established light breeds also fall into this classification. So how does one distinguish between ponies and horses? Technically, the various breed associations make this decision. One general observation may assist the novice horse enthusiast: a horse's height is referred to in hands (1 hand equals 4 inches) while a pony's height is expressed in inches. A horse's height should be stated in hands, say 15.3, while a pony's height should be stated in inches, say 48 inches.

TYPES

Use of the horse has dictated that several types evolve from the classes of light horse, draft horse, and pony. While drafters are used for logging, farm work, and other heavy pulling chores, the light horse and pony have much more latitude. Types are divided into *riding*, *racing*, and *driving* horses. Additionally *donkeys and mules* are covered as a type of equine.

RIDING HORSES

Five-gaited horses. These riding horses are usually taught two extra gaits in addition to the natural gaits. Natural gaits for most horses are the *walk, trot,* and *canter*. Five-gaited horses additionally use the *slow-gait* and *rack*.

The walk and trot gait are commonly recognizable to most people. The canter is a slow, smooth, rhythmic three-beat gait as opposed to the high action four-beat trot. The slow gait is a high stepping four beat gait also referred to as the amble, stepping pace (slow pace), running walk, fox trot, and perhaps other terms, but of these only the stepping pace is accepted as a slow gait for show purposes. The rack (also called single foot) is a fast, showy, four-beat gait free of pacing action. In most cases, the slow-gait and rack are learned responses while the walk, trot, and canter are natural gaits. There are some instances, however, in which certain breeds or types of horses are naturally five-gaited and do not have to be trained to develop the slow-gait and rack. A distinguishing characteristic of any five-gaited riding horse when shown is that it is always shown with a long, flowing mane and full tail. Examples of breeds of five-gaited horses are the American Saddle Horse and Racking Horse.

Three-gaited horses. The walk, trot, and canter are natural gaits of horses and many light breeds from the Arabian to the Thoroughbred fall into this category. Three-gaited riding horses are usually distinguishable from five-gaited horses because the three-gaited types are shown with mane clipped (or roached) and a clipped tail. Five-gaited horses, as previously mentioned, are shown with a full, flowing mane and tail.

Stock horses. The open range and rodeo arena are home to the stock horse. Examples of these breeds are Arabians, Grade horses, Quarter horses, Thoroughbreds, and many other light breeds that also qualify for working equines.

Polo horses. This fine athlete must have tremendous stamina, strength, and speed. The breeds that dominate the polo field are the Thoroughbred, cross breeds involving the Thoroughbred, and many grade horses of all types. The prime prerequisite is athletic ability.

Hunters and jumpers. These horses are also great athletes, noted for their strength, stamina, and natural ability to jump. The breeds that dominate the hunter/jumper classes are the Thoroughbred; and especially important in recent years has been a cross between the Thoroughbred and Cleveland Bay. Jumpers are horses that are bred for jumping competition and steeple chase races. Hunters are strong jumpers used to follow the hounds such as in fox hunting. Hunters and Jumpers differ little except the purpose for which they are used.

Ponies. This is a very popular category for children and short adults. There is a tremendous variety of breeds available in the riding pony type. A few examples of breeds are the Pony of the Americas, Shetland, Connemara, and Welsh. Other pony breeds are also discussed in this chapter.

RACE HORSES

The layman normally thinks of a race horse as a Thoroughbred animal ridden by a jockey in the Kentucky Derby. Although this is understandable, there are other types of race horses, such as harness race horses (trotters and pacers), and Quarter race horses. The Thoroughbred dominates the running races to the exclusion of virtually all other breeds. The Standardbred is exclusively used in harness races and the Quarter horse is the breed developed for quarter races.

Table 2-1 Equine Population Data

State	1996 Estimate By Author	1980 AHC Estimate
Alabama	63,000	173,000
Alaska	15,000	11,000
Arizona	166,500	158,000
Arkansas	160,500	171,000
California	943,000	843,000
Colorado	220,000	170,000
Conneticut	58,000	43,000
Delaware	10,000	11,000
Florida	300,000	178,000
Georgia	250,000	165,000
Hawaii	16,000	13,000
Idaho	191,000	171,000
Illinois	200,000	308,000
Indiana	146,500	130,000
Iowa	230,000	63,000
Kansas	250,000	199,000
Kentucky	200,000	213,000
Louisiana	210,000	190,000
Maine	50,000	37,000
Maryland	100,000	68,000
Massachusetts	45,000	39,000
Michigan	259,000	219,000
Minnesota	54,000	210,000
Mississippi	157,000	189,000
Missouri	200,000	228,000
Montana	175,000	218,000
Nebraska	150,000	108,000
Nevada	100,000	78,000
New Hampshire	15,000	30,000
New Jersey	60,000	44,000
New Mexico	99,000	131,000
New York	182,000	202,000

North Carolina	177,500	152,000
North Dakota	25,000	52,000
Ohio	185,000	237,000
Oklahoma	325,000	294,000
Oregon	110,000	160,000
Pennsylvania	250,000	135,000
Rhode Island	14,000	11,000
South Carolina	100,000	66,000
South Dakota	37,500	116,000
Tennessee	160,000	226,000
Texas	1,067,000	792,000
Utah	183,000	141,000
Vermont	25,000	17,000
Virginia	163,000	152,000
Washington	300,000	172,000
West Virginia	15,000	53,000
Wisconsin	100,000	148,000
Wyoming	135,000	67,000
D.C. & Terr.*	39,000	32,000
TOTALS	8,686,500	8,197,000

*Includes Puerto Rico, Virgin Islands, Guam, and American Samoa.

DRIVING HORSES

Horses hitched to a vehicle of several designs is described as the driving horse type.

Heavy harness horses are categories dominated by the Hackney breed, and to some extent in England, the Cleveland Bay. Heavy refers to both harness and carriage, the Rolls Royce of carriage driving. Ponies are also used for driving in harness shows and heavy harness categories. The ponies most often used as a driving horse are the Hackney, Shetland, and Welsh.

Fine harness horse breeds are predominately American Saddle Horses, although not exclusively restricted to this breed. Fine harness refers to fine horses as well. The vehicle, harness, and horse are elegant, refined, and flashy, giving the impression of first class luxury.

Roadster type horses include the Standardbred and the Morgan. Roadster carriages and horses are an intermediate harness type. In times past, the roadster was the upper middle class form of transportation—dependable, strong, durable, yet fast and comfortable.

Table 2-2 Major Breed Registration (1985-1994)*

Breed	1985	1986	1987	1988	1989	1990	1991	1992	1993	1994
Anglo & Half Arab	9,854	6,645	6,200	6,500	4,775	4,276	4,251	3,834	3,668	4,257
Appaloosa	16,189	14,551	12,589	12,317	10,746	10,669	9,902	10,033	9,079	10,104
Arabian	30,004	28,283	26,421	24,569	21,723	17,676	12,993	12,544	12,349	12,962
Hakney	744	791	621	866	779	809	731	464	701	790
Miniature Horses	N/A	N/A	N/A	3,986	4,636	5,760	5,278	6,500	6,500	6,500
Morgan Horse	4,538	4,329	3,803	3,526	3,732	3,618	3,392	2,408	3,120	3,038
National Show Horse	856	927	1,011	978	919	733	624	557	473	562
Paint	12,692	11,273	15,518	14,929	14,390	16,153	18,648	22,396	24,220	27,549
Palomino	1,301	1,518	1,719	1,747	2,080	1,598	1,564	1,358	1,671	1,664
Paso Fino	1,335	1,323	1,249	1,464	1,453	1,550	1,483	1,859	1,640	1,980
Quarter Horse	157,360	153,773	147,007	128,352	123,294	110,597	101,390	102,843	104,876	105,017
Racking Horse	N/A	N/A	N/A	4,475	3,500	4,500	4,500	4,500	4,500	2,664
Saddlebred	4,351	4,363	3,918	3,811	3,708	3,569	3,570	3,048	3,353	3,192
Standardbred	18,384	17,637	17,579	17,393	16,896	16,576	13,617	13,029	12,086	12,204
Tennessee Walker	7,812	8,750	8,712	8,983	8,850	7,972	7,852	8,123	7,510	7,856
Thoroughbred	50,429	51,293	50,917	49219	48,218	43,571	37,442	37,915	35,405	37,940
Total	315,849	305,456	297,264	283,115	269,699	249,627	227,237	231,411	224,276	238,279

* Compiled by the American Horse Council

Draft Horses

In recent years, there has been a tremendous resurgence of interest in the draft horse. The reasons are not clear for this renewed interest, although the energy crisis and advancements in recreational forms of leisure time management may be part of the answer. The Belgian Corporation recently reported over 2,100 registrations.

This renewed interest is true not only for the Belgians but for other draft breeds as well. Prices paid for these massive industrial-sized animals also reflect the intensity of interest by the buying public. A pair of matched registered Belgian mares sold for $9,200 each at a Columbus, Ohio sale in 1977. A couple of months later, a registered pair of Percheron mares, one with foal at side, sold for $15,600. Although these prices represent the peak of the market, they also reflect the supply and demand theory indicating that the demand for draft horses is on the upswing.

For instance, because of Japan's dependency on oil exports and its small farm acreage, the draft horse has gained in popularity for use as a farm animal in that country. One of the largest exports of Belgian fillies occurred in 1978 when 30 horses were exported to Japan from the Amish communities in northeast Indiana. Other exports have been noted from Canada. Apparently North America has established itself as a source of fine breeding stock for draft animals.

The use for draft horses is not confined to agricultural areas of the world but has expanded greatly as hobby teams and horse pulling contests gain in popularity, with purses averaging $500 to $1,200 for first place. An increase in prize money of this sort has prompted sportsmen and hobbyists to expand their efforts to participate in events of this type.

This resurgence of interest has prompted junior colleges, technical schools, various draft horse associations, and clubs to develop short-term "teamster schools" to meet the demands of a draft horse-hungry public. A marvelous response has been the case in virtually every short term or one-day session with most courses oversubscribed and additional sessions scheduled. Once an "old man's game" the revitalization of the draft horse events, shows, plowing matches, field days, or pulling contests now include a multitude of activities planned for the younger generation, who have discovered the magnificence of power under harness.

One unusual use for the draft horse is the production of pregnant mare urine (PMU) by pharmaceutical companies for the use in the manufacture of drugs. Although this demand fluctuates, when there is a need for the production of PMU, draft mares are most commonly used in a "urine line" because of their greater size and volume of production to meet the demands of the drug industry. In previous times when the demand for PMU fell off, excess mares might be sent to the dog food market but recent developments have shown that the demand for draft horses is such that mares not needed on the urine line find a ready place in the more humane market of individual ownership.

Draft horse breeds covered in this text include the Belgian, Clydesdale, Percheron, and Suffolk Punch. There are many other breeds of draft horses around the world but these are by far the most important ones in the North American continent.

Ponies

As previously mentioned, ponies are merely horses in miniature and are used for the same purposes. Interestingly enough, in addition to riding pony categories, there are also *racing ponies* (mostly a fun type diversion) and numerous events for ponies to be used in the driving horse category. Pony breeds covered in this chapter include the American Quarter Pony, American Walking Pony, Appaloosa Pony, Connemara Pony, Hackney Pony, Pony of the Americas, Shetland Pony, Welsh Pony, and White Horse Pony.

DONKEYS AND MULES

In addition to the types and classes of horses, a section on donkeys and mules is also included in this chapter. Although they should not be confused with breeds of horses, because of the long standing breeding practices of crossing *Equus caballus* (horses) with *Equus asinus* (donkeys), both are combined in the production of mules and, therefore, covered for purposes of organization in alphabetical order under Donkeys and Mules.

BREEDS

AMERICAN BASHKIR CURLY

One of the strangest, most unique breeds of horses in the United States is the American Bashkir Curly. The breed derives its name from the horse's kinky, tightly curled hair coat, which it develops in winter. Although the coat sheds off during the summer to little more than a wave, the breed has found acceptance mainly because of the curled hair characteristics which first came to the attention of a Nevada rancher who found them running wild.

History

The history of the American Bashkir Curly is pure speculation. When or how these horses arrived in the United States is a complete mystery. Although many theories have been advanced on the subject, no factual proof has yet been found. It is probable that the American Bashkirs are related to an almost identical breed of horse that has been reared for centuries on the southern slopes of the Ural Mountains in Russia (Fig. 2-1) by the Bashkiri people. The Russian Lokai breed also produces offspring with curly coats, some of them even exhibiting Appaloosa color markings. Some authorities speculate that the Russians

FIGURE 2-1. Mamai II, age 5, 1954. Bashkir type 147-152-169-210. Awarded Certificate of Second Degree, Agricultural Fair, Moscow, Russia. (American Bashkir Curly Registry)

brought them into Alaska and they remained undiscovered for many years, running wild in the mountains. Others think that the Mongols, who have been historically linked with the Navajo, may have brought them across the Bering Strait when the short distance across the water was frozen over with ice. The later theory would put the Curlies on American soil before the advent of Spanish horses, possibly making them the oldest breed of horses to be introduced into modern times in the United States.

Horses with curly coats are most certainly an ancient breed and have been sketched by artists in early China. The Bashkiri people of Russia probably utilize this breed of horse more than any other in the entire world, using them for transportation, clothing, meat, and milk. As with most ancient cultures, when times are hard, animals are used for transportation until they get too old to be effective in their work. Then they are slaughtered and the meat used for sustaining life; bones and other waste matter may be used for handtools, weapons, ornaments, etc. For centuries the Bashkiri have kept the Curlies in herds much like cattle. In addition to recreation, transportation, and meat, mares have been traditionally milked, giving from three to six gallons of milk per day. Although it is well known around the world that the horse is a great milk producing animal, the Curly certainly goes above and beyond the call of duty in production. The milk is highly prized by tribesmen who use it not only as a drink but also to make cream, butter, and cheese. The horses provide recreation in more than one form since the milk is also fermented into Kumiss which the natives drink in great quantities both as an intoxicating drink and for medicinal purposes.

The long, silky, curly hair (Fig. 2-2) is put to good use in weaving ropes, clothing, etc. The hides are used for producing the traditional leather goods. Because of a rugged build and great stamina, the horses are able to pull large Troikas (sleighs) upwards of 75 miles a day over the snow.

FIGURE 2-2. The American Bashkir Curly is characterized by its unusual curly or wavy hair coat, which is shed in warm weather. Peter J—ABC-P1, Chestnut Stallion. Owner: Glen Kugler, Dayton, Ohio. (Photo by Jill Cannefax)

The known history of Curlies in the United States goes back to 1898, when Peter Damele and his father discovered three wild horses running in the Peter Hanson mountain range of central Nevada. The three horses were smaller than average with tight, curly ringlets over their entire bodies. These three animals were an intriguing mystery but the Damele family preserved and bred them somewhat out of curiosity in the beginning. Their unique traits began to be recognized, however, and the lost breed was preserved for more lasting qualities. Many of the horses found throughout the United States today can be traced back to the Damele herd.

The breed was actually a curiosity for over 70 years but as more and more of the animals were discovered, because of encroaching civilization it became necessary to save them from extinction because of wild horse hunters who were slaughtering them. In 1971, the American Bashkir Curly Registry was established to save these animals from extinction and to establish breed traits. Interested owners of American Bashkirs were asked to list the characteristics in their horses which they found different from other breeds. These lists, when compiled, brought out some highly unusual traits that helped to establish them as a true breed and not just a freak of nature.

Characteristics   It is somewhat more than a strong assumption that American Bashkirs are related to those developed in Russia. Two different sizes of Curlies are commonly known in Russia. There is a small Forest pony and a larger Lowland horse, the difference in size probably due to adaptation to an abundance or absence of available feed in their respective areas. Their curly coat gets from 4 to 6 inches long in the extreme winters of Russia, and an extra layer of fat is a peculiar characteristic to the breed, making them able to stand very cold weather, survive on scant rations, and not have to roam far even on open range. These horses can work at very high altitudes and are extremely sure-footed in rough terrain. Their nostrils are much smaller than average (Fig. 2-3) giving them the ability to cope with the cold by limiting and controlling intake of super-cooled air. Because of this physical characteristic, they tend to breath faster than other breeds when at work but the restriction does not affect their endurance. One characteristic noted in endurance rides is that the American Bashkir Curly cools out rapidly, its pulse and respiration returning quickly to normal as compared to other horses.

One especially odd feature of the breed is that the mane hair and sometimes the tail hair can shed completely out during the summer and grow back before cold weather sets in. Even though the mane hair is as fine and soft as the hair of a human child, it is very kinky. Since it would become almost impossible to manage if matted through years of growth, the shedding of the corkscrew curls is probably nature's way of coping with an unmanageable situation during warm weather. The body coat also sheds during the summer and horses may show straight or slightly wavy hair on their bodies. However, their unique curly coat returns in late fall. Winter coat patterns range from a crushed velvet effect, to a perfect marcel wave, to extremely tight ringlets over the entire body. A puzzling fact about this breed of horse is that curly hair is known to be flat, yet when the hair of the Curlies was tested, it was found to be round. Another interesting characteristic about the hair should be mentioned. Many horse owners who have previously suffered allergic reactions to their horses find that Curlies

FIGURE 2-3. Note the curly hair coat, mane, tufts of hair inside ears, and the small nostrils. Dan J. T-70. Owner: Glen Kugler, Dayton, Ohio. (Photo by Jill Cannefax)

do not affect them the way other horses do. This could be of real significance to people with allergies to know that there is possibly one breed they could enjoy without problems.

The basic color of the Bashkir breed in Russia is sorrel with flaxen legs. This rather unusual color pattern is seen in the American Bashkir but because of out crossing with other breeds, every color has been seen, even Appaloosa and Pinto markings, brought about of necessity because of the scarcity of the foundation breed.

Curlies are medium size (15 hands or so), somewhat resembling the early day Morgan in conformation. They also have a number of traits that link them to the more primitive horse such as the Tarpan and Przewalskii's horse. Many individuals have been found without ergots (chestnuts). Others have small, soft chestnuts.

The eyes have an unusual, rather oriental slant to them, giving them a larger range of vision to the rear as compared to most other breeds. There hoofs are usually black, unusually tough, and almost perfectly round in shape. Even Curlies with white legs usually still have black hoofs. The foals are born with thick, krinkly coats almost resembling astrakhan fur. This fur may even extend to the inside of the ears. Foals also usually have long, beautiful curly eyelashes.

One of the finest features and the most enduring quality to breeders of the Bashkir breed is their extremely gentle disposition. Many of them are taken off the open range and within a few hours gentled in a way that would take other horses days or weeks to accomplish. There have been several cases where breeders of Curlies have found their horses entangled in wire, fences, or other potentially tragic situations in which the horses merely remained calm without kicking and waited patiently for their owners to find and free them.

Uses

In the relatively few years since the Registry was started, the American Bashkir Curlies have made great strides in promoting this breed in a multievent area. As might be expected, because of their rugged build and ability to traverse mountain terrain, they have excelled in the fifty- and one hundred-mile endurance trail rides. However, the breed has also been used in barrel racing, pole bending, western riding, reining, gymkhana events, hunter, jumper, roping, English equitation, western pleasure, and gaited pleasure classes.

Common Criticisms

The most common criticism of the breed is that it has almost no known history, and breeders who formed the Registry have often guessed at the background of the origin of this breed. Also there has been little attempt to maintain the purity of the breed in the beginning because of scarcity of the type of horse that showed the curly characteristics. Some have even criticized the breed as being a freak of nature: the curly coat is perhaps the result of ill breeding, rather than a characteristic of a rare breed. However, the striking similarity to the Russian Bashkir would indicate that many foundation animals are indeed descendants of this rare breed. As with the development of most any breed, in the beginning the herd book must be left open to draw from other selected breeding stock to increase numbers while maintaining the desired characteristics of the original breed. The American Bashkir Curly Registry points with pride at its accomplishments. The association can be justifiably proud since it contains 2,485 registered horses to date.

AMERICAN BAY HORSE ASSOCIATION

This association is not an organization of horses within a specific breed but rather a registry of color (an association in which a specific color is mandatory and sometimes the only requirement). The only color allowed is, of course, bay.

History

The American Bay Horse Association (ABHA) was founded in 1976 for the betterment of all bay horses. Any bay horse is eligible for registration regardless of breeding. Many old established breeds such as Arabians and Quarter horses have outstanding bay horses that have been registered by the association. Any purebred individual from another breed association is registered by the American Bay Horse Association if it has the conformation characteristics of its breed.

Horses with no traceable ancestory are also accepted within the association. Offspring of horses with unknown ancestory may be registered at birth and will receive a number marked with a -T. If the horse measures up to the minimum height of 14 hands at two years of age, he will then be issued a new set of papers.

Characteristics

All horses registered by the association must be bay in color, ranging from light brown and red to the darkest brown. Black manes and tails are mandatory. Although socks and stockings are permitted, any white markings except for the face must be below the knees and hocks. White hairs elsewhere on the body are not permitted unless caused from old scars. Draft type horses are not permitted and all animals must be 14 hands or taller at two years of age.

The association at this writing has registered slightly over 300 horses. Mares, geldings, and stallions may be registered and shown at halter classes and performance classes throught the United States.

Uses

The American Bay Horse competes in any halter or performance class for its own breed or in open shows. The most common performance classes are English Pleasure, Western Pleasure, Reining, Barrel Racing, Pole Bending, Trail, Working Hunter, and Cutting Horse contests.

Common Criticisms

Since this association is so new, the only criticism that could be leveled against bay horses is that they do not represent any breed or any pure breeding. Some might argue that color alone is not sufficient reason to separate these horses from others. The association might answer this criticism with the philosophy that their organization is a color registry, nothing more. Their philosophy is well stated in the foreword to their official rule book: "The ABHA is devoted to horses, better conditions, better judges and better shows where, hopefully, there will be as little politics as possible."

AMERICAN PART-BLOODED

Although the average American can trace his family background little further than grandparents, he can often recite flawlessly the pedigree of his prized registered horse back to the foundation sire centuries ago. Unfortunately many excellent horses have a "one sided" history because of only one full-blooded, registered parent, but increased demand and interest by breeders has led to a Part-Blooded Registry for half-blooded, grade, or cross-bred horses. The reason for establishment of such an association is to enhance the value of an outstanding animal through certification of a "papered" horse, often increasing sale price making the moderate fee for registration a good investment. These papers also authenticate age, breeding, color, and markings.

History

John C. Abbett, former general manager of the Oregon State Racing Commission, founded the original American Part-Blooded Horse Registry (APB) in 1939 to organize a system of recording fine Part-Bloods. Over five decades of success indicate the popularity of the movement. Top states in volume of business are New York, California, and Ohio. Canada, if treated as a U.S. state, would rank number one since it consistently furnishes 11 to 13 percent of the registration.

Interesting European breed registries are represented by the APB. They include such well-known Part-Bloods as the Lipizzaner Spanish Riding School in Austria and the New Forest Pony Breeding and Cattle Society in Hampshire, England. Other breeds represented are Spanish Mustang, Morocco Spotted, Ysabella, Paso Fino, Missouri Fox Trotter, Pony of America, Connemara, Peruvian Paso, and Bashkir Curly. Numerous contributors of fine genetic material include the Morgan, American Saddlebred, Standardbred, Quarter Horse, Walking Horse, Hackney, and Welsh.

Characteristics

Since the various breeds that make up the association vary so tremendously, characteristics are difficult to define. All colors and sizes are represented. The typical Part-Blooded Horse accepted for registration simply certifies breeding, age, color, markings, and the fact that it is 50 percent or better pure-blood stock of some recognized breed.

Most horse registries have their origin in a variety of contributing bloodlines and the Part-Blooded Association will no doubt give rise to new developing breeds. One notable exception is the Morab which is receiving recognition now both in the Part-Blooded Registry and as a breed in itself.

Uses

As might be expected from the numerous breeds involved, the Part-Blooded Registry involves virtually every aspect of use from pleasure, showring, cow horses, endurance rides, to a children's pet.

Common Criticisms

The Part-Blood Registry may be criticized by established breeders as merely being a melting pot of horses unacceptable by other associations. These criticisms are answered by the association, approaching its 16,000th registration, as a needed development in the horse business and point out that most horses are traceable to stallion owners of recognized breeds who represent a cooperative element in producing and registering good Part-Bloods and crosses, as well as to repeat owners who often up-breed to 3/4, 7/8, and higher grades.

AMERICAN SADDLE HORSES

This breed has long been known for its many gaits and such refined training as to be able to change to one of five gaits at the command of the rider. Most horses only have three gaits: walk, trot, canter. Still other breeds exist that only pace, fox trot, or amble. The finished American Saddle Horse of today (Fig. 2-4) is the result of mingling the hot blood of the Thoroughbred with the best of pacing, racking, ambling, fox trotting saddle horses to result in a five-gaited animal of beautiful proportions. This is truly an American innovation in horse breeding. At a recent U.S. sale the average price for Saddlebreds was $5,000 and the top seller brought $275,000 in 1995.

History

The American Saddle Horse was born of a need to produce the best saddle animal that would meet the tests of early day transportation. The Saddle Horse might be compared to the first "five-speed transmission." This is the only breed of horse that was developed in the United States without importing blood from outside the country. Early breeders merely utilized existing bloodlines from early importations.

The first horses brought from the east coast of the United States were natural-gaited utility animals, Galloways and Hobbies, which had fallen from favor in England in the early 1600s because of the developing Thoroughbred breed. Similarly, in Canada, Norman French Horses, quite similar to Galloways and Hobbies, were imported for gait and appearance. Breeders in Virginia and New England selected from these three breeds to produce a horse known as the Narragansett Pacer, named for Narragansett Bay, Rhode Island. The northern counterpart was known as the Canadian Pacer, a cross between Norman French and Narragansett Pacers.

These horses were shipped by the thousands to every part of the United States and to many other parts of the world. Early horsemen of Kentucky were pioneers in selection and development of a horse from this stock which became known as the "Kentucky Saddler." Infusions of both Thoroughbred and Morgan blood were to play a major part in the development of the American Saddle Horse.

The modern American Saddle Horse can be traced back to a Thoroughbred sire, mated to a Pacer, the daughter of a Pacer. The sire, Denmark, was mated to the Stevenson Mare, a daughter of Cockspur, of Canadian Pacer stock. In 1851, a jet black horse called Gaines Denmark was foaled. He became the greatest of Saddle Horse sires, and all registered Saddle Horses of today may be traced back to him.

Fame came early for the American Saddle Horse during the Civil War, 1861-1865. Saddlebreds served as mounts for Generals Lee, Grant, Sherman, and Stonewall Jackson of the Union Army. However, most Union cavalrymen were mounted on Thoroughbreds. This proved to be a distinct disadvantage because Confederate commands

FIGURE 2-4. The American Saddle Horse, a genuine product of the United States. (Kentucky Horse Park, Lexington, Kentucky)

such as those of Generals John Hunt Morgan and Nathan Bedford Forrest were mounted almost exclusively on American Saddlebreds and these horses became known for their legendary feats of endurance. The American Saddlebred proved a far superior war horse because in the clash of a cavalry charge, it could easily knock down the lighter Thoroughbred. Because most Confederate horses were privately owned, General Grant's order to allow men to keep their horses at the close of the war perhaps saved the breed from extinction.

After the Civil War, the Saint Louis Fair became the focus for horse breeders who vied for showring winnings. Because of this keen competition started in 1866, the blood of other animals was introduced into the "Kentucky Saddler." This included Morgans, Thoroughbreds, Canadian Pacers, Bellfounder (a Hackney), and Hambeltonian (a cross between Messenger and Bellfounder who became foundation sire of the modern Standardbred). This produced a better animal but records were not kept until 1891 when the National Saddle Horse Breeders Association and a Saddle Horse Registry was founded in the United States consisting of members who were stockholders. Through the next 17 years, much deliberation was voiced as to the type of horse desired and the specific bloodlines that should make up the American Saddle Horse. In 1908, Denmark, through his son, Gaines Denmark, was given the technical designation of foundation sire because over 60 percent of the horses in the first Studbook could be traced to him. Thus, he is still referred to as Denmark F.S. (foundation sire). Another outstanding animal, Bourbon King, a trotting colt that could be traced back to Justin Morgan and Messenger, played a significant part in Saddle Horse development. Bourbon King was a five-gaited show sensation, living to the ripe old age of 30, and siring many offspring. These offspring became known as the Chief Family of Saddle Horses. When the Denmarks (of Thoroughbred background) and Chiefs (of Morgan background) were crossed, the resulting offspring were to-day's modern American Saddle Horse.

Because of breeders' fascination with the showring, which could be traced back to the Saint Louis Fair in 1866, American Saddle Horses became known as the "peacock of the showring" and gained many critics who complained the breed was good for little else. Unfortunately, this attitude prevailed until 1957 when the American Sad-dlebred Pleasure Horse Association was formed to reestablish the po-sition of this breed as a pleasure and using animal in addition to its pleasing characteristics in the showring. In 1978, the old stockholder system of membership was abandoned in favor of an annual member-ship corporation to create a more active membership, which now exceeds 7,400. American Saddle Horses are sometimes more appreci-ated around the world than they are in the United States. The breed has, however, come to be known nationally and internationally as "the horse America made."

Characteristics   The early requirement that the horse be a pleasure to ride has never changed. Original standards of conformation have been adhered to since the beginning and anyone familiar with the breed finds it a most comfortable, light-footed animal, with the five-gaited trait remaining true to the original qualifications of the breed.

Exceptionally versatile and intelligent, the American Saddle Horse is characterized by high head carriage and a thin refined throatlatch, often made thin by the use of a "neckwrap." This is a "showring maneuver" for which this and other breeds have drawn criticism. The first place a horse collects fat is in the neck and the neckwrap simply prevents the formation of a "double chin." An arched neck with sloping shoulders and a level croup with the tail "standing high" are also distinguishing characteristics. The tail is not actually "broken" in order to achieve the erect position although the term is a slang word used to imply this operation. When horses are very young, trainers daily push up on the tail to stretch the muscles to a higher position. Then the muscles that pull the tail downward are "nicked" slightly with a scal-pel. Although not cut through, the small cut allows the higher posi-tion. Then a "tail set" is used to keep the tail in the proper position. The horse still has normal use of the tail and after the show career is finished, the tail is allowed to return to its normal position.

Hindquarters are well muscled, and legs are straight with long sloping pasterns providing the springiness necessary for a smooth ride. Hooves are sound and open at the heels.

Uses

The American Saddlebred Horse is usually divided into three divisions for showing. Within these three divisions are many subdivisions.

The first division is the Three-Gaited or Walk-Trot Horse, which performs the walk, trot, and canter (Fig. 2-5).

FIGURE 2-5. A typical Three-Gaited American Saddle Horse is characterized by high head carriage, refinded throat-latch, arched neck, and high tail carriage. (American Saddle Horse Breeders Association, Inc.)

The second division is the Five-Gaited Horse (Fig. 2-6). This is the aristocrat of the showring, the exciting spectacle of American Saddle Horse Shows. In addition to the walk, trot, and canter, this breed of horse adds two exciting gaits almost unknown to other breeds—the slow gait and the rack. These two gaits require a good trainer to teach the horse these maneuvers even though the American Saddle Horse has inherited the ability to learn these additional gaits as a part of his genetic makeup. Since these are taught movements, the American Saddle Horse is often seen with a variety of weights, bandages, chains, protectors, etc., which are used in assisting the trainer to achieve these disciplined gaits.

The third division is the Fine-Harness Horse (Fig. 2-7), a beautiful, fine, and exceptionally eye pleasing horse that executes the gaits of walk and park trot. Horses are shown hooked to a four-wheeled, fine-harness buggy.

The largest of the "subdivisions" are the pleasure classes. Interest in the pleasure division was so high that the American Saddlebred Pleas-

FIGURE 2-6. The Five-Gaited American Saddle Horse in action. (American Saddle Horse Breeders Association, Inc.)

FIGURE 2-7. An American Saddle Horse shown in Fine-Harness division. (American Saddle Horse Breeders Association, Inc.)

ure Horse Association was formed in 1951, not to serve as a registry but to promote the American Saddle Horse as an ideal pleasure mount from the backyard to the showring. Membership is currently about 600.

Pleasure classes cover all of the previous divisions discussed but simply in a pleasure form. Included are three-gaited, five-gaited, and pleasure driving divisions. The most obvious difference distinguishing pleasure classes from show classes is that horses do not have to have the exceptional motion and brilliance of a trained show animal. Emphasis is placed on manners and the ability of the horse to give its rider a smooth ride.

In addition to these uses, the Saddlebred is well represented in the olympic jumping contests, along with many championships in western cutting contests. The kind and quiet disposition of the breed make it an ideal, safe horse that children and the entire family can enjoy. Many endurance contests have also seen Saddlebred mounts take home the honors. The breed is truly a versatile animal whether it is cutting cattle, carrying riders over mountain trails, or pulling a hack on a pleasant Sunday afternoon. The stylish head carriage and stepping action also make it one of the most pleasing of horses to own when one is just "showing off."

Common Criticisms

Because of their showy abilities, the American Saddle Horse has long been criticized as the "peacock of the showring", considered good for little else by horsemen not familiar with the breed. The uninitiated complain that American Saddlebred Horses are too highly specialized, used mostly as an entertainer. Breeders point out that no one criticizes the Thoroughbred for specializing in racing, the Quarter Horse for a short stretch racer, or the Standardbred for being a harness racing specialist. Just as these fine breeds have other outstanding qualities, the American Saddle Horse claims the additional title of "superb athlete" outside the showring. The Association is constantly striving to reestablish its worth as a pleasure and using animal. After all, prior to its "showring reputation", this is why the breed was developed.

AMERICAN QUARTER PONY

As is the case with most breeds, there are some outstanding individuals from a conformation standpoint that do not measure up to the qualifications of larger animals. The normal classification for "pony" is any horse that stands less than 14.2 hands at the withers. Because Quarter Horses are rather small to begin with, it is not unreasonable to expect a certain number of individuals that do not measure up to "horse" standards. For this reason, to preserve many outstanding horses as children's mounts, and other reasons, numerous pony associations have developed. The American Quarter Pony Association is just one of many.

History

Quarter Ponies are Quarter Horses in miniature sharing the same origin. The National Quarter Pony Association, Inc. was organized in

1975 to record and preserve the pedigrees of outstanding animals of Quarter breeding that failed to meet minimum standards in height. Because of the tremendous size of the parent association and the exploding growth and popularity of Quarter Horses, the Quarter Pony Association found a ready market among people who were interested in smaller mounts for whatever reason. The association provides information for the general public on matters pertaining to shows, contests, and projects to improve the breed.

Characteristics   The head of Quarter Ponies should be proportionate to the body with clean-cut features. The same type of compact, well proportioned, heavily muscled body is expected in the Quarter Pony (Fig. 2-8), a smaller version of the Quarter Horse.

It should be kept in mind that the Quarter Pony is not a genetic malfunction, or a dwarf. All parts must blend together in correct proportions to make up good balance, substance, ruggedness, quality, and refinement. The same pride is taken in Quarter Pony conformation that has led to the popularity of the Quarter Horse.

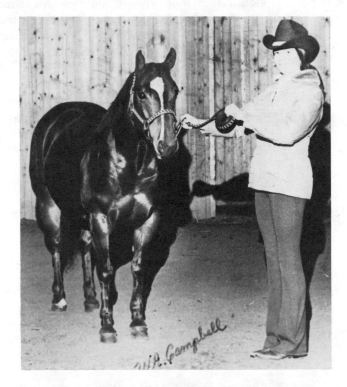

FIGURE 2-8.   Cowboy's Super, outstanding Quarter Pony mare owned by Edward Ufferman, Marengo, Ohio. (National Quarter Pony Association)

Small, alert ears, doglike, furry coat, swishing tail, it needed a rather long face to accommodate its 44 teeth (today's horse has 36 to 42 teeth, depending on age and sex). The teeth still were not capable of handling coarse, abrasive materials so Eohippus munched on leaves and other browse.

The distinguishing characteristic of Eohippus as compared to its theoretical predecessor is the direction of growth of the feet. Front feet, adapted from the original five toes, had been reduced to four. One of the toes on the front feet had retracted to become a splint. The rear feet had been modified also, now containing three toes with one splint indicating the withering away of toes not needed. Both the front and back toes had been replaced, however, by tiny hooves instead of the original claws.

**MODIFICA-
TION—
MESOHIPPUS**

About 40 million years ago, the evolutionary process began to change the horse even more. At this time, during the Oligocene Epoch, appeared Mesohippus (Fig. 1-3). As the temperature and climate changed, forests began to dwindle and grass became more prevalent. Mesohippus developed larger than its ancestors, standing 24 inches high at the shoulders, about the size of a collie dog. The 44 teeth remained, however, and legs and face began to lengthen. Its feet were still clinging to pads but tiny hooves had developed on three toes on the front and three toes on the back feet. It was better suited to running fast to escape the enemies that pursued. Because the swamp had given way to soft ground, Mesohippus no longer needed its toes so much as Eohippus did. The lateral supporting toes gradually decreased in size while the middle toe gained strength. Some of these horses migrated across the Bering Strait to preserve the species, which were eventually wiped out on the North American continent for unknown reasons.

**TOTALLY
NEW
ADAPTA-
TION—
MERY-
CHIPPUS**

During the Miocene Epoch, about 25 million years ago, Merychippus (Fig. 1-4) appeared as a totally new, adapted type of horse. This was a sleek, three-toed animal with erect mane, about 40 inches high with three toes on both front and back feet. Merychippus was the most startling development of all the ancestors of the horse. It evolved in North America and adapted to the hard grasses of the plains region. This was the beginning of the grazing horse of today. The development that made this possible was the remarkable capacity of its teeth to grow out from the socket as they were worn down from the coarse grass, which contained silica and other abrasive elements. Had these complicated grinding molars not developed, it would not have been possible for Merychippus to survive on the plains. Other changes were also beginning because of its lateral toes, which continued to diminish and no

FIGURE 1-3. Mesohippus, stage three in evolutionary development of the horse. The face and legs had begun to lengthen, feet still clung to pads, but tiny hooves had developed on each of the three toes on front and back. Size had increased to about 24 inches at the withers.

longer reached the ground. The main toe thickened and hardened and swift travel on the dry ground was made possible. The pad on the feet had modified to the "frog" and the weight was carried on the enlarged single hoof of the central toe.

"ONE TOE"— PLIOHIPPUS About 10 million years ago, during the Pliocene Epoch, the horse evolved into Pliohippus (Fig. 1-5). This ancestor had only one toe, or hoof, on each foot. At the beginning of this era, one branch of horses crossed into Asia and quickly multiplied and spread to Europe. Meanwhile, in North America, the horse developed into the final model. Pliohippus was the first true monodactyl (one-toed animal) of evolutionary history. This horse had an increasing need for speed to evade predators so the hoof evolved from the middle toe. Its denture and

All ponies must measure between 11.2 and 14.2 hands. No two-year-old measuring more than 14 hands will be accepted for registration and two-year-olds in excess of 14.2 hands will have their registration revoked because it would fall into the Quarter Horse category. As in its larger counterpart, no animal may be registered that exhibits excessive whited spotting from the ears back, or evidence of Pinto, Paint, or Appaloosa color characteristics.

Uses

The Quarter Pony Association was established for the sole purpose of promoting a registry for small, Quarter-type horses and Quarter-type ponies. They are obviously well suited as a child's mount and have found acceptance in 50 states and Canada as cow ponies, pleasure mounts, halter show participants, and youth events ranging from the rodeo arena to the most elegant equestrian event.

AMERICAN WALKING PONY

This unusual breed of horse was the dream of one individual spurred on by a desire for a mount between horse and pony size with a smooth saddle gait. Joan Hudson Brown searched in vain for "the ideal pony" until she and her father realized that nothing was available that suited her needs and taste. In the words of association promotional material, "Have you ever seen a dream walking? Well, we have!" Membership is small and approximately 328 ponies are registered as of 1994.

History

In the mid-1950s, the Browntree Stables of Macon, Georgia under the direction of Joan Hudson Brown and her father began a breeding program to produce a small mount with the characteristics of the Tennessee Walking Horse. Crosses involving the Welsh Pony (Arabian type conformation and refinement) and the Tennessee Walking Horse (gait and calm disposition) resulted in several outstanding animals. After years of experimenting with the crosses, the American Walking Pony Registry was established in 1968 in Macon, Georgia.

Registration requirements designate a sire or dam to be registered Tennessee Walking Horse and the other parent a Welsh Pony not to exceed 52 inches in height. First generation cross is still acceptable for registration. All horses must be able to do the Merry Walk, a fast four-beat gait with slight head motion in order to be registered.

Characteristics

The Walking Pony ranges in height from 13 to 14.2 hands, has a smaller head, more level croup, and higher tail carriage than the Tennessee Walking Horse. The back is short and overall conformation resembles the Arabian, from the Welsh Pony heritage.

For show purposes, the Walking Pony must wear long, natural unbraided mane and tail and have a natural unset tail. Artificial appli-

FIGURE 2-9. The American Walking Pony, a breed developed from the Welsh Pony and Tennessee Walking Horse. (Mrs. Joan Brown, Macon, Georgia)

ances, boots, etc. are prohibited. Shoes must not exceed 16 ounces in weight, no pad is allowed between hoof and shoe, and length of toe must not exceed 4½ inches including the shoe.

The natural gaits of the American Walking Pony are the pleasure walk, merry walk, and canter. It can trot and is easily trained to rack.

Perhaps two of the most outstanding characteristics in addition to the small size, are the "rocking chair gait" and a calm, lovable disposition suitable for children.

Uses

The American Walking Pony is shown in harness at the pleasure walk and merry walk, informal and pleasure driving, and at the trot in roadster classes. Breed rules include Western and English pleasure, harness, pony hunter, and jumper classes.

It is especially suited as a riding horse for children and smaller adults but has the durability to be ridden also by most average size adults.

ANDALU-SIAN

Although the Andalusian breed is a very old and aristocratic horse, it is a relative newcomer to the United States. While a few were here before 1965, none were registered in the United States until that date. The Andalusians of today have been refined from the original breed and retain the great strength, learning, and elegance of their ancestors. The unique color characteristics are reminiscent of the Lipizzan, understandably so, because of the contribution the Andalusian made in the development of that breed. There are fewer than 500 purebred registered Andalusians in the United States. California leads the nation in the number of registered Andalusians and owners consider them priceless. However, every product has its market value and Andalusians are commonly sold in the United States at prices averaging ten to fifteen thousand dollars for a mature, well-trained animal.

History   Ancestors of this magnificent animal can be traced to the cave dwellers of the Mezolitique Age, about 8,000 years ago, in the mountains of the Iberian Peninsula. Promoters of the breed claim that, based on their historical research, the Andalusian was the first horse ever ridden in the entire world. Long before the Christian era, this horse was used as a cavalry mount against the Greeks, Carthaginians, Barbarians, Visigoths, Romans, and many others. In 218 B.C. Hannibal made his famous crossing of the Alps using elephants and a cavalry consisting of Andalusian horses. About 100 B.C. the French and the Romans simultaneously started importing these horses to improve their own mounts. They were used both under saddle and hitched to the chariot.

When the Moors invaded Spain in 711 A.D., they faced the Spanish Andalusians and were immediately impressed with their strength and versatility as compared to the Moorish Barb horse. Historians speculate that it was only because of the much greater size of the Moorish army that they were able to defeat the superior mounted Spanish defenders. The Moorish commander Tarik gave orders to first capture the horses of Spain and then their riders. The remainder of their campaign was successful but the success was greatly attributed to the captured Spanish horse.

The ruling Caliphs of the different provinces prized this horse so greatly that they sent an Andalusian stallion, richly adorned and escorted by one hundred of the small Moorish horses, as gifts to the orient. During the eighth and fifteenth centuries, the Moors remained in Spain and adopted the training methods of the Spanish, utilizing "La-Jineta," the forerunner of the present-day "dressage" (the teaching of exotic, complex, or gymnastic movements). This art of war had existed for about 5,000 years previously.

Sir Walter Scott put his great Ivanhoe astride a white Andalusian. Richard the Lion Hearted rode to victory on an Andalusian and the Duke of Newcastle wrote, "It is the noblest horse in the world, the most beautiful, the most worthy to be ridden by the king on a day of triumph."

Grenada, the last Moorish possession, was retaken in 1492, the same year that Columbus discovered America. On his second voyage, Columbus carried Andalusian horses with him and disembarked several head in this newfound territory, making the Andalusian "the first horse of America."

It can be argued that this horse was instrumental in reintroducing the equine species into the new world. In 1893, it became a law that every ship that left Spain for America must carry at least 12 horses in the hold. Within a few years, Spain had sent more than 3,000 head of horses to the new world, and founded herds on the Caribbean Islands. The choice of the islands for breeding establishments was no accident. The islands were ideal since most of them were relatively small and the herds easily contained without the use of fences or the possibility of horses establishing wild herds that could not be caught. From these herds, during the next 80 years or so, the Spanish transplanted horses across most of the American continent.

It was the Spanish who taught the Indians and, later, the Vaqueros and cowboys of the Americans to ride, using the "La-Jineta" horsemanship style that exists today. The horsemanship style of the Spanish dictated that the reins be held in the left hand, leaving the right hand free for lance, sword, and later, the lasso.

The Spanish empire was carried over most of the world on the backs of the Andalusian horse, which took the Conquistadors into battle, outmaneuvering the heavy cavalry horses used by the rest of Europe. Because of this agility and the La-Jineta style, "La Maddalene" was founded in Naples. It was here that the famed Spanish Riding School had its beginning, using "La Maddalene" (School of Equitation) as the basis of horsemanship.

The Andalusian was the forerunner of the Lipizzan breed. The Archduke Carlos, son of the German Emperor Ferdinand I, employed horses imported only from Spain to found a new, high-class breed of horse. The Imperial stud in the village of Lipizza, part of the former Yugoslavia, was chosen because it so closely resembled Spain in climate and terrain. From these Spanish horses, primarily Andalusians, the present-day breed of Lipizzan evolved. In like manner, the Spanish Riding School took its name in honor of these founding Spanish sires and mares. Periodically, fresh, pure Spanish blood was regularly brought in from Spain to help keep the Lipizzan standardized in type, color, and temperament. At one time, a four-year-old stallion of the Carthusian line of Andalusians was imported from Cadiz, Spain to rejuvenate the present line of Lipizzans in Austria.

The International Andalusian Horse Association was recently formed to promote the breed in the western hemisphere. About 300 Andalusians are registered with the association.

Characteristics

The Andalusian has one of the most unusual color patterns in all the horse kingdom. Although blacks, roans, and chestnuts exist, they are extremely rare in this breed. The vast majority of Andalusians are born steel gray or chocolate brown (Fig. 2-10). Within a few weeks, they start to change color. The brown to dark grey, the grays into a lighter gray.

One notable exception to the color pattern is Charro, the only pure black Andalusian stallion in the western hemisphere who qualified for the Regional Finals of the U.S. Dressage Federation, taking first honors in AHSA trials over a field of Thoroughbreds. Most Andalusians will whiten with age. Although color may appear to be a unique characteristic of this breed, it is by no means an indication of basic selection principals.

Andalusians (Fig. 2-11) generally stand 15.0 to 16.0 hands high but no objection is made to horses above or below this height so long as they subscribe to conformation standards. The association looks for "a noble aspect" to the head, a reasonably long and broad neck, well crested in the stallions. The withers should be prominent, with long sloping shoulders. The back is short-coupled and well connected at the loin. The body should be deep ribbed and strong; the chests are strong, with extreme broadness or narrowness being a fault. They have strong quarters, with the croup being gently rounded. The tail setting is rather low.

Uses

The Andalusian certainly is among the most versatile horses in existence. He is used as a pleasure horse, working horse (stock work,

FIGURE 2-10. Andalusian mares with typical chocolate brown foals. These foals will turn to dappled gray at maturity (8-10 years) and will have a life expectancy of 30 years. (The Sugarman Ranch, Thousand Oaks, California)

reining, roping, cutting), harness horse, jumping, hunting, fine harness, carriages and carts, show horse, circus horse, and dressage horse. Andalusians are trainable to any level, including performance of all the famed "Airs above Ground" made famous by the remarkable Lipizzan stallions of the Spanish Riding School.

One of the rare uses to which few, if any other horses, are used is in the bull fighting arena. It is a most common sight in bull fighting to witness the confrontation of the Andalusian and the bull. The process is repeated over and over each afternoon in the bull ring. A mounted rider called the "rejoneador" must ride close to the bull's horns to place a "banderilla" (small flag) in the bull's neck. This animal athlete is used almost exclusively in bull fighting arenas around the world. Rarely will any other breed of horse but the Andalusian be seen in a confrontation with the dangerous Spanish fighting bulls.

With their noble stature and beautiful long mane and tail, the Andalusian is also an attention getter and show stopper at any parade or gathering. It is a stunning, but not unusual, sight to see several Andalusians with riders dressed in authentic Spanish costumes being featured in such exclusive parades as the Annual Tournament of Roses in Pasadena, California. This old and noble aristocrat, although laying claim to "the first horse of the Americas," is only recently being rediscovered in North America.

FIGURE 2-11. Admirado, Andalusian stallion embodying the physical ideal in conformation and bearing. (The Sugarman Ranch, Thousand Oaks, California)

APPALOOSA

History

The Appaloosa was first hunted as a game animal about 20,000 years ago. Cave dwellers in France depicted spotted horses on the walls of their caverns as a form of "magic" to draw their quarry near enough to be killed for food.

These spotted horses were well established before the dawn of history according to this ancient artwork found throughout Europe. Similar cavern murals illustrated spotted horses in ancient China, Persia, and Egypt.

Archaeological excavations in Austria have unearthed artifacts dating back to 1,000 B.C. buried with invading warriors from the steppes of Asia that depicted spotted horses mounted by Asian warriors.

The first appearance in recorded history is found in the account of Persian wars written by the Greek historian Herodotus. This writer described the spotted horses as "sacred", used to pull the chariot of King Xerxes of Persia when his armies invaded Greece in 1480 B.C. This striking animal was a special breed reserved for the king and high ranking nobles.

Emperor Wu Ti of the Han Dynasty of China learned of the "sacred" horses in Persia about 126 B.C. He first tried to buy horses from Persia offering many treasures of gold and precious gems. When his efforts at negotiating a trade were thwarted, the Emperor sent his armies into Persia, fought battles for many years costing an estimated 40,000 men and 100,000 horses before the spotted horses were captured. The Chinese were victorious in bringing this treasured animal home about 101 B.C. The victorious Emperor was so elated that he was inspired to write the poem "The Heavenly Horses From the Extreme West." Artists also depicted this event in numerous paintings throughout China which have since proven beyond a doubt that the color pattern was that of what we now call the Appaloosa.

From Persia, the spotted horses spread to the west across southern Russia, Germany, and the Netherlands. They reached northern France by the year 1600.

King Louis XVI recognized the beauty of the breed by using a matched pair to draw his hunting sleigh in 1774. He further added a matched pair of identically spotted Dalmatian dogs to trot along behind, adding regal color to royal travel. Strangely enough, Appaloosas were never popular in Africa where they remain unknown to this day. Horsemen in South America also did little to promote the breed because of a hostile attitude toward the color pattern.

Some breeding stock was imported to the state of Chihuahua, Mexico about the seventh century. It was from these Mexican herds that the Appaloosa breed developed and spread into this country. Navajos probably traded for spotted horses in Chihuahua and brought them to other tribes as barter.

About 1730 some of these beautiful horses reached the Nez Perce in the Columbia basin of Washington state. The Nez Perce were excellent stockmen and began raising horses, improving them by selective breeding, by the hundreds. When the first white man visited their country, which included parts of Washington, Oregon, Idaho, and even Montana, the Nez Perce had herds of spotted horses that were greatly admired by the early fur traders. Originally called the Nez Perce horse, concentrations of these spotted animals were noted predominating the rolling hill country along the Palouse River in southeastern Washington, which took its name from the French word "peluse" (grassy sward). White settlers then began referring to the horses as "Palouses," which in time was anglicized to Appaloosa.

The history of the Appaloosa and that of the famous Indian leader Chief Joseph are inseparable. Chief Joseph, his missionary given Christian name, was the leader of the Wallowa band of Nez Perce in northeastern Oregon. The Wallowa band suffered under English expansion and was finally driven from their homes in 1877. Thus began one of the most stunning feats of horsemanship in the history of the United States. For 1,300 miles, Chief Joseph led his band of tribesmen, women, children, and possessions across mountain terrain while outmarching and outfighting four armies. Although the Wallowa band was finally surrounded and captured in northern Montana, the feats of their Appaloosa horses became legendary. Declaring that he would "fight no more forever," Chief Joseph surrendered to the U.S. Cavalry and was returned to the reservation. After this war, the Appaloosa became a "lost" breed. To keep the Indians from revolting again, and because missionaries and Indian agents thought it was sinful for Indians to own such speedy and beautiful horses, the white men took away their horses and dispersed them throughout the country. Many were killed, others were given to Crow scouts or sold to farmers in the Midwest.

A renewal of interest in recreational horse riding after World War I led to a revival in many horse breeds including the Appaloosa. In 1938, the Appaloosa Horse Club was formed and a search began to reassemble horses with the characteristic patterns that had come to typify the Appaloosa (Fig. 2-12). Registrations now exceed 75,000 animals, making it not only a horse of another color but one of a rare history as well. It might well be argued that the Appaloosa is the oldest breed of horse known to man, with the possible exception of the Arabian.

Characteristics Appaloosas are more than just a color pattern. They have very definite physical characteristics recognized in 1950 by the National Association of Stallion Registration Boards, the final authority as to what constitutes a breed in this country.

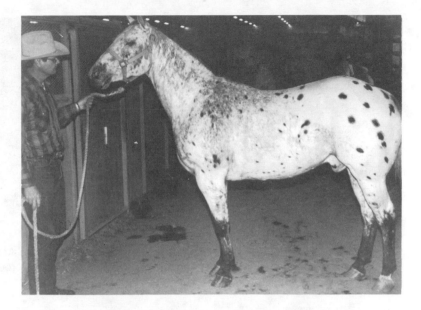

FIGURE 2-12. Appaloosas vary in their coat color. Some have almost no spots; others like this one are more preferred.

The Appaloosa is one of the most interesting of the horse breeds because of the definite physical characteristics required in addition to desired color.

Not all Appaloosas have to be spotted in order to be registered. In fact, so many different color patterns exist that color is merely a genetic hope in most cases. Disregarding for a moment the color patterns, there are several physical breed characteristics that distinguish the Appaloosa from some other breeds.

White sclera around the eye. The iris of the eyeball should be surrounded by a white sclera somewhat resembling the human eye.

Striped hoof. The typical Appaloosa frequently shows vertical stripes or laminations in one or all four of its hooves. This is the normal, expected pattern although horses are not discriminated against if they have only one hoof with stripes. These laminations also are not always readily visible. They are easier to see when the hooves are wet or cleaned (Fig. 2-13).

Parti-colored skin. For an Appaloosa that does not have a distinct color pattern, this is one of the most tell-tale physical characteristics of the breed. Mottled skin (beneath the hair coat) on the Appaloosa is most evident in the genital region and may also be seen around the soft skin of the lips, muzzle, nostrils, or eyes (Fig. 2-14).

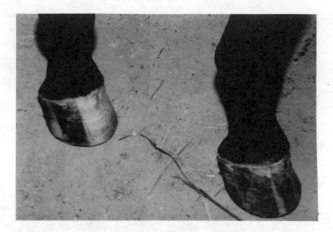

FIGURE 2-13. Striped hooves are characteristic in the Appaloosa breed. Some horses may have one light-colored hoof, three dark-colored hooves, or a striped combination.

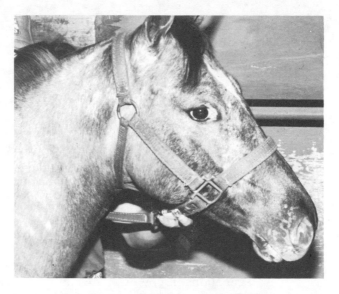

FIGURE 2-14. The skin of the Appaloosa, especially on the nose and around the eyes, may lack pigmentation giving a mottled appearance. This is characteristic of spotted horses.

Sparse mane and tail. Although not all representatives of this breed have the characteristic "stump," "finger-tail," or "rat-tail," the horse as a rule tends to have very few tail hairs as compared to the average equine (Fig. 2-15). The mane also tends to be rather whispy.

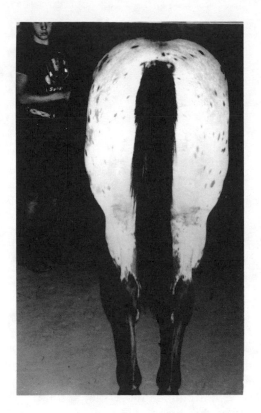

FIGURE 2-15. The tail of the Appaloosa is naturally shorter and thinner than other breeds, giving rise to the term "rat tail."

Varnish marks. Imagine brush stroking a light colored horse with a dark paint and you will get some idea of the term varnish marks. This is a grouping of predominantly dark hairs within an area, usually on the nose, face, above the eye, on the point of the hip, and/or in the gaskin and stifle region. At a distance, these varnish marks may be the first tell-tale sign of Appaloosa blood (Fig. 2-16). Closer examination of the sclera around the eye and the parti-colored skin will add clues to possible Appaloosa breeding. Add a striped hoof or two and there is a definite suspicion even with a traditionally colored solid coat.

Appaloosa coloration. Not only does the Appaloosa have different colors but it has six different color patterns that are recognized by the association. These are spotted blanket, white blanket, leopard, snowflake, frost, and marble. All these colors are basically variations of the size, shape and distribution of the spots.

Strangely, there is a "color pattern" which has almost no color pattern. It is identified as a *marginal* color pattern. These horses may show typical characteristics of the Appaloosa breed but have a lack of the coloring or show only a faint trace of the spots. Some marginal horses

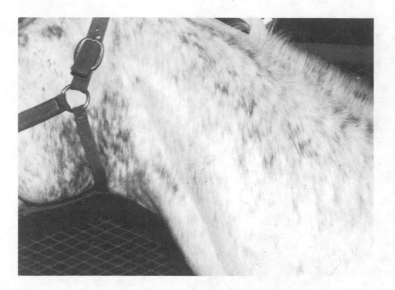

FIGURE 2-16. Many light-colored Appaloosa horses have streaks or "varnish marks" or darker hairs that do not conform to a spotted pattern.

cannot be distinguished from other breeds except upon close examination. A good marginal specimen is kept for breeding purposes because most Appaloosa breeders believe in "horse first, color second."

Another interesting characteristic of this breed is that many foals at birth do not have any of the typical spotted patterns. This may develop at a later age. Also, some horses will change dramatically in their color pattern with advancing age. Another observation worthy of note is that the male, like many wild animals and game birds, is characteristically the more colorful of the species. Other than these interesting deviations, the Appaloosa horse is judged in the traditional manner, using specific conformation standards set forth by the association.

The typical Appaloosa weights 1,000 to 1,150 pounds and stands 15 to 15.2 hands in height.

Animals under 14 hands at 5 years of age (maturity), pintos, albinos, ponies, or draft horses are not eligible for registration in the association. There is, however, an Appaloosa Pony Association which accepts the smaller version of the breed.

Uses

The desirable qualities of the Appaloosa have lead to its use in virtually every phase of business and recreation where a horse is needed or desired. This breed has for centuries been adaptable to rough terrain and rugged treatment. It is noted for qualities of endurance, speed, agility, and easy riding. In addition to its distinctive color pattern, the Appaloosa has proven to be a performance horse. The tribes of Central Asia prized the spotted horses for use in war and races. The Nez Perce treasured the Appaloosa as a hunting horse for buffalo. Early fur traders prized them as the best in mountain transportation. Northwest cattlemen still use them to this day for "rough country" horses.

The day of the war horse has past. So has the influence of the fur trader, but the horse for recreation has become a most important factor in animal husbandry. The Appaloosa is used in riding clubs, posses, gymkanas, trail rides, horse shows, rodeos, cutting contests, pleasure-riding, and many other facets of equine showmanship. The most recent addition to the long list of accomplishments for the Appaloosa is the development of the Appaloosa as both a quarter bred racing horse and a Thoroughbred racing horse. This versatile animal with its distinctive color pattern has made itself known in virtually every phase of the horse kingdom.

Common Criticisms

The most common fault that most horsemen complain about when discussing the Appaloosa breed is a desire on the part of many breeders to put the color pattern above considerations for physical development. However, this is contrary to the desire of the better Appaloosa breeders. Most conscientious horsemen will strive to produce a horse with the most desirable physical characteristics first and play genetic roulette with the color pattern second. Appaloosa breeders in recent years have made tremendous strides in breeding through the infusion of bloodlines with the desirable muscling coupled with the beautiful color pattern that is so sought after by horse lovers of this breed.

APPALOOSA PONY

History

A relatively recent development in the horse breeding field, the Appaloosa Pony Association was founded in 1962 and has since registered over 5,000 ponies. Membership in the association is currently estimated at about 3,000. Approximately 45 shows are held annually throughout the U.S. but the breed appears to be most heavily concentrated in Indiana, Illinois, Oklahoma, and Pennsylvania.

Characteristics

The same conformation type and distinctive physical characteristics of the Appaloosa horse are standards in selection, including the unique color patterns. The chief distinction of the Appaloosa Pony, separating it from its larger foundation breed, is the maximum height of 56 inches. Height is measured, including shoes, as with all horses, at the withers.

Uses

The Appaloosa pony is used mostly for recreation and is obviously well suited to the needs of the young rider. Many ponies, however, show exceptional powers of endurance, agility, and speed found in its larger counterpart and find use in every phase of the horse industry.

ARABIAN

There are two associations that deal with Arabian horses: The Arabian Horse Registry of America, which handles purebred registrations only, and the International Arabian Horse Association, which handles registrations for Half-Arabs (Fig. 2-17) and Anglo-Arabs (the cross between registered Thoroughbreds and purebred Arabians). The IAHA also handles all the promotion, clinics, shows, and public relations work for both associations.

The IAHA was founded in 1950 and has since grown to a membership of approximately 26,000. It is estimated that about 500 IAHA-approved Arabian shows are held in the United States each year.

The Arabian Horse Registry is unique in that it has never been open. Most horse associations leave the doors open for entry until a certain number of superior animals have been obtained. This is not so with the AHR. The only way to produce a purebred Arabian is with registered purebred parents having pedigrees stemming from the purebreds of the Arabian desert. Naturally, because of this stiff regulation, there are many fine horses, from one-half to seven-eighths or greater proportions of Arabian blood that are not eligible for registry. These animals are taken care of by the IAHA. Before World War I, the U.S. Cavalry needed mounts that would compete favorably with their allies and enemies. Recognizing this, Congress appropriated funds in 1920 to purchase Thoroughbred and Arabian stallions to upgrade the mili-

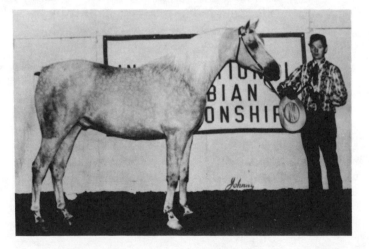

FIGURE 2-17. My Mystic Mirage. 1972 U.S. National Champion, Half-Arabian Gelding. Owner: Mr. and Mrs. George Albin, Lincoln, Nebraska. (International Arabian Horse Association)

tary horse. Known as the United States Remount Service, the program officially registered the Half-Bred (a Thoroughbred crossed on a non-Arab mare), the Half-Arabian (a cross between an Arabian stallion and a non-Thoroughbred mare), and the Anglo-Arab (a cross between Arabians and Thoroughbreds). This initial development lead to the Half-Arabian Registry, which is in existence today. In addition to the United States, most of Europe maintains Half-Arabian registries. Poland has a Half-Arabian registry that is broken down into five or more divisions of types.

Most of the "light horse" breeds as we know them today have Arabian blood in their veins. The classic example is the Thoroughbred. All Thoroughbreds racing in the world today are descendants from three Arabian sires—the Godolphin Arabian, the Byerly Turk, and the Darley Arabian. Some of these same bloodlines were also used in the development of the Standardbred, the Saddlebred, the Morgan, the Appaloosa, the American Quarter Horse, the Tennessee Walking Horse, and many others. Arabian horse owners can justifiably point in pride to their horses as the "sire of nearly all fine horses."

History

The Arabian horse is unique in that it is not considered a man-made mixture of bloodlines which we refer to as a breed. The Arabian horse is considered as a subspecies, one that developed on its own from *Equus agilis*, the hot-blooded horse of the South.

The late professor Henry Fairfield Osborn of the American Museum of Natural History stated that the Arabian horse was clearly depicted on cavern walls in southern France that date back 25,000 to 40,000 years. Although the exact origin of the Arabian horse is lost in antiquity, it is safe to assume that the breed has maintained its unique physical characteristics almost unchanged over a period of 20 centuries or more. Through natural selection, the Arabian developed unassisted by man for many centuries in the high, dry plains of Arabia and Africa.

The Arabian horse was found in Asia Minor at least 3,000 years ago and on the Arabian peninsula 2,500 years later. The silhouettes painted on Greek jars about 600 B.C. are undoubtedly Arabian bred horses. Greek artists carved statues using Arabian models. Mohammed and his disciples rode Arabian steeds as they conquered most of the world. The growth of the Mohammedan religion resulted in the introduction of the Arabian horse to France, Spain, and North Africa. The prophet Mohammed was so enchanted by his marvelous horses that he declared it a religious duty for all Moslems to love their horses. The Koran is even filled with tips on caring for horses.

The Bedouin nomads were as responsible as any group of people for the development and training of the Arabian horse. Desert bred horses were raised as part of the family, carrying the master of the household into battle and hauling tents and other possessions from oasis to oasis through blistering hot days and terribly cold nights. However, when night fell and tents were pitched, the horses, as a part of the family, were invited inside the tent with the family to drink camel milk from special cups and to share barley and dates in the family tent. The nomad riders did not use bits and rarely found a need for halters or bridles. The horses were trained to react to the voice command or a small amount of pressure from a heel, toe, or knee. This was important to the warring Bedouins who needed to have hands free for combat. The Arabian horse was never mistreated or handled with unnecessary force. So prized was this horse that he was never sold or traded, but was occasionally given as a gift exemplifying the utmost in friendship. Legend has it that some enterprising breeders, fearful of retaliation if the horse was stolen, clandestinely stole semen from superior stallions to artificially inseminate their mares. If this is true, the desert nomads were the first to recognize and practice the science of artificial insemination.

The bloodlines were recorded and kept pure for hundreds of years. The heritage of many horses even today can be traced back almost a thousand years. The impure blooded horses, known as Kadisches, were looked upon with scorn and could be readily sold or traded at common prices. A legendary Arabian horse, Bucephalus, was ridden by Alexander the Great.

In the year 1580, the Archduke Carlos, son of the German Emperor Ferdinand I, established the Imperial stud (breeding farm) using Andalusian (Spanish) and Arabian stock at Lipizza, part of what was Yugoslavia. From these horses came the famous Lipizzan breed, a mixture of Arabian and Andalusian blood.

In 1689, the Byerly Turk was imported into the British Isles for use on Barb (itself part Arabian) or Royal mares. The Darley Arabian was imported in 1706 and the Godolphin Arabian came in 1724 to continue the line of breeding that led to the English Thoroughbred. Practically every Thoroughbred racing horse in the world today stems from one of these great foundation sires. A classic example is the famous steed Man O' War.

About 1765, the purebred Arabian Ranger was imported to America. This horse, later called Lindsay's Arabian, was purchased by General George Washington after noting the superiority of the stallion's offspring. George Washington purchased this fine Arabian from a breeder in Connecticut and took him to Virginia for his own personal use.

General U.S. Grant was presented with two fine Arabian stallions by the Sultan Abdul Hamid, II.

During the Chicago World's Fair in 1893, Bedouins brought 29 pure-bred Arabian horses into the United States.

Before 1908, Arabian horses were registered by the Jockey Club of America. However, the Jockey Club allowed only registration of horses that were from the General Stud Book of England on the basis of their British papers. This left control of the American Arabian Registry in the hands of the British. This policy was changed as a result of Homer Davenport's trip to the Arabian desert in 1906 to search for Arabian horses. The expedition was sponsored by President Theodore Roosevelt. Davenport was successful in obtaining a shipment of 27 Arabian horses, which the Jockey Club would not accept except under the rules of the General Stud Book of England. Since the English Arabs actually carried a trace of native English horse blood, it occurred to some in this country to develop an American Arabian Registry. In 1908, in New York City, the Arabian Horse Club Registry of America was formed to maintain the purity of the old and distinguished breed. However, there were others in the country who wished to have an association that would represent an Arab on the basis of physical appearance if not genetic purity. A group of Arabian owners and enthusiasts in California formed the Arabian Horse Breeders Society of California. Soon after this, other associations sprang up across the country which lead to the development and formation of the International Arabian Horse Association in 1950.

Characteristics   The Arabian has many unique characteristics that set it apart from other breeds. The classic dished face (Fig. 2-18) with large eyes set wide apart shows a comparatively short distance between the eye and the muzzle. Although the muzzle is so small that it will ordinarily fit in the human cupped hands, the nostrils are very large allowing great quantities of air to be inhaled. These horses have a very high arch to the neck and tail. The mane and tail are customarily quite long. The croup is long and very flat in comparison to many other breeds. Like all purebred Arabians, they have 23 instead of the normal 24 vertebrae (5 instead of 6 lumbar) in their backs (Fig. 2-19), making them close coupled and capable of carrying heavy loads over long distances without back trouble.

Because they evolved under desert conditions, they are known for their ability to travel long distances without water or vegetation. The large barrels on the horses indicate that they are "easy keepers" able to utilize large quantities of forage rather than the more expensive grain.

In color, Arabians are bay, grey, and chestnut, with an occasional roan or black. Duns, piebalds, or yellows are never seen in the Arabian breed. However, the skin is black underneath the very fine coat, ex-

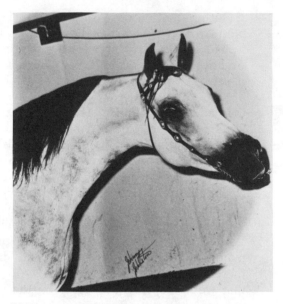

FIGURE 2-18.   Destiny's Desire #A35674. Champion Half-Arabian Mare, 1970 Nationals. Owner: Marjie Sammons, Kirkland, Washington. (International Arabian Horse Association)

FIGURE 2-19.   Arabians have one less vertebra in the back than other breeds, making them close coupled, capable of carrying heavy loads. (International Arabian Horse Association)

cept on stockings or facial markings. Foals may change shades of color as they grow older and one can never depend on the coat color at birth for an accurate appraisal of adult coloring. In addition to the common colorings, markings may include stars, stripes or blaze faces, snip noses, and white stockings on one or more feet.

The height of the Arabian is 14.1 to 15.1 hands with an occasional individual over or under this range.

Since Arabians are the foundation for virtually every light horse breed, it might be expected that they compete favorably in nearly every category. The Arabian cannot run as fast, however, as a Thoroughbred, or trot as high and fast as a Saddlebred, but he averages out well in overall competition.

The stamina and toughness of the Arabian make him the leader in Endurance Riding, a one-day race against time over a 50 or 100 mile course of grueling terrain. This activity is nothing new to the Arabian breed, whose ancestors faced similar obstacles over many centuries of use in the rugged desert. The world endurance record for competition in one year by one horse is held by an Arabian. One famous example is El Karbaj, a six-year-old, fourteen-hand gelding, ridden over 650 miles in sixteen endurance rides. The Bedouins were well aware of the Arabian horses' ability to excel over long distances at amazing speeds. For this reason, they affectionately refer to their Arabs as "drinkers of the wind."

Although the Arabian wins the toughest of endurance trials, he is a versatile showman. Beauty, refinement, and eloquence compliment the English attire of Pleasure Horse and Park Horse competition (Fig. 2-20). The flash and charm of this natural show horse is also taken advantage of in Driving Harness classes.

Of great interest to western riders is the discovery that Arabian horses adapt well as a stock horse. The Grand National Championship Reined Cowhorse Stake, long determined by the Quarter Horse, was won in 1961 by Ronteza, an Arabian. The prestige of the Arabian was greatly enhance by yet another example of his versatility. Although the Arabian is from a desert floor environment, he is used as a stock horse in elevations ranging to 8,000 feet without noticeable difficulty.

Cutting horse contests have increased in popularity over the last few decades and the event has become so popular that the versatile Arabian has also capitalized on this spectacular event (Fig. 2-21). Arabians compete in open competition as well as within the IAHA.

Because of its intelligence and long association with man, the Arabian is a favorite as an entertainer. The famous Lipizzan Stallions are of Arabian descent so it might be expected that the purebred Arabian would be used in dressage. Arabians can be taught leaps and pirouettes to create equine ballet, a demonstration of highly skilled rein

FIGURE 2-20. The Arabian—beauty, refinement, eloquence. (International Arabian Horse Association)

FIGURE 2-21. Arabians make fine cutting horses. (International Arabian Horse Association)

FIGURE 2-22. 1969 U.S. Nationals Arabian Racing. (International Arabian Horse Association)

work. The army of Alexander the Great was trained in teaching their part-Arabian horses a technique of warfare that included caprioles and leaps, performing highly specialized maneuvers to create awe and fear in their enemies. Because of these tremendous leaps and bounds the enemies of Alexander the Great often thought they were facing supernatural horses mounted by supernatural men. Dressage requires a horse that is a natural athlete, intelligent, agile, supple, and responsive to the slightest, almost hidden, command.

The Arabian also excells as a racehorse (Fig. 2-22). This should come as no surprise since for more than 127 years, every winner of the famous English Derby descended from an Arabian. The Darley Arabian, imported in 1706, accounted for nearly 87% of the winners. Although the Arabian is not as fast as the Thoroughbred, in recent years, special racing contests have been held for the Arabian counterpart of the Thoroughbred race.

Finally, the Arabian reputation for intelligence, affection, gentleness, and tractability have made him an ideal horse for children. The breed is one of the most docile of all horses. Because of their many centuries of close association with man, the Arabian appears to have developed a genuine affection for the human species and it is not unusual to see a stranger walk into a pasture of Arabian horses and soon have them crowding around him to muzzle their affection. This trait alone might

FIGURE 2-23.   Ansata IBN Sadan, AHR 32342. 1971 U.S. National Champion. Bred and owned by Donald and Judith Forbis, Ansata Arabian Stud, Chickasha, Oklahoma.

FIGURE 2-24.   Serenity Sonbolah, AHR 50737. U.S. National Champion Arabian Mare, 1971. Imported and owned by Serenity Farms Limited; Mr. and Mrs. B.D. Heck, Queensville, Ontario, Canada.

very well convince many people who in the past have been frustrated by a horse that could not be caught without trap or trickery of the desirability of the Arabian.

Common Criticisms

A most devastating genetic disorder, an incurable disease called combined immunodeficiency (CID), is found exclusively in the Arabian and Half Arabian horse. Although CID has been found in man, to date, it has not been discovered in other horses.

Foals are born with a severely defective immune system, making them susceptible to any type of infection. The slightest infection by a virus, bacteria, fungus, or protozoa is fatal. No amount of medication or care has in the past made the slightest difference. With the exception of two experimental foals receiving tissue transplants to restore their immunological systems, affected foals have not been known to survive past five months of age.

The genetic disorder is estimated to be carried by approximately 25% of the adult population making it a disease of great concern to breeders.

At present, there is no known treatment or management system to prevent CID. A blood testing program of all foals is recommended by the International Arabian Horse Association to detect the foals having the condition, and through a system of parentage tracing, the carriers could be detected and conceivably eliminated from producing more foals. A qualified laboratory using a small amount of blood drawn any time after birth is used as the basis of diagnosis. An air dried blood smear and five ml of serum are needed for diagnosis in the live foal. This blood testing and early diagnosis of CID is of tremendous value in preventing repeated matings between carriers. It is a well accepted fact that when two carriers are mated four times, the ratio of foals to be expected would be one normal, one CID foal, and two CID carriers (normal in appearance but perpetuators of the disease).

Since the disease is not known to occur in other horses, the IAHA has taken steps to raise funds exclusively through their own membership to provide grants to universities in Colorado, California, and Washington to discover ways of combating or eliminating CID. The association is also active in soliciting donations of carrier mares and stallions to assemble a carrier herd, to be donated to a university for further study of the disorder.

BELGIAN

The Belgian (Fig. 2-25), like the Percheron (Fig. 2-60), is one of the clean-legged draft breeds. The Shire (Fig. 2-73) and the Clydesdale (Fig. 2-29) are known as the feather-legged or hairy-legged breeds. Compared to the other draft breeds, the Belgian is a more recent newcomer to the United States but has made tremendous strides in estab-

FIGURE 2-25. The Belgian breed is the most popular draft horse in the United States and Canada. (Big Ed's Photos, Davenport, Iowa)

lishing itself as the most numerous of the draft horse breeds in the United States. Of course, the day of the draft horse breed as a necessary work animal in many parts of the world is basically a thing of the past. The Belgian still retains its popularity in the United States and Canada for such crowd pleasing spectacles as team pulling contests.

History

The Belgian breed originated in Belgium, a descendant of the ponderous Great Black Horse of Flanders. The humid soil of the low lying farm areas in Belgium required a heavy horse with strong and heavy bones. The Belgian was developed to farm this extremely difficult-to-manage soil. Breeding practices resulted in a deep bodied, rather short legged type of draft horse. Further selections from these war horses produced a strong horse to till the heavy soil.

For centuries since, the Belgian draft horses have been used for plowing and general farm hauling in their native land. The breeding of the horse is still promoted by the government, with annual prizes and awards being given to the best animals from each province. So prized is this breed that stallions standing at stud must be approved by a special government commission designed for this purpose.

The first importation into the United States was around 1885 or 1886. However, it was not until the turn of the century that the breed attracted much attention. The word soon spread among farmers about the Belgian's superior pulling characteristics and the breed prospered through the horse drawn agricultural implement stage. Although it does not get the favorable publicity of the high stepping Clydesdales, the Belgian still leads the field in numbers of registrations for draft animals in the United States.

Characteristics

Belgian horses have numerous outstanding characteristics, among them an easy going disposition. They are good feeders and good workers and travel well in trailers.

This breed has perhaps the ideal build and conformation for a truly draft-type animal. One of the Belgian's most outstanding traits is the ability to stamp their characteristics on their offspring. Belgian stallions, when bred to most any type of mare, have the ability to sire foals that are uniformly drafty. Very few mature Belgians are classified as "cherry pickers," a term used to denote draft type horses that are slim-bodied, leggy, or rangy.

The preferred colors are chestnut, roan, or bay with flaxen manes and tails. Browns, grays, and blacks are occasionally seen however. With advancing age, some of the horses grow walrus-shaped mustaches. Many Belgians also have a white-blazed face.

The Belgian averages 15.2 to 17.0 hands in height and weigh 2,200 pounds or more on the average. Although there may be variations above and below this height and weight, the Belgian is noted as being the widest, deepest, and lowest set of all draft breeds.

Uses

Originally used as a working plow horse, the Belgian has made its reputation in the horse pulling contests. In the old days, and even today in some places, horse pulling contests involve pulling a boatlike sled loaded with weights of stone or sacks of sand. The team that could pull the specified weight, which was standardized for all teams according to the weight of the team, the greatest distance in one straight pull was hailed as the champion. In recent years, horse pulling contests have become more scientific by using a dynamometer, which has iron weights similar to a scale, to register the exact pounds a team pulls. This "great equalizer" always remains the same for each team. The resistance of the dynamometer never varies. The Belgians consistently set the heavy weight records, currently in excess of two tons of dead weight in a straight pull. In national pulling contests, there may be as many as 125 matched pairs entered in the contest. The Belgians are consistently competitors and winners, there being more Belgian teams in competition than any other draft breed.

FIGURE 2-26. A beautifully matched pair of Belgian horses are used for draft recreation. (Kentucky Horse Park, Lexington, Kentucky)

Close examination of the Belgian will explain why it is a weight puller. Its compact body and muscular hind quarters furnish the power to propel it for these great tasks. Because of its short legs, it is able to double down into its harness, to draw strength from the core of its body. Although the Belgian does not have the high action and flashy way of going that other breeds have, its strong sense of determination and willingness to work make it a champion difficult to replace in a field of competition.

Common Criticisms Because of his extremely wide build in front, most Belgians roll or paddle and may be criticized for their way of going. Some of these horses are a little sluggish in temperament compared to other breeds.

In the early days of Belgian breeding in the United States, these horses were criticized because of small feet, short pasterns, high hips, short necks, and steep croups. Although these features are still very common to the breed, great strides have been made in developing the American Belgian into a truly great draft horse.

These defects not withstanding, the Belgian is recognized as a quiet, docile individual with strong, powerful determination.

BUCKSKIN The International Buckskin Horse Association (IBHA) was incorporated in 1971 to suit the needs of Buckskin horses throughout the world. Horses are registered on a world-wide basis. Currently, Buckskin horses are registered in Australia, Bahama Islands, Canada,

France, Iran, New Zealand, South America, and the United States. Although the Buckskin is not a definite breed as such, the association feels that the strong genetic linkage with the color type is related to qualities that are not common to all horse breeds. The main qualities promoted by owners of Buckskins are strength of muscles, bone, and determination. The stamina of the horse is legendary. There is some evidence to suggest that even the feet of most Buckskins are extremely hard and do not chip or wear down easily. Although the Buckskins might be considered a "color" association by some, breeders offer some interesting historical evidence to document the strength of an ancient type of horse that offers other dominant characteristics than color alone.

History

Buckskin horses in America do not, at this time, belong to any one pure breed. Historical evidence indicates that the Buckskin is a strong breed type. The color is an indication of strong heritage from antiquity. Nearing the end of the evolution of horses as we know them today, there were two main types which served as a springboard for all living horses today. The first was the Norwegian Dun type which exists today almost unchanged from prehistoric times. This horse developed in the cold northern countries and is still a dominant force in the equine world of Norway. The second type was the Barb, represented today by Arabs, Barbs, and Thoroughbreds.

The Norwegian Dun is not a product of man's selective breeding. It has always been the same, a Buckskin with a dark dorsal stripe. It is believed by some authorities that the Norwegian Dun may have inherited its color from the Sorraia, the original Buckskin colored horse of Spain. The Sorraia is also believed to be one of the oldest and most primitive breeds. It still exists in Spain today, a fine boned, hardy, small horse that is believed to have contributed greatly to the Buckskin dominant color.

When the Spanish Conquistadores came to America, they brought with them many horses from Spain of the Andalusian type. Many of these horses were Buckskin or Grulla due to the strong influence of the Sorraia. The influence of these Spanish horses is thought to be the reason for so many Buckskin and Grulla Quarter Horses in this country today. Although this color pattern cannot be traced back in pure form to either the Norwegian Duns or the Spanish Sorraia, they are the strongest living decendants of these breeds in America today. Since the Buckskin color, or some variation thereof, is such a dominant force in so many horse breeds in America, the International Buckskin Horse Association was formed to strengthen the bloodlines of horses carrying this color pattern and subsequently the other enduring qualities of the Buckskin. Breeders of Buckskins feel that their color is an indication of the superior genetic heritage they possess. Legendary rumors that a Buckskin with weak or spavined legs is a rarity lend some credibility to claims by the association. Promoters of this true Buckskin claim that he is "tough as wet leather."

Characteristics

The IBHA convention and national show is now referred to as the Dunarama. Approximately 16,000 horses are now registered by the association.

Although certain color restrictions are adhered to for registration in the association, the color is by no means the sole criterion for registration. Although there is no preferred type of conformation by the IBHA, a horse should be a good representative of the type it represents. Eligible horses can vary from the Arabian type to the "Bulldog" Quarter Horse type. The western or stock horse type saddle horse is considered the ideal.

Mature horses under 14 hands are not eligible although in some countries there are associations that handle Buckskin pony registrations if they do not measure up to this standard at maturity. Any horses having albino, appaloosa, paint, or pinto horse characteristics are not eligible. Even though the horse may be Buckskin in color, if it shows a predominance of gray hairs or roan hairs throughout the body, it is not eligible.

The color classification is rather broad and varied; colors may be classified under one of seven categories.

Buckskin. The true-colored buckskin is golden tanned (similar to deer hide) with black points (Fig. 2-27). The shade of buckskin may vary from yellow or light gold to dark gold. The points (mane, tail, legs) can be dark brown or black. A dapple bodied buckskin is acceptable.

Dun. The dun differs from the buckskin in that the body color is a duller shade and may appear to have a smutty appearance. This is caused from a dark hide with an abundance of pigment in the hairs. Shoulder and dorsal stripes belong to the Dun and often there will be leg barring.

Grulla (pronounced grew-ya or grew-yo). Body color is a mouse color or blue or dove or slate color with black points. The hide is well pigmented and the Grulla has a dorsal stripe in most cases shoulder stripes and leg barring. This color is considered the most rare of the Buckskins.

Red dun. Varying degrees of body shades of red with darker red points and a definite dorsal stripe are characteristics of this color pat-

FIGURE 2-27. Grand Champion Stallion "Lil Sage Scotter." David C Miller, Scottsdale, Arizona. (International Buckskin Horse Association)

tern. Leg barring and shoulder stripes are common. The dorsal stripe is usually dark red.

Copper dun. This is a dun with a copper tone shade to the body color. The points will be chestnut or dark copper in color and a dorsal stripe is required for registration. Some shadowing over the withers is often seen in place of the shoulder stripe.

Claybank. This is a lighter shade of the copper dun caused by less pigmentation. The eye of the claybank is amber. Being a dilute color, the claybank is in the same category as the Palomino. Claybanks are usually bred to Buckskins with a more intense color to produce offspring with more pigmentation.

Perlino dun. A very light shade of yellow body, almost white, with red points and a dorsal stripe with shoulder stripes and leg barring necessary for registration.

All Buckskins have a dark skin underneath whatever color type it may possess. The skin of the Buckskin, Dun, or Grulla is always black. The eyes are dark and rarely show white sclera.

An interesting fact about the Dun factor is that color indicating Buckskin breeding can actually be seen in the hair of a horse, when viewed under a microscope. In all other colors, the pigment granules in the hair are distributed rather evenly, with the color depending on the density of the granules. In the Buckskin, Grulla, or Dun the color or pigment granules are located only down one side of the hair shaft, the color running lengthwise of the hair, with the other side of the shaft being transparent. This is true even in the case of the horse of some color other than Buckskin, if he has close Buckskin breeding.

Horses having blue eyes (glass-eyed) or white spots on the body are not eligible for registration. Horses showing a predominance of draft blood and mules are also not admitted to the registry although there is a Buckskin Mule Registry Association.

White markings on the face and lower legs are permissible although leg markings are not allowed to go above the knees or hocks.

Although color is never judged at horseshows, there is one interesting exception in a special "dun factor" class which is held as an informative session for the Buckskin enthusiast. The dun factor points stress the variation in color patterns of the mane, tail, dorsal stripe, leg markings, etc. The darker shades of hair pigments in the various points of the Buckskin lend beauty to the overall color. The nine specific points covered in a dun factor class are dorsal stripe, leg barring, ear tips and ear edging, shoulder stripe or shadow, neck shadow, cobwebbing, face mask, mane and/or tail frosting and guard hairs, and mottling. In this educational session, no one body color is preferred.

Uses

Since Buckskin horses are found in virtually every breed, it stands to reason that their use is as wide as the breeders' imagination. Buckskins may be found in every type of horse show or horse event but the ideal type is considered to be the western or stock horse type saddle horse.

CLEVELAND BAY

The Cleveland Bay was bred to fulfill a wide range of needs, varying from pack horse to hunters, jumpers and carriage horses.

History

The breed derived its name from the Vale of Cleveland in Yorkshire in Northern England. It was influenced by developing Thoroughbreds in the neighboring Vale of Bedale. A direct ancestor known as the Chapman Horse was originally bred as a pack animal in Yorkshire for use by traveling merchants (chapmen) in late medieval times. The Chapman Horse was crossed on lesser quality horses that had been bred for centuries to produce a general purpose animal that could work the steep hills of Yorkshire farms, trot smoothly to market towns, and also be used for recreation as a fox hunting horse. From this cross, the Cleveland Bay eventually emerged to upgrade other breeds by supplying stamina and weight carrying ability. The Studbook was closed in 1883. It is the only surviving breed of general utility horse.

FIGURE 2-28. Cleveland Bays were used by Buffalo Bill Cody's wild west show. More recently they have been crossed with Thoroughbreds to produce heavy-weight hunters. (*Horses*, The Ridge Press, New York)

The first importation to America occurred in 1820 and the Cleveland Bay gained great popularity at that time. Buffalo Bill Cody used them to pull the Concord Coaches in his wild west shows. More recently the Cleveland Bay has been crossed with Thoroughbreds to produce heavy weight hunters.

Characteristics

The breed is bay in color, as the name implies, with black points on the mane, tail, and lower legs. The height normally varies from 16 to 16.3 hands and weight from 1,250 to 1,500 pounds. The body is wide and muscular. It has a long neck, substantial shoulders and withers, a free movement with excellent hock action, and a quiet temperament.

One of the outstanding characteristics of the Cleveland Bay is the ability of stallions to prepotently mark their offspring for consistency in type.

Uses

The Cleveland Bay has proven to be an excellent weight carrying hunter, an outstanding show jumper and event horse, and a superb competitor in harness and international combined driving events.

CLYDESDALE

Of all the draft horses, the Clydesdale is the showman, noted for its style, beauty, and action. If the big Clydes could talk, they would have a Scottish accent in their voices, being the national horse of Scotland. Action and stamina have made him the popular dray horse still to be seen on Scottish city streets, but more often in pairs or multiple hitches pulling wagons and working farm land all over the world. In the United States and Canada, they are more noted for their appearance in parades and flashy exhibitions but Clydesdale teams still plow, harrow, and harvest in Australia, New Zealand, and the Pampas of Argentina. In the early 1900s it was not unusual to see six or seven or even twelve horse teams hauling tremendous harvest loads to the railroads. Although not the most popular horse in terms of numbers, the Clydesdale is probably the most often remembered because of its beautiful color markings and stylish way of action.

History

Although its origin is lost in antiquity, there is no doubt that the Clydesdale was developed by Scottish farmers of Lanarkshire, through which the River Clyde flows. The former name for Lanarkshire is Clydesdale. The heavy mists that billow into these valleys from the Atlantic Ocean kept the earth always moist. This necessitated a healthy hoof. The soundness of the feet and legs brought about by these conditions are still among the chief assets of this breed.

Some writers credit a Scottish nobleman, the Sixth Duke of Hamilton, with the importation of six Flemish stallions from England, about 1715, to improve the quality of native Scottish mares. Other historians credit John Paterson, a farmer of Lochlyoch with the importation. Few, however, will dispute the evidence that a black stallion with a wide stripe down his face and knee-length wide stockings, named Blaze, foaled in 1779, had the most lasting influence in establishing the characteristics of the Clydesdale. When Blaze trotted, his long white stockings appeared to give him the stylish action of lifting front feet very high into the air and slapping them down with extraordinary strength and vigor. Most of the descendants of this outstanding sire inherited his stylish action and showy white markings which are still to be seen in the breed today (Fig. 2–29).

The Clydesdale was bred not only to meet the needs of the farmers, but the demands of commerce for the coal fields of Lanarkshire and for heavy hauling chores on the streets of Glasgow. An early feature of Scottish agriculture that did much to standardize and fix the type within the breed was the district system of hiring stallions. Outstanding stallions stood at stud in every district making easy access to superior sires. The records of these hiring societies can be traced as far back as 1837. The Clydesdale Horse Society, formed in 1877, has been an active force in promoting the breed throughout the British Isles and the world. As Scottish settlers began to emigrate to the United States and Canada, many of their superior draft horses accompanied them. The first Clydesdales brought to North America probably came into

FIGURE 2-29. Among draft horses, the Clydesdale is noted for style, beauty, and action. (Big Ed's Photos, Davenport, Iowa)

Canada in the 1870s. The United States drew from both Canada and Scotland for its importation of Clydesdale horses.

Characteristics   In average condition, mature stallions range from 1700 to 1900 pounds and stand 16 to 17 hands in height. Compared to other breeds of draft horses, the Clydesdale is not as wide, compact, or as heavy. The most enduring quality of the breed is its underpinning. Two old Scotch adages illustrate this philosophy: "No foot, no horse" and "Tops may go, but bottoms never." A thoroughly well built, typical Clydesdale exhibits the chief characteristics of strength and activity, with a minimum of superfluous tissue. The goal of breeders is quality and weight, rather than grossness and bulk. Although he is not bred for action, he must have action. Clydesdale judges look for high lifting of the feet, not scuffling along, but a clean lift off the ground with every step. Action also means "close" movement. The forelegs must be planted well under the shoulders—not a "bulldog action" as may be seen in other draft horses. There must be no openness at the knees, and no inclination to knock the knees together. Likewise, hind legs must be planted closely with points of the hocks turned inward rather than outward. Straight, "plumb" feet and legs are extremely important. "Sickle" hocks are a very bad fault, leading to a loss of leverage.

With so much emphasis on underpinning, it is to be expected that the merits of the Clydesdale are estimated by first examining the feet.

Bay and brown are the most common colors in the Clydesdale with black favored by some. Roans are also seen. The preferred markings are four white socks to the knees and hocks, and a well defined blaze or bald face.

As one of the more famous feather-legged breeds, the Clydesdale is expected to have a moderate quantity of fine silky hair from the hocks downward.

The custom of braiding the Clydesdale's mane in an Aberdeen roll (Fig. 2–29) is lost in antiquity but, like kilts and bagpipes, seems to be a part of Scotland. The Scots developed a different style of braiding, starting between the horses' ears and braiding horizontally along the crest, weaving into the mane long strands of brightly colored bunting. The result is a roll along the crest with the remainder of the mane hanging free. Rosebuds stand erect on long spikes at equal distances along the roll. To this day, the custom of the Aberdeen roll is carried out wherever Clydesdales are seen in the show ring. The tail is also usually fashioned into a knot with rosebud adornments.

Uses

The Clydesdale was originally developed as a farm horse, and a heavy dray (cart) horse. Developed for use in the farming districts in Scotland and for pulling heavy loads in the coal fields and commercial districts of Glasgow, his distinctive beauty and action has expanded his popularity to include recreation and entertainment. Farmers in the midwest of the United States and many Canadian provinces still use the Clydesdale for general agricultural needs. Some Clydesdales are kept by fanciers of the breed as saddle horses but the most famous use for this breed in the United States is as a multiple-hitched team to pull wagons. Perhaps the most famous draft horses in the world are the matched Clydesdale teams that pull the famous Budweiser Beer Wagon (Fig. 2–30).

COLORADO RANGER HORSE (RANGER-BRED)

The Colorado Ranger Horse Association (CRHA) is a small but growing association. It was established in 1938 and for 30 years restricted to 50 members. Membership has since been expanded and now registers more than 2,000 horses. In appearance, the Rangerbred is quite similar to the Appaloosa and most horses carry a double registration. However, the Rangerbred has always carried specific bloodlines in which the color has not been a requirement for registration. Even the best and most beautifully spotted Appaloosa is not eligible for registration in the Rangerbred association unless it carries specific bloodlines. Membership is nationwide in the United States and has spread into Canada, Australia, Belgium, and the Kingdom of Jordan. Four regis-

FIGURE 2-30. The world famous eight-horse hitch of Clydesdales, probably the most famed exhibition in the world. (F.L. "Kirk" Kirkendall, Wharton, Texas)

tered Rangerbreds are in the Royal Stables of King Hussein where they have been interbred with the Royal Pure Arabian Horses. More and more horse owners are discovering the Rangerbred as a distinct breed, not just another spotted horse.

History
    The distinguished cornerstone for the Rangerbred horse was laid by General U. S. Grant in 1878. While visiting Sultan Abdul Hamid in Constantinople, Turkey, General Grant was shown through the personal stables of the Sultan, which contained over 100 stallions whose ancestry could be traced back over 600 years. The Sultan asked General Grant to make a selection of any horse in the stables to be presented to the General as a gift. Grant selected a dapple gray, five-year-old purebred Arabian named Leopard, a translation from Turkish. After signifying his choice, the Sultan personally selected another horse to be included in the gift. The four-year-old blue-gray stallion Linden Tree, a purebred Barb, indicated the Sultan's admiration for the famous U.S. general. Both horses were shipped by the Turkish government to New Haven, Connecticut. These horses were so outstanding that $10,000, a handsome fee for those days, was refused for a halfbred son of Leopard.

    These two great desert stallions were used by Randolph Huntington of New York and Virginia in the development of a light-harness trotter which he proposed to name the Americo-Arab. Many improvements to the horse were made by Mr. Huntington but financial troubles spelled the end of the Americo-Arab and complete dispersal of his efforts. General Colby, a retired army general and a friend of General Grant, persuaded Huntington to lend him the use of the aged stallions, Leopard and Linden Tree, for a single breeding season in Nebraska. In only one short summer, these two stallions left an indelible mark on the native mares from the Colby ranch. This was actually the beginning of the breed. In the latter part of the 1890s, several Colorado horse breeders heard of the Colby horses and sent A. C. Whipple of Kit Carson County, Colorado to the Colby ranch with instructions to buy several mares and a stallion. Mr. Whipple selected a snow-white stallion with black ears named Tony, a double-bred grandson of Leopard. These crosses met with remarkable success in the years that followed.

The aim of the Colorado horse breeders was to produce a working cow horse with no interest whatsoever in creating a particular color pattern. However, because of the intensive line breeding program, the high plains horseman produced a wealth of barbaric color patterns. The breeders were pleasantly pleased to find so many color patterns deriving from the Barb breed—leopard-spotted, rain-dropped, blanket-hipped, snow-flaked patterns of every conceivable color. These flashy horses created a stir in the hearts of horsemen wherever they were seen. The W. R. Thompson Cattle Company of Yuma County, Colorado further strengthened the Barb blood and distinctive traits of these horses in 1918 through the stallion Spotte, a purebred Barb stallion presented to their daughter as a wedding present. Spotte figures in the pedigree of many Rangerbred horses today. In the same year, a stallion colt named Max was born on the ranch of Governor Oliver Shoupe at Colorado Springs, Colorado. Max, a snow-white stallion completely covered with black leopard spots, and his offspring were noted for a trim build and capacity for speed. Max was purchased by Mike Ruby, an emigrant from Ontario to the Colorado plains. Mike Ruby perhaps did more for the establishment of the Rangerbred Horse than any other man in its history. It was he who founded the association and served actively in it until his death in 1942. The origin of the unusual name for the breed can be traced back to the efforts of Mike Ruby who in 1934 was extended an invitation by the National Western Stock Show Commission in Denver to bring a pair of his stallions for an exhibition. The two spotted stallions that Mike brought from the home ranch created a sensation at the Denver show and caught the eye of Colorado State University faculty members who suggested the name Colorado Rangers—Range horses bred in the open environment of the state. Thus, the name Colorado Ranger Horse, or Rangerbred.

Characteristics

Rangerbred horses are more often than not spotted in color. The wild, widely variegated colors are due to the influence of the Barb horse. Old records indicate the Barb to have carried every color imaginable for horses.

Although the spotted colors so characteristic of the Colorado Ranger Horse are striking in appearance, it is neither the objective nor a prerequisite for entering a horse in the CRHA Stud Book. The association makes it quite clear to the general public that an owner may pursue any color his heart dictates but there is only one requirement for registration: all horses must trace an unbroken pedigree to the original stallions Leopard, Linden Tree, or Max. To quote from association literature, "color is a fickle jade. It is merely pigment in the skin. It cannot be ridden. Fads fade. Bloodlines endure."

This young association still uses the time honored method of maintaining an open herd book in order to allow outcrosses with other superior bloodlines to improve the breed. Although ponies and draft outcrosses were barred in 1947, the association still allows outcrosses from Thoroughbreds, American Saddle horses, Tennessee Walking horses, Quarter horses, Appaloosas, Arabians, Morgans, and Standardbreds. The purpose for this provision is to allow for the infusion of outstanding bloodlines to more quickly improve the developing breed. Like all associations, it is anticipated that the books will one day be closed and breeders will be restricted to selecting horses from within the association registry.

Because of the many bloodlines that have gone into the Rangerbred, it is difficult to establish a particular set of characteristics that would identify the horse separate from other breeds. The average Rangerbred is 15 to 16 hands high, of Quarter horse type conformation, although some closely resemble the Thoroughbred or Barb when bred for uses other than originally intended. No draft horses or ponies are eligible for registration. Figures 2–31 and 2–32 show some of the typical visual characteristics to be expected by outstanding representatives of the breed.

Uses

The Rangerbred horse was developed primarily as a working cow horse on the open ranges in Colorado. The basic purpose for the association still clings to this guideline as a major purpose. However, some unusual individuals have been used in other areas as well. "The Spotted Wonder" was a racing type Rangerbred that was undefeated in his lifetime. The stallion "Rio Dinero" won the National 100 Mile Endurance Trail Ride, and numerous Rangerbreds are used on the rodeo and show horse circuit. The primary use might be expected to be as a hard working range cow horse.

FIGURE 2-31. (a) Welcome Sting, Rangerbred stallion. (Courtesy of John E. Morris, Colorado Ranger Horse Association). (b) Rangerbred Mare. Although color patterns such as this are quite common in the Rangerbred, the association puts no emphasis whatsoever on color. (Courtesy of John E. Morris, Colorado Ranger Horse Association)

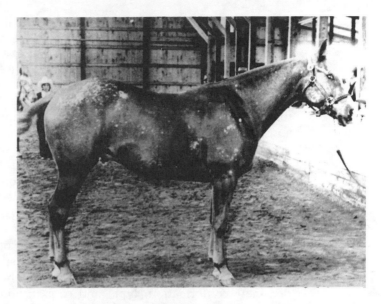

FIGURE 2-32. Rangerbred Gelding. A typical horse in good working condition. Note the extreme variations in color patterns from Figure 2-31. (Courtesy of John E. Morris, Colorado Ranger Horse Association)

CONNEMARA

The Connemara is the largest of the native pony breeds and because of their relatively large size on the small end of the scale, they have proven invaluable as a youth horse in the United States. They are large enough to be rugged yet small enough to serve as an intermediate size horse for more advanced riders.

History

The wild, windswept hillsides of western Ireland is the native home of the Connemara pony. Because of the harsh climate created from storms arising from the Atlantic Ocean, the Connemara had to develop a tough constitution. This pony had no shelter and had to rely on gorse and heather for forage. The original hardy native ponies grew from birth to maturity in the rough terrain around County Galway. The harsh rocky inhospitable land developed a native pony that grew up very sure footed, a trait which enthusiasts say makes for a natural jumper. The history of the ponies before 1600 is a combination of fact and some Irish folklore. The truth probably lies somewhere in between what is known and what is speculated. It is known that the tough native ponies probably developed on their own without the help of mankind or infusions of other breeds for centuries. However, Irish legends indicate that the stormy seas that developed the original Irish indigenous ponies also washed ashore the breeding stock to improve the natives. Legend has it that shipwrecked Andalusians washed ashore in County Galway to run wild, mixing and mingling with the native ponies. Legend also tells us that a Spanish mare, a refugee from the 1588 Armada, washed ashore to cross with a native stallion of questionable background. According to this Irish rumor, the result between the native stallion and the Spanish mare was a fine dark dun riding mount that was presented to King James I from County Galway to London and housed at the Royal Stables in Greenwich. The year was 1606 and the pony at that time was referred to as a Connemara "hobby." He was a 5-year-old stallion at the time of the gift.

By the close of the eighteenth century, some stocky, large-boned black horses of French origin were introduced into County Galway along with Arab strings. These too were mixed with the blood of the hardy native ponies.

Because of the dun color that crops up so often in the Connemara pony native to Ireland, it is reasonable to speculate that the breed sprang from the original wild dun horse, whose blood continued to dominate conformation, type, and constitution in the Irish pony. In 1900, a study was made of the actual condition and potential possibilities of the native Connemara pony. The report of Dr. J. C. Ewart of Edinburg University described the old dun type of Connemara as "capable of living where all but wild ponies would starve" and "strong and hardy as mules." Dr. Ewart made no secret of the fact that the breed was so valuable "and fertile and free from hereditary disease" that their extinction would be a national loss. From that time onward, the breed began to receive much more attention and breeding practices became more controlled and formalized.

In short, the Connemara pony seemed to have developed by chance, a combination of wild horse, gifts from the sea in the form of Andalusian, Spanish, and perhaps other breeds that washed ashore, Arabians, and a few outstanding horses of questionable origin that were thrown in with the native ponies. A mixture of fine "blooded" stock and "wild," hardy strings led to the development of a most unusually gifted horse.

The Connemara did not receive much recognition in this country until 1956, when a sufficient number of ponies existed to create a demand for a society for this hardy breed. The first Stud Book was published in 1959. About two-thirds of the original entries were imports compared to the current 18% imported horses. The Stud Book currently has registrations of more than 1800 purebred Connemaras. The association also maintains a supplement to the American Connemara Pony Society for registration of half-bred Connemaras. If consistently bred to purebred Connemaras, descendants of half-bred parents, after the fifth generation, may be registered in the ACTS.

FIGURE 2-33. Michelle Hood and Shaun Cyoilin, July 1976 Chagrin Valley P.H.A. Show, Cleveland, Ohio. (Photo by Mrs. John E. O'Brien, American Connemara Pony Association)

Characteristics

Connemaras in the United States may vary in size from less than 13 hands to more than 15 hands. However, the average horse should range around 14 hands.

The conformation of the Connemara is closely akin to that of a Hunter with a well balanced head and neck, prominent withers, good sloping shoulders, lots of substance and quality, and a symmetrical body. Legs should be especially rugged with clean, hard, flat bone measuring approximately 7 to 8 inches below the knee.

Colors of Connemaras, in addition to the expected dun, include gray, bay, brown, with some roans and an occasional black, chestnut, or palamino. Piebalds, and Skewbalds are not eligible for registration. Neither are blue-eyed creams foaled after 1972. Stock is not eligible for permanent registration until it is two years of age.

Uses

In Ireland, the Connemara was bred for utility purposes and characteristics such as docility and intelligence were as important as hardiness and constitution to Irish breeders. A consistently gentle temperament with children combined with their native jumping ability made them desirable mounts for children's horses in show jumping and fox hunting. They are so docile that even children may show Connemara stallions in horse events. Of course, the size of this largest of

FIGURE 2-34. Connemaras excel as children's show jumpers. (Photo by Mrs. John E. O'Brien, American Connemara Pony Association)

FIGURE 2-35. Hideaway's Hustler by Hideaway's Erie Suithereen and his dam Hideaway's Centerfield. (Photo by John E. O'Brien, American Connemara Pony Association)

the native pony breeds also makes it a very respectable adult pony and is used by many around the world where a smaller horse is desirable or necessary.

The American Connemara Pony Society was formed in "recognition of the need for a pony of great stamina and versatility, capable of carrying an adult in the hunting field, yet gentle and tractable enough for a young child, fearless as a show jumper (Fig. 2–34), yet suitable and steady as a driving pony." The horse is reported, therefore, to be a mount not only for novice riders but for adults of any age or height. The Connemara has built a reputation in America as a family animal, willing and able to pull buggies and sleighs, to be used on trail rides and in show events, or just to be the neighborhood pet. Because of their gentle, even disposition, they have proven invaluable in demanding, competitive situations whether ridden by adults or younger riders.

DONKEYS AND MULES

With very few exceptions, mules are infertile, incapable of producing offspring. It has been said that "the mule is without pride of ancestry or hope of posterity." However, the mule has persisted because of its unique contribution to mankind. The breeds of donkeys available and types of mules produced from them are as varied as the genetic base from which they came.

History of the Donkey (Ass)

The domestic donkey is most likely a descendant of the wild ass found in North Africa. Other theories are that it descended from the Kiang of Asia or even the Zebra. It is probably the oldest beast of burden domesticated by man, basically because of its docile nature and friendly, even loving disposition.

The scientific name for donkey is Equus asinus. The proper name for all donkeys is Ass; most English speaking countries, however, refer to it as the donkey. This name comes from the old English term meaning dun-colored animal. In America, both north and south, most people have adopted the Spanish word "burro," which is donkey in the Spanish language. Whether called donkey, ass, burro, or some other name, they are all of the species Equus asinus.

Historical research reveals that donkeys were a vital part of living many years before the time of Christ. Findings from Egyptian tombs indicate that asses were ridden, harnessed to chariots, and driven by rings inserted in their noses long before bridles were known or horses had even been put to use. Many ancient kings favored the all white donkey as a source of purity and prestige. As early as 2,000 B.C., donkey caravans were recorded and Hebrew nomads were completely dependent on donkeys. Donkey-riding Arabs conquered Palestine in 635 B.C. In 40-67 A.D., Roman legions were mounted on donkeys and in the eleventh and twelfth centuries European peasants depended upon them. Certainly the most famous of all animals was the donkey that carried Christ into Jerusalem just prior to his crucifixion.

Some historians claim that donkeys came to America with Columbus on his second voyage in 1493. Although there is no conclusive evidence to support this, there is general agreement that donkeys were brought to America by Spanish colonists through Mexico and Florida in the 1500s. Records do indicate that Ferdinand II of Spain sent four jacks and two jennets to the West Indies about 1495.

Without a doubt, the expansion of America from the east to the west coast and from Canada to Mexico came about partially because of the donkey packing endless goods on its back through the whole exploration and development of North and South America. Who can think of the old gold prospectors of this continent without his trusty donkey, the Mexican peasant without his burro loaded with firewood, the mountain pack train without its share of longears?

Characteristics of the Donkey

A wide variety of types, sizes, and colors (Fig. 2–36) of donkeys exist throughout the world. These range from the Miniature Mediterranean Donkey, less than 36 inches at the withers, to the giant Mammoth Ass, 13–16 hands or more. All of them have been used at one time or another in crossing on horses to produce various sizes of mules.

FIGURE 2-36. A superior type standard donkey jack. George Kolb, Southlake, Texas, owner and handler. (Betsy Hutchins, Denton, Texas)

The basic color is a dun gray with a dorsal stripe, a dark cross stripe on the withers, and perhaps stripes on the legs. This is a common color because it is the original color of the ancestral wild ass. However, the donkey is found in most horse colors including chestnut and appaloosa. Another common color is black or dark brown with a light muzzle, rings around the eyes, and a light belly, and the insides of the legs light. Very rarely do donkeys not have these light areas in its coloring.

The Miniature Mediterranean Donkey was originally imported from Sicily and Sardinia. These small asses have strong conformation, broad heads, and dun or brown coats. They are rarer than the other donkeys and usually more expensive because of their small size.

The American Spotted Ass is basically a donkey in a pinto coloration. It is of normal size. Because of its colorful coat it has some unusually attractive aspects of ownership.

In America, the ass is usually referred to as a donkey or burro. The standard size is widely spread throughout the United States and comes in a variety of colors.

The Mammoth strain of donkey is highly prized in the United States. It stands 13 to 16 hands high and was selectively developed for crossing on horses to produce a strong, draft-type mule. It is also referred to as the American Jack and Jennet.

The most famous French ass, and perhaps the most famous in the world, is the Poitou Ass. Although there are only about 200 in the world today, they are heavy boned with huge feet and heads and thick, long, shaggy hair. They are excellent draft mule breeders and highly prized around the world. Other large breeds include the famous Spanish Catalonion Jacks. It is also referred to as the Spanish Jack.

Other large breeds exist, one of the more famous of which is the Andalusian.

The following terms are associated with donkeys:

Jack.   The mature male ass.

Jack colt.   A male ass under three years of age.

Jennet or jenny.   The mature female ass.

Jennet filly.   A female ass under three years of age.

Burro.   A spanish word adopted by Americans to denote ass.

Donkey.   A word coined from the English "dun-key" meaning small, dun colored animal.

Jackstock.   Used to refer only to the standard American Jack and Jennet otherwise known as the "Mammoth" Jack and Jennet. These are very large asses never referred to as donkeys or burros. The minimum size for the smallest is 13.2 hands at the withers. This is the American breed started by George Washington and steadily developed in quality and numbers since that time.

Spanish jack. Usually a term used to denote the American ass or burro that shows a substantial amount of the bloodlines imported from Spain. This is usually a tall animal with good quality, balance, and style which makes a useful Jack for producing mules in crossing on horses.

The most outstanding characteristics of donkeys compared to horses include the fact that they are generally more sure-footed with more elastic and stronger hooves. Donkeys are also more narrow and up-standing and for this reason, their feet usually do not wear down and chip off.

Donkeys will almost never overdrink water and founder themselves even when brought in hot. However, the same cannot be said for overeating, as most donkeys are gluttons about grain. They have to be watched carefully in this respect as much as a horse.

Normally, donkeys do not have to be shod and their ability to carry tremendous loads in comparison to their relative size is well documented.

If the donkey is kept out in the weather, it should proably not be groomed heavily as the dust of its daily dust bath protects it from the elements. A donkey's coat is coarser than a horse's in winter and bur-ros normally establish a regular "dust bowl" somewhere in their enclosure and roll in the dust several times a day. Unlike a horse, a donkey does not shake the excess dust from its coat because the dust provides protection from the heat, a mechanism from its desert days.

Donkeys also vary from horses in that their gestation period is 12 months instead of the 11 of the horse. Most donkey breeding is done by leaving the animals in a pasture together for a month, as the jennet comes into heat every three weeks on the average. When ready to accept the jack, the jennet will "mouth," or click her teeth together several times in a unique action not found normally in horses.

A unique consideration in working donkeys is to make sure the bridle and halter fit. Donkeys usually have a horse-size head and a pony-size mouth. Care must be taken that the tender mouth is not irritated by a bit that is too large. The bit must not pinch.

Uses

The use of donkeys as a beast of burden is legendary throughout the world and they are still used in many underdeveloped countries for mining, packing, agricultural work, etc. In the United States, it is also well known that they make wonderful pets and companions to children because of their gentle, kind nature. They are unequaled as a family pet by any other animal with the possible exception of the dog. They make an ideal first mount for a child. Although they have a reputation for being stubborn and "mean" on some occasions, they resort to this form of rebellion only when mistreated or forced into a situation they fear.

Donkeys are driven, ridden, packed, shown, and loved throughout the world. No equine has such an intense affection for people. In training, rewards of food are not necessary. Petting and kind gestures are the most effective means of rewarding for proper behavior.

However, the most widely accepted use for the ass is for crossbreeding a jack and mare to produce the mule or a stallion on a jenny to produce a hinny. A hinny looks like a mule but has a little more of the horse characteristics, conformation, and agility.

History of the Mule

The use of the mule can be traced back to accounts of the Trojan War but was first popularized by George Washington in the United States. The king of Spain presented an outstanding Jack (Ass) to President George Washington in 1787 as a gift from the country of Spain. This Jack had a very docile temperament. Using another Jack of the Maltese breed that had great size and conformation but a rather nasty disposition, Washington was able to combine, through the use of his jennets, a strain of donkeys (Ass) having the best qualities of both outstanding sires. Their offspring were eventually crossed with horses to develop the first good quality mules in the United States. The descendants live on to this day and are now differentiated from the more common donkey by the name Mammoth Jack. Mammoth Jacks when used on draft type mares produce the famous "Missouri Mule."

However, a cross between any Jack and mare will produce a mule. If draft mares are on the maternal side, the result is a heavy work mule (Fig. 2–37). Crosses on light horses result in lighter animals sometimes referred to as "Cotton Mules", so common to the old plantation states. And Jacks crossed on ponies results in "mini-mules."

The reciprocal cross results in a Hinny. That is, using stallions crossed on Jennets results in a mule type animal also but it is referred to as a Hinny. The Hinny is more horse-like in appearance, agility, and temperament. The Hinnies are normally not as large as the mules and most approach the appearance of a mule in its head characteristics, ears being rather long. One of the most common uses for the Hinny is as a mount for rodeo clowns. Unsuspecting spectators might think they are seeing a "mini-mule" but most likely it is a Hinny resulting from the cross between a horse or pony stallion and a Jennet.

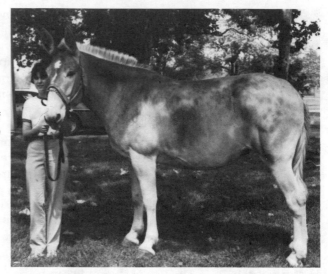

FIGURE 2-37. An excellent example of a large draft type mule. (Kentucky Horse Park, Lexington)

CHARACTERISTICS OF THE MULE

The mule has long been known for its sure-footedness and docile temperament in situations that would bring about disaster with horses. For instance, when a horse gets excited, it normally panics. This seldom happens with a mule, who is generally calm and collected under the most stressful situations. For this reason, mules are seen almost exclusively as tourist mounts descending the spectacularly narrow trails to the bottom of Grand Canyon. Legend has it that the mule is also much brighter than the horse. Evidence of this superior intelligence has been reported on many occasions when the mules walked too close to the edge of the canyon. Nervous tourists tended to dismount. Mules discovered this fact very quickly and soon learned that an easier descent to the bottom of the canyon and back could be had as the result of careful placement of feet very close to the edge of disaster.

Compared with the horse, the mule can withstand much higher temperatures, is less subject to founder or other digestive disturbances, and may be used in many places where a horse cannot. In the days of the old South, a horse was rarely used to pull tobacco sleds into a barn because if a foreign object should accidently touch the horse's head, it would rear up, injuring itself and possibly handlers. On the other hand, an object touching the head of the mule simply causes it to lower its head quietly away from the object.

The mule is generally considered stronger than the horse but slower. Contrary to popular opinion, it is quite capable of running since one of the most recent developments in the use of mules includes mule racing.

There has been only one or two documented cases in which mules have been able to reproduce. For all practical purposes, we can say that the mule is infertile. Because of its hybrid vigor, strength, longevity, sure-footedness, and resistance to digestive disturbances, the mule has long held a place of fondness in the heart of man.

Mules come in assorted colors, normally brown or black, but may even be spotted (Figure 2-38). Sizes vary according to the following types:

Small miniature.   40 inches or less at withers

Miniature.   40 inches to 54 inches

Saddle.   54 inches and up with saddle type conformation

Light work or pack.   54 inches up with heavier conformation

Heavy draft.   60 inches up with draft characteristics

FIGURE 2-38.   An excellent saddle mule. Pennie Maxson of Michigan, owner and handler. (American Donkey and Mule Society)

It should be noted that mule production is not as simple as just turning any jack in with a mare. The two normally do not associate socially or sexually unless they have been trained to do so. The time honored method has been to raise a jack to be used for producing mules with a band of horses. The theory is that he thinks he is a horse and can even convince a mare to accept that philosophy. Of course, other methods using handlers and breeding crates, artificial insemination, etc., may be preferred.

Uses

The uses of mules in show and specialty events throughout the United States is astounding. Although originally thought of as a work animal for use in plowing, draft work, and as pack animals, the mule has become somewhat of a novelty sport animal. For purposes of show and this discussion, Hinnies are also included as mules. Some of the more interesting classes are as follows:

Pleasure Western Riding. The rider is dressed in appropriate gear. Mules are shown at a flat-footed walk and a slow easy lope.

English Pleasure Riding. Rider and mount are dressed in appropriate English tack and judged at canter.

Trail Mule. To be tested for manners and obedience over a series of obstacles.

Saddled Jumper. Jumps are from 2 to 4 feet over an appropriate course.

Pack Strings over Obstacles. This is a ridden class in which a rider is mounted on one mule leading another over a set obstacle course.

Walk, Trot, and Git Race. Animals walk 200 yards to a marker, trot 200 yards to the second marker, turn and "git" to the finish line at the fastest pace possible.

Pony Express Relay Race. Each team uses three saddled mules and one rider. Each animal is ridden once around the track with the rider changing animals in front of the grandstand.

Driving classes with mules are also conducted and include the following:

Single Hitch Pleasure Driving. A walk and trot are required in this event with the mule hitched to a suitable wheeled vehicle.

Open Hitch Driving. Two or more mules in a team, pulling a suitable wheeled vehicle.

Parade Class. Fancy parade style equipment using mule hitches is a popular event in the show ring or down main street.

Sled Mules. A single hitch is used using a mule to pull a sled over an easy obstacle course. This is a spinoff event from plantation days when mules were used to pull tobacco on wooden sleds.

Chariot Race.   A distance of one-half mile, a timed event, with no more than two mules per vehicle constitutes this colorful event.

Mules are also entered in specialty classes such as:

Junior Exhibitors Obedience Class.   An event for the youngsters which illustrates the calm obedience of the mule. All four hoofs must be raised by the youngster, the tail is grabbed without the animal getting excited, then the mule is lead over a special course, commanded to jump a small obstacle, and loaded into and unloaded from a trailer.

Lead Line.   This demonstrates the obedience and calm disposition of the mule when carrying the very young rider on its back. A child usually rides and may hold the reins but must not control the animal. The handler does the work through a lead line.

Coon Hunters Mule Jumping.   In this colorful event, a mule will be shown saddled. Animals are allowed to jump without the rider, a command to clear the object given through a lead line. Coon hunting mules are expected to walk up to a barrier, test it with their nose or chest and rear up on hind legs, jumping almost flatfooted over the barrier. This makes for a very practical illustration of the versatile use of a calm beast of burden.

Pulling Contest.   Mules are weighed on the day of the contest, and, if pulling in teams, will move a percentage of their combined weights, which may range from 150 to 350 percent of their weight as needed to determine the winner.

Authentic Costume Class.   Mules and riders have authentic native and occupational costumes suitable for a colorful show much to the delight of spectators.

Obstacle Pack Course.   The animal is fully packed in the arena with a top cover to be tied down. This illustrates the age-old use of mules in rough or mountainous terrain. Mules were used in this way as recently as World War II in the mountains and jungles of Burma.

Packing Race.   In this event, men pack three bales of straw in an arena. The top pack must be tied down using one continuous rope. This is a timed event but neatness and tightness are also judged in the packing race.

Mule Foot Race.   The mule may be packed or not, but the prime consideration is to have one person lead a mule on foot, with the assistance of one other person, in a timed event to the finish line. The mule may be pushed, lead, or dragged but no whipping is allowed.

Perhaps the most unusual and imaginative use for which the mule has been selected is the recently developed Lincoln County Mule-O-Rama race in Ruidoso, New Mexico. Known as the Mule Futurity, a 30-race card with more than $25,000 in prizes was first held in 1979. Since than plans have been set in motion to enlarge the event and at least double the prize money.

Two substantial differences between mule and horse racing involve the age of eligible animals and the weight carried.

While the horses are allowed to race at two years of age, the mule futurity restricts racing to three-year-olds.

Since there are very few professional mule jockeys, the second consideration was primarily based on logic. Most mule races are still stock saddle races, and rather than eliminate the heavier, nonprofessional riders, the sponsors of the mule futurity chose to use a higher weight limit.

Although some might think this event to be pure entertainment and lots of laughs, the owners are dead serious. Most racing mules are out of Thoroughbred or running Quarter Horse mares and as with any sport, the object is to win. The heyday of the racing mule is at hand.

GALICENO

The Galiceno Horse Breeders Association was established in 1959 and at present lists over 6,000 horses in the registry. Breeders are found in California, Florida, Illinois, Indiana, Kansas, Kentucky, Maryland, Missouri, New Mexico, Ohio, Oklahoma, Oregon, Texas, Utah, Washington, and Canada.

History

Known as "the beautiful little horse with the proud history," the Galiceno (Fig 2-39) originated in Galicia, a province in Northwestern Spain. As with most Spanish horses, the breed undoubtedly contains Arab and Barb blood, in addition to the now extinct Spanish Jennet. It is thought that these small horses were among the first 16 equines landed on the mainland of America when Cortez invaded Mexico from Cuba in 1519. Although the Galicenos probably contributed to the original Mustang herds, they were absorbed by crossbreeding and lost to the "melting pot" of horse flesh that contributed to so many breeds and types in what is now the United States. However, the pure-bred Galiceno remained for centuries along the coastal regions of Mexico, prized by Mexicans for their riding ease, courage, endurance, and relatively small size. Great strength combined with small size and endurance made for a tough, versatile horse that was an easy keeper. Pure economics dictated that the Galiceno would be less expensive to feed compared to the larger breeds.

The Galiceno went unnoticed by most of the rest of the world until 1958 when Glenn H. Bracken saw them in Mexico. He liked the horse for its ability, versatility, and stamina. Bringing 40 head of horses into

FIGURE 2-39. "Canta," a Galiceno mare owned by Shareen Allen, Kyle, Texas, is an association champion having earned eight register of merits in open classes and three in youth classes. (Galiceno Horse Breeders Association; photo by R. L. Falkner, Tyler, Texas)

the United States that same year, he established the Galiceno Horse Breeders Association in 1959 and the popularity of the horse has spread throughout the United States and Canada.

Characteristics   The Galiceno is characterized by its small stature; gentle, easy manners, and good disposition.

Although lacking size (it is usually 12 to 13.2 hands high at maturity), breeders reject the idea of referring to the Galiceno as a pony. Owners point to a hardiness, courage, and stamina which is not easily matched by larger horses. The structural makeup and way of going allow the Galiceno to outlast many larger competitors and to be less tiring on the rider as well. Galicenos have a natural running walk, very fast, producing an easy rhythmical ride which breeders point to as a characteristic setting them apart from the pony class.

Solid colors prevail in the Galiceno breed and include bays, blacks, sorrels, duns, buckskins, roans, grays, chestnuts, browns, and a few palominos. No albinos or pintos are allowed in the registry.

Uses   Although the Galiceno is relatively small, it makes an excellent jumping horse, and is used in western pleasure, English pleasure, barrel racing, pole bending, cutting, trail riding, endurance races, and a colorful event in Galiceno horse shows known as the Costume Class, putting the small horse in its most beautiful and interesting element. Riders wear native Spanish costumes and groom their horses accordingly.

Galicenos are excellent youth horses because of their small size but adults also use them in calf roping, breakaway roping, and cutting.

Common Criticisms

Detractors from the breed might argue that it is just another pony breed with a good public relations program. Generally speaking, any equine less than 14.2 hands is considered a pony. However, there are numerous exceptions to the rule and breeders point to the natural running walk of the Galiceno as an outstanding characteristic that sets it apart from the pony class. Semantics aside, the breed, no matter how diminutive its size, is a tough, durable, versatile, easy keeper with a classy appearance and functional use.

GOTLAND

The Gotland is a descendant of the Tarpan breed and traces its history back over 10,000 years to the Swedish Island of Gotland in the Baltic Sea.

History

In the first century A.D. the Goths from Sweden began to emigrate into eastern Europe and spread all the way down to Italy and Spain. Ties with the mother country were maintained for many centuries. The Goths and Swedish Vikings used the prized horses from the Island of Gotland in both battle and their trade system. These Swedish warriors on their fast, maneuverable horses were also credited as being the first Europeans to use stirrups. This rather simple innovation gave the Swedish warriors an advantage against their stirrupless opponents, making the unseating of a stirrupless enemy a much easier task. One battle in 1632 credited the defeat of 4,000 Russians to only 800 Swedish horsemen mounted on their swift ponies.

After the decline of their warlike ways, the Swedish cavalry declined and Gotland horses were used primarily to pull carriages. The breed has only recently found itself in the United States.

Characteristics

The Gotland is considered a pony by some, but breeders would rather refer to it as a true small horse.

The average Gotland stands between 12 and 14 hands high, has a gentle temperament, and some individuals are naturally five-gaited with a fox-trot, rack, walk, trot, and canter.

The most common colors are bay, dark dun (both charcoal and blue), sorrel, buckskin, and occasionally palominos, creams, and roans. Solid colors are most common but the color may be lighter on the muzzle, around the eyes and flanks. As a throwback to the Tarpan breed, dorsal and withers stripes and barring on the legs are found. They are greatly prized for their speed, maneuverability, endurance, and "easy

FIGURE 2-40. Gotland horses' ancestry may be traced back 10,000 years to Sweden. (Leeward Farms, Elkland, Missouri)

keeping'' qualities. Endurance is an inbred factor since the Swedes expected their cavalry mounts to travel at least 35 miles in 5 hours.

Uses

The Gotland Horses in Sweden are used for horse show events, in jumping, dressage, pleasure riding and driving, flat racing, and harness racing.

In the United States, Gotlands have shown impressive wins in open competition against both horses and ponies in western pleasure, trail, pole bending, barrel racing, hunters, jumpers, and harness racing. The Gotland is very well suited as a child's mount but their endurance, speed, and substance make them equal to far larger horses for adult riders. Many are used as stock horses in cattle operations in this country. They are excellent pony trotters with times that challenge the fastest pony breeds in harness racing. They are also used as chariot racers competing favorably against full-sized horses.

GRADE HORSE

Although grade animals are not considered a ''breed,'' many of them carry excellent bloodlines, and function extremely well within our society. The specific meaning of ''Grade Horse'' refers to horses without papers that are not listed in a registry or association. One might reason that these horses are of inferior quality because they lack proper identification papers. Nothing could be further from the truth. Some horses have no papers because the owners neglected filling out the necessary forms; others may have only one registered parent, and while even Half-Blood Registry Associations exist, some horses may fall short of requirements simply because of color, markings, or some other minor blemish. However, the Grade Horse is included in this book because the number of Grade Horses in the United States exceed the combined registration of all breeds put together.

History

It is not possible to provide specific historical data of the Grade Horse but two events helped to create the types of Grade Horses generally in use in the United States—the Army Remount Program and the Dude Ranch Industry. The Army Remount Program can be traced back to the U.S. Cavalry when inferior horses could have caused a military defeat. The Grade Horses being used at that time left much to be desired in comparison to enemy cavalry. An intensive campaign was developed, considered to be the quickest way to improve U.S. mounts. Thoroughbred stallions of the finest quality were brought in to breed on the native military mares. With thousands of fine, half-blooded foals developing under government care, the system proved quickly effective. Superior sires were continued in service to descendants to retain the "hot-blooded" outcrossing. These latter horses, even though almost full blooded, were nevertheless considered Grade Horses. Battles were won, traildrives were started, and the West was developed with the aid of the Grade Horse.

The second major event in the spread of Grade Horses can be attributed to the Dude Ranch Industry, a more recent development. The Eaton Ranch in Wyoming is credited with founding the idea of "tenderfoot transportation," necessitating gentle, dependable horses that could carry a child or a 200-pound adult with equal confidence. Looks didn't count but the horses had to be of gentle disposition and with strong feet and legs to stand the rigors of constant use.

Of course, the farming and ranching industry contributed to the development of the Grade Horse along with the dudes and the military. For hundreds of years, the Grade Horse has been found on farms and ranches. Call him work horse, fun horse, cold-blooded, unregistered, cowpony, cayuse, or "hoss," the Grade Horse was around before the registered equines, provided the foundation for the majority of associations and registries in the United States, and continues to outnumber his more carefully recorded peers.

Characteristics

Since the Grade Horse history is so ill-defined, it would be even more difficult to describe the horse's characteristics. The Grade Horse is a horse, a pony, a draft horse. Its height ranges from under 14 hands to over 17 hands, and may weigh from a few hundred pounds to over a ton. Its color is its most definite characteristic—it is allowed to be whatever color God decides to make it.

Uses

The Grade Horse is primarily a working and pleasure animal. In addition to the Dude Ranches, Grade Horses are used on trail rides, endurance rides, cattle ranches, etc. One of the most widely used animals in the United States, the Grade Horse may be found everywhere, from wilderness to the back yard.

HACKNEY HORSE AND HACKNEY PONY

Selective breeding, starting in the 1880s, has produced the Hackney Pony from the Hackney Horse. Both have the same conformation and gait and are registered in the same Stud Book. The history of the Hackney Pony is that of the Hackney Horse.

History

For many years before 1800, the term Hackney was used to describe a type of English horse of strong Arabian bloodlines with a flashy trot, both under saddle and in harness. The Hackney breed was formalized in 1883 when a Stud Book was begun, although ancestors can be traced back to the Middle Ages. The Hackney's immediate ancestor is the Norfolk Trotter, which was a descendant of a halfbred horse named Shales, a son of Blaze, who was a descendant of Flying Childers, a son of the Darley Arabian. Blaze had two important sons, Scot Shales and Driver. From Driver, foaled about 1780, the modern Hackney descended. A Norfolk Trotter imported to the United States in 1922 (Bellfounder) was also influential in the creation of the Standardbred by siring the dam of Hambletonian, so Hackneys and Standardbreds may lay claim to similar origins.

Characteristics

The Hackney (Fig. 2-41) is distinguished by a small head with a straight or convex face, large eyes, and small ears. The neck is muscular, the body is compact with powerful shoulders and clean legs. In the showring, Hackneys are usually docked and have their manes pulled.

Colors of the Hackney range from bay, brown, sorrel, black, blue, and red roan to the predominating and most preferred color, chestnut. White snips, blazes, and stockings are frequently seen.

Hackney horses usually range from 14 to 15.3 hands. Those under 14 hands are considered ponies.

Uses

The Hackney's spectacular trotting action has insured its lasting popularity in the showring. It is known as the leading heavy harness horse in the world. The Hackney Pony, of course, is a smaller version

FIGURE 2-41. The Hackney breed is the leading heavy harness in the world. (Kentucky Horse Park, Lexington, Kentucky)

of the outstanding harness qualities desired in a horse. Both are unequaled in style and action.

HALF SADDLEBRED   As previously discussed with the grade horse, improvements in horse breeds have traditionally been made by infusion of the blood of superior animals, most of whom originate in registries and associations. Noting the outstanding qualities of a truly American innovation, the Saddlebred breed, improvements have been made with both grade and registered horses to produce a specific type of horse that has found a niche in many areas of horse recreation and work.

History   Any history of the Half Saddlebred Registry would naturally have to include the entire history of the Saddlebred breed. The history of the Half Saddlebred breed is much easier to pinpoint. So many breeders had noticed the great improvement in breeding virtually every breed and type of horse to the Saddlebred that a move was made in 1971 to found a registry for offspring with Half Saddlebred blood. The reason for this move is simply that many horsemen consider the Saddlebred to be the greatest utility breed alive. Although many consider the Saddlebred as a rich man's horse, a peacock for the showring, the Half Saddlebred Registry Association was founded to explore this myth and "in truth" to promote the full Saddlebred horse as one of the better buys in the country.

Characteristics   The characteristics of the Half Saddlebred differ from the full Saddlebred in that color patterns, size and scale, and uses vary so much. The Half Saddlebred may range from below 14 hands for a pony type to more than 16 hands for the mature animal. However, most of them carry the flashy style, appearance, and qualities that are so evident in the full Saddlebred (Fig. 2-42 and Fig. 2-43).

FIGURE 2-42. Golden Jewel HSRA 1022. Half Saddlebred-Half Morgan. Reserve Champion 1977–1978. Owner: John and Martha Bigrigg, Coshocton, Ohio. (Half-Saddlebred Association)

FIGURE 2-43. Crescendo HSRA E-1043 Saddlebred Pinto Breeding. Grand Champion Mare, 1977–1978, Halter and Performance. Owner: Laura Barnes, Coshocton, Ohio. (Half-Saddlebred Association)

Uses

For many years, breeders have utilized American Saddlebred stallions and mares to cross on other breeds and grade horses to produce mounts with stronger bone, finer heads and necks, more desirable conformation, and numerous other qualities of the full Standardbred breed.

Perhaps no other breed in the United States is used as widely as the Saddlebred cross for such a variety of accomplishments. The Saddlebred has been crossed on the Appaloosa as well as the Thoroughbred to produce jumping horses of fine quality, the Standardbred to produce a superior Roadster horse, the Morgan for show and pleasure, the Tennessee Walking horse for pleasure riding, the Hackney for a five-gaited and three-gaited pony, the Welsh for small jumpers, and the Shetland for small jumpers.

The Saddlebred-Thoroughbred cross is without a doubt producing the greatest dressage horses, producing conformation and stamina that is necessary for this grueling event. This cross is the best jumper, since both breeds are noted for this natural ability. The stronger feet, legs, and bones produced in this cross produce a horse able to take the demands of pounding during jumping competition. It is also a favorite mount for fox hunts.

The Half Saddlebred can be used as a trail horse, pleasure mount, cow horse, endurance racer, or even a child's horse. Perhaps one of the outstanding qualities of this breed is its excellent ability as a jumper. This fact has been proven many times with the United States Olympic Teams.

The sole requirement for registration in the Half Saddlebred Registry is that one parent be a full registered Saddlebred, duly registered with the American Saddle Horse Breeders Association, with papers in order.

One of the more interesting uses for the Half Saddlebred horse is in the improvement of fledgling associations that are in the developmental stages of the so called "color breeds." Color breeds are referred to as Palomino, Buckskin, Pinto, Paint, Appaloosa, Spotted, American Albino, American White, and American Creme. When a breed association is based on color, in the beginning it may be necessary to bring in outstanding sires from many breeds until a population is large enough from which outstanding individuals may be selected. The Saddlebred has been used in this respect on the "color breeds;" this situation has lead to double registration in the Half Saddlebred Registry as well as the developing color registry. One such outstanding example is the American White and the American Creme breed developed in the United States on White Horse Ranch in Naper, Nebraska. These horses are not to be confused with the Albino, which usually has red or pink eyes and spotted skin marks. Using Arab and Morgan blood as a foundation, the White Horse Ranch produced not an Albino but a truly white breed, the horses having white hair, pink skin, and hazel, blue, or brown eyes. With color patterns set, the American White Registry began using Saddlebred blood to produce better conformation resulting in strikingly beautiful, well-proportioned animals. The most famous of these American White, which can also be classified as Half Saddlebred, is the famous ABU BEKR Patrol of the Shriners, forty outstanding examples of a Half Saddlebred improvement program.

INDIAN HORSE

The American Indian Horse Registry was established by a native American Indian in California in 1961. The registry has since moved to Texas and exists for the purpose of collecting, recording, and preserving the pedigrees of 2,413 American Indian Horses. As of 1996, the membership for the wild horse adoption program was 305 with the largest representation from Oregon, Montana, California, and Arizona.

History

The American Indian Horse can be traced back to the wild horses of the plains that were brought to this country by the Spanish. The Spaniards brought many horses from Europe and the Arabian desert. Actually, Indian Horses may be traced to the foundation of most horse breeds—the Arabians and the roaming Bedouin tribes. The Indians, at the time of the discovery of America, had no horses and had never seen them. However, the horse was made for the Indian and the Indian was made for the horse. The love affair has existed over many centuries and remains intact to this day. The typical Indian Horse or pony is generally thought of as a Paint, Pinto, Appaloosa, or some wildly multicolored horse. This is not unusual since the Barb, with its wildly varying color patterns, was instrumental in the development, along with Arabians, of so many of the horses brought over by the Spanish Conquistadors. Horses became a way of life for the American Indian. "Indian ponies" prospered under the wild, free life of the plains and were ideally suited for that lifestyle. The horse was worshipped in a strange sort of way by the American Indian. He was sought after, hunted, eaten, ridden, and used as a form of barter, and quite often his possession in numbers was an indication of great wealth among Indian tribes. Some tribes, such as the Nez Perce, practiced selective breeding to produce the Appaloosa, but most merely let the horse develop under the survival of the fittest technique. Through centuries of mismanagement and neglect, the Indian Horse survived. Called Cow Pony, Buffalo Horse, Mustang, Indian Pony, Cayuse, they are all the same animal.

Characteristics   The Indian Horse, although many have unknown sires and dams, is sturdy, well made, close to the ground. He may be Appaloosa spotted, Paint, Pinto, or solid color (Fig. 2-44). Indian Horses are prized for their color, easy gaits, and ability to get by on less feed and pampering than the average breed of horses. The average size is about 15 hands.

The Indian Horse Registry has three classifications: class *O* for the original type and breeding of the Indian Horse; class *AA* for horses that need special qualifications of ability, breeding, etc; and class *A* for horses under two years of age who do not measure up to class *AA* standards.

FIGURE 2-44. Cochtaw Me-Hin-Gen, a gray stallion, is an example of Indian Horse descendants. (Photo by American Indian Horse Registry)

Uses   Because of the tough, hardy, inbred nature of the Indian Horse, the registry emphasizes one of the outstanding qualities of this animal—stamina. These mounts make excellent trail horses, and because of the colorful haircoats characteristic of so many Indian Horses, they are used as a pleasure horse and as an impressive parade horse. Several registered Indian Horses are seen nearly every year in the Rose Bowl Parade. An Indian Horse mounted by a native American in colorful regalia is an unforgettable sight in any parade.

LIPIZZANER

Without a doubt, the most highly trained breed of horse is the Lipizzan. The famous Lipizzaner stallions and the executions performed by the Spanish Riding School of Vienna (Fig. 2-45) are among the most magnificent spectator events imaginable in the demanding field of animal obedience. The Lipizzans are truly the superior stars of the field of equine athletics.

History

The history of the Lipizzaner is closely entwined with that of the Andalusian, forerunner of the Lipizzan breed. The Archduke Charles, in 1580, imported Andalusian horses into Yugoslavia to found a stud at Lipizza. The stud imported other Spanish horses until about the seventeenth century when Spanish stock began to dwindle. One notable addition to the original foundation stock was that of the Arabian stallion Siglavy. Andalusian blood is occasionally still introduced into the Lipizzan breed to maintain a standard type, color, and temperament. In 1968, a four-year-old stallion of the Carthusian line of Andalusians was imported from Cadiz, Spain to add fresh blood to the line of Lipizzans.

Because of the predominant Spanish bloodlines, principally Andalusians, the Archduke Charles founded a riding school in Lipizza and named it the Spanish Riding School. Eventually, the Spanish Riding

FIGURE 2-45. A Lipizzaner stallion executing the capriole, one of the "airs above ground" movements that characterize these amazing equine athletes. Rider is Professor Ottomar Herrmann. (The Royal International Lipizzaner Club)

School and its famous Lipizzan stallions and mares were moved to the famous Piber Stud in Vienna, Austria. However, the traditional name of the Spanish Riding School continues to be used to this day.

The modern history of the Lipizzan is perhaps as exciting as the original beginnings. During World War II, the Lipizzaners faced possible extinction because of the extensive fighting that threatened the lives of all living things. Only the love of good horses on the side of both enemy and allies saved the Lipizzans from possible extinction. In 1945, Colonel Alois Podhajski, director of the Spanish Riding School, moved his prized Lipizzan stallions from Vienna to St. Martins in Austria. While the stallions were protected for the time being, the mares so necessary for the continuation of breeding practices were left behind in Hostau, Czechoslovakia. Colonel Podhajski, who was an acquaintance of the famous American General George Patton, called upon his old friend to save the mares from possible seizure or extinction at the hands of the oncoming Russians. General Patton, who had competed in equestrian events at the Olympic games, was sympathetic to the project and approved an attack on Hostau to save the horses. Much to the surprise of the invading Americans, it was found that the Germans also greatly admired the Lipizzan horses and wanted them saved as much as Podhajski and Patton. According to one report, the German troops formed an honor guard and saluted as the Americans advanced on the stables where they captured 150 mares, foals, and a few stallions. The Americans continued to hold the horses for eventual return to Podhajski. Later, as the Russians arrived in Czechoslovakia, it became increasingly clear that the new government was intent on seizing the horses for themselves. Sensing this move, the Americans spirited the horses across the border into Germany in a clandestine move to thwart this operation. The Americans returned the Lipizzan horses to the control of their rightful owners, the Spanish Riding School, which remains active today.

The Royal International Lipizzaner Club of America, Inc. was founded in 1968 by Colonel Ottomar Herrmann for the purpose of perpetuating the breed in America. Colonel Herrmann, a native of Austria, and his family had been engaged in the breeding of Lipizzaners for four generations. Although only a few hundred horses are registered in America, the breed holds tremendous popularity in this and every other country of the world. Requirements in the United States include proof of a parentage tracing to importations from Austria.

Characteristics   Lipizzans are compact horses, strong of back and quarters and short but strong of leg. The average height is 15 to 15.2 hands.

The predominate color is gray although bays and browns occur. This is one of the more obvious connections to the Andalusian breed because many Lipizzaner foals are born black or brown and change color with age, eventually turning gray. Some Lipizzaners take up to ten years to acquire their gray coats.

The Lipizzans are noted for their docile temperament, making them an ideal, although very expensive, horse to use in crossing with other more highly strung breeds.

Uses

The Lipizzan is truly a magnificent, athletic animal and can be used for a variety of purposes, excelling in every phase of horse activities. The dominant use, however, is as a show animal executing the world famous movements developed by the Spanish Riding School. These whirling, leaping movements are not entirely natural, although the Lipizzan is one of the few breeds that appears to have the ability to learn these extremely difficult motions, which take years of training to perform. These magnificent horses truly are in a class by themselves in the horse kingdom.

MINIATURE HORSES

One of the most unusual breeds of horses is the true Miniature, not to be confused with Shetland ponies or the dwarf. A revival of interest by hobbyists in the Miniature Horse has led to a recent rediscovery of these small animals, which are found in increasing numbers throughout the United States, Republic of South Africa, England, Canada, and Australia.

History

During the sixteenth century, heads of state and royalty considered their horses as a part of the national treasury. Horse breeding was a source of great pride, social standing, and wealth. Stable masters, under the direction of European royalty, were encouraged to breed smaller and smaller horses as a novelty, pets for the royal young, showpieces of the palace. The natural evolution of the horse was from a size approximately that of a dog to the current mature horse of today. European breeders used this principle in reverse, breeding the smallest to the smallest to produce a true Miniature Horse, perfect in conformation. It was a project which occupied several generations of both men and horses.

After the decline of royalty, many of the horses survived in circuses, but much of the breed died out. Some that survived did so because of the useful function, much like the Shetland, of pulling iron ore carts in the mines of Bolivia and Peru. About 1900, some were imported for use in West Virginia coal mines. When the mines were automated in the 1930s, the breed nearly vanished again. However, a few admirers of these small horses continued to maintain individual herds. There are now about 52,000 in the United States.

Stables of Miniature Horses have been kept by notables such as

Queen Elizabeth II, King Juan Carlos, the Kennedy Family, and the late entertainer Dean Martin. There are two general types of miniature horses today: the draft horse and the finer boned Arabian type.

Although Miniature Horses may be found around the world, a breed registry did not exist until 1972, when Rayford Ely of California funded the project and established the standards for the registry. Ely's horses are considered so valuable that they are all insured by Lloyd's of London. It is not unusual to expect a range of prices from $5,000 to $25,000 per individual.

Characteristics

Since these tiny horses were bred only for size, they represent every color imaginable (Fig. 2-46). In addition to solid colors, there are numerous Paints, Pintos, and even a few Appaloosas within the association. Much of the stock is of obvious Arabian descent, and it might be surmised that because of the wild color patterns that the Barb bloodlines are also carried.

A registered Miniature Horse with permanent papers cannot exceed 34 inches in height at the withers when full grown (36 months). The characteristics and conformation of a full-sized horse, only in miniature, are stressed.

One peculiar aspect related to the world of Miniatures is that the smaller they are, the more valuable they become. Only about 200 horses worldwide are less than 32 inches at the withers, and those that are below this height vary from "expensive to priceless." One mare (Silver Dollar) owned by Rayford Ely measured at maturity 26½ inches at the withers. She was so prized that the owner confessed a concern for even breeding her for fear of foaling complications that could result in her death.

The Miniature Horse, unlike some other small breeds, is characterized by an even temperament. They do not bite or kick normally, and are considered to be completely safe pets for the smallest children. They vary in size from 26 inches to 34 inches (Fig. 2-47).

The purpose of the registry is to improve the breed by applying strict registration standards to those finer Miniature Horses measuring 34 inches and under.

One of the outstanding characteristics of this tiny pet is that it may be kept, studied, and worked with, just as a mature horse but for only a fraction of the expense. A dozen or so horses of the Miniature variety can be kept for the cost of one standard horse. A bale of hay can last, for one horse, up to three months. They eat everything the larger horses do only in smaller quantities.

Uses

This horse is strictly a pet, a hobby for those who are intrigued by its unusual size. Although a few breeders advocate very small children

FIGURE 2-46. "Arabian King's Champion," a four-month-old miniature red and white pinto colt. (International Miniature Horse Registry, Palos Verdes Estates, California)

FIGURE 2-47. "Ramundo," a 10-year-old black miniature stallion. Sire of "TD", the AFC Denver Broncos mascot, 28½ inches tall. (International Miniature Horse Registry, Palos Verdes Estates, California)

riding them, most owners think that the horse is simply too small to bear much weight on its back. They have been used to pull specially made carts for children, or for miniature harness racing, a more commonly accepted practice.

This horse is ideal for those who have little acreage available for pasture; even a backyard will suffice. Two or three may be stocked per acre, and fences need only be about two feet high to contain them. They are often hauled to Miniature Horse Shows in the back of station wagons, vans, even riding in the back seat of Cadillacs between two adults.

One of the more notable uses of the Miniature Horse is to draw attention from the news media. "TD," a registered Miniature Horse, has been used as the mascot for the professional football team the Denver Broncos.

Perhaps one of the chief advantages of this tiny equine is that a horse lover, restricted by lack of funds or space, can study every aspect of horse production from breeding to nutrition and management on a very small budget. The expensive price tags to get started may be a deterrent; the expensive prices paid for offspring, however, may be an incentive to invest.

Common Criticisms

As with most horses, conception rates are not as desirable as with other species of animals. The Miniature Horse has an even less impressive record than modern mature horses. Foaling rates of less than 50% are common. Foaling difficulties are to be expected with the Miniature. As foaling time approaches, mares are often kept in small stables, even baby beds, and watched closely in order to save the foal. They are watched around the clock at foaling time as assistance is inevitably needed.

Why would anyone want such a tiny horse? One breeder explains his hobby of raising the Miniature by stating: "It's like a Porsche, nobody needs one but everyone wants one."

MISSOURI FOXTROT- TING HORSE

The Missouri Foxtrotting Horse has existed since the very early beginnings of western expansion in the United States. Breeders developed an easygoing, fast moving, gaited horse for smooth, efficient transportation. The breed developed largely from the blood of Arabians, Morgans, and plantation horses from the deep South. Later infusions have included the American Saddlebred, Tennessee Walker, and Standardbred. In 1996, registrations were reported to exceed 46,000 horses.

History

Although Missouri may lay claim to the Foxtrot breed, the characteristics of this unusual gait are found in many breeds of horses. Missouri breeders simply utilized this natural tendency by breeding the best to the best. Many breeds contributed to the development of the foxtrot gait. Breeders had specific standards for this "grade" horse in the beginning which has since become recognized as a breed with an official registry. Early breeders demanded a horse that could travel long distances at a comfortable speed of five to eight mile per hour. The result of breeding for this particular function led to the Missouri Foxtrotting Horse, a favorite of pioneer doctors, sheriffs, stock raisers, businessmen, and others.

The move to preserve this type of horse, originally bred in the Ozarks, was initiated in 1948. As with most developing breeds, the foundation stock was allowed to enter into registry with the association as long as the foxtrotting standards were met. The success of the registry is obvious since over 46,000 horses are now recorded by the registry and the books remain open, at present, to allow for additional blood to further improve the breed and secure a firm foundation of breeding stock. As is the case with all breeds, it is anticipated that the registry book will one day be closed.

Characteristics   The most distinguishing characteristic of the Foxtrotting Horse is its unusual, broken gait. The horse walks with the front feet and trots with the back feet (Fig. 2-48). Although it is not a high stepping horse,

FIGURE 2-48. Zane's Bobbin Robbin, a Missouri Foxtrotting Horse, champion three- and four-year-old mare. Note the front and trotting rear stride. (Freda and Skeet Beisner, Everton, Missouri)

the Foxtrotter is sure-footed because of the sliding action of the rear feet, as opposed to the hard step of other breeds. Because of this peculiar gaited action, the horse is extremely easy on the rider. Spectators especially enjoy watching the Foxtrotting Horse because although it is not a high stepper, it travels with animation, a Foxtrot rhythm that denotes a special flair or style. The head and tail are held slightly erect producing a graceful carriage with a slight nodding of the head, giving the horse a poised, relaxed appearance. Usually the rider holds the horse in a "collected" manner—a small amount of rein tension on the bit.

Although conformation is similar to other horses, the Missouri Foxtrotter has as its chief characteristic the way of traveling: a flat-foot walk, foxtrot gait, and canter. The height averages 15 hands with an expected range of 14 to 16 hands.

Although numerous colors, as might be expected, exist because of the variation of breeds used in the foundation stock, the Foxtrotting Horse can be expected to show the following colors: bay, black, blue roan, brown, buckskin, chestnut, dun, gray, palomino, red roan, and sorrel. In borderline cases, the predominant color is used.

Uses

The Foxtrotting Horse has gained much popularity recently as a show horse because of his flashy characteristics and appeal to the crowd. The demand for the breed, however, is also found as a pleasure horse and a cross-country trail horse; and it is readily adapted, because of its easy gait, to younger riders. It is often described as the common man's pleasure horse because of its gentle disposition and ease of training.

Not all horses have a natural foxtrot gait. There are methods used by trainers to teach the foxtrot rhythm to some nonfoxtrotting individuals descended from Foxtrotting Horses. Some trainers may use weights and other mechanical aids to develop the desired gaits. However, the foxtrot gait and canter are usually naturally found characteristics of the Missouri Foxtrotting Horse.

MORAB

The idea to cross the Morgan and the Arabian horse to produce a Morab was probably first conceived in the early 1800s. However, an organized effort to produce the horse on a broader scale did not develop until after World War I when more people began to experiment with the cross.

History

The blending of two great breeds of horses, the Morgan and the Arabian, had long been practiced by avid horse owners to produce a family pleasure horse and a ranch horse. The move to designate it as a breed, however, did not occur until 1973 when James Allan Miller, of Fresno County, California formally established the American Morab Horse Association, Inc. The foundation stock was contributed by Martha Doyal Fuller, who had been practicing selective breeding since 1955 on her ranch in Clovis, California. Using big, heavily muscled mares and outstanding Arabian sires, she produced some distinct characteristics in the offspring of this cross. Called "Morabs," these horses were bred primarily for use as pleasure, ranch horses, and show animals. Previous to 1973, some of these half-bred horses were registered in half-bred or color registries but not as "Morab." Although the name implies strictly Morgan and Arabian bloodlines, it may contain Thoroughbred blood; however, it must show no other breed characteristics. Less than 800 Morabs are registered in the United States today with California being the leading state in numbers. Other significant concentrations are mostly on the East Coast.

Characteristics   Mature Morabs stand between 14.3 and 16.0 hands and may be any color without spots on the body, with black eyes and skin. Conformation goals are powerful muscling with well-defined refinement and grace of movement. The Morab is distinguished by a stylish head, arched neck, short back, round powerful hindquarters, and high tail set (Fig. 2-49). The short back, an Arabian-Morgan trait, and longer croup of the Morgan account for their great strength. Morabs inherit

FIGURE 2-49. Dahman Najib, a Morab stallion 15.2 hands high, is touted as an outstanding example of Morab conformation. Note the refined, arched neck, closely coupled back, and strong, powerful hindquarters. (Morab Horse Registry of America)

the medium-length pastern and sound bone formation from the Morgan, and the sound feet and hoof of the Arabian. One unusual characteristic of the Morab is the heavy shinbone inherited from the Morgan. The shinbone of Morgans and Morabs weigh more than any other horse of similar size, a factor which is said to account for the lack of leg and foot troubles found in both the Morgan and Morab.

A most important trait of the Morab is the round, powerful hindquarters—a genetically recessive trait in the Arabian and a dominant trait in the Morgan. A Morab with over three-fourths Arabian blood often does not show this trait; the Morab therefore, is designed to carry approximately half blood of the Morgan and Arabian for best results.

Morabs inherited from the Arabian a short back, five lumbar vertebrae—instead of the usual six—to give it the close coupled look.

Morabs have a classy, free-flowing way of moving, giving the impression of a powerful horse moving off of strong hindquarters.

The Morab, like the Morgan and Arabian, has a longer life expectancy compared to other equines. Accepted colors are bay, black, buckskin, chestnut, dun and palomino, gray, grulla, and roan.

Uses

Because of the high-stepping, natural, animated park action and lower, quieter, pleasure action, the Morab has distinguished itself in a variety of events. Conformation, disposition, and way of traveling make them excellent for adults or children. Morabs are used in dressage, cutting, endurance rides, equitation, gymkhana, hunting, jumping, parade, park, pleasure, roadster, and stock events.

Common Criticisms

Although owners would justifiably argue with the criticism that Morabs are not a true breed, merely a half-blood horse, the fact remains that characteristics of the Morgan and Arabian in the Morab are difficult to maintain in a breeding program once bloodlines deviate significantly beyond half-blooded animals. The Morab may also be faulted as a late maturing horse, not unexpected since this is a criticism of both the Arabian and Morgan from which the breed was derived.

MORGAN HORSE

The Morgan Horse story is one of the most unusual in all the horse kingdom. The "pride and product of America" is very likely this country's oldest breed of light horse. It is as much a part of America today as it was in the beginning back in Vermont, in 1789.

History

The foundation of the Morgan Horse breed was a nondescript stallion, thought by many to be too small, rough coated, originally named Figure. The owner of Figure was a quiet spoken school teacher by the name of Justin Morgan. Justin Morgan and Figure left Springfield, Massachusetts in 1789 to make their fortune in Vermont. Figure was a stylish, magnificently proportioned horse but he was only about 14 hands high, too small to be taken seriously by breeders or other competitors. Justin Morgan had hoped to sell Figure for a small profit to make a new start in Vermont. Few people and no buyers took the small bay stallion seriously or recognized the tremendous potential in this little giant.

Although Figure never weighed much over 1,000 pounds, he accomplished some amazing feats. There was a time that he alone, in draft contests, pulled a log that no other draft type horse could budge. At other times, he was entered in traditional races and became the winningest quarter-mile race horse in central Vermont history. It was the custom in those days for an outstanding animal to take on the name of his owner. Thus, Figure became Justin Morgan, the foundation sire for every Morgan Horse in the world today. It was said of Justin Morgan that he could outrun, outtrot, outjump, outpull, and outwork any horse in any competition. Records show that he seldom, if ever, was beaten in any contest. The original Justin Morgan was barely 14 hands, never weighed over 1,000 pounds, and never carried, according to historians, an ounce of excess fat. His muscling, elegant carriage, tremendous stamina, and longevity are legendary. Only such a gifted animal could live almost 30 years and set all of the records he did, as well as do the work of a good draft team for some 28 of those 30 years.

Although most literature claims that the original Justin Morgan was of Arabian and Thoroughbred breeding, there is some indication that he was a Dutch horse of Spanish-Barb blood. Randolph Huntington of New York and Virginia, about 1879, wrote in a letter to a friend that "the best way to bring back the undiluted blood of the Morgan is to infuse the blood of Barbs since the original Morgan was a Dutch horse of Spanish-Barb blood." Since the Thoroughbred is known to be derived from Arabian and Barb blood, this comment is not to be taken lightly. Whatever the bloodline, Justin Morgan is known in genetic terms as a sport or mutation, an unusual stallion possessing the ability to transmit characteristics unique to himself on to his offspring. Morgans maintain that characteristic to this day.

Three sons of Justin Morgan, Sherman, Bulrush, and Woodbury, formed the foundation for America's first breed of light horse. Every Morgan in the world today can be traced back to one or more of these fine stallions.

Justin Morgan, the little bay stallion who took the name of his master, was to become one of the greatest breeding horses of all time. Countless sons and daughters took on his image and way of going.

Because of his versatility, stamina, and longevity, the Morgan has contributed to many famous individuals as well as numerous developing breeds. Brood mares earned their oats on farms and ranches and sons were sent along with their descendants to Boston and New York financiers as roadster horses. Trotting racing became a popular sport in the 1850s and again a Morgan, Ethan Allen 50, a bay great-grandson of Justin Morgan, became the world's fastest trotting stallion.

Other American light horse breeds that use Morgan blood are the Standardbred, which has never produced a horse that can beat 2:00 minutes for a mile that has not had Morgan blood, the American Saddlebred, Tennessee Walking Horse, American Albino, Palomino, and contributions to the State of Texas where many Morgans lost their identity in the developing Quarter Horse.

Perhaps one of the most famous horses of all time was the only survivor of Little Big Horn, Comanche, a Morgan-bred horse. Longevity again showed up in Morgan bloodlines as Comanche lived to be about 40 years old.

It is interesting to note that the Morgan Horse is the only horse ever to be perpetuated by the United States Government. The U.S. Department of Agriculture, in 1907, established the U.S. Morgan Horse Farm in Middlebury, Vermont. The purpose was to continue in perpetuity the Morgan breed by providing stallions for Remount Stations at various points throughout this country. Although the horse farm is no longer operated by the government, it still stands in Middlebury as a monument to the Morgan Horse. If it is true that the pathway of history is paved with the bones of horses, surely the Morgan has provided his share for the United States.

Characteristics

The Morgan type of today (Fig. 2-50) varies very little from the original Justin Morgan of the late 1800s (Fig. 2-51). One of the more unusual physical characteristics of the breed is that the neck appears to be more highly arched, with a cleaner throatlatch, allowing the head to appear more directly over the top of the shoulders rather than in front of the withers as with most other breeds. A bit more prominence in the withers has been bred into modern Morgans allowing for a better fit for saddle purposes.

Height ranges from 14.2 to 15.2 hands with some individuals exceeding these figures in either direction. The Morgan is, of course, one of the most versatile animals, one that will pull, jump, and race, yet is gentle enough to be a good child's horse. Morgans have stamina, vigor, adaptability, and longevity as outstanding characteristics.

The beautiful Morgan head is one of the most characteristic features of this breed.

No horse is eligible for registration in the association if it has natural white above the knee or hock, except on the face. Colors include chest-

FIGURE 2-50. Mantic Balladeer, bay Morgan stallion foaled in 1974, typifies the form and elegant grace of the Morgan breed. (J. W. Crawford, Wilsonville, Oregon)

FIGURE 2-51. The Morgan horse is characterized by a beautiful head and a highly arched neck and clean throatlatch, allowing the head to appear more directly over the shoulders as compared to other breeds. The original Justin Morgan looked much like this. (American Morgan Horse Association, Inc.)

nut, bay, brown, black, palomino, dun, and buckskin. Colors that are not accepted are pintos, appaloosas, any type of spotted horse, and white horses.

Uses

As might be expected, because of the versatility ranging from the pulling of plows to winning on the race tracks, the Morgan has a multitude of uses. Among them are included park horse, roadster, pleasure horse, road hack, trail horse, working stock horse, cutting horse, hunter and jumper, and dressage. In addition, there may be still isolated cases of Morgans being used as draft animals but by far the most common use of the Morgan today is as a pleasure horse.

MUSTANG

The Spanish word "mesta," meaning a group of horse raisers, and the suffix "eno," meaning belonging to, is the root of the American term mustang. Horses that escaped from "mestas" in Old Spain or its new world possessions were thus referred to as "Mestenos" which means belonging to the mestas. The settlers who followed the Spaniards in the development of North America, Americanized Mesteno to Mustang. Sometimes referred to as the Spanish Mustang, the breed has been preserved more recently by two associations, American Mustang Associations, Inc. in California and Southwest Spanish Mustang Association in Oklahoma. About 2,200 horses are currently registered.

History

The Spanish Mustang (Fig. 2-52) or American Mustang (Fig. 2-53) can be traced back hundreds of years to the Spanish Conquistadors who brought over the now vanished Spanish Jennet, Barbs, Andalusians, and Arabians. Descendants of the Royal horses of Andalusia contributed greatly to the original foundation stock. The Andalusian was developed by crossing a small, coarse native horse of Spain with Barbs or Arabian horses introduced into Spain in 710 A.D. by the Moors invasion.

To supply the Conquistadors, and later Spanish settlements, with horses, Spain established breeding stations throughout the Caribbean. From here, horses were taken to the new world, and by 1520 exploration was causing such a drain on Spanish horses that an embargo was imposed. After this, it was entirely up to island breeders to supply horses for further conquest of the new world.

It wasn't long before horses bred at island remount stations were superior to those in Spain and became known as the finest "Barbs" in the world, not only in looks but also in performance. Reference to the Barb was due mainly to the flashy, wild color pattern that characterized inclusion of Barb bloodlines. These horses were taken by the Spaniards to North America where they eventually became the first Indian pony and "wild" horse.

FIGURE 2-52. A typical Mustang of early foundation stock, Old Dunny Boy, and Gilbert H. Jones, Albuquerque, New Mexico, 1938.

FIGURE 2-53. Bock's Al Borak Pam 850 Permanent Registered American Mustang. 1974 and 1977 National Grand Champion Stallion and 1975 Champion of Champions Stallion and 1978 Pacific Coast Champion Stallion. (Mustang Manor, Lake Elsinore, California)

Several hundred years of roaming wild and some selective breeding by Indians somewhat changed the appearance of these Spanish horses. Some Indian nations such as Choctaw, Chicasaw, Cayuse, Nez Perce, Pawnee, Shoshoni, and Comanche retained the beauty as well as the enduring qualities of the Spanish or American Mustang.

In many cases, inbreeding or uncontrolled breeding lead to the hang-dog appearance of Indian horses immortalized by western artists. Yet, even today the magnificent look of the bright-eyed, well-conformed, refined Spanish-Barb and Arabian still breeds true in most Mustangs. The common idea that Mustangs gradually degenerated through uncontrolled breeding is contrary to fact. Because only the fittest stallions had a chance to breed, the Mustang developed distinctive, hardy characteristics that only nature could dictate. According to some old timers, the only defect in the natural system lay in the indiscriminate practice of stallions breeding any mare in the vicinity. Old timers claim that Mustang stallions were as indiscriminate as the frontier cowboy, who never tasted bad whiskey or saw an ugly woman.

Many races of people had an influence on the development of this wild horse of the plains. A common saying indicates the influence of different nationalities: "A white man will ride the mustang until he is played out; a Mexican will ride him another day until he thinks he is played out; then a Comanche will mount him and ride him to where he is going." The American Indian did as much to preserve the character and toughness of the Mustang as any race of people.

The history of America was practically written from the back of the Mustang. He carried the Indian on his nomadic ventures ranging hundreds of miles from home on raiding sorties. He carried the mountain man into the wilderness, helped the pioneer make his trek westward, followed thousands of cattle drives northward, and became legend throughout the west.

Contrary to popular opinion, the Mustang was not a degenerated wild horse but one with extremely important bloodlines that contributed much to the development of other American horse breeds, either as the foundation or partly the foundation stock. Colors such as Appaloosa, Paint/Pinto, Dun, Buckskin, Grullo, and Palomino all came from the Spanish Mustang. The Morgan, Quarter Horse, Standardbred, American Saddle Horse, Tennessee Walking Horse, and some other American breeds were founded on partial use of the Spanish Mustang blood. In the Caribbean and South America, the Paso horses also originated from the Barb stock and the true Crillo horse of South America. Although these breeds carry a little more Andalusian blood, they are brothers of the Spanish Mustang.

At one time in the history of the developing west, the Spanish Mustang was the most numerous horse. Old historical reports indicate that herds of 10,000 upwards were not uncommon. In 1754, an English Jesuit writing about a trip made on the plains told of great numbers of Mustangs passing him at full speed, "for two or three hours together, during which time it was the greatest difficulty that I and four Indians who accompanied me on this occasion, preserved ourselves from being trampled to pieces by them." Although reports cannot be authenticated, it has been rumored that herds of 40,000 to 50,000 Mustangs existed in the mid-1700s in North America. The Mustang was hunted by "Mustangers" who slaughtered these magnificent animals for meat, hide, and tallow. Wild horses became such a nuisance that a bounty was placed on their heads and numbers eventually dwindled.

There was a $25 bounty on each stallion killed and only $2 for a wolf. Untold thousands of free Mustangs were shot, drowned, speared, poisoned, and clubbed until the vast herds of Mustangs were almost depleted. The few that got away escaped to the mountains where no one dared to follow. Civilization later took care of many of the outstanding stallions and mares by preserving them in breeding operations. Those who knew their courage and respected their abilities domesticated many of the best Mustangs and preserved the "type" by careful breeding. Thus, nature and man combined to produce a trait that neither man nor the elements have been able to erase from the characteristics of the Mustang—incredible stamina, endurance, and hardiness. Only within the last few decades did an association develop to preserve the existing outstanding individuals that have come to be known as the Mustang breed. The aim of Mustang breeders currently is not to create a new breed, but to restore and preserve the Mustangs as they are. Emphasis is not so much on upbreeding within the breed, but on taking care not to breed down.

Characteristics   Mustangs are basically gentle and sensible in disposition, and many have a smooth way of traveling and convenient size to make them ideal as a child's horse or for use by the grown-up.

The Mustang stands from 13.2 to 15 hands. They mature slowly but have a long, useful life span. Brood mares usually produce up into their twenties. Full size and development is not normally reached until five years of age. Average weight is from 700 to 950 pounds.

Mustangs are attractive, short coupled, deep bodied horses. Glass eyes and scleras are not uncommon, especially among the roans, appaloosas, and paints. The muzzle is tapered and refined, the mouth shallow, and the lips firm. The head profile is either straight, slightly dished, or has a slight bulge above the nostrils. Some individuals have mustaches.

The legs are strong and straight and appear rather delicate in some individuals. Skeletons of Mustangs have shown that they have dense bones as well as round front cannon bones, instead of the oval shaped bone found in most other breeds. This type of leg structure explains why Mustangs seldom have leg problems. When raised on pasture with good solid ground and rocks, hoofs are small but ample and hard as iron.

Endurance is legendary among Mustangs. An old cowboy legend states that "they would stay—stay till hell froze over and a little while on the ice." One story related by frontier historians is that of a little girl named Aubry who was placed on the back of a Mustang mare named Dolly to escape an Indian attack. Although her entire family was massacred, little Aubry rode Dolly at a gallop for 200 miles in 26 hours to safety. Some historians claim this is a world record which has never been equaled.

Coloration in the Mustang covers the spectrum of possibilities. Along with all the typical solid colors (browns, sorrels, black, white) the Mustang runs in various shades of Duns, Buckskins, Grullas, Clay Banks, Palominos, Roans, Blue Corns, Pinto/Paints, both Tobinano and Overo, Medicine Hats, and Appaloosas. Wild gene markings are very common (dorsal and zebra stripes, crosses over the shoulders). Coloration has no bearing on purity.

Uses

The Mustang is used as a child's horse, as a show, pleasure, and trail horse, and because of their natural herding instinct and cow sense, they make fine ranch horses and cow ponies. Of course, because of their legendary stamina, they excel in endurance rides.

Common Criticisms

Breeders of other fine horses may argue that the Mustang is simply a wild horse that is being preserved because of historical sentiment. They are also criticized for being small in size and slow to mature. Few, however, would argue with the need to preserve examples of a fine American tradition and a living reminder of America's glorious frontier past.

NORWEGIAN FJORD

The Norwegian Fjord (pronounced fee-ord) Horse is Norway's oldest and America's newest breed. All breeding in Norway has been controlled by a government agency. It was not until 1950 that exportations were allowed to the United States. Approximately 25 Fjords have been imported to North America, all of which had to be designated champion stock by the government of Norway.

History

One of the most ancient breeds of horse is the Norwegian Dun or Fjord Horse (Fig. 2-54). The ancient duns are said to hold the same position among the cold-blooded breeds as does the Arabian among the hot-blooded ones. Although it is unknown where or how the breed

FIGURE 2-54. The Norwegian Fjord Horse is small, rugged, an easy keeper, and always dun colored. (The Norwegian Fjord Horse Association of North America)

came to Norway and the Scandinavian peninsula, it is known to have occurred over 4,000 years ago with domestication occurring about 2,000 B.C. Some researchers believe the Fjord to be related to the small northern Celtic ponies found in Ireland, Shetland, or The Hebrides. Others maintain that it is a direct descendant of the wild, prehistoric breeds that roamed Asia and Russia. The prehistoric theory has received most consideration backed primarily by the color theory, which claims that the dun color is a true primitive trait, found today only in the last remnants of the steppe horse.

Very little is known, other than its mere existence, about the Fjord Horse until the sixteenth and seventeenth centuries. Ancient records during this time show that the horse was rather small. Documents dated 1750 indicate a height of 10 to 12 hands and 1850 records show maximum height of 13.5 hands.

During the 1850s, a national breeding program was designed by the government to select good stallions and place them in the best breeding areas. A unique program of corporate stallion ownership evolved and has been the mainstay of Norwegian breeding efforts to date. Mare owners and interested breeders simply join forces to secure a superior stallion for their district. Supervision of breeding practices and the keeping of the Stud Book has been in charge of the government since the very beginning.

The name is derived from the fact that many small farms of two acres or slightly greater exist in the mountainous terrain and fjords of

Norway. These small, tough, native horses had managed to survive for several thousand years in a hostile climate and were ideally suited for farming the small acreage in summer and hauling firewood and other things during the long, cold winters.

The little duns are still needed for jobs that machines cannot handle, especially in the western parts of Norway, the traditional home of the duns. This area of mountains and moors, deeply cut by great fjords, prevents the use of even mechanized transportation to some areas. Surprisingly, the Norwegian army maintains pack trains to get supplies to troops where all other transport fails.

Export laws by the government of Norway allow only champion stock to be sent abroad. Less than two dozen Norwegian Fjords have been exported to different parts of the United States, but they have found a ready acceptance among horse lovers who use them for children's mounts, among other uses.

Characteristics

The Fjord horse was never bred to be a saddle horse although it has been used in the mountains for trail riding purposes when needed. For centuries, Norwegian breeders and now their American counterparts have emphasized the calm, gentle temperament, and unequaled dependability of this small horse.

These dun colored horses, with their distinct and spectacular markings, look nearly identical to the untrained eye. Contrary to popular opinion, the association is not a color registry. All Fjord horses simply have the dun color, which may vary from brown dun, red dun, gray dun, and yellow dun. A light brown or buckskin dun is the most common color, accounting for 80% of the horses. Regardless of the shade, each has a dark dorsal stripe, starting in the center of the forelock and running through the center of the mane, back, and tail. Dark bars on the legs and black fetlocks finish out the color pattern. Stallions stand 14 to 14.2½ hands while the mares are 13.1 to 13.3 hands.

The Fjord is an outstandingly thrifty keeper. Grass and hay alone will provide sufficient nutrition. The historical, natural habitat of the breed makes them able to stand even the coldest and snowiest winters in pasture. Instances in Norway have been reported of Norwegian Fjords being ridden 20 miles per day, for many days, without carrying a single morsel of feed for them. The horses are simply turned loose at night and allowed to forage among the rough, rocky pastures for themselves. Centuries of natural and unspoiled breeding have produced a fertile, hardy animal, one with tough feet and legs, seldom affected by the more common equine problems or ailments.

Uses

The Fjord's strength, clean lines, and exceptional adaptability have made it equally well suited to harness (Fig. 2-55) or saddle. In Norway,

FIGURE 2-55. Pair of two-year-old stallions, Norwegian Fjord Horse. Although selected for farming and pack purposes, Norwegian Fjords are excellent for cart and carriage uses as well as for riding. (The Norwegian Fjord Horse Association of North America)

they are used mainly for farming, logging, and packing purposes. However, in England and the United States, they are often ridden English or Western, hunted, or driven in shows, parades, and down country roads. Their temperament makes them an ideal family horse, ridden or driven easily by young or mature horseman.

For adults or children, the show circuit or the small family farm, the Norwegian Fjord horse is a tough, small, thrifty, all-purpose horse.

PALOMINO

Most breeds of horses are classified according to their lineage, but the Palomino is determined by its color. Various breeds of horses are registered as Palomino although they may or may not be recognized by their breed association: Quarter horses account for fifty percent; the remainder are Thoroughbreds, Standardbreds, American Saddle Horses, Arabians, Morgans, and Tennessee Walking Horses.

History

The place of origin of the Palomino cannot be conclusively determined. Myths and legends of various countries shroud the beginnings of this golden horse with the ivory colored mane and tail. This color pattern has been preserved in ancient tapestries and paintings of Europe and Asia, as well as in Japanese and Chinese art. The history of the horse is actually a history of its color. The color is historically agreed upon as coming from the Arab and the Barb which produces all light colored horses.

Numerous theories exist as to why golden horses with white manes and tails are called Palominos. Palomino is a fairly common family name in Spain. It is possible that a family with a golden horse gave rise to "El Caballo de Palomino"—the horse of Palomino—which was eventually shortened to "Palomino." Another suggestion is that the Spanish word "Paloma," meaning dove, was the origin. There is also a Spanish grape called Palomino which is said to be golden. It is not known for certain which is the correct theory. For whatever reason, the name has come to denote a particular, beautiful color coat that is distinctive in several breeds.

It is believed that the first Palomino was introduced to America in the fifteenth century. The horses later became prized by wealthy Spanish landowners, particularly in California.

In an effort to produce a distinct breed, the Palomino Horse Association, Inc. was orginized in 1936 to perpetuate and record bloodlines of horses that produced the Palomino color. Today the Palomino has become popular not only within its own bloodlines but in several other breeds as well.

Characteristics   Although color is the major characteristic and the chief consideration in Palomino horses, they do not breed true for this trait. Bred to one another, Palominos produce on the average 50% Palominos, 25% Albinos, and 25% Chestnuts. A Palomino can virtually be assured, however, by crossing a Chestnut with an Albino.

Although they do not perpetuate their coloring genetically, the Palomino has specific standards for color. The body color must be natural, the color of newly minted gold coins. The shade may vary from light to dark gold. They also must have a full white mane and natural white tail. White on the face is permitted but must not exceed a blaze, strip, or star. White on legs is acceptable to the knees or hocks. Skin pigmentation is either dark or golden in color. Dark skinned Palominos' coats often turn white in winter while light skinned examples maintain the gold coloring year around.

The eyes must be brown, black, or hazel, and unlike some other color breeds, glass eyes or different colored eyes are not allowed.

Height restrictions range from a minimum of 14.1 hands to a maximum of 16.0 hands and weight varies considerably depending upon the breed association with which the Palomino is associated, although 1,100 pounds is considered the ideal.

All horses with blue, moon, or pink eyes, or with white or dark spots on the body (such as Pinto markings) are refused registration.

FIGURE 2-56. The typical Palomino color is a golden body with white mane, tail, and stockings. (Kentucky Horse Park, Lexington, Kentucky)

No horse whose sire or dam is an Albino, Pinto, or Appaloosa shall be registered.

Uses

The Palomino is a multipurpose horse. They are admired not only for beauty but also for versatility, maneuverability, and endurance. Uses include ranching, racing, rodeos, pleasure riding, parades, shows, fiestas, jumping, trail rides, and many other equine activities.

PAINT

The words "Paint" and "Pinto" are synonymous, both referring to spotted or two-tone horses with body markings of white and some other color. Although they share a mutual history, the modern terms paint and pinto are vastly different because of the two registry organizations that represent them and the restrictions the organizations placed upon their registry. The Pinto Association registers horses of all breeds and types, including Ponies, Saddlebreds, Parade, and Fine-Harness horses. The American Paint Horse Association is devoted to only three types of horses: Registered Paints, Quarter Horses (as approved by the American Quarter Horse Association), and Thoroughbreds (as approved by the Jockey Club of New York).

History

As long as there have been horses, there have been Paints as evidenced by drawings, paintings, and lore of Asian, European, and African civilizations. The distinctive color pattern can be traced back to the Oriental and African Barbs. Egyptian tombs depict Paints as far back as 4300 B.C.

It is believed that when Hernando Cortes led his Mexican expedition from Cuba to Mexico in 1519 that at least one of the sixteen horses taken was a Paint. Large numbers of Paints later developed in the American Mustang herds, due no doubt to Spanish horse foundation blood. The Comanches, who were superior horsemen, favored the Paint horse for its speed, durability, and bright colors.

As the solid-color breed registries developed, Paints gradually receded from prominence and were mostly forgotten until the early 1960s. Because the strong inherited color pattern persisted, interest was rekindled, and in 1962 Mrs. Rebecca Tyler of Gainesville, Texas and E.J. Husdpeth of Era, Texas formed the American Paint Stock Horse Association, now the American Paint Horse Association (APHA). Originally, the association worked out of Rebecca Tyler's kitchen. Offices were moved to Amarillo, Texas in 1963 and in 1964 to permanent offices in Fort Worth, Texas. The association currently has over 286,000 horses in its registry, membership exceeding 34,000 with over 2,000 registrations per month coming into the Fort Worth office. Over 1,000 state and regional shows and 271 approved races are sanctioned by the APHA each year.

Paint registrations outside the United States boast horses in the countries of Australia, Canada, Denmark, England, France, Guatemala, Ecuador, Holland, Honduras, Japan, South Africa, Switzerland, and Germany.

Characteristics   Since the association is primarily a color registry, allowing Quarter Horses and Thoroughbreds, the most obvious outstanding characteristics are the two color patterns—"tobiano" (Fig. 2-58) and "overo" (Fig. 2-59) patterns. Tobiano comes from the old Argentine word *tubiano* meaning "large spots of two colors." Tobiano horses usually have a head marked like a solid-colored horse, with legs that are white at least below the knees and hocks, and with large regular spots.

The original meaning of overo meant "peach colored or golden colored." As used in America, however, it came to mean "several colors and many spots." Another term used to describe this pattern is "calico." Whether the color pattern is referred to as paint, pinto, piebald, skewbald, tobiano, or overo, these colorful horses are referred to by the Paint Association as "sport model of the horse world" (see also discussion covered under Pinto Horse).

The APHA was founded on the proposition that color alone is not sufficient basis for a Paint and that the indiscriminate use of all breeds

FIGURE 2-57. Long Tall Texan, 16 hands, 1400 pounds, six times Grand Champion Paint Stallion. (Al and Patt Edwards Ranch, Austin, Texas)

FIGURE 2-58. A Paint with the Tobiano color pattern. This form of spotting is often thought of as a brown horse enclosed by a white frame. (American Paint Horse Association)

FIGURE 2-59. A Paint with Overo markings. This pattern may be thought of as a white horse enclosed by a brown frame. (American Paint Horse Association)

would be undesirable. The registry is based upon a combination of breeding, conformation, and color.

A gaited horse that single-foots or paces is not eligible for registration in this association. However, a foxtrot or running walk is eligible. Horses with Appaloosa or Arabian characteristics are not eligible for registration. Size of the Paint horse is variable with the minimum height of 14 hands required for registration.

Solid colored horses of Paint extraction are allowed registration in the Appendix Breeding Stock Registry of the association, provided they are eligible for registration in the American Quarter Horse Association or Jockey Club of New York Association.

Uses

The Paint is an agile, versatile horse able to perform well in a wide variety of events. They are used for arena performance, trail riding, pleasure riding, family use, show ring competition, racing, youth activities, and as cow horses.

Common Criticisms

As with most color registries, there is the inclination for detractors to claim that color pattern is insufficient for selection purposes. The American Paint Horse Association has nullified some of this criticism with its strict adherence to conformation requirements of the Quarter Horse and Thoroughbred standards.

PERCHERON

A most famous draft horse around the world is the Percheron breed from France. This work animal, on the average, is somewhat smaller and of a more refined nature than other draft breeds. When one delves into history, it is not difficult to understand why the Percheron carries a more refined appearance than the average heavy horse.

History

The Percheron originated in the ancient province of Le Perche near Normandy, France, a district about one-fifteenth the size of Iowa.

Although it is speculation, Arabian sires most likely played an important part in the early refinement of the breed. By the time of the Crusades, the Percheron had already achieved a reputation not only for substance and soundness, but for style and beauty. Much of the ancient descriptions of "chargers" mounted by knights in gleaming armor can be credited to the classy lines of the Percheron.

These large horses of the Perche district during the seventeenth and eighteenth centuries were in great demand for a variety of uses. The ancient Percherons were lighter in weight, more active, smaller in scale, ranging in size from 15 to 16 hands. They were used as a general purpose horse for a saddler, hunter, and a carriage horse although all horses had a drafty conformation. Since foundation sires were thought

FIGURE 2-60. The Percheron is noted for its clean head and neck, a long croup, big round hips, and extra heavy muscling in the thighs. (Big Ed's Photos, Davenport, Iowa)

to have been the Arabian, English Thoroughbred type, and some Turkish horses, this is not to be unexpected.

The French government established an official stud at Le Pin, during the nineteenth century, to encourage the horse industry and to develop army mounts. Horses were selected with great care over a long period of time to develop and fix the characteristics of the Percheron. About 1823, a tremendous prepotent sire named Jean-le-Blanc was born that became the most famous Percheron sire of all time. All Percherons today trace their bloodlines back to this outstanding animal.

While the French were busy establishing the breed, it was the Americans who were instrumental in motivating the French to establish an official breed registry. The first Percheron arrived in America in 1839 as the result of an American traveler in France, Edward Harris of Morristown, New Jersey. The American Stud Book was published in 1876 under the name of Norman Stud Book, but the name was soon changed to "Percheron." The Percheron Horse Association of America, as we know it today, was established in 1905. It was not until the appearance of the American Registry in 1876 that the French were inclined to establish a registry for French horses in 1885.

The late 1800s were busy years for the Percheron business. America had a tremendous impact on the development of this breed of draft horse through the production of Brilliant 1889, and his son, Brilliant. These two sires had as much influence on the Percheron breed as any others in the history of the development of this breed of draft horse. It was not unusual for individual Percherons of the late 1800s to sell for the then fabulous sum of $5,000.

Just before the turn of the century, a depression struck America which had a lasting effect upon breeding stock in the United States. Many large breeding herds had to be dispersed because of economic collapse, but the Percheron horse industry actually benefited because of dispersion evenly throughout the United States. By the early 1900s, with breeding stock available throughout the country, the horse business boomed once again and the Percheron prospered as a draft animal.

Once referred to as the "nearly perfect draft horse," an outstanding individual named Calypso was once chosen as the all time ideal Percheron stallion and many judges proclaimed him to be the perfect draft animal of any breed. Other outstanding sires of this era were Carnot, sold at a record high price of $40,000, Dragon, Laet, Lagos, Hesitation, and Don Degas. Of course, numerous other outstanding sires also contributed to the wide distribution of the Percheron.

Characteristics   In 1936, breeders arranged a conference to discuss and decide on the ideal conformation and characteristics that should guide breeders of

Percherons throughout the remainder of the association history. As a result, 100 prominent breeders established criteria for Percheron type. The ideal Percheron is medium sized, heavy boned, and upheaded. Sires are expected to range from 1,800 to 2,000 pounds, mares from 1,500 to 1,600, and sires normally range 16 to 17 hands high, mares 15 to 16 hands high. One of the outstanding characteristics of the Percheron is the heavy muscling in the lower thighs which gives an unusual amount of strength and power to the breed. Percherons are also clean legged and of quality conformation of the feet and legs. The ideal horse has large, round hips and a fairly long croup. He is wide and deep through the chest, showing plenty of back rib, and close coupled. Ease and balance of gait are stressed. He is also expected to be of a gentle temperament and an easy keeper. Among draft breeds, the Percheron carries his head and neck with animation and shows a great deal of style and grace for a large animal, suggesting influence of the early Arabian breeding.

Although browns, chestnuts, and roans are sometimes seen in the Percheron breed, grays, blacks, sorrels, and bays are predominant.

Uses

Percherons are used in the United States as typical draft animals valued for their ability to pull heavy loads and do heavy farm work on relatively light rations. They are also used as carriage horses and because of their relatively small draft style, are occasionally ridden as saddle animals. The Percheron, although a draft type horse, is truly a versatile, all-around individual.

PONY OF THE AMERICAS

An all-around youth performance pony for any event is the Pony of the Americas (POA). This breed emphasizes its ideal size: it is not too big (13.2 hands), not too small (11.2 hands), but just the right range in size to fit most youth best.

History

Les Boomhower, George Barrett, and Nick Litzel laid the original plans for founding a new type of pony to meet the demands of active young horse people in the United States. These breeders admired the Shetland for its small size yet rugged characteristics and the Appaloosa with its colorful markings. Initially using only these two breeds, crosses were made to develop a pony with more scale than the Shetland but with the colorful markings of the famed spotted horse (Fig. 2-61). The first approved POA was born in 1954, a foal of an Appaloosa mare by a Shetland stallion, and was named Black Hand #1.

Since 1954, bloodlines have continually been improved but the POA breeding standard called for a conformation between that of the Quarter Horse and Arabian, with Appaloosa color and characteristics.

FIGURE 2-61. A Pony of the Americas (POA) gelding. POA's are a miniature version of the comingling of Arabian and Quarter Horse with Appaloosa color patterns. Note the spots and striped hooves. (POAC, Inc., Mason City, Iowa)

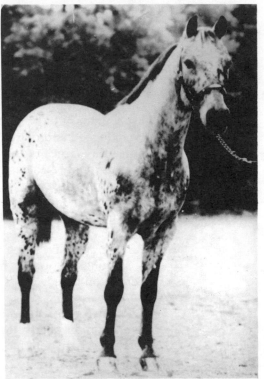

FIGURE 2-62. Pony of the American ponies were bred to fit the young rider 18 years of age and under. Competitions are held for numerous events in thirty-five states. (POAC, Inc., Mason City, Iowa)

Infusion of Arabian and Quarter Horse blood commingled with earlier crosses gave the desired results.

The POA was developed as a "using pony for youth" and designed for young riders 18 and under (Fig. 2-62), although it is suitable for many adults. The emphasis has always been on a pony that the entire family as a unit could enjoy but especially one that would fit the formative years of a child, teaching him or her sportsmanship, responsibility, and good horsemanship.

The POA Club membership has grown to include 57 active POA Clubs and Chapters in 35 states. There are more than 45,000 registered horses belonging to the association.

Characteristics   Although Shetlands figured in the initial cross, the POA of today bears little resemblance to its somewhat smaller ancestor. The "ideal type" is described as a miniature cross between a Quarter Horse and an Arabian with the color markings of the Appaloosa.

Arabian characteristics are emphasized especially in the head of the POA. A slightly dished face is desirable to accentuate Arabian characteristics. Another striking feature of the breed is the rather heavy muscles of the quarters and gaskins. The breed standard calls for a heavily muscled pony, not as well muscled as a Quarter Horse but heavier than an Arabian.

The association is still allowing some breeds of unknown ancestry to enter the registry but for the most part, a POA pony must have at least one parent which is registered by the association. To be eligible for registry, the pony must have a visible Appaloosa type color, sclera around the eye, and some mottled skin. Striped hooves are desirable but not essential.

Color is heavily emphasized and in order for a pony to participate in approved shows and sales must have visible Appaloosa type color at a distance of 40 feet.

Accepted color patterns of the POA are the following: Leopard pattern, white with black spots on hindquarters, body; Frost pattern; Marbleized Roan pattern; Blanket pattern; and Snowflake. All the color patterns are variations of Appaloosa type markings. The cosmetic emphasis is on a spotted pony.

These ponies were developed for youth age 18 and under and as such POA selections have been for an even temperament and great versatility to compete in youth events of every type.

The best results for a youngster occur when a mount suits the rider best in size and disposition. For that reason, the POA was developed to meet a maximum size of 13.2 hands and the minimum of 11.2 hands at maturity.

Uses   Activities of POA Clubs constantly strive to emphasize sound horsemanship for youth. Contestants compete in age groups of 8 and under, 9 through 12, and 13 through 18. Adults do not compete with youth but are allowed to enter a pony in halter, adult cart, and fun classes. An Annual International Show is held for championship events in western pleasure, gymkhana, jumping, leadline, calf daubing, halter, trail, English, costume, and cart classes.

Common Criticisms   As always, when a new breed develops, there are detractors. Criticisms have been leveled at the POA as a glorified color registry, a slightly larger version of the Shetland, or a "breeding down" of the Arabian, Quarter Horse, and Appaloosa. However, few will argue with the POA philosophy, "If you love horses—and youth—you will enjoy the POA." Any POA show is an inspiring spectacle to watch, with its sportsmanship, competitiveness, and ability of youthful horses and riders.

PASO FINO   The Paso Fino has to be classified as among the smoothest riding horses in the world. The breed developed in the Caribbean, especially Puerto Rico, and South America over the last 400 years. Although recognition and popularity in the United States began as recently as 1959 when the first importations were made, it has gained a strong stable of admirers.

History   The name Paso Fino can literally be translated to "smooth ride" or smooth gait. This smooth gait is brought about by a natural tendency to do a lateral, broken pace; right rear, right fore, left rear, left fore (Fig. 2-63). Almost all of the jarring action of riding is absorbed by the hind quarters giving the rider unequaled comfort.

Horses with this peculiar gait were the pride of Spanish provinces like Cordela and Andalusia, from whence Columbus gathered 20 stallions and 5 brood mares for his second voyage to the new world. These horses were taken to the Caribbean Islands for use in remount stations to provide horses for the new world. One of the chief strains of horses exported during this time was known as the Spanish Jennet breed, noted for its comfortable saddle gait and the ability to pass this gait on to its offspring. Although the Spanish Jennet is most often referred to as a "vanished breed," there are those who would argue that the breed still lives on in the bloodlines of a horse with a different name—Paso Fino.

The horses brought by Columbus were first unloaded in the Dominican Republic where they became foundation stock for the Conquistadors. Others were taken to Puerto Rico in 1509, to Cuba in 1511, to

FIGURE 2-63. Marichal, a Paso Fino, in this action shot exhibits the broken pace. Note the leg movement of right rear, right fore, left rear, left fore. (Elna Hayward White, Weimar, Texas)

Mexico in 1518, and by 1515 many large horse breeding centers were established throughout the Caribbean area.

Although some Arabian blood may have been in the very early stock, it is the blood of the Barb, Andalusian, and Spanish Jennet coupled with selection for the natural tendency to do a lateral gait that lead to the development of the breed now known as Paso Fino.

In the later 1500s, different breeds began to emerge, but in South American countries and particularly on the island of Puerto Rico, breeders highly prized the stylish action and smooth ride of the small horses with the lateral gait. Island breeders became increasingly interested in a stylish show horse and to date have developed one of the more outstanding strains of the Paso Finos. Pasos also developed in Peru, Columbia, Dominican Republic, and elsewhere in South America. Prized for their gait and bred for it, Paso Finos made a comfortable mount for use in sugar cane fields, plantations, mountainous trails, and in colorful horse shows which are so much a part of the Latin culture.

During the 1960s, many servicemen stationed in Puerto Rico became attached to their Paso Fino horses and introduced them into the United States. In 1964 a need for a stateside registry became apparent and the American Paso Fino Horse Association was formed. There are approximately 23,000 Pasos registered in the United States. These horses should not be confused with the Peruvian Paso, a breed with a similar history which will be discussed separately.

Characteristics   Paso Finos are a distinctive breed of horse based on the primary natural gait—a lateral broken pace. The Paso movement is a broken gait in which the two legs on the same side move together, but the hind hoof touches the ground a fraction of a second before the fore hoof. This produces a smooth, syncopated, four-beat gait that gives comfort to the rider and a characteristic "pitter patter, pitter patter" sound to the passing of the horse.

The Paso Fino characteristically may do three or more of the Paso gaits. All of them are natural and no training with the use of weights or other artificial measures is ever allowed to induce the gait. Some horses do only one gait while others may do all of them. The three basic gaits are known as *Paso Fino*, the very collected showring gait; the *Paso Corto*, the same gait but more relaxed, slightly faster, and considered a pleasure gait; the *Paso Largo*, a speed gait in which the horse may cover the ground at 15 to 18 miles per hour yet producing a smooth effortless ride. Two additional gaits worthy of note are the *Sobre Paso*, the most relaxed form of gait allowing a completely loose rein and little or no style; and the *Andadura* gait, used when a Paso horse is pushed for top speed. The horse does not go into a gallop, but rather a pace because of his strong lateral gait. This gait has none of the comfort or popularity of a Paso. Paso Finos are also unusual in that they are expected to produce their natural gait with natural feet—that is, the use of shoes is frowned upon by breeders and horse shows. Shoes are recommended only on occasions when Paso Finos are used in endurance rides, and even then only very light plates are recommended.

The Paso Fino is a relatively small horse being close in size to the Arabian. The ideal size is between 14 and 15 hands high. Much effort has been made in the past to increase the size of the horses but to little avail, because the natural gait is often lost when crossing Pasos with larger scaled horses.

Pasos come in every color including paints and albinos, but bay, gray, and chestnut are the most common. Some of the more famous Paso Fino horses are what the Spanish call zaino oscuro—black or very dark bay. Many breeders try for horses marked with four white socks because this has a tendency to show off the lateral gait in the showring. Legend has it that Queen Isabella favored this marking, because she decreed that horses with four white feet could pass toll-free through Spanish gates. Various shades of roan have been noted, including one example which a breeder referred to as purple. Although colored photographs indicated that his color was not far from wrong, the registration papers were amended to read "red roan."

Uses

This extremely versatile horse can be used for any purpose where a trot is not required. They are generally used, at present, in modified western classes, trail riding, pleasure, gymkhanas, pole bending, pick-up races, mounted drill teams, etc. However, the major and most colorful use of these horses is in the traditional Caribbean horse shows. In this latter event, riders are always costumed in the traditional Spanish Riding Habit (Fig. 2-64). Spanish costumes are required for showing and although tack may vary, the traditional saddle is English or Dressage saddles.

FIGURE 2-64. Paso Finos are shown with English or Dressage saddle. Riders wear traditional Spanish costume. (Nan Redding, Houston, Texas)

Common Criticisms

Paso Finos are often criticised for being small. Some horsemen might also complain that there is little difference between the Paso Fino, the Tennessee Walker, the American Saddle Horse, the Missouri Fox Trotter, and the Peruvian Paso. However, fanciers of the Paso Fino believe their breed to be distinctively unique, and to substantiate their claim readily point out finer points of equine performance and heritable traits not readily observed by the untrained eye.

PERUVIAN PASO

Although several horse associations exist that include the Spanish word "Paso," such as American Paso Fino Horse Association, International Paso Fino Society, Paso Fino Owners and Breeders Association, etc., these should not be confused with the Peruvian Paso Horse Registry. The Peruvian Paso has a distinct origin and unique characteristics, and should not be confused with Paso Fino breeds.

History

The Peruvian Paso is original only to Peru. Some confusion exists because of the translation of the Spanish word "Paso" which means gait. Note that the Peruvian Paso deletes the word "Fino" from its title. This has caused some confusion in differentiating between the Paso Fino breeds and the Peruvian Paso. While the Peruvian Paso and the Paso Fino breeds had similar foundation stock, the similarities soon ended there.

The Peruvian Paso is descended from the Andalusian, Barb, Spanish Jennet, and Friesian, breeds brought to Peru by Pizarro. These horses were directly responsible for the fall of the Inca Empire and were so prized by the Spaniards that many were shod with silver and so valuable that porters carried young foals in "hammocks" on the long, forced marches. Over the centuries, selective blending of only these breeds, plus climatic and environmental changes, have produced the Paso of today. No bloodlines other than the original foundation breeds have been introduced into the Peruvian Paso. It is a point of pride with Peru that this fine animal is designated the National horse of Peru.

The reason for the development of the Paso horse in Peru is quite simple. The terrain is extremely rough, making road building an economically difficult task, as well as physically impractical. While other parts of the world after the seventeenth century were developing trotters to pull wagons and other types of wheeled vehicles, the naturally gaited horse was still in demand in Peru. A smooth riding horse was a necessity, and still is to this day in that country. Since a horse that trots is more desirable for pulling a wheeled vehicle, the breeding of trotting horses through the nineteenth century exceeded by far that of the breeding of gaited horses. At the same time, world wide acceptance of horse racing was taking place, an event at which the gaited horse does not excel. One of the most complete transformations of horse breeding the world has known was taking place virtually everywhere except Peru. For centuries, the Peruvians have maintained their interests in selective breeding for a smooth gaited horse. Of course, selection for desirable characteristics has continued to the point that this is the only gaited breed in the world that can guarantee the transmission of its gait one-hundred percent to its offspring. The trademark of the Peruvian breed is an inherited Paso gait in every purebred offspring. A major principle with Peruvian breeders is that their horses are born, not made.

The Peruvian Paso was relatively unheard of in North America until

1960 when some importations were made. Peruvian breeders are noted for their unselfishness in sharing this unique horse with other horse lovers. After 450 years of selection, the breed was shared with others outside of Peru. Peruvian breeders are such avid admirers of the horse that no money exchanges hands when the horses are bred in their native country. If an owner admires the stallion of some other rancher, he is usually giver the service of that stallion free. If an owner admires a certain mare, he is loaned "the belly of the mare." The mare is then returned after the foal is weaned.

In Peru, there are two distinct and separate bloodlines—the southern and northern bloods. Most of the large haciendas are located in northern Peru and a plantation type horse that is capable of traveling many miles a day was developed for this area. The northern Pasos are large and strong and have great endurance. In southern Peru, the haciendas are smaller and the horse is used more as a pleasure animal. They are bred for finer characteristics such as fine type, animated action, etc. To help insure natural action and gait, no horse is allowed in the show ring with shoes or hooves longer than four inches.

The history of the Paso breed in the United States can be traced back to the early importations in 1960 and more recently the foundation of the Peruvian Paso Horse Registry of North America, established in 1970. Currently 11,500 horses are registered in North America. There is also a Peruvian Paso Half-Blood Association.

Characteristics   The Peruvian Paso (Fig. 2-65 and Fig. 2-66) is one of the few breeds that has had a long-range program of breeding for disposition, second only to the selection for the Paso gait. Culling is done to produce an animal that is spirited, yet quiet and docile in hand.

The Spanish word "pisos" defines the gait and way of traveling for this breed. The gait of the Paso was originated by the Peruvians who wanted to travel great distances between haciendas, and in order to get the smoothest ride possible, never allowed their horses to do anything but walk. As time passed, the stride lengthened, legs became more flexible, and movement was increased. The natural tendency to pace, because of the original foundation stock, was inherited by these Peruvian horses and the fore and hind legs of the same side began more and more to move together, producing a smoother, cat-like movement. Through the centuries, selective breeding maintained and refined this four-beat gait. In essence, the horse does a broken pace—the hind foot touches the ground before the fore foot on the same side. All breeders use basically the same training methods and equipment so that no advantage is gained through the use of artificial devices or aids.

One very unusual characteristic of the Paso is the movement of the

FIGURE 2-65. Santos Placintia, 1968 champion Paso gelding. Good action is captured in this photo. Notice the "tapa ojos" (blinders) just above the eyes, used to prevent horses from running away on the treeless plains of Peru. (The American Peruvian Paso Horse Registry)

FIGURE 2-66. El Cid, Champion of Champion Stallion three straight years in Peru. Owned by Senor Fernando Peschiera. Note the typical stirrup, crupper, and breechings, a part of traditional attire. (Western Horseman)

fore leg, an original trait found only in Peruvian Pasos. This movement is termed a "termino" and is neither a wing nor a paddle. It is a flashy, natural rolling action of the Paso, very desirable in this breed for show purposes. The termino is an outward rolling of the fore legs in a high exaggerated manner, much like the arms of a swimmer. It is most desirable when the movement comes from high in the shoulders.

Each Peruvian horse has a gait at which it is most comfortable, termed a road gait. Speed variation ranges from six to eight miles an hour, with the horse being able to maintain this for extended periods of time.

Although the Paso gait is not too different from the rack, running walk, single foot, and even four beat gait familiar to the American Saddlebred and Tennessee Walking Horse, the difference is that the gait is one-hundred percent transmissible in purebred offspring. Chains, boots, special weights, special training, etc. are not required or allowed.

The Paso averages 14.3 to 15 hands high, about the size of Morgans and Arabians, and weighs from 900 to 1,200 pounds. The hair is fine and silky, the mane and tail long and luxurious. Pasos come in all colors: black, brown, bay, chestnut, gray, palomino, buckskin, and roan.

The Paso horse wears a special bridle made of plaited goat hide (Fig. 2-67), which is fitted with a special set of blinders called "tapa ojos." Translation is roughly "over the eyes" and is an important function of the head gear. Since few trees are found on the plains of Peru, the horse simply has his blinders pulled down over his eyes and is prevented from running away when the reins are dropped.

FIGURE 2-67. A Peruvian Paso showing head gear, in bit, complete with "tapa ojos." (The American Peruvian Horse Registry)

Other interesting uses of gear were developed for functional purposes because of the harsh terrain or people. An interesting modification of tack is the Peruvian stirrup (Fig. 2-66). It is a pyramid shaped block of solid wood, the toe hollowed out, with four sharp corners covered with metal. It was made to be easily detached from the saddle, to be used as an effective bone-crushing weapon for discouraging bandits or ruffians.

The Peruvian horse is also shown with unusual trappings—the crupper and breechings on the hind quarters. These serve no function, but can be traced back to the Spanish draped tapestries and other decorations used centuries ago.

Uses

The Paso is still used as a plantation horse in Peru and has become a point of national honor in Peruvian Horse Shows where the breed is always shown with tapestries and other paraphernalia indigenous to Peru. Riders are always dressed in native costume in Peru and other countries where Peruvian Paso Horse Shows are held. In North America, the horse is used for a pleasure horse, for dependable transportation, for children's horses, for endurance rides, etc.

**Common
Criticisms**

The Peruvian Paso has been criticized as a "cult" by some because of Paso breeder's determination to maintain the "termino" which many consider to be an unnecessary trait. Other criticisms include a strict determination to allow no infusion of outside blood to increase the size of the Paso. Still others are critical of the gait, claiming that it is little different from walking horses, fox trotting horses, etc. These criticisms are answered by avid admirers of the breed who point to the flashy style that has been bred for centuries to "travel like a conquerer."

PINTO

In recent years, there have been two active associations for the registration of the colorful spotted pattern known as Pinto or Paint. The Pinto Horse Association, located in California, differs from the Texas based American Paint Horse Association covered separately. The main difference is that the Pinto Horse Association accepts any colored, spotted horse or pony that meets requirements of color, conformation and breeding for four basic types of horses: stock type, predominantly Quarter Horse; hunter type, predominantly Thoroughbred breeding; pleasure type, predominantly Arabian or Morgan breeding; saddle type, American Saddle Horse, Hackney or Tennessee Walking Horse breeding.

The Paint Horse Association, on the other hand, recognizes only horses with Quarter Horse and Thoroughbred conformation (Fig. 2-68) and breeding, and has no registry for ponies.

FIGURE 2-68. Pinto horses and ponies are registered according to stock, hunter, pleasure, or saddle type. (Kentucky Horse Park, Lexington, Kentucky)

History   Although the Pinto is commonly associated with the American Indian, who according to legend, considered the loudly marked horses to be a special magic or "good medicine" for effective warfare, it is generally agreed that these wildly spotted horses can be traced back to the African and Oriental Barbs. The standard Pinto patterns were introduced to America by Spanish explorers through Barbs of largely Arabian background imported to Southern Europe by way of North Africa, and crossed with native European stock.

Since many horses escaped from the Spanish conquistadors, herds were lost or simply abandoned because of early expeditions that met with disaster. The American Indian eventually selected some of the wild stock that developed in frontier times. Because the American Indian held the Pinto markings as a special "magic" from the great spirit, their selectivity increased the incidence of Pinto markings.

The Pinto normally is not a true breeding horse, that is, the pattern unexpectedly appears on numerous occasions from solid colored horses due to the Barb influence.

However, by selectively breeding only Pinto colored horses, the incidence of Pinto markings is increased to approximately three out of four foals having the characteristic markings of the Pinto. A Pinto bred to a solid-colored horse will produce only about 50 percent spotted foals.

Centuries passed on the American frontier, tribes were defeated, herds dispersed, but the Pinto had already established a foothold and its characteristic markings had taken on a special kind of "white man's magic" in the eyes of many beholders. While the Indians' use of horses faded with their civilizations and the Anglo-Americans continued to import much foundation stock from Europe, wild horses of the frontier were more readily available and better suited to strenuous working conditions and developed into a type of western horse that became a fixture of America.

In the 1940s, several attempts were made to register Pintos, but all failed because of restrictions on conformation. In 1956, a move was made to organize the Pinto Horse Association of America, Inc. which has since overcome the difficulties of conformation and has as its goal improvement of the Pinto horse. Although it may be considered a color registry by many, the association has approximately 80,000 horses in the United States and Canada, a fact indicating the desire for this type of registry by a large number of people.

Characteristics   Since color and eye-catching appeal are so prevalent in the minds of Pinto horse breeders, it is reasonable to assume that the most outstanding characteristic of these horses is their color pattern. Although there are countless variations of patterns and colors that make up the patterns, the Pinto may best be described as a horse of any color with white marking on his body. Two distinct patterns emerge from the confusion of marking to the untrained eye. The patterns have been greatly simplified by the terms Tobiano and Overo, the Spanish designations for these color markings. (See also the discussion and illustrations covered under Paint Horse.)

Tobiano marking (Fig. 2-58) are large and bold and constitute the most common pattern; the Overo (Fig. 5-59) is generally a more fine, often lacy-edged pattern.

While the untrained observer may consider the designation Tobiano and Overo to be confusing, it can be simplified for the majority of cases. If one thinks of a "picture frame" in the shape of a horse, it will greatly facilitate the necessary mental process for determining the basic difference between the two patterns. Fig. 2-59 illustrates the Overo, a "picture frame" type of marking. Note that the basic Overo marking is a dark outline, seeming to run all the way around the horse, even though the belly is often white. This pattern may also be thought of as a dark colored horse with white markings overlaying that color.

The most common Tobiano pattern (Fig. 2-58) is just the opposite. The white appears to start from the top of the horse and spread downward. The Tobiano pattern may also be thought of as a white horse with dark spots overlaying that color.

Pintos may also be referred to as piebalds (an English term meaning black and white), or as skewbalds (another English term meaning all pintos other than black and white). The Spanish term "pintado" also translates to the English "pinto" or is translated to the English version "paint." Although they are all of a similar background, the Paint Horse term is not used because of another association which has some characteristic requirements that differ from the Pinto Association.

Pinto heights range from 14.1 to 16.2 hands and weights vary from 750 to 1,300 pounds.

Animals under 14.1 hands are also registered by the association but are designated as Pinto ponies.

One peculiar characteristic of Pinto breeding is the "glass eye" which is a part of the color inheritance and is not discriminated against by the association.

Uses

Since the Pinto Association divides their conformation standards into four basic types, it is not unexpected to find that their uses cover the gamut of activity between stock type, hunters, pleasure horses, saddle horses, show animals, endurance rides, racing activities, and any other activity that requires the use of either horse or pony. In the words of the Association, this animal is versatile, a high achiever, and one that "stands out in a crowd." Established primarily as a color registry, today it has grown to offer four conformation types in horses in addition to a separate registry for ponies.

Common Criticisms

Breeders of Pinto Horses may justly be criticized for selecting a color pattern as their most outstanding feature. However, the association has made great strides in improving type and conformation through the use of other outstanding breeds while maintaining this colorful part of America's legendary past. As one breeder so aptly put it, "horses don't register horses, people register horses."

QUARTER HORSE

The American Quarter Horse Association is the world's largest and fastest growing horse registry. Over 1.33 million Quarter Horses are registered in the United States and 57 other countries. Although still found as a working cow-horse on ranches in the United States, Canada, Australia, Mexico, Africa, and South America, the largest growth in the industry has been recent, created by men, women, boys, and girls for use in pleasure riding and contesting in shows, races, and rodeos.

History

The American Quarter Horse Association was the first breed developed in America. It originated in the Carolinas and Virginia during the colonial era more than 300 years ago. Early day colonists enjoyed match-racing as the leading outdoor sport. Since the towns were small and the wilderness great, often the longest stretch of open raceway was the "main street" through the center of town which seldom exceeded 440 yards, hence the early designation "Quarter Miler" for frontier racers. From this colloquial beginning, comes the Quarter Horse.

The Arab, Barb, and Turk breeds brought by Spanish explorers to North America were the foundation breeds for the Quarter Horse. Stallions selected from these breeds were bred in 1611 to a band of imported English mares. The cross produced compact, heavily muscled horses that could run faster than any other breed for the short 440 yard distance. As more colonists began to arrive in North America, these short sprinters were cast aside because of the wealthy landowners' fond remembrances of the racing days in their native lands with the Thoroughbred. Always eager for something new and different, horsemen in the colonies turned to long distance racers, hunters, and jumpers.

However, the "Quarter Miler" was not forgotten by the pioneers who continued westward in the quest for adventure. This tough, compact, dependable horse went up the trail with cattle drives, carried preachers on their circuits, and rushed doctors to their frontier patients. Because of its gentleness, intelligence, and multiple abilities, the Quarter Horse was prized more in the development of the West than was a man. The Southwest was the eventual proving ground for the fulfillment of the Quarter Horse's destiny. On the unfenced, limitless prairies, this horse earned its keep and won the respect of cattlemen, whose fortunes, even their lives, depended upon this four-footed companion. The horse survived time and changes in the Southwest because he excelled in qualities that were of major importance to persons of diverse backgrounds. The "cow savvy" of the Quarter Horse is legendary and still ranks as one of the primary attributes of the breed.

In the early part of the nineteenth century, the Quarter Horse, established in the Southwest, left its offspring along the way spreading its influence throughout the nation. The cattle drives that were pushed by Quarter Horses into the North and West explain the reason for spread of the breed in those areas. As a descendant of true "hot-blooded horses" (Arabs, Barbs, Turks), it is not historically difficult to explain this kind of dominating influence.

As important as this unique equine was to the developing frontier, however, it was not until 1941 in Fort Worth, Texas that a move was made to establish a registry and perpetuate Quarter Horse bloodlines for posterity through the American Quarter Horse Association (AQHA). In the following years, because of the organized association, the breed spread rapidly throughout other parts of the nation, into Canada,

Mexico, and numerous other foreign lands. The registry currently grows three times faster than any other breed registry in the world.

The association headquarters was moved to Amarillo, Texas in 1946 and has experienced continual growth since its foundation. The AQHA boasts 312,544 dues-paying members as of 1996.

Characteristics   Quarter Horses are rather stocky in build (Fig. 2-69), as were their ancestors. There are now two types of Quarter Horses: the more recent Racing Type Quarter Horse, which developed through the addition of American Thoroughbred blood, and the Working Type Quarter Horse used for working cattle and for utility purposes.

The Working Type Quarter Horse is the older of the two types. These horses are rather short-backed, close-coupled, shorter legged, and very heavily muscled. The head is rather distinct because of the small, erect ears and heavily muscled jaws. This type of Quarter Horse makes an ideal cow horse because it is strong and agile and capable of outrunning the fastest of cattle in a very short distance. For this reason, they excel in roping, dogging, and other rodeo events where a strong, durable, fast horse is needed.

The Racing Type Quarter Horse has evolved in past years to a more lean build because of the infusion of some Thoroughbred blood. This is the more prevalent type in Quarter Horse racing.

FIGURE 2-69. The ideal Quarter Horse is close-coupled, agile, and heavily muscled. (Quarter Horse Association)

Height of Quarter Horses will vary somewhat, but on the average they are 15 hands at the maximum and 1,000 to 1,200 pounds in weight.

Color is of no importance to Quarter Horse breeders except for personal preference. Recognized colors include bay, brown, black, sorrel, chestnut, dun, red dun, buckskin, grullo, palomino, gray, blue roan, and red roan. However, no animal with one or more spots of such size and in such location as to indicate Pinto, Appaloosa, or Albino breeding is eligible for registration as a Quarter Horse.

Uses

The Quarter Horse is one of the most versatile of all animals, being intelligent and gentle and possessed with multiple abilities. It has the capacity for hard work and superb "cow sense," and may be seen participating in barrel racing, cutting contests, trail rides, chariot races, western pleasure, steer roping, western riding, calf roping, jumping, pole bending, working hunter, pleasure driving, racing events, and youth activity programs.

More Quarter Horses compete at more shows and more places before more people than do all other breeds of horses combined. Perhaps the fastest growing facet of the AQHA is the youth program, which enables boys and girls 18 years of age and under to compete at approved horse shows. Thousands of these youth shows are sponsored annually by the AQHA.

One of the outstanding events honoring the Quarter Horse is the world's richest horse race held each Labor Day at New Mexico's Ruidoso Downs.

With the exception of a Paint Horse in 1986, only Quarter Horses have ever won the contest for the Annual World Championship Cutting Horse Contest held in Fort Worth, Texas—a contest open to all breeds.

Of course, countless thousands of adults and children do not compete in events or race on the track, preferring the pastime of riding or driving for fun. One of the fastest growing uses for the Quarter Horse is as a status symbol among urban people of all ages.

RACKING HORSE

One of the newest and fastest growing breeds of horses in the United States is the Racking Horse, not to be confused with the American Saddlebred Horse. Although the two breeds are similar in appearance, the Racking Horse is distinguished from the American Saddlebred by the unusual and unique "natural" gaits of the walk, slow gait, and rack. The Racking Horse is one of the few show horses that has always had a natural rather than an induced show gait.

History

The Racking Horse, known from colonial days as the Single Foot Horse, has a history as old as our nation and may have had ancestors

FIGURE 2-70. Go Boy's Road Runner, 1972 World Grand Champion Racking Horse. (Racking Horse Breeders Association)

common to the American Saddlebred Horse. The southeastern states are credited with the selection and development of this breed.

Large plantation owners of the south selected for natural gaited characteristics known as the "single foot."

After two centuries of competing in horse shows, the Single Foot Horse earned a reputation as a show animal and has competed in the showring with the showiest of American Saddlebreds.

In the ring, the Single Foot, later to become known as the Racking Horse, performed naturally in three gaits: the pleasure walk, an easy ride that would cover acres of plantation terrain; the slow rack, a smooth, four-beat gait with style and action—not a pace or a trot, but a great ground gainer; the fast rack, in the same form as the slow rack, which gives the rider the appearance of "sailing" above the ground in an easy, rocking gait.

The Racking Horse had long been known in the showring and had competed with other show horses but without the prestige or protection of an official registry. In the late 1960s, Joe D. Bright, a native of Alabama, had visions of establishing a registry for the Racking Horse. This lead to the development in 1971 of the Racking Horse Breeders Association of America, recognized by the U.S. Department of Agriculture as representing an established breed. Qualified horsemen of experience were licensed as commissioners and authorized to qualify horses for registration. Over 77,000 horses have since been registered, and the books remain open with provisions for foundation sires and dams to be named upon completion of closing of the books. To be registered, a horse must be able to perform the natural rack, the four-beat gait with no animated hock action. There is nothing artificial about the Racking Horse. It requires no special training or attention for the performance of his gaits. In the showring, horses are shown with English tack and exhibitors dressed in English attire.

A long history of post performance and confidence by breeders for a bright future led to the designation as "The Horse of Yesterday, Today, and Tomorrow." Alabama shared this enthusiastic endorsement when in 1975 the Racking Horse was named the official state horse by proclamation by the legislature.

Characteristics

The essential characteristics stressed by the association are gentleness, intelligence, and affection for man. Conformation standards, including elongated hooves, are quite like the American Saddlebred. However, the most outstanding characteristic is the inherited ability to instinctively perform the racking gaits without artificial methods of inducement.

The Racking Horse is small to medium size, averaging 15 hands in height, and about 1,000 pounds in weight.

Colors are black, white, gray, chestnut, bay, brown, sorrel, roan, and yellow.

Uses

The Racking Horse is basically a show horse that can compete in the ring by performing the pleasure walk, slow gait, and rack. In addition, the Racking Horse is touted as an outstanding pleasure horse.

SHETLAND PONY

Perhaps the oldest breed of horse in Britain is the Shetland Pony. Named after the islands where it survived as a distinct breed, the hardy characteristics of the shaggy little Shetland were probably conditioned by its harsh environment. The body of the British Shetland is full and furry, while the American Shetland is bred to be larger and sleeker, with conformation more like a Hackney Pony. *Breeders Gazette Magazine* has for the past several years determined that the Shetland is among the most popular 21 breeds of horse and pony.

History

The islands whence the breed draws its name are some 200 miles north of Scotland. Legend has it that sometime in the sixteenth century, ships of the Spanish Armada were shipwrecked on the Shetland Isles, having had on board some fine horses belonging to an admiral famed for his stable of Arabs. This cross, it is said, on native horses imparted much of the beauty and fleetness to the Shetland. The rough and rocky terrain was unproductive of anything but heather and salt grass. The horses existed on this slim diet, under unfavorable weather conditions, and those that survived at all were stunted in size. From this "survival of the fittest" came a breed renowned for its long life, sound feet and legs, good eyes, and endurance. Many of the young ponies were treated as dogs and given the run of cottages with children and other animal, which is said to have resulted in the Shetland's good temper and kindly disposition.

The Shetland Ponies have been natives to the isles for more than a thousand years. Shetlands have been there for as long as there has been any knowledge of the country. Although ancestors are unknown, it is believed that the original stock can be traced to the small pony stock also found in the adjacent countries of Iceland, Scandanavia, Ireland, and Wales.

Importations to the United States from the Shetland Isles began in the late 1800s where ponies were used to work in coal mines. In 1888, an association of 20 persons met in Chicago to form the American Shetland Pony Club. Today more than 9,000 persons hold membership in the club, with extensive records on more than 139,000 ponies.

Characteristics   Technically, a pony is a horse that is under 14.2 hands at the withers. The official maximum height for a registered Shetland is 46 inches (11.2 hands) in the United States, 42 inches (10.2 hands) in England, and 44 inches (11 hands) in Canada.

There are two kinds of Shetlands. One is a small copy of the draft horse (Fig. 2-71), which is referred to as the "Island" type. The other, the "American" type (Fig. 2-72), is more delicate, refined, with a higher head and slimmer lines.

Shetland Ponies are characterized by small size, hardiness, and good disposition. They are "as sure-footed as mules, as patient as donkeys." They are accustomed to doing without, for grazing is sparse in their native land.

The Shetland of the draft type gives a maximum of power in the smallest package. Shetlands have long been employed for draft purposes in coal mines, where they are able to draw half a ton of coal and cover up to 30 miles per day. English records indicate that Shetlands were used for packing peat, their customary load being 120 to 140 pounds, a remarkable feat considering the average height of these equines. Working under adverse weather conditions and insufficient forage, the Shetland is without equal.

Colors are varied, with bay, brown, and dull black, the most prevalent colors. There is often a mixture of white such as paint, pinto, etc.

FIGURE 2-71. The English Shetland is the draft form of this famous pony. (Kentucky Horse Park, Lexington, Kentucky)

FIGURE 2-72. The American Shetland Pony has evolved through selection to a pleasure type. (Kentucky Horse Park, Lexington, Kentucky)

The spotted horses find a ready market in America, especially for children's ponies.

Uses

There are hundreds of uses for Shetlands in addition to the familiar halter classes. A most popular outlet is multiple hitches for publicity work in parades, at fairs, trail rides, and other gatherings.

Of course, the Shetland has long been known as a superb children's pony because of its diminutive size and reasonably good temperament under ideal conditions. Pony rides are popular at fairs, carnivals, and amusement parks where the children invariably flock for this popular event.

Harness racing has become very popular in recent years as a growing sport, governed by the United States Pony Trotting Association.

It is not inconceivable that Shetlands are still used for their original purpose, that of hauling coal and peat in some parts of the world.

Common Criticisms

Although Shetlands are noted for their gentle disposition they can become rather aggressive under harsh treatment by unkind individuals. Biting, kicking, or pawing may be common criticisms of "spoiled" ponies. This occurs most often with children's mounts when the child has no prior experience with ponies and mistreats an animal.

SHIRE

Numerous draft breeds exist around the world but one breed is noted for being the biggest, tallest, broadest horse in the world (Fig. 2-73). Although other draft breeds often lay claim to more size or weight, there is little dispute that the tallest draft breed in the world is the Shire. While he may resemble other horses at first glance, even the novice is soon in awe of the outstanding characteristic that sets the Shire apart from other draft breeds—size.

History

The Shire, like most other draft breeds, is a descendant of the medieval horse ridden by knights in armor. This was the ponderous Black Horse of Flanders. When lighter weapons and faster cavalry changed the course of warfare to include a lighter, swifter type of horse, the old "war horses" were relegated to farm chores. From the beginning, lost in antiquity, selections were made in various parts of the world to develop a type of horse that could cope with the peculiar terrain and needs of the farming community. The low lying areas of east-central England had need for a type of horse that could stand up well under marshy, wet fens covered with rushlike sedge grass, extremely sharp and abrasive to man and animal. Men of the Fenland wore leather britches, or leggings, but the horses had to be tough enough to get by without protection. Perhaps for this reason, the Shire was selected on the basis of its extremely large feet and coarse hair covering from the

FIGURE 2-73. The Shire is characterized by its great size and heavily feathered legs. (Photo by the author)

knees downward. The shaggy, coarse hair, appearing much like bell-bottom trousers, protects the knees, back of the legs, and fetlocks from being cut by the sharp blades of sedge grass. Originally called the Great Horse, War Horse, Old English Black Horse, or Cart Horse, this breed developed in the counties (shires) of Lincolnshire and Cambridgeshire. Since there was some dispute as to just which shire developed the horse, including Kentshire, Derbyshire, Huntingdonshire and Leicestershire, it seemed proper to merely refer to the horse as "Shire."

The Shire horse can trace its present history back to the year 1066 when England was conquered by a Norman, William the Conquerer. The English were impressed by such a large man, fully clothed in heavy armor, riding a horse that carried not only this load but an additional 200 pounds of armor to protect the horse. The English quickly recognized the quality of a huge, stout animal and adapted the "Great Horse" as they called him, to pulling fully loaded carts. After sending to Belgium for more importations of the Great Horse, they crossed these stallions with native mares to produce the Old English Black Horse. The result was an even larger animal than the War Horse. During the reign of King Henry VIII of England, a decree was issued that all horses less than 15 hands high should be destroyed due to a severe shortage of pasture land. The King wanted to develop only large scale brawny horses and out of this decree came the foundation stock for the Shire breed. The breed was further developed by Robert Bakewell (1726–1795), known as the father of animal breeding, who sent to Holland for several mares which were mated to native stallions of the Shire breed. During this era, the breed became well established and is quite well known to the present day for its uniformity and ability to stamp its characteristics on its offspring when crossed with grade horses. The Shire breed is still used in many places in the world today to cross with native draft type horses resulting in size and bone improvement.

The first importations of Shire horses were to Canada about 1836. The first importation to the United States was reported to be a stallion, John Bull, about 1844. During the next 50 years, a steady stream of Shire importations came into the United States to "grade up" the smaller American horses. Although a lesser known breed in the United States, the Shire is still found in the cornbelt of the Midwest and on large ranches of the far West, where they are used for logging, farming, and wagon hitches.

Characteristics

The average Shire is awesome in size, invariably a full ton or more in weight. The typical Shire is 2300 pounds or more in average working condition. His size, bone, and brawn are clearly evident at first glance.

As the tallest of the draft breeds, the Shire ranges from 16 to 17.2 hands high.

One of the chief characteristics in a visual appraisal of the Shire is the heavy amount of feathering on the legs. Although the Clydesdale has heavy hair around the feet and legs, it is nothing compared to the extremely thick, coarse hair that grows not only around the lower part of the leg but as high as the knees as well. Long locks of hair grow from the front as well as the back of the legs. These shaggy tufts are in abundance and protect the feet and legs of this ponderous horse from harm. The Clydesdale also has feathering but the hair is very fine and covers only the backside of the legs.

The Shire is a hard worker, extremely docile, and generally very sound in body and strong of appetite. In spite of his tremendous strength, very little excites the Shire except a box full of oats. The hairy legs and heels insulate feet and legs to make this breed a good doer in cold or wet conditions.

Colors may vary from bay, brown, chestnut, or roan, but as might be expected from one of the original names, Old English Black Horse, the Shire is most often black with a white star, or white streak down the nose, as opposed to a broad blaze, and most often with white boots instead of long white stockings.

Uses

In England, the Shire was used as a cart horse and for various uses in the marshy Fenlands of central England. A general farming horse in the United States, the Shire has proven itself on Midwest farms for general agricultural purposes and for multiple horse hitches, and has been especially effective in the forestry industry for hauling tremendous logs to more acceptable terrain where other transportation can take over. His great strength, size, and heavily protected feet and legs make him ideal as a logging horse. The heaviest concentration of Shires in the United States today is to be found in the logging areas of Northwestern United States and Wisconsin.

The village of Oakham between Leicestershire and Lincolnshire has a custom that goes back hundreds of years. When a nobleman or other important person comes to town, he is expected to hang a horseshoe in the town hall as a token of his visit. The larger horseshoes are supposed to bring good luck. For this reason, shoes of the Shire almost exclusively dominate and decorate the walls of the ancient town hall.

Common Criticisms

Qualities which were noted originally as outstanding characteristics, mainly heavy bones and feathering, have lead to faulting the breed for quality and refinement. Additional criticisms in the past, have been a "shelly hoof" and a sluggish disposition.

SPANISH-BARB

The Barb is actually more of a type than a breed, its characteristics varying widely, having been developed in the Barbary states of northern Africa—Algeria, Tunisia, Morocco, Tripoli, Fez. The Barb was probably originally an offshoot from the Arabian, being somewhat larger in size and coarser in conformation but speedy and with exceptional endurance. Some historians have referred to the Barb as "The African Arab."

History

The history of the Spanish-Barb must be traced back not to America or Spain but to the scrub brush mountains and the dry plains of North Africa. Bred in North Africa, they took their name from the Barbary States of Africa, later to become known as the Barb Horse of the Moors. This breed varied between 14 and 15 hands high depending on whether they were bred in the dry mountain area or on the plains nearer the coast. The Barb, likes its Arabian cousin, usually carried only five lumbar vertebrae. This trait was very strong and has continued to be retained into modern times.

In 711 A.D. the Berbers and the Muslims joined forces to invade Spain and the 700-year occupation by the Moors brought about monumental changes in the breeding of horses. The Berbers and Moors crossed their superior Barbs on the native stock of Spain. The 700-year occupation was eventually ended when the Spanish regained possession of their country and drove the Moors back into North Africa by

1492. However, the superior horses that had been bred and selected by their foreign invaders remained in Spain to become known as the Spanish-Barb. This is the 'horse that enabled the Spaniards to conquer South America and Mexico and establish the first white settlements in North America. Because of continued exploration by the Spanish Conquistadors, the drain on Spanish horses from the motherland became unbearable and a law was eventually passed prohibiting further export of Spanish horses. However, by this time, the Caribbean Islands had become a breeding station for the Spanish and provided stock to expeditions that explored Florida, Mexico, South America, and numerous other areas of North America that stretched to the Pacific Ocean.

The Spanish-Barb was instrumental in developing breeds of horses throughout the New World. In South America, Spanish horses displaying a smooth, lateral gait resulting from centuries of selection for this characteristic, became known as Paso Fino horses. Others valued for their agility and hardiness came to be called South American Crillos.

The first Indian horses were of Spanish-Barb stock. Numerous tribes became expert breeders of horses and selected for color patterns as well as conformation and hardiness. One type of horse, the Chickasaw, was a forerunner of the Quarter Horse. The Chickasaw Indians were expert horsemen and secured their foundation stock from Spanish-Barb blood out of Spanish Florida. Crosses involving Chickasaw mares reportedly contributed to the original "Quarter Horses" so popular with early colonists. These same Quarter Horses were later used for crossing with imported Oriental/Barb English Racers in the development of the American type of Thoroughbred. Even the famous Justin Morgan could trace ancestory back to the old time Spanish-Barb.

One of the most unusual and colorful histories of the horse world involves the American Indian horse which also sprang from the Spanish-Barb, the foundation for later huge Mustang herds. Contrary to popular theory, Indians did not obtain their horses from "wild" herds. They first obtained them solely from the Spanish. The distribution of the horse among Indians was gradual but complete. Although many tribes were not wise in the ways of professional breeding, the Choctaws, Chickasaw, Nez Perce, Pawnee, Commanche, and Osage retained the beautiful color patterns found in the Spanish-Barb as well as their enduring qualities. The Chickasaw and Choctaw nations developed superb strings of horses by inbreeding methods that even today remain a mystery. However, out of the Indian influence came one of the most unusual color patterns in the horse world. Virtually all flashy, spotted breeds can be traced back in some form to the Spanish-Barb, the wild color pattern being a characteristic of the early North African strains. Paints, spotted, and roan spotted horses were favorites among many tribes. These horses were considered "good medicine" and the man who rode a "sacred horse" into battle believed he would be protected from harm. This color pattern has been preserved into the Spanish-Barb of today and is referred to as the unique Medicine Horse Strain. It is interesting to note that all color phases of Appaloosa, Paint, Palomino, Buckskin, Dun, and Grullo were originally introduced to America through the Spanish-Barb.

As the development of the West continued, Spanish-Barbs, Indian Horses, Quarter Horses, virtually every remnant of the Spanish-Barb contributed to a "melting pot" which in time almost absorbed the original Spanish-Barb into extinction. It was almost cross-bred out of existence. The breed's survival today is due to the efforts of a few individual families and ranchers.

Although no records were kept until 1972, several interested owners of Spanish-Barb horses incorporated the Spanish-Barb Breeders Association to perpetuate, selectively breed, and register the several surviving proven strains known to exist. Foundation sires represent two major strains: the Scarface horses (Fig. 2-74), an isolated strain kept intact since the mid 1800s by the Romero family, currently owned by Weldon McKinley of New Mexico; and the Rawhide horses, a strain of Spanish-Barb selectively bred by Ilo Belshy of Nebraska. In addition, several outstanding proven Spanish-Barb individuals outside these strains serve to strengthen the breeding programs. Foundation mares Coche Two and A-ka-wi and the stallion Sun perpetuate the unique African Barb coloration known as Medicine Horse.

Approximately 321 Spanish-Barb horses are registered with the association and probably no more than 150 exist in the country to date. The breed is being revitalized by a breed standard based upon documented descriptions of Spanish-Barbs in the fifteenth through the eighteenth centuries.

Characteristics

Spanish-Barbs are famed for hardiness, survivability, good temperament, and cow sense, and their feats of strength, stamina, and courage are endless.

Spanish-Barbs are smooth and deep in body, possess great balance, style, and action. The breed possesses a distinctive, triangular, well-formed head with a straight profile, being slightly convex above the nostrils.

They are short coupled, possessing only five lumbar vertebrae and stand on short, clean limbed legs. Spanish-Barbs are rather small, standing 13.3 to 14.1 hands in height. Weights range between 800 and 975 pounds. They are rather slow to mature, and seldom reach full development and growth before five years of age.

All color phases are represented in the breed although it is basically

FIGURE 2-74. Three-year-old Spanish-Barb stallion, Taw-ka Quieto, SBBA PF-34, bred and owned by Susan E. Field of Hot Springs, South Dakota, is a fine example of the Spanish-Barb breed. His sire, the SBBA foundation sire, Scarface, SBBA PF-1, is from a strain of Spanish-Barbs kept intact since about 1846 by a family who ranched in an isolated area of New Mexico. Quieto's dam is the foundation mare, A-ka-wi, SBBA PF-4, one of the finest producing mares of the breed.

The Spanish-Barb is a deep-bodied breed of rounded croup and hip, full neck, refined head, and strong, correct legs. They have great endurance and are natural cow horses. This highly intelligent breed is smooth gaited, and possesses a gentle, personable disposition. (Photo by Susan Field)

a solid-colored horse. Dun, grullo, sorrel, and roan are the most prevalant colors. There is a paint strain, most commonly represented by the "Medicine Horse" coloration or the splashy overo paint. Appaloosa markings are rare. Line backs, zebra stripes, and a cross over the withers may be found in the duns and grullos, and occasionally in other colors.

A rather peculiar characteristic of this breed that has helped to preserve the existing strains is the tendency of Spanish-Barb stallions to associate only with Spanish-Barb mares. Many instances have been observed in the past of Spanish-Barb stallions refusing to breed mares of other breeds, on pasture, or by hand.

The breed possesses a shallow mouth, making it responsive to feather-reining. Most have a lower than normal respiration rate and heartbeat as compared to other breeds, making them specialists in endurance.

Chestnuts of the Spanish-Barb are small and flush with the leg if they exist at all. Spanish-Barbs with white leg markings usually have striped hooves.

Uses

The Spanish-Barb is a truly versatile animal having the reputation of being the "original Spanish horse of the Americas." They excel as cow horses, and endurance and ranch mount as well as range or pasture kept horses. They are used as working and pleasure horses and because of their athletic, highly maneuverable trait, they are well suited for all-around use by adult or child.

STANDARD-BRED

Standardbred Horses are descendants of trotters and pacers that have been used for over 200 years in harness racing. Standardbred racers annually draw an estimated 29 million fans to the almost 5,000 pari-mutuel race and fair tracks. Latest figures available indicate almost 42,000 horses competed for over $389 million in purses with fans wagering over $2.6 billion on these magnificent sport horses.

Ancestors of the Standardbred are found alongside famous persons in American history. Paul Revere rode a Narragansett Pacer on his famous ride in 1775, George Washington used a number of trotters and pacers, and President U. S. Grant was a harness racing fan, driving his own trotters in road races in the 1870s.

Standardbred breeding farms are located in two prominent areas, around Hanover, Pennsylvania and Lexington, Kentucky. An average price of $14,000 per horse and individual sales as high as $600,000 attest to the popularity of the sport.

History

The history of the Standardbred Horse is closely entwined with that of the Thoroughbred, American Saddle Horse, Norfolk Trotter (now extinct), Hackney, Arabian, Barb, Morgan, and some natural pacers of mixed breeding. Evidence exists that men have been racing horses to harness for over 3,000 years. It is generally agreed that harness racing began in America in 1806 when records began to be kept and a gelding named Yankee trotted a mile in under 3 minutes for the first time. Early American colonists chose natural pacers and trotters for road driving and racing from these various horses, resulting in improvements in type and ability. But it was not until the great Thoroughbred

Messenger, imported in 1788, that the final destiny of the Standardbred was established. A grandson of Messenger, Rysdyk's Hambletonian, Hambletonian, or Hambletonian Ten (all three names refer to the same outstanding sire) was a stallion foaled in 1849 that had the greatest influence on the Standardbred breed. This horse carried the blood of Messenger, a Thoroughbred, and Bellfounder, a Norfolk Trotter, and during his 21 years at stud sired 1,321 foals. Every Standardbred in America today is related to Hambletonian and through him to Messenger.

Through the use of outstanding bloodlines from Hambletonian and native foundation mares that were trotters or pacers, a breed developed that could adapt to fast driving in harness. The breed was originally called the American Trotter but this designation was later dropped because both trotters and pacers were among foundation animals. The name Standardbred came about because of original requirements for registration eligibility to trot the mile at 2:30 or pace at 2:25. This requirement became standard practice in 1879 but has continually decreased in time as breeding methods and horse flesh has improved. Today, harness horses race much faster than that, around 2 minutes for the mile, and now all are born Standardbreds, the standard time no longer a factor in eligibility.

About 1850, shortly after the effect of Hambletonian began to be felt, harness horses were raced "under saddle" rather than in harness. By 1850, as roads began to develop, heavy wagons and high wheeled sulkies replaced the saddle. For 42 years, the high wheeled sulkies were used for road transportation and harness racing. Then the bicycle tire sulky (or bike) replaced the old style cart and reduced the world record by four full seconds. Just as the term "sulky" describes a person wanting to be alone, in harness racing parlance it refers to a bike made to carry one person. Just before the turn of the century, transportation depended almost totally on trotters and pacers in this country in order to conduct the necessary business of transportation. Just as harness racing was flourishing, the automobile came on the scene and replaced the horse as the chief means of transportation. This took the Standardbred off the roads and placed more emphasis on the recreation of sport fine harness racing. One of the greatest horse heroes of the twentieth century was a Standardbred named Dan Patch. He set world speed records from 1904 until 1910. He had his own railroad car to transport him from track to track, and it is reported that as many as 70,000 people would come out at one time to see him race.

In 1935, a gray trotter also made a name for the Standardbred. Greyhound, nicknamed the "Grey Ghost," burst on the scene as a virtually unbeatable horse.

Until 1940, harness racing was a daytime sport, then night racing began under the lights right after World War II, about 1946, and harness racing boomed as an unparalleled recreation.

It is interesting to note that the Standardbred breed is one of the few breeds of horses developed in this country that have been exported rather than imported. Interestingly enough, although trotters and pacers are about equally famed in this country, pacers are unknown in Europe, Scandinavia, and Russia. Harness racing survives in these countries, but only the trotter is used. Conversely Australia and New Zealand use the pacer, having very few trotters.

Characteristics

Selective breeding has produced a harness horse that resembles the Thoroughbred but is generally more compact and more ruggedly built than his galloping cousin.

Standardbreds are generally between 15 and 16 hands high and weigh between 900 and 1,100 pounds. Size, however, has relatively little bearing on the finish in the race of an outstanding individual.

Colors are variable with most falling into the bay, black, brown, chestnut, gray, and roan categories.

The most distinguishing characteristic of Standardbreds is the movement of feet and legs in a pattern known as either a trotter or a pacer. A trotter strides in such a way that the left front leg and right hind leg move together. A pacer is a horse with a lateral gait that moves both legs on one side of its body at the same time. It is generally agreed that the pacer has a very slight advantage over a trotter in terms of speed.

Trotters and pacers do not race against each other. A few rare individuals have been known to both trot and pace and, therefore, compete in trotting as well as pacing classes. Even the novice can tell the pacers from the trotters from the equipment they wear. Most pacers (Fig. 2-75) wear hopples (also called hobbles), a plastic or leather restraining hoop worn around their thighs. This is a training device to encourage the horse to maintain a pace rather than a "break" into some other form of gait, such as a gallop or trot. Trotters (Fig. 2-76), on the other hand, do not wear hopples but often wear bell and elbow boots to prevent injury by the racing stride. Racing regulations have penalties for pacers or trotters that "break" into a gallop. This may include disqualification in a race. A long training period of approximately 9 months is needed to insure that an animal will respond to racing commands of a sulky driver.

Uses

The Standardbred is strictly a harness racing horse. However, it does not compete totally at pari-mutuel tracks. The U.S. Trotting Association serves races as well as over 400 fairs at which millions of fans witness harness racing throughout the nation. The nation's two most

FIGURE 2-75. Bret Hanover, a Standardbred pacer. Note the movement of left front and left rear legs in unison, absence of footwear, use of hopples. Blinders and nose banks are often used to guard against "breaking" into a nonpacing gate due to unexpected movement of objects blown by wind, etc. (Photo by George A. Smallsreed, U.S. Trotting Association)

FIGURE 2-76. Nevele Pride, Standardbred Trotter in action. Note movement of left front and right rear legs in unison, and protective footwear. (Photo by George A. Smallsreed, U.S. Trotting Association)

prestigious Standardbred tracks for three-year-olds—the Hambletonian (Du Quoin State Fair, Illinois) for trotters and the Little Brown Jug (Delaware County Fair, Ohio) for pacers—are hosted by fairs.

SUFFOLK

The Suffolk (Fig. 2-77) has two rather unique characteristics. It is the only breed of horse ever developed exclusively for farm work (as opposed to dray work) and it is the only all-chestnut colored breed.

History

Suffolks were developed in East Anglia, the countries of Norwich and Suffolk, England. The original name "Suffolk Punch" was derived from Suffolk County and the rotund "punchy" conformation. Private records were kept for many years in the English counties but it was not until 1880 that the first volume of the Stud Book was published. Crisp's horse of Ufford, foaled in 1768, is the foundation stallion of the breed.

For generations, Suffolks were bred for their usefulness on the farm, for strength, stamina, docility, longevity, and soundness. There is great uniformity among Suffolks not only for their chestnut color but for conformation. Beginning in the late 1800s and lasting for about 50 years, Suffolk horses were imported into this country although never in very large numbers. Although it gained popularity during the 1930s, it did not have the numerical base necessary to withstand the mechanization of post World War II advances. In the early 1960s, as the draft horse market began to recover, a few widely scattered breeders continued to provide stock to a very limited number of breeders now active.

Characteristics

The Suffolk is the only breed of horse that breeds completely true to color. In over 12,000 matings investigated, not a single foal of any color but chestnut was discovered. Several shades of chestnut are recognized ranging from dark liver to light golden sorrel. White markings occur but in general are not as predominant as in other breeds. Most white is confined to a star or snip and white ankles or fetlocks.

The original name Suffolk Punch can be traced back to the characteristic conformation of punchy (pleasingly round) without flatness anywhere. This pleasing roundness remains an important feature of the breed to this date.

Height averages about 16.1 hands with some stallions going 17 hands or more.

The rotund Suffolk, bred for farm work, exhibits a willingness to work, great endurance, and a quality known as "heart."

Uses

Although the Suffolk was developed as a farm working animal, not intended for other draft purposes, it has become a popular matched team horse in many parts of the world. The chestnut color that always

FIGURE 2-77. The Suffolk or Suffolk Punch is a rotund, muscular, "punched up" breed of English origin. (Kentucky Horse Park, Lexington, Kentucky)

breeds true makes it relatively easy to select from among numerous horses to develop a pair that is matched in size, conformation, and markings on a standard chestnut color coat.

Suffolks have developed the reputation among draft animals as "the using horse," a symbolism prized and promoted by breeders of the association.

TARPAN

The Tarpan breed is one of the most unusual in the world today in that it was previously a prehistoric wild horse type that became extinct in 1876 but was later genetically recreated in 1933.

History

The prehistoric Tarpan ranged from southern France and Spain eastward to central Russia. It was domesticated in Russia by Scythian Nomads about 3,000 B.C. The original wild Tarpans were pests and hunted out in Europe and Russia during the late 1800s. The last Tarpan horse died on a Russian game preserve in 1876. In an effort to recreate the breed, the Polish government created a preserve and rounded up all animals that looked like Tarpans but their efforts came too late to save the breed from extinction.

The modern Tarpan is a genetic recreation of the original wild breed. Two German zoologists, brothers Heinz and Lutz Heck working at the Tierpark Hellabrunn (Munich Zoo) in Germany, believed that the genetic makeup of the Tarpan could be recreated by rearranging existing genes of descendants of the animal. The Heck brothers selected from pony breeds believed to have descended from the prehistoric Tarpan,

Polish Koniks, Icelandic ponies, and Swedish Gotlands. Drawing on mares from these three breeds, the brothers crossed the wild Przewalski stallion to serve as a catalyst to draw out Tarpan characteristics dormant in modern descendants. The first successful recreation of the bred-back Tarpan was born May 22, 1933 in Munich.

In 1954, a stallion descended from the newly established Tarpans was imported to the Chicago Zoo, and in 1955 two mares were imported to the same zoo. In 1956, the Catskill Game Farm in New York imported a pair of Tarpans and the Fort Worth Zoo imported a mare in 1962. All Tarpans now in the United States trace back to these six animals imported from Germany. The American Tarpan Stud Book Association was formed in 1969 to locate and register all Tarpan horses in the United States. The Stud Book was published in 1975. A registry for Half-Tarpans is also maintained. The most popular cross seems to be with Welsh-Arab mares to produce quality ponies for children. To date, the American Tarpan Stud Book Association has registered 98 animals. There are about 50 Tarpan horses in the United States and at present only 15 owners of registered Tarpans, and 3 individuals who have registered Half-Tarpans.

The largest breeder of Half-Tarpans in North America is Dr. Peter Neufeld of Manitoba, Canada. Utilizing bloodlines of the Tarpan, Welsh and Arabian, he is developing what he calls the Canadian Rustic Pony.

Characteristics

The recreated Tarpan approximates the original prehistoric horse, standing about 13 to 13.2 hands tall, a semi-erect mane, with large head and massive jaws and thick neck (Fig. 2-78). The back is short and strong, and has very low withers. Hooves are dark and believed to be the toughest found on any breed.

The Tarpan has a calm disposition but is independent and quite stubborn.

Tarpans are Mouse Dun or Grulla in color. The body is a smokey gray color, with the face and legs being darker than the body. The mane and tail are flaxen, but dark in the center. A dorsal stripe passes through the back beginning at the poll and running through the tail.

Uses

The Tarpan is an attempt by man to recreate a previously extinct type and is mostly a novelty item in zoos. However, the majority of Tarpans are in the hands of individuals and attempts are being made to domesticate them for endurance rides and similar purposes. In Europe, they are frequently crossed with larger breeds such as the Thoroughbred to produce hunters.

FIGURE 2-78. The Tarpan, represented here by the stallion Kublai Khan, is the recreated version of an extinct wild breed. (Photo by Kent Benedict)

Common Criticisms

Some Tarpans adapt to being ridden, but most do not take to domestication. If extreme patience is used, they do eventually respond to directions but if the rider resorts to force, the Tarpan simply turns into a statue and refuses to move.

TENNESSEE WALKING HORSE

The Tennessee Walking Horse is well-known in the showring. It also proves a snappy carriage horse and general purpose saddle horse.

History

Originating in the heart of Tennessee by plantation owners, the versatility of the Tennessee Walking Horse is due to its heritage, with its foundation sire, Allan F-1, a Kentucky pacer who had a Standardbred sire, Allendorf, and a Morgan dam, Maggie Marshall. These breeds are evident in the Tennessee Walking Horse, with its quick, clear gait from the Standardbred and the strength and stamina of the Morgan. Later, Thoroughbred, Quarter Horse, and American Saddle Horse blood were added to this breed. The Tennessee Walking Horse Breeders and

Exhibitors Association (TWHBEA) was founded in 1935 as the official breed registry. Current membership in TWHBEA exceeds 14,000.

Characteristics   Careful breeding of the Tennessee Walking Horse has led to the inheritance of the unique "running walk." The running walk is notable in that the hind legs overstep the front legs by a foot or more. This breed also performs at the walk and canter.

The predominant colors of the Tennessee Walking Horse are bay, black, chestnut, often with white markings. The body is muscular, the barrel full and the neck thick. The legs have low-angled pasterns and elongated hoofs.

The Tennessee Walking Horse averages 15.2 hands in height and 1,000 pounds in weight.

Uses   Primary use of the Tennessee Walking Horse was originally intended to be an easy riding mount that could carry a rider over the large plantations on which it originated, pull a plow, or take the family to church on Sunday. Modern uses include a pleasure horse, showring animal, trail rides, field trials, and even endurance rides.

FIGURE 2-79. Tennessee Walking Horses are known for their famous "running walk," hind legs overstepping front legs by a foot or more. (Kentucky Horse Park, Lexington, Kentucky)

THOROUGH-BRED   Little is known of Thoroughbred history before 1700. However, in a general way, the equine historical events before the sixteenth century were significant in molding the breed. Development of lighter horses came about at this time because of a change in medieval warfare methods. With the advent of daring invasions, light weaponry, and later gunpowder, it became necessary for cavalry units to be able to outflank an enemy instead of charging over him. Compressing the history of several centuries, speed rather than strength became the standard selection practices for the typical horse of war.

The English knights in armor were mounted on very heavy horses. When the shift in breeding practices came, England, always in the thick of medieval warfare, found her "lighter" horses too small, under 14 hands for the most part, and not capable of sustaining the rigors of continuous battle. The obvious need was for a horse type roughly as tall as the heavy breeds but lighter, with strong bone, back, and muscle. The combination of speed and stamina was found when the English turned to the "Eastern Horses" (Arabian, Turk, Barb). By the 1700s, these horses were already well known for endurance as well as speed. Eastern horses of every description were brought into England to "breed up" the native English mares.

In the early 1700s, many fine breeding studs were established but record keeping systems were such that most of the pedigrees were usually known only by memory. By the end of the century, it became obvious that great improvements were being made in the native English but there was still no organized system of registration. Although most records were private, John Cheny, in 1727, attempted to record as much of the known facts as possible in a publication that was the foundation for a later publication by James Weatherby, Jr., titled *An Introduction to a General Stud Book*. From this information, volume I of the General Stud Book appeared in 1793. Stud books of all countries, to this day, are based on this publication. The book still remains in the Weatherby family.

The General Stud Book is also the foundation for answering the question "What is a Thoroughbred?" It is a horse that can be traced back, in all branches of its family, without flaw, to the General Stud Book of England. This is because the General Stud Book is "closed," that is no blood not already in it can be admitted.

The first edition of the General Stud Book lists the names of 174 imported eastern sires and 100 mares that were registered in volume I. The most startling aspect of Thoroughbred history is that only three of these 174 sires have lived on in their tail-male line. The "tail-male" term means from sire to son, to grandson, to great-grandson, etc. It is a mystery why only three horses survive in the tail-male breeding but every Thoroughbred in the world today can be traced, in this fashion, to either the Darley Arabian, the Byerly Turk, or the Godolphin Barb (sometimes called Godolphin Arabian). Without question, these three names are among the most famous in all the world of horses.

The Byerly Turk was the earliest of the importations, arriving about 1679 and showing up in the Stud Book as late as 1698. Although this horse was called a Turk because it is believed he was captured in wars fought in Turkey, there is evidence that he was in fact an Arabian. At the time of King Williams' wars in Ireland, this horse was ridden by a Captain Byerly and became famous as his personal charging horse. Thus, the name Byerly Turk. Although he was captured from the Turks, little else is known about him. He was foaled about 1679.

The Darley Arabian has a very certain origin compared to the other two. This fine sire was purchased in Aleppo by Thomas Darley who sent the stallion to his father in England. The 15-hands-high stallion arrived in 1704, at the age of four. Although it is often speculated that records are in error, the Stud Book shows him to have sired foals as late as 1735.

The Godolphin Arabian (sometimes called the Godolphin Barb) has the most obscure history of any of the three foundation sires. He was foaled in 1724 and at maturity stood about 15.1 hands. According to one legend, he was a present to Louis XIV of France from the Emperor of Morocco. However, another tale indicates that he was rescued from pulling a water cart in Paris about 1728 by a Mr. Coke. Accordingly, Mr. Coke presented the horse to a Mr. R. Williams, keeper of the Saint James Coffee House, who in turn presented him to the Earl of Godolphin. At any rate, he stood at stud for the Earl of Godolphin and became known as either the Godolphin Arabian or Godolphin Barb.

Although it may seem confusing to indicate that Arabians are mistaken for Barbs or Turks, it was not uncommon in those days because all three of the breeds were so visually similar. Add to this confusion of using native English mares and there develops a real genetic puzzle.

The Barb derived its name from Barbary (North Africa) from where it was brought by the Moors into Spain. Barbs are generally more coarse than the elegant, fine lined Arabian but are known for speed and endurance.

The Turk is a mixture of Arab, Persian, and other Asiatic breeds, somewhat larger than Arabians and Barbs, and is more like the modern Thoroughbred in size and general appearance. Its name is derived, of course, from their origin in Turkey.

It is speculated that the Thoroughbred breed also had an assist from the Galloway, Scotch Pony, Cart horse, Draft Breeds, Highland Dun, and numerous other bloodlines but it is from the Arabian, Barb, and Turk that Thoroughbreds are most commonly traced. After the circle of breeding was closed, the descendants were mated solely on the criterion of racing for appoximately 250 years. Breeding stock is to this day primarily selected on the basis of their performance on the race course.

In modern pedigrees, male lines are traced only to three descendants of the Godolphin Arabian, Byerly Turk, and Darley Arabian. Eclipse (1764) is the great-great-grandson of the Darley Arabian, Herod (1758) is the great-great-grandson of the Byerly Turk, and Matchem (1748) is the grandson of the Godolphin Arabian. In the male line, horsemen trace pedigrees back to these three horses since no other branches of the original male lines exist.

The origin of the Thoroughbred in the United States began as early as 1625 when horses were brought into New York. By 1665, races run by horses from questionable bloodlines were held on Long Island. Racing in the traditional English style among pedigreed horses began at Annapolis, Maryland in 1745. This date approximates the beginning of Thoroughbred breeding and racing in North America.

As the United States began its westward movement across the Appalachians, the Thoroughbred moved along with it and spread into Tennessee and Kentucky where famous breeders developed and still exist to this day.

Racing continued in the United States as a fairly disorganized sport until 1894. At that time, the Jocky Club was established to provide a central ruling body for the "sportive teams." The American Stud Book was purchased in 1896 by the Jockey Club, and all registrations since that time have been handled by them. The primary purpose of the Jockey Club, in the beginning, was to standardize rules and customs so that the variation from track to track could be eliminated. Racing in America today closely follows the rules and regulations as established by the Jockey Club. The name, frequently misunderstood, was derived from a racing track authority in England of the same name. This registry association is limited to less than 100 members, making it one of the most exclusive groups of sportsmen in the United States and Canada. All Thoroughbreds from the United States and Canada are registered by the Jockey Club.

History of the Thoroughbred cannot be written without more thorough mention of this organization. Every Thoroughbred born in this country must be registered and its parentage properly verified by the Jockey Club before it can be raced. Over 38,000 foals are born each year, and the club must determine that no other duplicate name in sound as well as in spelling has been previously used. Racing colors, stable names, partnerships, and apprentice jockey contracts are also handled by the club's staff. One of the major innovations is the School for Racing Officials. Students from around the world are educated in all aspects of Thoroughbred racing from foal registration through the functions of the Steward.

Characteristics   An old saying around the race track is "They run in all shapes and sizes." Thoroughbreds (Fig. 2-80) range tremendously in size, from about 14.2 to 17 hands from 700 to 1,400 pounds in weight. However, the great majority of Thoroughbred horses range from 15.1 to 16.2 hands and from 900 to 1150 pounds in good training condition. Stallions in good breeding condition may range upwards to 1400 pounds.

Colors among Throughbreds are most commonly bay, brown, chestnut, black, and gray, although most any color, even paint, may occasionally be seen. One unusual characteristic concerning gray Thoroughbreds is of interest. A gray stallion, Alcock's Arabian, living at the time of Queen Anne of England, seems to be responsible for virtually all gray Thoroughbreds now living. Students of horse breeding should note that a gray horse must have at least one gray parent, and if all Thoroughbred grays are followed through on their pedigree, they will, with very few exceptions, be traced back to the Alcock Arabian.

One characteristic that separates the Thoroughbred from its Arabian, Turk, or Barb ancestry is that the Thoroughbred has grown in speed and can easily outrun any of their current ancestors. Furthermore,

FIGURE 2-80. Man o' War, a king among Thoroughbreds and a champion among racehorses, raced only 21 times, and he won 20. As a 3-year-old, he competed in and won 11 races. In 8 of those he set or equaled the track record time, in 5 he set new American records and in 3 he set new world records. Man o' War was the first horse in modern history to be embalmed. His likeness, by sculptor Herbert Haseltine, stands over his grave at the Kentucky Horse Park in Lexington. (Photo by Department of Public Information, Frankfort, Kentucky)

FIGURE 2-81. The Trakehner, represented by Rantzau, winner of the USDF silver medal rider award for 1976 in dressage. The rider and owner is Mrs. Margaret Gafford. (Daniel S. Gafford, Sankt Georg Farm, Petersburg, Virginia)

there. The area was known for its short, warm summers and vicious, cold winters. The Trakehner breed of horse, therefore, evolved to a strong, hardy, sturdy individual.

For over 240 years, Trakehners have been bred especially for riding purposes, never as a carriage horse or for other utility purposes. Originally a military mount, it quickly found acceptance in other areas where riding skills and competition were required. Since 1912, when the first Trakehner competed at Stockholm in international competition, they have dominated the areas of dressage, jumping, and three-day eventing in Europe. Starting in 1964 and for the following decade, the Trakehner breed won every Olympic dressage gold medal.

Olympic medals were a natural for the Trakehner because of the German cavalry training maneuvers which consisted precisely of those exercises needed in developing military horses that could compete on the battlefield or in the similar maneuvers required in dressage, jumping, and three-day eventing. The German cavalry and the Trakehner breed dominated the Olympics prior to World War II.

History has not been kind to the Trakehner breed. Because they were primarily a light cavalry horse, literally thousands of them were lost in battle; fifty percent of German military horses were killed in battle during World War I.

In the short years that intervened between world wars, the Trakehner survived and expanded only to have 90 percent of their number lost in World War II. One of the most amazing marches ever forced on man and animal was "the Trek" that involved Prussians fleeing before advancing Soviet armies over 600 miles of frozen terrain, three months of nightmarish hardships and unbelievable suffering, from east Prussia to northwest Germany. The Prussians loaded everything of value on the backs of their beloved Trakehners in an effort to save something of their heritage in the closing days of World War II. Over 1,500 Trakehners and their owners lost their lives due to starvation and enemy attacks. At one point, the survivors, making their way across the East Sea, were caught on the frozen ice in open daylight. Allied bombers spotted the retreating colony and strafed and bombed the ice. Wagons, horses, men, and equipment sank to the bottom of the sea in the savage days of World War II. A few horses and men swam the bone chilling waters, clawed their way out of danger, and stumbled exhausted into northwest Germany. Supporters of the breed claim that these hardships helped to strengthen the breed because only the strongest and fittest survived. The government of West Germany revived the breeding farms now known as "Trakehner Verband," which are distributed throughout West Germany. The breed prospered under government supervision, and in 1969 a few were allowed to enter the United States. The Trakehner Breeders Association and Registry of America, Inc. was formed the same year. In 1974, the breeders and friends of the breed voted to form a nonprofit corporation, The American Trakehner Association, Inc., to record, promote, and preserve full-blooded and part-blooded Trakehners. Registrations exceeded 8,000 in 1994.

Characteristics

The Trakehner breed is an unusually large horse, standing 16.1 hands on the average with ranges of 15 to 18 hands.

One of the most unique characteristics of the horse is its "floating" gait. The deep sloping shoulder provides an extraordinary freedom allowing the unusual extension of the trot for which the Trakehner is known. Hindquarter muscles are carried well under the horse providing excellent impulsion and forward thrust. In less technical terms, the Trakehner appears to "float" in a trot, gliding with its rider.

Trakehners are not bred to run; they're not bred to race flat out. They're bred to trot, to turn, to flex, to collect, and they do it with a style and grace that is admirable.

Another outstanding asset of the Trakehner is its mild temperament. This is especially important in performing the difficult disciplines involved in dressage. Riders of Trakehner horses praise them for not "blowing up" at difficult times.

The breed has some variation in colors being mostly chestnuts, bays, grays, and blacks. White markings on the face and lower legs are not uncommon.

Uses

The primary use of the Trakehner is in Olympic competition, for dressage, jumping, hunting, and three-day eventing. These are wonderfully disciplined horses with a long tradition of stamina, endurance, style, and grace.

Additional uses in the United States have included cross-breeding with the Thoroughbred, Arabian, or Quarter Horse, not an unusual idea since all three share common ancestors with the Trakehner. Size and bone, along with a larger hoof, are the result of crossing Trakehners with Arabians and Quarter horses. This cross produces outstanding animals with a light, well-balanced trot, natural impulsion, smooth canter, good disposition, and the ability to jump.

WELSH COB AND WELSH PONY

The Welsh Cob (Fig. 2-82), like the Welsh Pony (Fig. 2-83), originated in Wales but the Cob is heavier and stands taller than the ponies, usually between 14 and 15.1 hands.

History

Evidence of the existence of the Welsh Cob in the middle ages and even earlier can be found in old Welsh literature. The horse was a hardy breed, small but durable, capable of drawing loads of timber from the forest and doing the general work on upland farms before the introduction of the heavier animals. Even an edict by King Henry VIII that all horses under 15 hands high be destroyed failed to exterminate the hardy Welsh Cob. Herds of these horses ran wild in the rough terrain and valleys of Wales and are reported to have crossed with Hackneys and Arabians. Their background also contains the blood of the now extinct Norfolk Trotter, which was tested at a trot against time over a 20 mile hill-and-dale route.

The Welsh Cob was a favorite mode of early day transportation for doctors, tradesmen, and others eager to get from place to place in the shortest period of time. Businessmen in south Wales were known to select a Cob by trotting it all the way from Cardiff to Dowlais—a distance of 35 miles uphill all the way. The best Cobs would do this without changing pace in under three hours.

Importations of Welsh Cobs and Ponies began as early as the 1880s. The Welsh Pony and Cob Society was founded in 1901 to record this ancient breed along with the Welsh Mountain Ponies and the larger Welsh Ponies in the Welsh Stud Book, dividing them into four sections according to height and type. The Welsh Pony and Cob Society of America (the word ''Cob'' was dropped in 1946) was formed in 1907. Today two societies exist in the United States, the Welsh Cob Society

FIGURE 2-82.   Dafydd Y Brenin Cymraeg, Welsh Cob stallion. Cobs are strong with clean legs, heavy bones, have attractive ground covering gaits. They are used for driving, jumping, and riding. (Welsh Cob Society of America, Inc.)

FIGURE 2-83.   Welsh Pony, also known as Welsh Mountain Pony. When crossed with the Welsh Cob, they produce the famous trekking pony, or Welsh Pony of Cob type. (Welsh Pony Society of America)

of America (formed in 1974) and the Welsh Pony Society of America. The English Association still retains the name Welsh Pony and Cob Society. The Welsh Cob may be bred to any of the following English or American types and registered with the Welsh Cob Society of America: registered Welsh Mountain Pony, registered Welsh Riding Pony, registered Welsh Pony of Cob type, registered Welsh Cob. This interesting angle allows for breeding for local size demands.

Characteristics

All Welsh horses are tough, versatile, and long-lived trotters. The Welsh Cob is a heavier and larger version of the pony, standing between 14 and 15.1 hands.

In the United States, the terms Welsh Pony and Welsh Mountain Pony are interchangeable. They are distinguished in the British Stud Book by height alone. In the British Welsh Stud Book, ponies listed under the "A" division cannot exceed 48 inches (12 hands). In the American Welsh Stud Book, the limit is 50 inches (12.2 hands). Ponies exceeding this height but not more than 14.2 hands are listed under the "B" division of the American book.

All colors are acceptable with the exception of skewbald and piebald. Gaudy white markings are not popular.

Uses

Although a trotting horse considered primarily a harness type animal, the Welsh Cob is also a good riding horse noted for its endurance and soundness. The Welsh Cob has made an outstanding record in Britain in "four-in-hand" harness competition, singles, pairs, and tandems in driving events. The Welsh Cob Society was formed in 1974. It is often crossed with Thoroughbreds to produce hunters, jumpers, and three-day event horses.

The Welsh Pony in America is the more popular of the Welsh strains, having registered animals in all 50 states and Canada. It is a most popular "child's pony" that is finding acceptance in 4-H, vocational-agricultural projects, and as a family horse. Uses include pleasure, harness racing, driving, and jumping.

WHITE HORSE AND CREME HORSE

For centuries man has been aware of the occurrence of white or creme colored foals often resulting from the mating of darker colored sire and dam. As the study of genetics developed and the correlation of breeding results in other species was compared, these equines were given the erroneous classification of albino. The true albino, however, has no pigment; it has white hair, pink skin, and pink eyes that appear red in artificial light. True albinos in this sense, so far as known literature dictates, are not found, the condition probably accompanied by a lethal gene. What man has in the past classified as an albino horse has white hair and pink skin, but the eyes have been dark or some shade of blue. For these reasons, the AAA (formerly the American Albino Association), strictly a color registry, now distinguishes its registrants as White or Creme horses.

History

From 1918 to 1936, twin brothers Caleb and Hudson Thompson of West Point, Nebraska produced many snow-white, pink-skinned foals using a circus stallion, Old King, as the foundation sire. All their horses were direct descendants of this prolific stallion. In 1936, Caleb and Ruth Thompson organized the American Albino Horse Club, Inc. on their White Horse Ranch and opened their registry to allow addition of all snow-white, pink-skinned horses, regardless of breed or type. Although registrations swelled to 3,000 animals in the years to follow, it was the Thompson foundation stock and the colorful annual horse shows at the White Horse Ranch, often drawing 10,000 spectators, that propelled the Great Whites into national celebrity status even attracting a feature story by *Life Magazine* in 1945. Warner Brothers filmed *Ranch in White* in 1945 and *Ride a White Horse* in 1951 also featuring these horses.

With the death of Caleb Thompson in 1963, the White Horse Ranch was leased out and its 150-head foundation herd was sold at public auction. Some of the herd was sold without pedigrees because identification was difficult. Mrs. Ruth Thompson, however, moved the rec-

FIGURE 2-84. R. R. Snow King T-1073, National Grand Champion American White Horse stallion at 1971 show, White Horse Ranch, Nebraska. The owner is Mrs. John Simmering Jr., Washington, Iowa. (AAA, Inc.)

ords to Oregon, set up a new organization, American Albino Association, Inc. and continued with the family tradition of recording Whites. Further changes came about in recording procedures because of genetic findings that many horses previously referred to as White were in reality some variation of creme in color, a recessive trait, the pure white being a dominant trait. The association, in 1963, incorporated these findings into the registry by promoting only the dominant white characteristic but making provision for creme color in an auxiliary known as the National Recording Club. Because of continued interest in the creme color, the board of directors voted in 1970 to give them a distinct registry and name of their own. Since 1970 the American Albino Association, Inc. (AAA) has color registered (neither parent need be registered) the American White Horse and the American Creme Horse under the AAA. The designation "Albino" was officially dropped in 1980, changing the parent association to twin registries, White Horse Registry and Creme Horse Registry, and adopting the motto "Action Always Achieves." AAA was thus phased out and the Whites and Cremes are kept as separate color breeds. The association currently has a membership of approximately 110 with registrations since 1936 totaling about 4,000. Headquarters for the association is located in Crabtree, Oregon.

Characteristics
The American White Horse has white hair and pink skin and eyes of any color, although dark is most desired. All breeds are represented by this color registry including Quarter, American Saddlebred, Belgian, Arabian, Morgan, Pony, etc.

Size varies with the breed although the standard for stock and saddle types calls for 15.1 hands and about 1,100 pounds.

The American White Pony has the same color characteristics as the larger Whites but is of miniature and refined characteristics from 36 to 58 inches in height—preferably 52 inches or less.

The American Creme is fast becoming popular. Although they are often mistaken for the pure Whites, the difference is obvious when they are shown side by side. Cremes may be of any breed: Arabs, Morgans, Quarter, Thoroughbreds, etc. Size and scale will vary according to the breed standards from which they come.

Four color classifications have been assigned for acceptance in the Creme Horse Registry.

A. Body ivory white, mane white (lighter than body), eyes blue, skin pink.
B. Body creme, mane darker than body, cinnamon buff to ridgeway, eyes dark.

C. Body and mane of the same color, pale creme, eyes blue, skin pink.

D. Body and mane of same color, sooty creme, eyes blue, skin pink.

Combinations of the above classifications are also acceptable. Dark eyes are generally preferred by breeders.

Uses

Without exception, the most outstanding use of these horses is as a show animal (Fig. 2-85). The famous foundation sire of White Horse Ranch stock, Old King, was a circus horse; the Emperor of Japan, known once as the Son of Heaven, rode astride Silvertip, an American White originating in California; and the Texas White Horse Troupe, owned by JoAnn and Don Anderson, tours the United States as an attraction at fairs, horse shows, and Shrine circuses. Roman riding, chariot races, trick horses, and parades are just a few of the uses for this specialized, eye catching animal.

Other uses include everything from stock work to pleasure rides since every breed and type may be represented.

FIGURE 2-85. American White Horses excel in the circus and show ring because of their uniform eye appeal. (AAA, Inc.)

Common Criticisms

Light colored horses, especially with pink skin, are sensitive to prolonged high intensity exposure to rays from the sun and tend to sunburn. Horses with the lighter colored eyes especially may develop problems such as watering or irritation. However, these conditions vary greatly from horse to horse and some actually stand heat and light much better than darker breeds because of reflection of the sunlight.

3
Reproduction in Horses

The horse is by nature a nomadic, free-spirited, far-ranging animal. In the wild, it was accustomed to having the choicest environment, including freedom. Perhaps this atmosphere creates the conditions necessary for high reproduction rates, for in the wild reproduction approaches 90% or more. Under the conditions imposed upon it by man, however, the reproduction rate usually falls far short of this mark, 50% not being unusual. Such a condition is common with many zoo animals captured from the wild. Their physiological system and psychological system simply cannot adapt to lack of exercise, change in nutrition, restricted living quarters, etc. For these reasons, it is important to understand the horse's physiology, nutritional requirements, psychology, and other factors that may contribute to an overall breeding program of excellence.

The first place to start would be the reproductive systems of the male and the female. In order to know what can go wrong and how one science may influence another, it is important to have a basic understanding of the mechanics of reproduction in both sexes.

MALE REPRO-DUCTIVE TRACT

The male reproductive tract is illustrated in Fig. 3-1. Sperm is produced by the testicles and stored in the epididymis, but the bulk of seminal fluid is added to the sperm by the secondary sex glands. For all practical purposes, the function of the male can be simplified by thinking of sperm production as an additive to fluids released through the act of copulation (breeding). The fluids act as a carrier for the se-

217

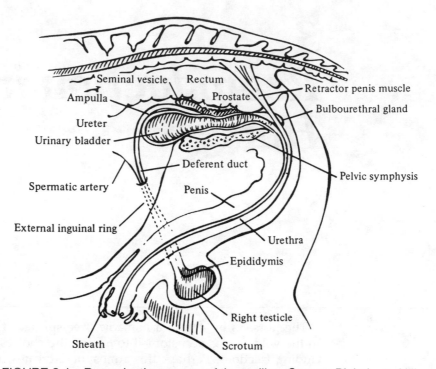

FIGURE 3-1. Reproductive organs of the stallion. Source: Blakely and King, *Brass Tacks of Animal Health* (Doane Argicultural Publication, St. Louis, MO, 1978). Drawing by P. G. Garret, DVM.

men which contributes the male half of inheritance. When problems occur with the male, it is advisable to check, through semen analysis, the live sperm count as well as the volume of fluid produced. A veterinarian can determine quickly if a stallion is functioning properly from a physiological standpoint. A layman's knowledge of the reproductive tract is essential for simple observations to detect any problem that could arise during abnormal behavior at breeding time.

The mechanics of sexual excitation in the stallion are rather simple once the anatomy is understood. Sight and smell play a part in the stimulation of the male. A mare that is in estrus (heat) triggers a reaction in the stallion. Adrenaline is produced when nerves are stimulated by the senses; the heart begins to beat faster, pumping blood into tiny caverns in the penis. This stimulates protrusion through the sheath. After mating with the mare, the retractor penis muscle is responsible for returning the organ to its resting position. Simple knowledge of this process can reward the layman with detection of problems such as an infected sheath, a weak retractor muscle, or a host of other problems that may be associated with temporary inability or unwillingness on the part of the stallion to serve a mare.

FEMALE RE-PRODUCTIVE SYSTEM

The female reproductive system is illustrated in Fig. 3-2. The ovaries normally shed one ovum (egg) at a time which is fertilized by one sperm from the male, creating a fertilized egg which attaches itself to the wall of the uterus and develops into the offspring. There have been numerous instances in which multiple ovulation has occurred. About 18% of cycles produce multiple ovulations. Occasionally, twins are born to mares but because of a peculiar physiology in horses, it is extremely rare for twins to be carried to parturition. Normally, twins are aborted and thus are a very rare occurrence in horse science.

The placenta (sac) surrounds the developing embryo (foal) in a protective amnionic fluid. The placenta is attached to the uterus by small cotyledons over the entire surface of the uterus. Growth and development of the foal to parturition (foaling) is carried out in the body of the

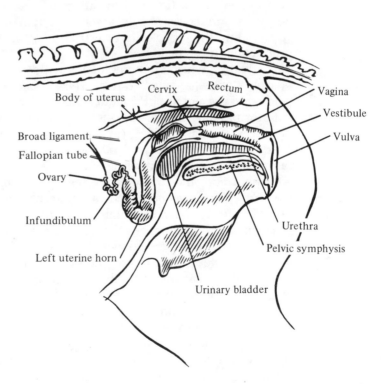

FIGURE 3-2. Reproductive organs of the mare. Source: Blakely and King, *Brass Tacks of Animal Health* (Doane Agricultural Publication, St. Louis, MO, 1978). Drawing by P. G. Garret, DVM.

uterus. The cotyledons connect the blood system of the mare by attachment of the uterus to the placenta (sac, afterbirth) connecting the mare's blood system with the blood system of the developing foal. The blood system of the mare traverses the placental membrane which terminates by funneling nutrients through the umbilical cord of the embryo (foal). At birth, the placental membrane breaks, releasing the amnionic fluid to lubricate the vaginal canal allowing for birth with as few difficulties as possible. The umbilical cord will often be crushed and will separate from the placenta without assistance. After foaling, the afterbirth must be shed if reproduction cycles are to be maintained in healthy condition. Under nature's system, the cotyledons gradually release their tension and "unsnap" allowing the afterbirth to be expelled. If this does not occur, a veterinarian is often needed to make sure the mare has "cleaned out."

Endocrine System

The desire to breed in both the male and female is under the influence of the endocrine system. Although this system is not as well understood in the horse as in other species, a general discussion on hormonal influences should assist the layman in understanding and appreciating the complexity of estrus (heat) in the female, and sperm production in the male.

The *ovaries*, which are homologous with the male testes, contain numerous "potential ova," called *primary follicles*, which are generally held to be present at birth. Under the influence of a hormone from the anterior pituitary gland, FSH (follicle stimulating hormone), the ovary produces a small "blister" (follicle, egg, ovum) on the surface of the ovary. The pituitary also produces LH (luteinizing hormone) which causes a rupture of this follicle and a release of an ovum. Immediately after ovulation, the cavity left by the vacated egg produces a scar-like structure, the *corpus luteum*. If the mare conceives, the corpus luteum retains its size under the influence of the anterior pituitary hormone *prolactin* and itself produces the hormone *progesterone*, which is responsible for maintaining pregnancy and suppressing further estrus (heat). If the mare does not conceive, the corpus luteum generally regresses to be replaced by another follicle which grows and produces ever increasing amounts of the hormone *estrogen* (actually estrogenic substances, including progestins), which is responsible for bringing the mare back into heat in about 21 days.

For all practical purposes, the male system can be condensed for the layman to represent a system under the influence of one major hormone, *testosterone*, produced by the testes. This male hormone is produced at a more constant level, as compared to the variable female estrogenic substances, producing a readiness to breed at every opportunity. Testosterone produces excitement in the male, estrogen produces excitement in the female. Upon copulation (breeding), the male ejaculates sperm into the female reproductive tract uniting with the egg to create the union of two individuals through an embryo.

Estrous Cycle

A filly normally will reach puberty (age of sexual maturity) at 12 to 15 months of age and will begin to exhibit estrus (heat) signs at that time. Even though the estrous cycle has begun, she should not be bred before the age of two years and some horsemen prefer waiting until after three years. A filly bred at the earlier age usually has a poor conception rate the following year. When bred at three years of age and properly cared for, a mare can be expected to produce 10 to 12 foals during her lifetime. It is not unusual for a mare to produce foals at twenty years of age or older.

The mature filly or mare normally has an estrous cycle of 21 days. However, the cycle may vary from 10 to 37 days, with mares remaining in estrus (heat) 4 to 6 days on the average, although this too will vary from as little as 1 day to as much as continuous heat in the case of maiden horses. However, under "normal" circumstances, a mare should be expected to exhibit signs of heat at 21-day intervals, remaining receptive to breeding for 4 to 6 days. If conception does not occur, the cycle is repeated until she "settles" (conceives).

Teasing

Detecting estrus in a mare or filly is not as easy as with other farm animals. Some clues of impending cycles are nervousness, nickering, walking up and down a fence line or stall, frequent urination, and swelling of external genitalia.

These symptoms may be obvious and pronounced in some cases but in others, there may be little hint of a desire for mating. Some mares do not exhibit any of these clues. Therefore, in order to obtain maximum conception at the time of breeding, many horse managers use the process of teasing to detect mares that are in estrus. Many horse breeding establishments use a teasing board (strong wall) and allow a stallion to be confined on one side of the board while a mare is held on the other side (Fig. 3-3). This has a tendency to excite both male and female if the female is exhibiting heat. Mares that are approaching or experiencing estrus will nicker, urinate, or show signs of nervousness that can be spotted by an experienced handler.

Some establishments use Shetland Pony stallions as teasers to prevent accidental mating. Although the national average is only 50% conception, using teasing methods and good management practices, it is possible to get 90% or higher foal crop.

BREEDING

The horse's reproduction rate under wild conditions approaches 90% efficiency or more but under the unnatural conditions imposed on

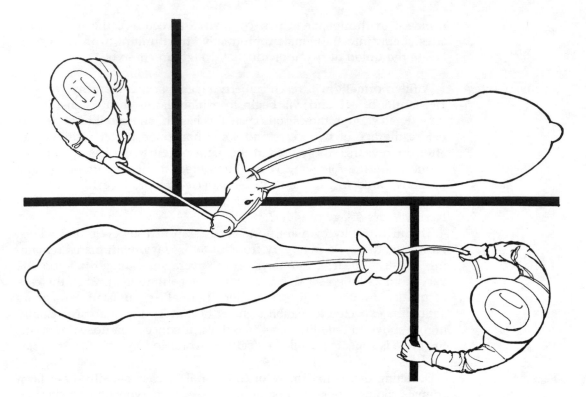

FIGURE 3-3. Teasing board such as this one allows a mare to be checked by the stallion without danger of injury to mare, stallion, or handlers.

it by man, the rate usually falls far short of this mark. One theory is that the reduced conception rate is the result of higher concentrations of animals for longer time periods. In the wild, horses had hundreds, sometimes, thousands of acres per animal on which to roam. Under domestication, this concentration has been reduced to, in many cases, several horses per acre. This concentrated system may also have concentrated organisms that affect conception in mares through improper sanitation. To reduce the possibility of microscopic organism contamination strict measures must be observed. The better establishments wash the stallion's and the mare's genitals with warm water and soap. A tail bandage of flannel or gauze is applied to the mare to prevent tail hairs from interfering with mating or introducing an organism into the reproductive tract. It is also not uncommon for the mare to be restrained by a twitch and hobbles to prevent a kicking injury to the stallion. Under wild conditions, there is a great deal of kicking and biting as a natural part of the "courting rites" but these precautionary measures are taken by man because of the obvious danger to an expensive animal. Precautionary measures such as twitch and hobbles are needed only about 10% of the time but it is considered good insurance.

Time to Breed

The shedding of the egg from the ovary of the female (ovulation) occurs during the latter stages of estrus. The egg is viable, on the average, for six hours. Since the sperm of the stallion remains viable for 24 to 96 hours, it is recommended that mares be bred every other day beginning with the third day of estrus. It is generally thought that the sperm must be in the reproductive tract prior to ovulation for conception to occur.

Gestation (Pregnancy)

The duration of pregnancy (gestation) is 336 days for the mare, with ranges of 315 to 350 days. Individual mares have a tendency to consistently foal at the same length of gestation, for example 315 days for mare A, 325 for mare B, 350 for mare C. Once the pattern is determined, rather accurate predictions can be made by experienced handlers.

Foaling

The time of approaching birth is especially important in the horse. Other domestic animals normally require little if any assistance during birth. In the case of the horse, however, although assistance is not often needed, when it is necessary, it must be given promptly. For some strange reason, foaling will invariably occur during the dark hours. Proper care, sanitation, and observation are necessary if high foaling rates are to be achieved.

One of the first signs of approaching parturition (birth) is the "making of a bag," an enlargement of the mammary glands. Close observation of the end of the teats will also disclose a waxy substance within 12 to 24 hours of birth. This "waxing" softens and falls away just prior to birth; sometimes milk will even stream from the teats. These signs occur two to three days or less prior to foaling.

Other signs of approaching parturition include relaxation of the ligaments in the hind quarters and a swelling of the muscles around the vulva. The muscles and ligaments begin their process of relaxation in order to allow for natural passage of the foal at birth. Mares appear "loose about the hips," a sign of approaching parturition to the trained observer.

The mare may also exhibit unusual traits, uncommon to her normal behavior patterns. She may leave the herd to be alone, show flares of temper, pin her ears back and kick when approached by other animals. The tail may be carried slightly away from the body, she may bite at her sides indicating some pain, urinate frequently, and alternate in lying down and standing up. She may also break out in a sweat from the induced labor.

Signs of more immediate urgency are when the placenta (waterbag, sac, afterbirth) breaks, allowing two to five gallons of fluid to lubricate the birth canal. If the foal is in the right position (Fig. 3-4), involuntary muscles contract and birth can occur with surprising ease. In most cases, delivery takes less than 30 minutes. If the foal is not delivered within 20 minutes after the breaking of the waterbag, the mare probably needs help and a veterinarian is highly recommended.

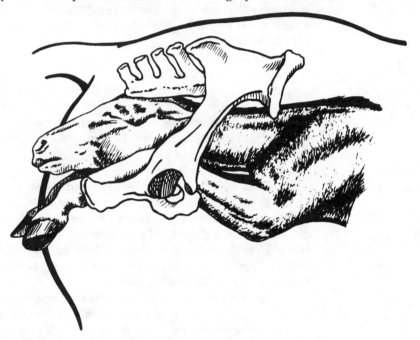

FIGURE 3-4. Normal presentation of a foal. From Blakely and Bade, *The Science of Animal Husbandry*, Reston Publishing Co., 1979. Drawing by Tom Stallman.

Care at Parturition

Only a few items are essential to have on hand at birth—a clean, well-bedded box stall; a dependable source of light; clean, hot water and soap (Ivory is suggested); tail bandages; approved disinfectant; a navel dressing such as Iodine or Merthiolate; an enema bag with a mild laxative such as milk of magnesia because of the peculiar digestive disorders that occur in horses.

When all doubt has passed that the mare is about to foal, the attendant applies a flannel or gauze tail bandage and hopes for the best. No assistance should be given until it is obviously needed. Often assistance can be simply a soft, thick rope tied around the foal's forefeet and used to assist the mare with gentle pulls that correspond with labor contractions. If both feet and the muzzle of the foal can be seen, then the foal is coming in the correct position and birth will generally be within 10 minutes to an hour without problem.

A difficult birth can bring about many problems that only a veterinarian is capable of handling. If within 15 minutes after the placental membrane ruptures, the muzzle or one or more legs of the foal cannot be seen, the attendant, preferably a veterinarian, may make an examination for complications. The attendant must wash hands and the vulva with soap, water, and antiseptic solution before examination. Some common difficulties are illustrated by Fig. 3-5 (head turned to one side), Fig. 3-6 (the dorso-transverse position), and Fig. 3-7 (breech position). The foal must be rotated to the normal position (Fig. 3-4) or suffocation can result. The breech position is the most dangerous malfunction because the time for birth must be extremely short since passage through the birth canal cuts off the flow of oxygen by crushing of the umbilical cord, resulting in separation of the foal from the placenta. This separation terminates the exchange of oxygen between the mare and foal. The foal can exist only about three minutes past this point without the danger of suffocation. Suffocation may also occur in other positions if delivery of the head is delayed.

Assuming a normal delivery, the foal should be checked for any membranes that could cover the mouth or nose. Membranes or fluids should be cleared from the mouth and nostrils.

Most foals will stand and nurse within 20 minutes but it may take two to three hours for the young foal to gain the necessary strength. If it does not nurse within three hours, the handler should assist it in nursing so that colostrum milk (the first-produced milk), which contains the necessary antibodies, and substances to provide added energy, can get the foal off to a fast start. Colostrum is extremely important with horses because of the many diseases and unsanitary conditions imposed upon the horse by modern confinement. If the foal does not receive ½ to 1 qt. of colostrum the first day of life, it has virtually no chance of survival. The antibodies in colostrum are absorbed during the first 15 to 24 hours of life and protect the new foal for 6 to 12 weeks. The horse is peculiar in this respect because it receives almost no protection from the blood of the mare, relying mostly on immunity that results from consumption of colostrum. As an additional safeguard, many veterinarians and horse owners recommend a tetanus antitoxin and a penicillin-streptomycin shot to the foal.

An enema should be given to the young foal shortly after birth, because of the development of *meconium,* a waste product developed in the foal due to swallowing of amnionic fluid. This is a normal fetal waste product, not particularly toxic as rumored by "old timers," but it can result in constipation, which can cause colic and which could be fatal. Therefore, the precautionary measure of giving 4½ ounces of

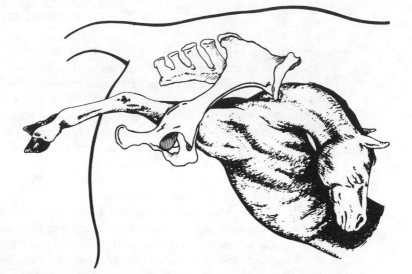

FIGURE 3-5.   Foal with its head turned to one side. From Blakely and Bade, *The Science of Animal Husbandry,* Reston Publishing Co., 1979. Drawing by Tom Stallman.

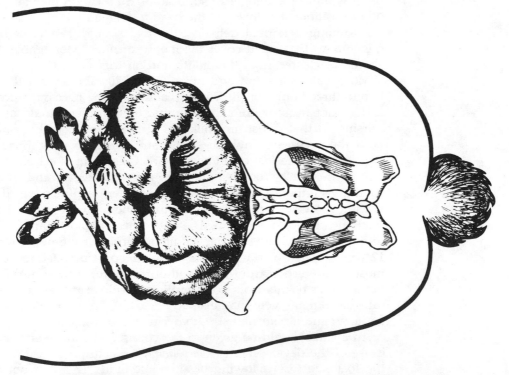

FIGURE 3-6.   Dorso-transverse position of a foal. From Blakely and Bade, *The Science of Animal Husbandry,* Reston Publishing Co., 1979. Drawing by Tom Stallman.

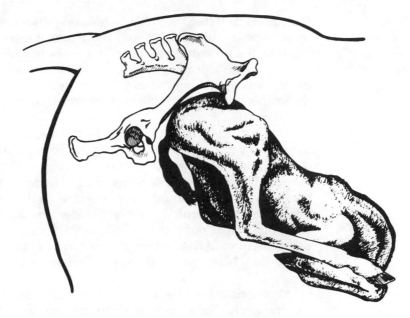

FIGURE 3-7. Breech position of a foal. From Blakely and Bade, *The Science of Animal Husbandry*, Reston Publishing Co., 1979. Drawing by Tom Stallman.

Fleet Enema™ or a warm, soapy water enema, and a dose of milk of magnesia is recommended.

The navel cord normally breaks without assistance from man. However, if it does not break on its own accord within 30 minutes after birth, it is recommended that it be cut approximately 2 inches from the abdomen and treated with 2% iodine to prevent infection through the navel. The cord should be repeatedly treated with the iodine solution until it dries up. It should not be tied off because this could result in infections.

The afterbirth (placenta, sac) should be shed within 3 hours. A retained placenta can cause founder or infection and is, therefore, important to be observed to make sure expulsion occurred. To determine if a piece of the placenta was retained, the sac should be recovered and filled with water. It is very easy to detect a missing piece in this way because there should be only one tear through which the foal was expelled. If any part of the placenta was retained, a veterinarian should be consulted for treatment recommendations.

Rebreeding

Unlike some other domestic farm animals, the horse should be rebred as quickly as possible after foaling because of the relatively high inefficiency of reproduction previously described. Usually mares exhibit a foal heat (heat occurring a few days after foaling), often referred to as nine-day heat. Although the name implies that there is little latitude, the nine-day heat actually ranges from 5 to 15 days for most horses with a duration of 1-10 days. Nearly all mares will rebreed during this period but will not "show" and may need to be exposed to the stallion or a "teaser" during that time period.

Although conception at this time only averages about 50%, especially if artificial insemination is being used, the practice is recommended by most establishments. Of course, common sense would dictate that no genital lacerations, bruises, or signs of infection be observed as a prerequisite to breeding. The reason for using nine-day heat as a rule of thumb for rebreeding is to try to gain breeding efficiency, a difficult goal even under the best circumstances. If conception does not occur at foal heat, the mare will return to estrus, usually within 21 days although some mares may take 50-60 days, and repeat the 21-day cycle until conception occurs.

Abortions

Abortions caused by virus, bacteria, and other causes are relatively common in horses as compared to other species. Most are preventable through the use of vaccines if a virus or bacteria is the cause.

Types of abortions that are not preventable through vaccines are the twisting of the naval cord of the developing fetus resulting in abortion and the previously mentioned unusual incidence of twinning, which is fatal to the developing foals in about 90% of the cases.

The two main reasons a mare usually aborts when carrying twins are (1) the uterus is inadequate in size of surface to maintain two placentas, (2) different genetic makeup of the developing fetuses create autoimmune responses.

Pregnancy Examination

Veterinarians can detect pregnancy in a mare within 18 days after conception by rectal palpation. A more recent development in pregnancy examination is through the use of ultrasonography. Breeders are generally most anxious to confirm pregnancy and determine the number of fetuses as soon as possible. As compared to 88 percent accuracy in rectal palpation, ultrasound is 94 percent accurate within 9 to 11 days of conception, and instances have been reported of a week or less by skilled sonogram interpreters.

Artificial Insemination (A.I.)

Although A.I. has not been used widely in this country for horses, it has in Japan, China, and Russia. There are several advantages to utilizing A.I. in addition to the obvious ones of extending the breeding of a superior sire to a larger number of mares than would be possible through natural means. A.I. has been used in some countries to eradicate venereal diseases; injured or crippled stallions may be utilized when other traditional methods would fail; valuable stallions can be protected from being kicked; mares with physical disabilities can still be used in a breeding program; and mares that do not show signs of heat may be bred without the possibility of a stallion being injured. Also, there is a condition known as wind sucking: the vulva of some mares is sutured to prevent contaminants from entering the reproductive tract, a procedure that prevents natural breeding without removal of the sutures. Artificial insemination allows breeding without removal of the sutures.

Collection of semen from the stallion can be by several methods, the most common of which is the use of an artificial vagina. This is basically a light-weight tube with an inner rubber liner. Water at a temperature of 42-44 degrees Celsius is used to fill the space between the liner and the tube, maintaining the necessary pressure and temperature to simulate the female reproductive tract. The rubber liner is lubricated with K-Y™ jelly at the penetration end. The opposite end contains a rubber collection bag for the semen. The collection procedure involves allowing the stallion to mount a mare, directing the penis into the artificial vagina, maintaining pressure until ejaculation is completed. The collector determines the completion of ejaculation by feeling the cessation of pulsations from the penis or by visually observing a flagging of the tail.

Once semen is collected, it can be used raw but is most commonly extended through the use of skimmed milk or cream-gelatin dilutors. Extension is desirable because semen from a superior stallion can be used in a greater number of mares than if it were used raw.

Insemination of the mare is coordinated with her observed position in the estrous cycle. When she is determined to be at the proper stage of heat, insemination is performed usually by one of two methods. The first method involves inserting a sterilized speculum into the vagina. Through this speculum is passed a sterilized catheter, which is passed through the cervix. Attached to one end of the catheter is a 50-cc sterile syringe filled with semen. This semen is deposited into the uterus. The other method involves the more simplified procedure of inserting an arm covered with a disposable arm-length glove into the vagina to guide a catheter through the cervix for deposition of semen in the uterus.

The major obstacle in the way of further use of A.I. in horse breeding is the development of a better method to store frozen semen. Current methods produce low conception rates compared to natural breeding, brought on by unknown conditions created by storage or extenders or both. Ongoing research in this area continues to solve problems of low conception rates, and improved artificial insemination techniques are beginning to show successful results.

Ova Transfer, Embryo Transplant

A technique that is gaining in popularity is the ova transfer or embryo transplant method. Through regulation of the estrous cycles by sexual hormone injections, a mare can be caused to superovulate, that is produce more than the normal number of eggs. This technique is well developed in cattle, producing an average of 16–30 ova (eggs) at one time. The ova are then fertilized by male spermatozoa, either in the mare or a test tube, and one of the resulting fertilized eggs or embryo is transferred to a recipient, which has also been manipulated by hormones to receive the fertilized egg.

The potential is obvious for the increase of foals from one outstanding mare by use of this method. For example, a prize winning Thoroughbred mare could be superovulated, fertilized by the desired Thoroughbred stallion, and the ova shipped under controlled temperature and other environmental conditions to be implanted in a grade mare, allowing the grade mare to give birth to a genetically pure Thoroughbred offspring. Using this technique, one outstanding mare could theoretically produce a dozen or more foals per year instead of one. Experiments utilizing frozen ova are also in the planning stages. Researchers anticipate one day being able to store both sperm and ova in the frozen state, to be united at the appropriate time, and surgically place the resulting embryo in a desirable recipient to give birth. If these methods are developed, it is feasible that one day foals could be produced from stored sperm and ova long after both sire and dam are dead. The major drawback to ovum transfer or embryo transplant at present is that the technique has not been well researched and it is a complex procedure involving extremely expensive surgery.

INHERIT-ANCE (GENETICS)

Although genetics is extremely important to every breeder, it is little understood because of the supposed complexity of the study. It is the intent of this chapter to explain as simply as possible a few basic principals to better understand and utilize selection principals to obtain the highest percentage of genetic advantage.

The body involves both biological and chemical activity. Combined, they are referred to as biochemical reactions. These reactions, triggered or controlled by genes, occur in the body by the thousands to control virtually every aspect of life. Genes and their subsequent influence determine conformation, color, temperament, behavior, and every other facet of an animal's health and behavior. Inheritance may be referred to as "genetic factors" that control how the animal will appear and perform. Of course, nongenetic factors can also contribute to the final outcome. Environment, training, nutrition, and diseases interact with the inherited factors to dictate what the final product will be. Since the average horseman better understands the nongenetic factors, the genetic factors are often shrouded in mystery because they are not visibly evident. Inheritance principals, however, are so important in determining size, appearance, and behavior of the individual that the basics should be revealed to every serious horse owner.

Body Cells and Sex Cells

Parents pass on to their offspring certain characteristics such as size and color, and even some behavior patterns. Perhaps it will help to explain how offspring inherit these characteristics from the parents by visualizing the horse at the cellular level. Horse flesh is made up of billions of tiny cells connected together, along with connective tissues, bones, etc. Genetics and the basis of heredity begins within each of these tiny cells. Located in or near the center of each cell is the nucleus (Fig. 3-8). Surrounding the nucleus and inside the cell wall is a substance known as cytoplasm. Most all body cells are arranged in this way.

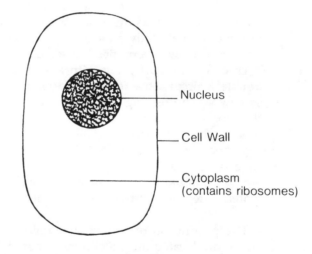

Nucleus

Cell Wall

Cytoplasm
(contains ribosomes)

FIGURE 3-8. The major parts of a cell are the nucleus and cytoplasm. Chromosomes and genes containing hereditary material are located in the nucleus. Ribosomes, located in the cytoplasm, are responsible for synthesizing proteins.

One exception is the red blood cell which usually has no nucleus by the time it reaches the bloodstream. Most all other cells contain a nucleus and cytoplasm but there is at least one notable exception, the male sperm cell. The male sperm cell has little or no cytoplasm, while the female cell (ovum or egg) contains lots of cytoplasm.

In fact, a common hen's egg is a good example of a nucleus (the yellow part) surrounded by cytoplasm (the white part). Cytoplasm varies widely from cell to cell but the nuclei of most cells are quite similar.

Chromosomes Much as the heart is considered the prime factor in controlling the reaction of the body, the nucleus is the "heart" of reaction within each cell. The nucleus is composed of long, microscopic, threadlike bodies (chromosomes) that are visible only under a microscope when specially prepared by a stain to make them visible. These chromosomes occur in pairs, 32 of them, for a total of 64 chromosomes. One notable exception is the Equus przewalskii, which contains 66 chromosomes. These chromosomes are designed in pairs so that the offspring will receive one-half of its chromosomes from its father and the other half from its mother. This produces a new individual, which contains the proper number of chromosomes to reproduce the same type of flesh. These chromosomes are not exactly alike, however, because they carry within them genes which determine numerous factors in the new individual.

In horses and all other farm animals, there occurs two "sex chromosomes" known as the X and Y. Stallions possess an X and a Y chromosome in their body cells, and mares have two X chromosomes. The stallion actually determines the sex of the offspring by passing on the Y chromosome. Offspring with a Y chromosome will be a male. If a double X occurs, the foal will be female. Since the Y chromosome is somewhat shorter (Fig. 3-9) than the X chromosome, it appears likely that foals may obtain slightly more hereditary material from their mother than their father. This may explain the observation that has long been known to ancient Arab breeders, that the female side of a tribe of horses is more genetically respected than the male side. It would seem likely that a male foal could receive slightly more genetic material from its mother than its father.

Genes The passing on of genetic material is actually a function of genes, which are located on the chromosomes. When the chromosomes split in reproduction, the new individual will receive half of its inheritance from each parent. However, the genes are not equally distributed on the chromosomes so there can be some variation in offspring due to chance. This is the reason siblings can favor but vary considerably in size, scale, conformation, etc. Genes might be thought of, in a crude example, as component parts of a zipper. Chromosomes might be likened to the zipper in the closed position. In the new individual, the zipper is opened, the chromosomes split, and one half of each zipper is recombined in the new individual. Each component part of the zipper might be further thought of as genes, layed down at random due to chance. With the genes lined up properly, the zipper is again closed

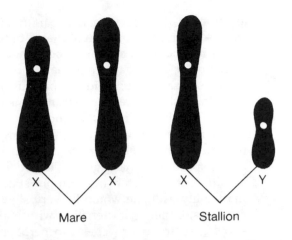

FIGURE 3-9. Sex chromosomes of the horse. Note that the X chromosomes of the mare are relatively larger, giving validity to the belief that the mare has more hereditary influence on the offspring than the stallion.

and a new set of chromosomes develops in the foal as a result of one-half of its inheritance coming from its sire and dam.

The main function of the genes is to control the synthesis of proteins in the cytoplasm of the newly created cell (growth, etc.). The gene sends out a "message" which determines the structure of a certain type of protein. These proteins are made up of "building blocks" normally referred to in technical terms as amino acids.

These amino acids are responsible for producing all of the thousands of different proteins in the body. Twenty specific amino acids are responsible for producing these reactions. Just as the 26 letters of the English alphabet can be arranged in different combinations to form thousands and thousands of words, these 20 amino acids can be similarly linked to form thousands of different proteins.

Proteins make up the tissues of virtually every part of the animal including hair, hide, skin, organs, muscles. Genes serving as a "messenger" are the supervisors that determine the type of structure that will be layed down throughout the body and should explain why genes can affect such things as conformation, color, and other biological functions.

Some Practical Applications

Robert Bakewell, considered the father of animal breeding, had a very simple philosophy of breeding the "best to the best." After selecting superior genetic stock from all over Europe, Robert Bakewell eventually closed his herd and began to develop the Shire horse by concentrating the characters and traits he desired in certain individuals. Observation plays a key part here and breeders should refrain from selecting any individual that is outstanding in some characteristic when its ancestors appear to be rather common. This would indicate a chance or haphazard combination of genes. On the other hand, individuals that are descended from outstanding ancestors and carry on their traits should be given strong consideration.

Another characteristic that should be kept in mind is the knowledge of "heritability estimates." These are known genetic estimates for the various heritable characteristics such as size, hair color, temperament, speed, etc. Many genetic textbooks provide heritability estimates of different characteristics. Simply stated, a characteristic with a low heritability estimate would be very slow to improve through breeding practices. Other characteristics, with high heritability estimates, would show dramatic improvement in perhaps the first cross. By combining outstanding individuals with high heritability estimated traits and breeding "the best to the best," the most rapid improvements might reasonably be expected.

Much confusion appears to exist between the processes of inbreeding, linebreeding, and outbreeding. Basically, inbreeding is the breeding of very closely related individuals such as a sire and daughter, dam and son. Although inbreeding is often used by trained breeders and knowledgeable geneticists, it is not generally recommended for the average breeder.

Linebreeding, on the other hand, is considered acceptable by a wide number of breeders. Yet it too is a form of inbreeding, somewhat less severe. Linebreeding is a special form of inbreeding (mating cousins for example) in which an attempt is made to maintain a close genetic relationship with an outstanding ancestor(s). This is the "concentration" of blood of superior animals which has been known to bring about some genetic defects and, therefore, most breeders prefer to use outbreeding systems.

Outbreeding, or outcrossing, is the tool used by the majority of breeders. This consists of mating individuals within the same breed that are not closely related within the last three or four generations. Although this method tends to decrease breeding purity, it has fewer genetic problems associated with it and ordinarily a bit more vigor can be expected using this process. For this reason, outcrossing is widely used throughout the world.

This oversimplified discussion of the use of genetics has been covered to illustrate some very basic principals in horse selection and breeding. For an in-depth discussion, the reader is referred to *Genetic Principles* by John F. Lasley, listed in the bibliography at the end of this chapter.

BIBLIOGRA-PHY

Blakely, J. & Bade, D. *The Science of Animal Husbandry*. Reston, VA: Reston Publishing Co., 1979.

Blakely, J. & King, D. *The Brass Tacks of Animal Health*. St. Louis, MO: Doane Agricultural Publications, 1978.

Lasley, J. F. *Genetic Principles in Horse Breeding*. Houston, TX: Cordovan Corp., 1976.

4
Nutrition

Nutrient requirements of the equine are unlike those of most other domestic animals. Since horses are used almost exclusively for sport, work, and recreation, owners should be cautioned against feeding prepared cattle feeds and other rations designed for production of meat, milk, etc. Cattle rations should be especially avoided because of the possibility of nonprotein nitrogen (NPN) content. Ruminating animals (cattle, sheep, goats, camels, etc.) can utilize some NPN, which cheapens the ration, but horses, because of their unique digestive system, have a very low tolerance for it and may develop toxic reactions. Specially prepared horse rations are available to meet every safety and dietary need, and numerous examples of rations will be given in this chapter that can be reproduced on the farm or ranch. Considerable skill and judgment are needed to feed horses for two reasons: so that their nutritional needs are met, and no digestive disturbances occur.

The horse, although a grazing animal like cattle and sheep, is not a ruminating (cud chewing) animal capable of the highest form of fiber digestion. As discussed in Chapter 1, the horse either evolved from a swamp living animal or was created to become adapted to prairie grasses. This adaptation caused certain modifications in the digestive system over thousands of years. The main modification appears to have been in the enlargement of the cecum (equivalent to the appendix in humans) where the major part of fiber digestion occurs. Note the size of the cecum in Fig. 4-1. The horse is physiologically unable to regurgitate, as cattle do, to break down fibrous roughage by additional

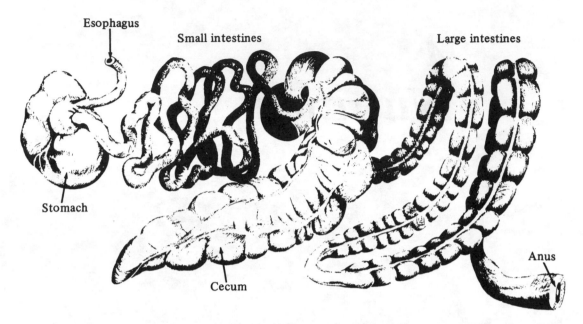

Esophagus

Small intestines

Large intestines

Stomach

Cecum

Anus

FIGURE 4-1.   The horse's digestive system. Note the size of the cecum. From Blakely and Bade, *The Science of Animal Husbandry*, Reston Publishing Co., 1979.

chewing. The large cecum, located at the end of the small intestine, houses not only a large volume of fibrous feed but many microorganisms that do the work of breaking down fiber, releasing absorptive nutrients. Because the cecum is near the end of the digestive system, it is not nearly as efficient in breaking down roughage as in the case of ruminants. This is evident in the droppings of horses, which are comparatively dryer and bulkier because of the passage of undigested roughage.

Equines might be thought of as monogastric animals similar to pigs and man, which have developed a large compartment (the cecum) that will house forages for later conversion to nutrients. Because this is a relatively inefficient system, it is necessary to provide nutrients through concentrated feeds such as grain, which provide energy and may be absorbed through the stomach, located, as in the human, in the first portion of the digestive system. If grain is not fed, horses must rely on more and more hay and grass to compensate for this lack of energy. This brings about an increase in the size of the cecum and consequently, the barrel. Some horses have a greater tendency than others to expand in this manner and are often referred to as "hayburners" or "easy keepers." One of the outstanding characteristics noted in the Arabian breed is the large barrel, which for centuries has been accepted as a sign of quality rather than a detraction from the appearance.

The horse has another peculiar characteristic due to its digestive system—the predisposition to founder and colic. This is brought about for several reasons, one of the most common of which is excessive feeding of grain or grain that is too rich (see Chapter 6 for further discussion of founder and colic). Because the horse has a high energy need but a very small stomach, it will often eat more grain than is necessary, bringing about compaction in the relatively small stomach, which leads to the digestive disturbances previously mentioned. For this reason, horse breeders have long recognized oats as a safe, superior grain source for horses because of its high grain content but moderate bulkiness. Perhaps the horse, too, recognizes this value because its desire to consume oats is exceeded only by the oldtime horseman's admiration for the safety of the grain. Most veterinarians will agree that the majority of digestive disturbances in horses is brought about by fancy, complicated horse rations and seldom, if ever, does the feeding of a simple oat ration in properly measured amounts create a problem. However, many horsemen, especially in the corn growing areas of the south, claim that ground ear corn (corn and cob meal) is equally safe and effective when substituting for hard-to-get oats.

The old song "Mares Eat Oats" hinted that there must be a reason why horses admired this grain so much and the song indicated that the owner was also pleased with this happy arrangement. There must have been a reason—there was, a lack of digestive disorders. Either oats or ground ear corn, mixed with a little common sense, is unexcelled in feeding horses without creating digestive problems. Table 4-1 gives some other safe mixtures that can be substituted for oats or ground ear corn.

DIGESTIVE PHYSIOLOGY

The digestive actions of the horse take place in the mouth, esophagus, stomach, small intestine, and large intestine.

Digestive Organs

Mouth The main functions of the *mouth* are to masticate feed preparatory to swallowing and to wet it with saliva. Saliva is important in providing lubrication of the feed and enzymes that aid digestion. Three pairs of salivary glands—*parotid, submaxillary,* and the *sublingual* gland—have experimentally been measured at as much as 12 liters per day of saliva.

Esophagus The *esophagus* of the horse, 50 to 60 inches long in the mature animal, is of such a tonus quality that it is almost impossible for a horse to vomit. In a digestive disturbance, this creates additional pressure on the digestive tract of the horse and explains why rupture

Table 4-1
Some Example Grain Mixtures for Horses

	Mixture No.[a]					
	1 %	2 %	3 %	4 %	5 %	6 %
Rolled oats	15.0	25.0	31.0	45.0	35.0	41.0
Cracked corn	15.5	20.5	29.5	25.5	25.0	35.0
Oat groats	15.0	—	—	—	—	—
Soybean meal	15.0	10.0	10.0	5.0	10.0	5.0
Linseed meal	10.0	10.0	5.0	5.0	10.0	—
Dr. skimmed milk	5.0	5.0	5.0	—	—	—
Dehy. alfalfa	5.0	10.0	10.0	10.0	5.0	—
Wheat bran	10.0	10.0	—	—	5.0	10.0
Molasses	7.0	7.0	7.0	7.0	7.0	7.0
Dical. phosphate	—	0.5	1.0	1.0	1.0	—
Gr. limestone	1.5	1.0	0.5	0.5	1.0	1.0
T.M.salt	1.0	1.0	1.0	1.0	1.0	1.0
Vitamin premix	+	+	+	+	+	+
	100.0	100.0	100.0	100.0	100.0	100.0
DE mcal/lb[b]	1.4	1.4	1.4	1.4	1.4	1.4
CP%[c]	20.2	17.8	15.9	13.2	16.1	11.9
DP%[d]	15.8	13.7	11.9	9.4	12.0	8.0
CA%	0.82	0.81	0.72	0.65	0.79	0.46
P%	0.53	0.57	0.54	0.49	0.58	0.37

Source: Blakely and Bade, *The Science of Animal Husbandry.* Reston, Va.: Reston Publishing Company, Inc, 1977. Courtesy of Dr. John P. Baker, University of Kentucky.

[a]Type of ration: (1) milk replacer; (2) creep feed; (3) postweaning; (4) grower; (5) broodmare; (6) maintenance and working.

[b]DE = digestible energy

[c]CP = crude protein

[d]DP = digestible protein

Note: All grain mixtures are to be fed with grass or grass-legume hay.

of the stomach can occur. Horses are the only domestic species which do not vomit. This should help owners understand why colic is such a serious matter.

Stomach The *stomach* of the horse makes up approximately 10% of the digestive tract. It is a relatively small organ and begins emptying soon after feeding, with food products moving into the small intestine and large intestine, having only minimal contact with gastric secretions from the stomach. This rapid passage perhaps explains why the horse appears to always be hungry and why it is recommended to feed even idle horses twice daily to prevent distention and possible rupture of the stomach or other digestive disturbances.

Small intestine Approximately 30% of the digestive tract is occupied by the *small intestine*. Pancreatic juices secreted into the small intestine supply enzymes to digest carbohydrates and protein. The small intestine is also the site for bile secretion from the liver. Horses have no gallbladder to store bile as in most other species. Thus, bile salts which emulsify fats (lipids) are secreted continuously into the small intestine. In spite of this apparent inefficiency, the horse is able to digest relatively high levels of fat in mixed feeds.

Large intestine Approximately 25 feet in length, the *large intestine* is made up of the *cecum, colon,* and *rectum.* The cecum is the primary site of microbial populations necessary for breakdown of fiber. However, the colon amounts to 40 to 50% of the storage capacity for the intestinal tract.

Sites for Digestion of Nutrients

The rate of feed passage in the horse is relatively fast, approximately 95% of undigested material passing through within 65–75 hours after feeding. The primary sites for the digestion of nutrients are as follows.

Protein The small intestine produces protein-splitting enzymes that reduce the protein faction of a feed into *amino acids* (the building blocks of protein), which are absorbed through the wall of the small intestine to be reassembled again into body proteins. Some bacterial action in the large intestine also appears to produce amino acids subsequently absorbed there.

Carbohydrates The fibrous part of a horse's carbohydrate diet (roughage) is digested primarily in the form of *volatile fatty acids* (VFA). The soluble carbohydrates are digested and absorbed in the small intestine.

Fat As previously mentioned, the horse does not have a gallbladder and, therefore, no method of storing bile salts responsible for reducing lipids (fats) to *fatty acids.* Apparently the direct continuous secretion of bile salts is an effective method for the horse since relatively high diets of 15% fat are digested by the small intestine without difficulty.

Vitamins Vitamins A, D, E, and K, the *fat soluble vitamins,* are probably absorbed in the small intestine. Carotene, a yellow plant substance, is a precursor to vitamin A and may be stored in the fat of the horse. Any animal which has yellow fat normally has this storage ability. The horse, having yellow fat, can draw on carotene supplies to provide it with vitamin A. It is interesting to note that two other members of the equine family, the donkey and zebra, do not have this ability and, therefore, have white fat.

Minerals   The small intestine has been shown to be the site of absorption of calcium, phosphorus, magnesium, and zinc. Although research has not defined absorption of other minerals, it is suspected that the large intestine probably absorbs them also.

Water   Water absorption takes place primarily in the *cecum* although the colon absorbs some water. Contrary to popular opinion, feeding a horse wet mash feeds will not produce wetter feces. The extra water is absorbed by the cecum. All material passing into the colon is of approximately the same dry matter content. Access to drinking water will affect the digestibility of most feeds, however. Some horses will not eat until they have been watered first. There is no evidence to indicate that watering horses after feeding will dilute or increase the rate of passage of the feed through the intestinal tract, reducing digestibility. The general recommendation is to water horses before feeding them since some will eat little or not at all unless they have been watered.

NUTRI-TIONAL REQUIRE-MENTS

Feed is a substance eaten and digested by the horse that provides the essential nutrients for maintenance (body repair), growth, reproduction (estrus, conception, gestation), work, and lactation (milk production). For purposes of discussion in this book, feeds can be divided into concentrates and roughages. Concentrates (grain-type products) and roughages (hay or grass-type products) make up the basic structure of a ration. The materials used to make up a ration are commonly referred to as feedstuffs. The feeding of horses is much more difficult and complicated than feeding other species because of the different use for horses: work, recreation, and the horse's peculiar digestive system which is subject to disorders. These peculiarities are taken into consideration when developing rations to meet the horse's needs.

Essential Nutrients

All classes of livestock require the following six essential nutrients:

Water   The cheapest nutrient, water, is a necessary part of adequate growth and lactation-type rations. A horse will consume five to twelve gallons of water per day depending upon the size of the animal. It can live for weeks without food but only a few days without the substance that regulates body temperature, dissolves and carries other nutrients, eliminates wastes, and constitutes up to 80% of the body. Water is necessary for the digestive processes both as a medium and a participant in body chemical reactions. Water is involved in the process of hydrolysis, the primary method of protein, fat, and carbohydrate digestion.

Circulating throughout the body, water carries dissolved nutrients to the cellular level and waste products through the excretory system. As a vital part of the blood, water has a temperature regulating function because of this circulation, just as temperatures are regulated in water-cooled engines by a circulatory system. One peculiar precautionary measure must be followed in dealing with horses. If they are extremely hot and are allowed full choice water without "cooling out," they may develop a condition known as founder or laminitis, discussed in Chapter 6.

Protein   Protein is the major component of tissues, such as muscle, and is a fundamental part of all living tissues. It contains carbon, hydrogen, oxygen, nitrogen, sulfur, and sometimes phosphorus. The protein molecule is composed of a number of smaller units linked together. These "building blocks" are called amino acids. Twenty-five different amino acids have been identified as constituents of the protein molecule, although most proteins contain from as low as 3 or 4 to as high as 14 to 15 different ones. The average protein contains 100 or more amino acid molecules chemically linked together by bonds known as peptide bonds.

Amino acids vary slightly in composition but average about 16% nitrogen, the major component of which protein is made. Because this figure is fairly constant, protein estimates are most often made by analyzing for nitrogen chemically and dividing by 16%, or the simpler alternative of multiplying by the constant 6.25. Feed samples are treated chemically to release ammonia, a form of nitrogen. Trapped ammonia is analyzed and expressed in percent. This is multiplied by 6.25. The resulting figure is called crude protein. This protein is not entirely digestible. Therefore, biological assays using live animals are conducted at research experiment stations. The feed that goes in the horse is chemically analyzed, as is the material that comes out of the horse, and the difference reflects a figure for specific feeds known as digestible protein.

Protein is extremely important with any animal and the reader might visualize its function better by thinking of the digestible protein as being composed of pieces of a picture puzzle. These pieces might be represented by different amino acids. When a horse eats a feed containing protein (of which there are many in both the concentrate and roughage form) the digestive system breaks down the pieces in the puzzle and transports them through the blood system to the cellular level where they are rearranged in their proper position to create the image, in this case, muscle and other body tissues.

Individual amino acids function as a necessary part of enzymes that aid in digestion, hormones that regulate body functions, hair and skin pigmentation, and metabolic body cell reactions, just to name a few examples.

Some plant protein sources (and therefore, amino acid) are soybean meal, cottonseed meal, linseed meal, and peanut meal (concentrates), and legume hays (roughage).

Carbohydrates The building blocks of carbohydrates are substances well known to man—sugars. Just as the sugar in a candy bar gives quick energy to young active humans, the carbohydrates in concentrates (grain) and roughages can produce the same effect in young, growing horses, or provide energy for work, lactation, etc. in older animals. Carbohydrates are the fuel used to drive the reactions necessary to maintain the fire of life.

The general grouping of carbohydrates into the sugar category is not exactly correct because this group contains other compounds such as starch, cellulose, and other, more complex substances, but for simplicity, it can be thought of simply as a source of energy.

Most of the carybohydrates in plants and feeds consist of the more complex carbohydrates, which include starch and cellulose.

Starch, which is the principle form of stored energy in grain (especially corn, wheat, and grain sorghum) is easily digested and, therefore, has a relatively high feeding value. Horsemen have long known the value of added grain to a ration.

Cellulose and related compounds, which comprise the bulk of plant cell walls and form the woody fiber parts, are less completely digested; however, the end product is the same. This yields energy to the horse but not as efficiently as grain and, therefore, a great deal of energy is lost in the work of digestion. Hay and related feeds typify cellulose-containing products. The feed tag term "crude fiber" represents these more poorly digested products.

For ease of analysis, discussion, and communication, chemists have divided the often confusing array of carbohydrates into crude fiber and NFE (nitrogen free extract). NFE, often seen on the feed tags and in horse nutrition publications, roughly indicates the more soluble products such as starch, sugar, and other complex carbohydrates.

Fats The building blocks of this nutrient are fatty acids, which are also used as a source of energy for horses. Fats are very concentrated sources of energy, having 2.25 times as much energy as carbohydrates. However, horses are rather sensitive to vegetable or animal fats and caution should be used when fats are considered to increase the energy content of a ration. The customary uses are to provide some energy, to improve flavor and texture, and reduce dust problems in a ration. Fat choices fall almost entirely in the concentrate category such as by-products of the oil seed crops.

Fat soluable vitamins, discussed later in this chapter, are also associated with this nutrient but are not a major factor in the utilization of fat in a ration.

The fat in a ration is broken down by the digestive tract to produce fatty acids which are linked together again at cellular levels to produce fat "finish" or "bloom" on horses. Although naturally occurring fatty acids may be found in common feedstuffs, without the need to add extra fat to a ration, essential fatty acids are necessary for life to the horse. Three fatty acids, linoleic, arachidonic, and linolenic are the three that are necessary for life. Normally, these are present in grains and other concentrates in sufficient quantity that the horseman need not be concerned about them one way or another.

Minerals Simply stated and easily visualized, minerals are the ashes of a substance that is burned, including feed. To analyze for minerals, feed is actually burned at an extremely high temperature until a constant weight is reached. All that is left is ash, often seen on feed tag information. The ash residue is the inorganic portion of feed, minerals. There are 15 minerals required for normal body function. Table 4-2 gives a condensed list of functions, deficiency symptoms, and sources of supply.

NUTRITIONAL DEFICIENCIES AND SIGNS

In spite of all we do in calculating rations and trying to feed the correct feedstuffs, occasionally situations develop that might appear to be a disease but often turn out to be a deficiency of one or more of the six essential nutrients. Normally, this does not occur when horses have access to pasture and are being cared for with supplemental feed. The most commonly occurring situations, their signs, and corrections follow.

Calcium and Phosphorus The functions of calcium and phosphorus are interrelated in the horse as with other species. Both are needed for proper bone development, and are especially important in horses because of the extreme pressures exerted on feet and legs through demands imposed by man. A deficiency or imbalance of either calcium or phosphorus can result in rickets in young animals, a condition of bowed legs and malformed bones. Mature animals may exhibit osteomalacia, a brittle development causing leg problems, even broken bones. This condition may be brought about not only from a deficiency of calcium or phosphorus but an improperly balanced ratio. The calcium–phosphorus ratio should be 1.1 part calcium to 1.0 part

Table 4-2
Minerals Required by Horses

Mineral	Function	Deficiency Symptom	Source
Salt (Na, Cl— sodium and chlorine)	Used in gastric jucies, maintains body water percentage	Lack of appetite, coarse coat, heat stroke, exhaustion	Salt
Calcium (Ca)	Role in blood coagulation, bone formation, and other vital functions	Fragile bones, rickets in young animals, osteomalacia in mature animals	Dicalcium phosphate; steamed bone meal
Phosphorus (P)	Formation of bones; aids in absorption of simple sugars and fatty acids	Depraved appetite, fragile bones, stiffness of joints, pica (chewing bones and wood)	Steamed bone meal; dicalcium phosphate
Potassium (K)	Muscle control and bone formation	Vague, seldom seen	Quality roughages; *potassium chloride
Magnesium (Mg)	Bone, teeth formation, and muscle coordination	Muscle tremors	*Magnesium sulfate (epsom salt)
Sulphur (S)	Synthesis of sulphur containing amino acids	Vague, seldom seen	Quality roughage; *elemental sulphur
Iodine (I)	Necessary for thyroid function	Goiter, poor growth, listlessness	*Iodized salt
Cobalt (Co)	Needed by bacteria to synthesize vitamin B_{12}	Loss of Appetite, weakness	*Cobalt sulfate
Copper (Cu)	Hair development, hemoglobin (oxygenated blood) formation	Severe diarrhea; weight loss; appetite loss; rough, coarse bleached coat; anemia	*Copper sulfate
Manganese (Mn)	Bone formation	Deformed bones	Quality roughages; trace mineral salt
Iron (Fe)	A part of hemoglobin (oxygen carrier in blood)	Anemia (paleness of blood vessels of eyelid)	Quality roughages; *iron phosphates

Zinc (Zn)	Skin and hair; a component of insulin	Rough skin	Quality roughages; *zinc sulphate
Selenium (Se)	Associated with vitamin E	Vague, seldom seen	Linseed meal, some soils have toxic levels that lead to poisoning
Molybdenum (Mo)	Stimulates fiber digestion, low level is required	Toxicity occurs more often than deficiency	Quality roughages

*Trace mineralized salt is a convenient source.

phosphorus to correct or prevent problems. The range of up to 1.4 to 1.0 is considered acceptable.

A deficiency of phosphorus can also lead to a condition known as pica, often called "cribbing" or a depraved appetite of the horse for chewing wood, bones, etc. Although most "cribbers" are simply nervous or bored horses, pica can be brought about by a deficiency of phosphorus. Cribbers of either type have been known to chew gates and fences completely through.

A ration of .6% to .7% calcium and phosphorus is recommended for a complete mixed ration. Bone meal is a source of calcium and phosphorus used in many feed mixtures, or it may be given free-choice mixed with an iodized trace mineralized salt. The salt not only controls consumption of the palatable bone meal but also provides iodine, sodium, and chlorine.

Salt   Because of the unique ability of horses to sweat, an uncommon condition among most other species, salt is extremely important to their "cooling system." Hard working horses often expel very large quantities of salt from their bodies. The white residues are readily visable on horses that have been lathered by sustained exercise. A deficiency of salt can cause heat stroke, tiredness, and physical exhaustion. If a complete ration is fed, it should contain .5% to 1% of the feed. Many owners prefer to leave a free-choice mixture of salt out for the horse and let it consume what its system craves. Table 4-3 gives an example of contents of a recommended trace mineral salt mixture.

Iodine   The horse utilizes iodine in the thyroid gland, which in turn regulates body temperature. A deficiency brings about an increase in the size of the thyroid gland, which tries to make up for a lack of production by increasing volume of the gland. This increase in gland size, about the neck, is called goiter. An unusual swelling around the throat-latch could possibly be a defective thyroid, or, a true case of goiter. If the condition is truly a deficiency of iodine, it can be corrected

Table 4-3
Trace Mineralized Salt

	Trace Mineral Content	
Mineral	T.M. Salt	Amount per lb of Grain Mixture
Iodine	0.007%	318 mcg
Iron	0.80%	36 mg
Copper	0.16%	7 mg
Zinc	1.00%	45 mg
Manganese	0.40%	18 mg

Source: Blakely and Bade, *The Science of Animal Husbandry.* (Reston, Va.: Reston Publishing Company, Inc., 1976.) Courtesy of Dr. John P. Baker, University of Kentucky.

easily by feeding iodized salt. For this reason, the precautionary measure of feeding trace mineralized salt mixtures (Table 4-3) containing iodine is quite common.

Iron and Copper   It is a well known fact that a deficiency of iron and copper can cause anemia in horses just as in humans. Owners of horses doing heavy work should be concerned about anemia, or iron poor blood, and supply the needed element in the feed or in a trace mineralized salt (Table 4-3) as a precautionary measure. Although most anemia is caused by a deficiency of iron, some types are also caused by copper or a combination of the two.

If in doubt, blood tests can be conducted by veterinarians to determine if there is a need and injections are simple and quickly effective to correct the condition.

Zinc   Although it is still open to speculation, there is some thought that zinc is needed by horses for proper skin and hair condition, and some even think zinc added to a ration has a positive influence on the well being of race horses. Precautions should be used in the indiscriminate use of zinc added to a home mixed ration. Competent nutritionists have calculated proper amounts in ready mixed feeds and the possibility of doing harm through the creation of an imbalance with other minerals is a significant factor in "tinkering" with prepared feeds. A very safe method of providing additional zinc is through a trace mineralized salt mixture as suggested in Table 4-3.

Manganese   Although manganese is required by the horse and is added to most rations, it is not well understood and deficiency signs are speculative. For safety reasons, it is generally added to rations and may also be found in prepared trace mineralized salt mixtures or the mixture given in Table 4-3.

Fat Soluble Vitamins Vitamins A, D, E, and K are referred to as the fat soluble vitamins. There should never be a problem with deficiencies of any of these if the horse has access to green pastures. However, stall-fed horses require green, leafy forages or a supplementary form of these essential vitamins. Alfalfa hay is high in fat soluble vitamin content but owners are cautioned against feeding large quantities of it because of resulting digestive problems. For this reason, a straight hay diet of alfalfa is never recommended. However, a small, supplementary amount is considered safe and extremely beneficial.

Water Soluble Vitamins Although not as necessary in the diet of the horse because bacteria synthesize these vitamins in the cecum, water soluble vitamins are essential to the horse. Most of these are grouped under the term B-complex vitamins. Deficiency symptoms are seldom ever seen but for safety's sake, the B-complex vitamins thiamine, riboflavin, pantothenic acid, and vitamin B-12 should be included in the horse's ration.

Table 4-4 gives a sample content of a vitamin premix recommended for horses. Commercially prepared premixes are available and more convenient for the average home horse feed mixer.

Table 4-4
Vitamin Premix for Horses

Vitamin	Per lb Premix		Amount per lb. Feed When Premix Added at: 5 Lb/Ton		1 Lb/Ton	
Vitamin A	1,000,000	I.U.	2,500	I.U.	500	I.U.
Vitamin D	100,000	I.U.	250	I.U.	50	I.U.
Vitamin E	5,000	I.U.	12.5	I.U.	2.5	I.U.
Thiamine	1.2	gm	3.0	mg	0.6	mg
Riboflavin	800	mg	2.0	mg	0.4	mg
Pantothenic acid	800	mg	2.0	mg	0.4	mg
Vitamin B$_{12}$	5	mg	12.5	mcg	2.5	mcg

Source: Blakely and Bade, *The Science of Animal Husbandry*. (Reston, Va.: Reston Publishing Company, Inc., 1979.) Courtesy of Dr. John P. Baker, University of Kentucky

RATIONS   The average horseman doing recreation riding will do well to forget about all the exotic sweet feeds that are on the market and stick to a relatively simple concentrate ration containing 95% oats and 5% linseed oil meal or soybean oil meal. A bright, clean, leafy grass hay is recommended for roughage. The grain portion is fed at a specified level to be explained later in this chapter. Of course, the rations given in Table 4-1 are considered a simple form of ration and not an exotic feed. An alternate ration suggestion for "picky eaters" is a grain portion of half oats and half commercially sweet feed (a mixture of molasses and grains) and free-choice bright, clean, leafy hay. This simplistic recommendation is not without foundation. There have been very few reports of digestive problems such as founder or colic with horses fed totally or largely on a simple ration such as oats and hay. Almost all digestive disorders come about when man begins to try to improve on nature by using very exotic mixtures. Unless one is thoroughly grounded in equine nutrition, these rations should be left to experts.

Every horse has to be fed as an individual because some are rapid eaters and others eat very slow. It is extremely important to keep feed boxes free of moldy feed because this can create digestive problems quickly. A horse should be allowed about 30 minutes to clean up its feed. If it does not, the feed should be removed so that it does not spoil and create problems later. Some horses are gluttons and will gulp their feed rapidly, consuming large quantities of air, and be subject to colic or "tummy ache." They can be slowed down by placing a few large smooth stones in the feed so the horse has to eat around them to consume it. Hay is, of course, made available free choice. To further guard against digestive problems, horses should be fed twice, or three times daily at the same times each day. For example, feeding times could be 6 A.M., noon, and 6 P.M. Select two or more times depending on how much work is expected of the horse. Idle horses are usually fed twice daily. Hard working plough horses may need 3 meals daily. Feeding once per day is not recommended because of the small stomach of the horse. Some horses have been known to gorge themselves rapidly when fed only once daily producing colic or rupture of the stomach.

Rations should not be changed abruptly, and a week's time should be allowed when gradually switching to a new mixture or a higher level of intake. For instance, many horses are taken directly out of a stall and ridden on trail rides of several days duration. The horse will naturally need more energy during this time but digestive disturbances can be brought on by this sudden increase in feed intake. Some advance planning of gradually increasing the horse's feed a week or so prior to the trail ride will have its system ready to metabolize the added energy without difficulty. Approximately another week should be taken after the trail ride to gradually reduce the feed level back to a maintenance level.

Table 4-1 gives the numerous mixtures proved to be safe and effective for the horse's digestive system when hand-fed at recommended levels. Tables 4-3 and 4-4 give the trace mineralized salt and vitamin premixes referred to in Table 4-1 for the horse owner who prefers to mix on the farm.

FEEDING HINTS

Whether the horse is a pony or a draft horse, its nutritional requirements are the same based on percentage of body weight. It is very important to know the weight of a horse and to feed according to this factor rather than feeding by volume or "eyeball." Some horse owners are "scoopers" and prefer to feed so many coffee cans or other such measure of feedstuffs. This need not be discouraged if it is convenient, but the proper amount should be weighed out first to determine what equivalent volume corresponds to it. Also keep in mind that when switching from one type of feed to another, the volume will vary greatly depending upon the concentration of the material. Therefore, "scoopers" should be aware of the changes in volume that occur when changing to heavier or lighter foodstuffs. It should also be mentioned that a horse that consumes an excessive amount of feed and still does not gain in condition (weight, hair coat, alertness) might be suffering from parasite infestations. This can be ruled out by having the feces examined by a veterinarian to determine if worming is necessary.

External parasites such as flies, mosquitoes, and ticks draw on the nutritional intake of the horse and must be controlled for efficient utilization of feed.

The horse's mouth should also be checked regularly because dental problems, especially in older horses, are quite common. Some horses have abnormal matching of the teeth which can cause pain and irritation to the gums and mouth. This is brought about when rough edges and sharp points develop, a common condition with horses because of the rough, abrasive materials in roughage that are commonly consumed. Veterinarians can easily correct the condition by filing down ("floating") the teeth so that they meet properly. If the condition cannot be corrected, then a choice of softer feeds is an alternate possibility.

Older horses also have a nutritional problem brought about by the natural aging process. As horses grow older, the angle of the front teeth changes (Fig. 4-2) to produce a longer and longer "V" shape where the teeth come together in front. This makes the sides of the teeth instead of the edges meet and makes it harder for the horse to bite off feed or to pick up loose feed. Older horses are fed softer rations to compensate for this problem. A simple ration consisting of

FIGURE 4-2. Natural wear of the back teeth due to aging, and a change in the angle of the front teeth, creating a longer "V," make the sides of the teeth meet instead of the edges.

90% oats, 9% bran, and 1% vitamin premix, fed with free choice, best quality grass hay is a simple recommended example.

Horses with respiratory problems have difficulty in breathing when eating dusty feeds. To minimize these problems, rations should be selected that are free of dust. If this is not practical, hay and grain can be moistened slightly with water to keep down dust and prevent materials being inhaled into the lungs while eating.

The horse that eats its bedding, or other unnatural material such as wood, may be either nervous, bored, or suffering from a nutritional disorder. With the exception of pica, a form of cribbing brought about by a phosphorus deficiency, boredom is most likely the cause of this action.

Owners should be aware of sand colic, a very common disorder caused by feeding hay on the ground. This is a digestive disturbance that can easily be prevented by providing hay in bunks or in the characteristic hay nets seen at eye level in many horse stalls (Fig. 4-3). Boredom may be combatted by using hay nets, or by providing something for the horse to play with, such as tin cans hanging from a string, a soccer ball, or some other movable, safe item. Leaving the top half of the stall door open is also effective; the horse can see out and observe activity much as a human would pass the time watching television.

The best safeguard against nutritional problems is good pasture grazing. Even this can create problems when lush spring grasses are full of moisture. Colic, diarrhea (scours), and even founder can result if the horse is suddenly turned on to these pastures without limiting grazing time. Gradual adjustment to changing conditions is the key to

FIGURE 4-3.   Hay net not only serves a useful purpose in combatting boredom, but also helps prevent sand colic.

avoiding digestive disorders. Feeding is as much an art as it is a science.

Feeding the lactating or pregnant mare requires special consideration. The normal gestation period (pregnancy) for mares is 335 days, with pony mares and jennies exceeding this figure to almost one year. If the mare's regular feeding program was sufficient prior to conception, it should remain sufficient for the first three-fourths of her gestation. The last quarter of pregnancy calls for some minor changes. For the standard size horse of approximately 1,000 pounds, this additional increase may amount to two pounds of hay and two-thirds pound of grain additional per day. An undernourished gestating mare at this stage may not be able to provide for the additional drain on her body because she is eating for two. Nature often compensates for this drain by abortion of the foal. A little extra feed, care, and observation should guard against this possibility.

The real drain on the mare's nutritional resources comes about after foaling when she is building her own body reserves back to normal and producing milk. For that reason, lactating mares must be fed at a special level recommended such as mixture #5 in Table 4-1.

Although the owner or handler will modify diets according to individual body and flesh conditions, the following helpful rules serve as a guideline:

1. Horses doing light work (under 3 hours)—0.5% of body weight in concentrate (see the sample rations in Table 4-1), 1 to 1.25% hay.

2. Horses doing medium work (3–5 hours)—1% of body weight in concentrate, same amount of hay.

3. Horses doing hard work (over 5 hours)—1¼% of body weight in concentrates, 1% in hay.

Breeding stallions should be fed as a horse doing hard work and should be exercised thoroughly prior to and during the breeding season.

4. Pregnant mares—0.75% to 1.5% of body weight in concentrate, 0.75% to 1.5% of body weight in hay.

5. The total combined consumption of concentrate and hay should be kept in the range of 2% to 2.5% of body weight.

6. Foals—The mare's milk will sustain adequate growth until about 6 weeks of age, when it is advisable to begin creep feeding. The foal should be consuming about .75% of its body weight in a good legume or grass hay and an equal amount of concentrate creep feed. The concentrate mix should contain a minimum of 12% crude protein and at least 5% fiber. A standard ratio is 9 parts grain to 1 part oil meal. No more than one-half the grain mix should be corn, milo, or wheat combined with oats or barley because of the possibility of compaction due to the heavier concentrates. This same mix can be continued after weaning to about 1 year of age. Consumption by this time will have increased to 1% of body weight in concentrates and 1.5% in hay. A suitable mineral mixture should be supplied free-choice as for other horses.

Management Suggestions

1. Withhold half of the grain ration and increase hay on days that working horses are idle.

2. Use only dust-free and mold-free feeds.

3. Water before feeding. If horse is heated, avoid excessive watering.

4. Feed hay before grain.

5. Do not feed a tired horse its total allotted diet of grain at one time. Feed half the grain, then feed the rest 1 hour later.

6. Do not work a horse hard after feeding a full grain allotment.

7. Feed and water regularly and not less than twice daily.

8. Observe the condition of the horse and feed accordingly.

BIBLIOGRAPHY

Blakely, J., & Bade, D. *The Science of Animal Husbandry*. Reston, VA: Reston Publishing Co., 1979.

Blakely, J., & King, D. *The Brass Tacks of Animal Health*. St. Louis, MO: Doane Agricultural Publications, 1978.

Bradbury, P., & Werk, S. *Horse Nutrition*. Houston, TX: Cordorvan Corp., 1974.

Cullison, A. *Feeds and Feeding*. Reston, VA: Reston Publishing Co., 1979.

Morrison, F. *Feeds and Feeding*. Ithaca, NY: Morrison Publishing Co., 1956.

5
Horse Selection and Judging

Most authors make a distinction between the terms selection and judging. Selection (such as in a purchase) of a horse may be done on the basis of visual appraisal, pedigree, or simply affection. Judging, on the other hand, is the comparison of one individual with an ideal model that the judge mentally keeps in mind. For purposes of discussion in this chapter, the terms judging and selection will be used interchangeably because judging plays such a big part in the selection decision. Judging a horse should be like looking at a beautiful painting, a beautiful woman, a handsome man, or any beautiful animal; everything there should be pleasing to the eye. To go one step further in the selection of horses, it can be said that everything seen has a direct relationship to the performance of that horse. The Thoroughbred looks the way it does because it has been designed for speed through selection and breeding. The Draft horse has a much different design and one would be able to guess simply from visual appraisal that a typical Draft horse would have little chance in a race against the Thoroughbred, and the Thoroughbred would have little of a chance in a pulling contest against a Clydesdale. The judging and selection of horses is one of the most fascinating arts in all of animal science. There is scarcely a single feature on the horse that is not related to performance of that breed, with the possible exception of color breeds, and even there the desired situation of conformation dictates the ideal model.

Every breed discussed in Chapter 2 was developed for some outstanding characteristic that breeders considered more important than features available from horses of another breed. The standards of judging and selection are, therefore, varied depending upon the breed of horse involved. Nevertheless, every breed has certain standards that dictate the desired conformation and type. Invariably, there is a direct relationship between this conformation, type, and desired function.

TYPES OF SELECTION

A knowledgeable horseman selecting an outstanding animal will normally be guided by pedigree, performance, and finally, visual observation. Certainly, the best method for selection would be to utilize all three types. In this chapter, the discussion will be limited to visual observation, normally referred to as judging or "halter" classes, commonly seen at horse shows and fairs.

Judging principles vary greatly between breeds. The association for the various breeds covered in this book determine the exact "ideal model" and instruct their breeders and professional judges to look for those features that are related to the desired conformation, type, and subsequently performance of the breed. Because of space limitations, it would be impractical to cover judging procedures for every breed. In order to simplify discussion yet show that variation exists from breed to breed, the two most popular breeds in the United States will serve as models—the Quarter horse and the Thoroughbred.

HORSE TERMINOL-OGY

Will Rogers once jokingly said, "There is not a single place on the human body that a person can point to that some doctor hasn't made up a name for." This statement can also apply to equines. It is important that the sincere horse fancier develop a knowledge of terms used in judging and discussing a horse. These terms are studied and memorized in order to simplify communications when expressing observations or listening to them.

A study of Fig. 5-1 and Fig. 5-2 will show the similarity of terminology used when expressing points of anatomy on the Quarter horse and the Thoroughbred. These figures are artists' conceptions because the appropriate association wishes to impress upon breeders the "ideal type." This ideal type is often never found but it serves as a mental model for the judge to compare against a common horse using a firm standard. Once the horses or classes of horses, regardless of breed, are assembled, they should always be judged in a logical sequence. The purpose of this judging is to place horses in the order of their excellence from the standpoint of conformation, soundness, and quality. It matters little whether there are numerous horses or only one because the judge is still comparing each individual against a standard model.

Among the first things judges look for in a halter class is the way a horse travels, keeping in mind the conformation standards of the particular breed. Imagine the horse leaving a set of tracks in a smooth

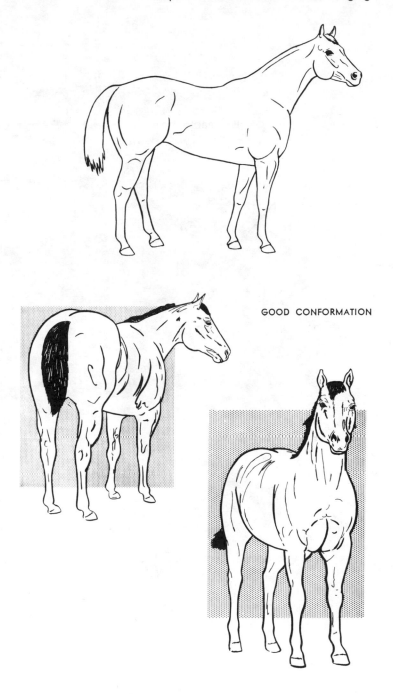

GOOD CONFORMATION

FIGURE 5-1. The ideal type of Quarter Horse. (American Quarter Horse Association, Amarillo, Texas)

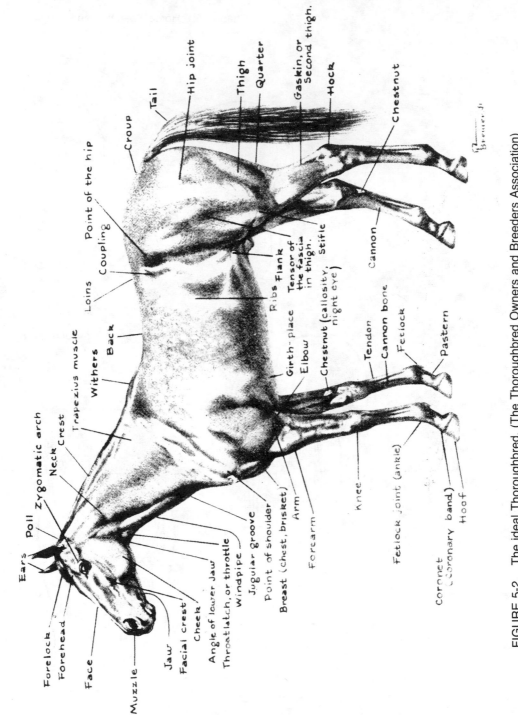

FIGURE 5-2. The ideal Thoroughbred. (The Thoroughbred Owners and Breeders Association)

sand lot and the image projected in the judge's mind becomes more clear. Fig. 5-3(b) illustrates what the judge is looking for.

After studying the horse's movements, the judge mentally records this and goes on to make other comparisons of a horse or many horses. If looking at only one horse, the judge mentally determines how that individual compares to the projected standard and decides what level of excellence it should receive. This may be determined by a blue ribbon, a title, or in numbers of dollars an individual is willing to pay for a horse. After the firm realization that judging is no more than comparing one individual against an ideal standard, judging becomes less complicated in the mind of the layman. If a group of horses is being judged, the judge has merely to decide the order of excellence according to the characteristics with which each of the horses has been blessed.

After watching the way of travel, the judge will normally follow a prescribed logical sequence. A common way is to look at the horse first from the side, then from the front, and finally from the rear. Many judges feel it is best to take a quick, overall view of the horse from all three positions, then start looking for the finer points. Figures 5-3 and 5-4 show what the judge is looking for and some of the faults that are commonly seen. Now for purposes of illustration, keeping in mind the wide variation between breeds, let's briefly observe a few differences between the Quarter horse type and the Thoroughbred type.

QUARTER HORSE TYPE CONFORMATION

Observe Fig. 5-1 for the side, front, and rear view of good conformation on a typical Quarter horse. Refer back to this figure frequently and the principles of selection in the show ring should become more clear.

The Head and Neck

A good quality head of the Quarter horse should include short, erect, and "fox like" ears. Ears pointed forward indicate a horse that is in good condition, alert, and paying attention, qualities necessary in performance of roping, cutting, or cattle herding. The eyes should be prominent and well set apart to give the horse visual latitude, enabling it to see forward and backward without moving its head. This allows quicker reactions for the horse because it is able to see in virtually every direction. The nostrils are also important; they should be large because air intake is very important in hard-working horses. Even with sufficient lung capacity, if the nostrils are restricted, the lungs cannot be filled, thus reducing endurance.

The jaw is a good indication of strength of bone and constitution. Commonly called a "dinner plate" jaw, being large and round, it is an indication of soundness of bone. The mouth should be shallow so that reaction to the bit is assured. A horse with a deep mouth may be dif-

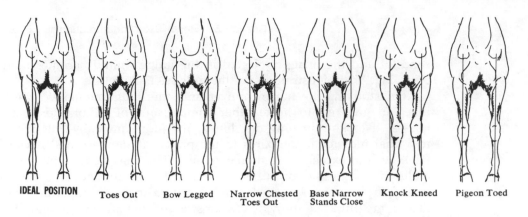

| IDEAL POSITION | Toes Out | Bow Legged | Narrow Chested Toes Out | Base Narrow Stands Close | Knock Kneed | Pigeon Toed |

Vertical line from point of shoulder should fall in center of knee, cannon, pastern, and foot.

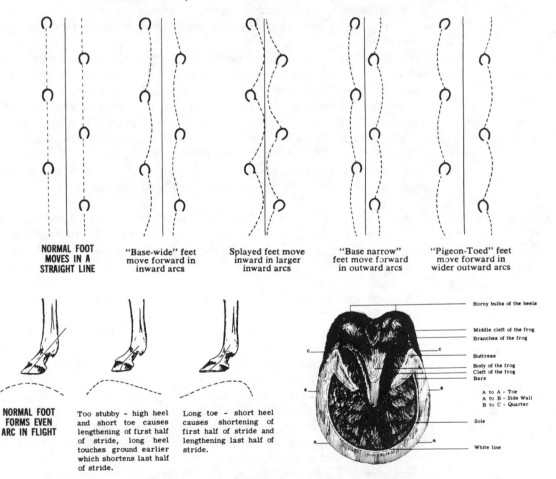

NORMAL FOOT MOVES IN A STRAIGHT LINE

"Base-wide" feet move forward in inward arcs

Splayed feet move inward in larger inward arcs

"Base narrow" feet move forward in outward arcs

"Pigeon-Toed" feet move forward in wider outward arcs

NORMAL FOOT FORMS EVEN ARC IN FLIGHT

Too stubby – high heel and short toe causes lengthening of first half of stride, long heel touches ground earlier which shortens last half of stride.

Long toe – short heel causes shortening of first half of stride and lengthening last half of stride.

Horny bulbs of the heels

Middle cleft of the frog
Branches of the frog

Buttress
Body of the frog
Cleft of the frog
Bars

A to A - Toe
A to B - Side Wall
B to C - Quarter

Sole

White line

FIGURE 5-3. Judging horses against an ideal standard is common practice. (Courtesy of the Appaloosa Horse Club, Inc., Moscow, Idaho)

IDEAL POSITION Stands Wide Stands Close Bow Legged Cow Hocked
Vertical line from point of buttock should fall in center of hock, cannon, pastern and foot.

50°

IDEAL POSITION Stands Under Camped Out Leg Too Straight
Vertical line from point of buttock should touch the rear edge of cannon from hock to fetlock and meet the ground behind the heel.

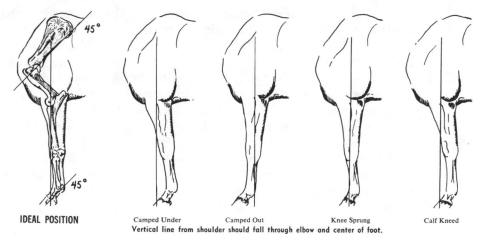

45°

45°

IDEAL POSITION Camped Under Camped Out Knee Sprung Calf Kneed
Vertical line from shoulder should fall through elbow and center of foot.

FIGURE 5-4. Comparison of one or many individuals is a matter of looking for faults and ideals in conformation. (Courtesy of the Appaloosa Horse Club, Moscow, Idaho)

ficult to control. The neck should be relatively thin because if the horse is unable to turn its neck, the body is unable to follow. An old axiom states "as the neck goes, so goes the horse." The throat latch must be clean with no excessive muscling or finish because this is the pivot point for the head.

The Shoulder, Forearm, and Withers

Notice the slope of the shoulder and the slope of the pastern shown in Fig. 5-4(c). This is a point missed by the average student Quarter Horse judge. These two slopes should correspond and be approximately 45 degrees because the pastern acts as a shock absorber to the front end and gives a smoother ride. The coordinated relationship with the slope of the shoulder is an easily understood example of biological engineering.

The forearm is a necessary muscle for moving the foreleg, and the more highly developed it is, generally the better movement the horse will have in the front end. A longer attachment is generally preferred to the heavier, more closely attached forearm muscle.

The Quarter horse's front legs form an inverted "V" from the front view. This is the most important aspect of the forequarter because it allows the horse to cross its front legs when running to give it the necessary agility. Think of the comparably flat-chested draft horse type and the picture becomes clear.

Notice also in Fig. 5-3(a) the standards for a set of legs. Imagine dropping a plumb line through the middle of a horse's leg, knee, and hoof and the common deviations and correct placement are made more meaningful.

From the side, withers should be prominent. This is a desired characteristic in order to give the saddle a place to hang and prevent it from turning. Although the layman may find a full, flat withers "pretty," it is not desired in performance Quarter horses. Also from the side, notice that the top line of Quarter horses should be shorter than the bottom line. This "close coupling" might be thought of as the rubberband principle. A horse that is "wound up tight" on top and able to stretch out underneath will have strength and speed. This is very important in Quarter horses. The croup should have a slight slope from the hip to the rear. This enables the horse to get its rear feet up and under it which is the source of power over a short distance. The muscling in the quarter should be well developed with a bulge that lets down to the area of the stifle muscle.

Hind Quarters

Perhaps the most important view of all is the rear view of a Quarter horse. Imagine the conformation lines of an apple turned with the stem down. Muscling in the rear of a Quarter horse is quite similar to this imaginary example. The horse should be wide through the stifle muscle and this should be the widest part seen from the rear. The gaskin muscle is the most prominent feature in descending order from the stifle. It should be full and bulging outward. Also, directly inside this muscle is the inside gaskin muscle which many horse breeders believe to be the most important, or one of the most important, and certainly one of the most difficult muscles to develop through selection and breeding. It is responsible for power from the rear end.

POINTS OF CONFORMATION OF THE THOROUGHBRED

The procedures followed by the judge of Thoroughbreds are similar to those previously discussed. The ideal standard (Fig. 5-2), however, is quite different, as it may be for the multitude of breeds in existence throughout the world. The comparison between Quarter horses and Thoroughbreds should give the reader, in as simplified a form as possible, the variation that can exist in the show ring between breeds. This is one reason "open" horse shows are seldom seen. Instead, shows are usually restricted to the particular breed in question such as Arabian, Appaloosa, Clydesdale, Belgian, Paso Fino, etc.

The general overall look of the Thoroughbred is one of greater refinement and quality in comparison to the Quarter horse. The Thoroughbred is lithe and clean and shows the prominence of the hot blood of the Arabians, Turks, and Barbs.

The Head and Neck

The head is small, well proportioned, and intelligent looking. In profile, the nose is either straight or slightly dished, as might be expected from its Arabian heritage. The muzzle is fine and cleanly cut, the nostrils are large to allow for great intakes of air while the horse is running or jumping—the two activities at which it is unsurpassed by other breeds. The eyes are large, prominent, and deep. The jawline is significantly different from the Quarter horse, not so heavily muscled, and the throat is fine and clean, attaching to a long, slender but well muscled neck. The neck is not only arched but also flexible, enabling the horse to use it to balance its actions.

The Withers, Shoulders, and Forearm

The withers are generally quite pronounced because they're the top of the shoulder that must be so long and sloping. The supposed ability of a Thoroughbred to jump well and stride out while galloping is often judged by the slope of the shoulder. The same 45 degree angle to the shoulder and pasterns is one common feature necessary to both breeds. Again, this is a conformation feature which determines how comfortable the horse is to the rider.

The chest is broad and deep, accommodating the big heart and expansive lungs. The forelegs should be well set on the chest, not too close together or out too far.

Long and slender legs make up the bulk of the Thoroughbred's height. The forearms should be well muscled but not stubby looking; the knee is flat; the cannon bone short but not as short as that of the Quarter horse. An excessively long cannon bone could spell early fatigue as do pasterns that are too sloping or too straight. Sound bone is extremely important in the Thoroughbred because the horse is normally pushed along in training to race at least by the third year of age. Unless there is good, strong conformation in the forearm, a Thoroughbred could break down.

The hooves of the horse should be fine and small. The previously discussed idea of visualizing a plumb line dropped down the foreleg and the rear leg apply to the Thoroughbred (or any other breed), too.

The Side View   Notice in Fig. 5-2 the flat and smooth muscles of the shoulder, neck, and hindquarters. This is a radical departure from the bunched muscular form of the Quarter horse. The back is on the long side with an underline slightly up-sloping on the well-conditioned Thoroughbred. Many Thoroughbreds are often referred to as "wasp waisted," which applies to horses carrying no fat with Thoroughbred conformation.

The croup is higher than the dock, giving rise to what some steeple-chase buffs call the jumping bump. It is often taken as an indication of a good jumper, and a horse that has been well schooled and jumped for several years may develop an even higher croup.

Hindquarters   The hindquarters are the most interesting aspect of the Thoroughbred. Note the great distance between the hip and the hock. Power in the Quarter horse is generated by a combination of this distance coupled with the overall length of leg and the angles at the hip, stifle, and hock. This determines the length of stride and power a horse may muster on the track and hunt field, or as a jumper.

Viewed from the rear, the Thoroughbred is pear shaped rather than square or apple shaped like the Quarter horse. Thoroughbreds normally have much longer tails, ideally kept at a length half way between the hocks and fetlocks.

Again, as with all other breeds, the hind legs should be straight and sturdy when viewed from the back. Refer again to Fig. 5-4a and 5-4b for a study in proper alignment of the hind legs.

Teething   Nearly everyone has seen the horse trader on the late, late western cast a suspicious eye on a prospective horse being traded or bought. After examining the teeth by opening the mouth, the trader calmly announces that the horse is much older than advertised. What did he see and what made him so sure?

Horses' teeth come in with such predictable accuracy that it is now quite common for race tracks to employ a specialist to determine age,

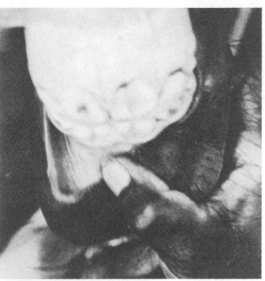

FIGURE 5-5.   Three-year-old's mouth. From Blakely and Bade, *The Science of Animal Husbandry,* Reston Publishing Co., 1979.

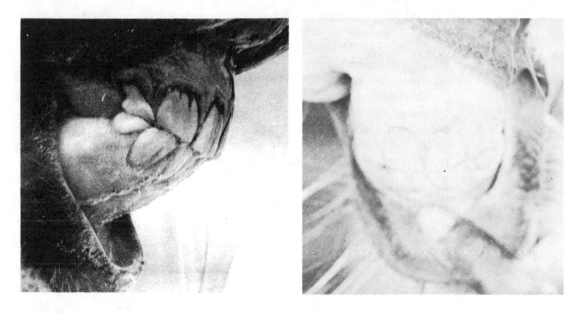

FIGURE 5-6.   Four-year-old's mouth. From Blakely and Bade, *The Science of Animal Husbandry,* Reston Publishing Co., 1979.

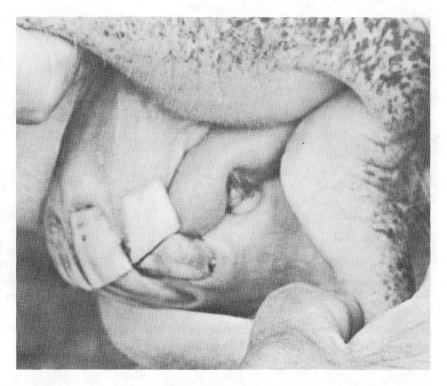

FIGURE 5-7. Complete mouth (age five). From Blakely and Bade, *The Science of Animal Husbandry*, Reston Publishing Co., 1979.

thus preventing unfair practices of running more mature horses against younger competitors.

Although age determination within a few months can be determined by the expert, a more simplified approach is taken in this text.

A young horse will have baby teeth that are replaced by permanent teeth. There are six upper front teeth and six lower front teeth. The permanent teeth start erupting in pairs, starting with the two middle incisors (the front teeth) around two to two and one-half years of age (Fig. 5-5). Note how much larger and longer these teeth are than the baby teeth.

At four years the next pair is complete (Fig. 5-6), leaving only one pair of temporary incisors.

Fig. 5-7 illustrates the complete set of permanent teeth that exists at five years. An interesting point is the development of canine teeth at about this age (although it may be as early as three and one-half). These canine or "wolf teeth" are always seen in a stallion or gelding but rarely in a mare. Fig. 5-8 is a picture of an eight-year-old mare's mouth with a rare, protruding canine tooth.

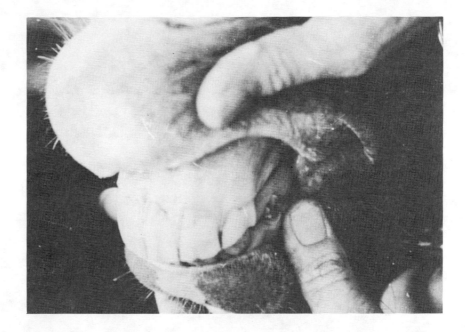

FIGURE 5-8. Eight-year-old mare's mouth with rare canine tooth. From Blakely and Bade, *The Science of Animal Husbandry*, Reston Publishing Co., 1979.

In summary, the average horse handler can tell the age of horses that are three, four, and five with little practice. Beyond five, more detailed observations are made with reference to the wearing of cusps and the angle of incisors. For the serious student of this neglected art, an excellent reference with great detail is published by the American Association of Equine Practitioners, Golden, Colorado 80401.

BIBLIOGRAPHY

American Quarter Horse Association, Amarillo, Texas. *Judging American Quarter Horses.*

Blakely, J., & D. Bade. *The Science of Animal Husbandry.* Reston, VA: Reston Publishing Co., 1979.

Estes, J.A., & Palmer, J. "An Introduction to the Thoroughbred Horse." Lexington, KY: *The Blood-Horse.*

Roberts, E. (ed.). *Horsemanship Manual.* Moscow, ID: Appaloosa Horse Club, 1971.

6
Diseases, Disorders, and Ailments

Not every horse disease known will be covered in this chapter. Instead, focus will be on those situations most likely to occur. For purposes of organization, diseases, disorders, and ailments will be covered under the following categories: respiratory diseases, reproductive disorders, viral and bacterial diseases, digestive tract problems, and finally, foot and leg problems.

**HOW TO DE-
TECT AN
ILLNESS**

The expression "healthy as a horse" may be misleading. Few know what signs imply health in horses or how to detect the opposite condition—"sick as a horse." Illness in the horse can be detected only after one understands normal health signs. Most horses will appear similar in many traits, but handlers learn that individuals have slightly different behavior patterns. Any deviation from normal behavior by a horse should be viewed with suspicion. Just as humans get irritable when suffering from a cold or some other disorder, horses may deviate from their normal behavior pattern for similar reasons. Diagnosis of a problem starts with a suspicion that an ailment of some sort is influencing the behavior pattern of the horse. Conclusions are later based on evidence through closer examination supplemented by conclusive tests.

Such deviations from normal behavior might include lack of appetite, extreme nervousness, listlessness, excessive sleepiness, laying down for long periods of time, or any variation in daily routine habits of an individual horse.

Early detection of diseases is very important because the condition can be treated and corrected more easily in the early stage, and the infected animal may also be quickly isolated to prevent spread of the disease to other horses in the herd.

A knowledge of some diseases is necessary to arrive at a reasonable diagnosis and a decision whether to call a veterinarian. For example, excessive laying down by the horse could be a warning sign. A horse seldom lies down, even to sleep. When it does lie down, it's usually sunning itself and will lie on its side. A sick horse, on the other hand, will often lie on its belly for long periods of time. If the horse does not offer to get up when approached by a human being, it could be a positive sign of ill health.

Foot disorders are quite easily detected but not all of them will intially appear as a lameness. A horse with a foot problem will naturally want to get the weight off its feet, and although it may not appear lame will often hold an aching foot off the ground and paw or nicker its disapproval. Closer examination of feet, legs, and hooves by noting unnatural odors or by testing the tender spots with a hoof tester may uncover possible inflammation or infection in the very early stages.

One of the classic signs to be alert for is profuse sweating, pawing the ground, groaning, and an unnatural desire to roll on the ground. This is a classic symptom of digestive disorders such as colic. It might be thought of as a "tummy ache" in humans. While the condition may only be discomfort to humans, it could easily spell death to a horse because of twisting of the intestines, and immediate attention must be given.

The stance of a horse reveals a great deal about its inner balance. A healthy horse will appear loose, with ears erect. If a clapping of the hands does not bring immediate attention with ears projected forward, it could be a sign of poor health. A horse that hangs its head down, arches its back, or droops the ears is quite likely suffering from some disorder.

Veterinarians observe the stance to detect early signs of particular problems, depending on the reaction of the horse to certain movements. For example, a "saw horse" stance is typical in horses suffering from tetanus. The legs will be spread abnormally wide and the horse will have difficulty in moving sideways. Sleeping sickness, on the other hand, produces a stance in which weight is shifted to the hindquarters and the horse exhibits a wobbly gait.

A horse "going off feed" could signal moldy feed, a change of feed, or a disease. Once the feed is determined to be good quality and a picky appetite is ruled out, the handler may suspect digestive disorders or a disease.

Rapid weight loss is a sure sign of problems and could include minor situations such as a sore mouth, tongue, or injured teeth; or, it could be the more serious condition of infestation with internal parasites or even deadly digestive disturbances.

Horses, like humans, may develop allergies, which show up as small bumps that look like mosquito welts on the skin. This could be a reaction to weeds, pollen, feed, etc. A dull hair coat is also an indication of internal disorders such as parasites, mineral deficiencies, or disease. Excessive scratching could be signs of infestation with internal or external parasites. The breath of a horse, like that of a human, should not be offensive. Unpleasant odors from the mouth or body parts, excessive salivation, or dry mouth are signs of many disorders.

One of the reasons medical doctors always look in the eye of humans is because the eye shows some of the first signs of disorders brought about by disease. The same is true in the case of horses. If eyes lose their moist appearance or the pupil fails to become smaller when a light is shined into it, it may be an indication of disease or disorder. Both eyes should also be checked to rule out the possibility that simply one eye has been injured.

Another good habit to develop is observation of the droppings of an animal. When a horse is ill, the digestive system is upset and droppings are often not in the normal round balls that break open upon hitting the ground. Observation of droppings for bad odors, severe changes in consistency, mucous or parasite content should give a further clue to problems.

Because of the very common problems of feet and leg disorders, the horse's underpinning should be observed frequently for swelling or obvious circumference of one limb as compared to the other.

The horse's vital signs—temperature, respiration, and pulse—are good indicators of health or impending problems. Normal body temperature of the horse should be between 100° and 101°F. Any variation from this norm should be viewed as conclusive evidence that a problem exists. A horse suspected of illness should have its temperature checked by placing a thermometer in the rectum. Be sure the thermometer is lubricated with Vaseline or a similar substance and it is recommended that a longer thermometer disigned especially for horses be used in order to reach far enough into the rectum to get an accurate reading. Because of rectal muscle movement, the thermometer should be secured by a string and clamp to the tail to prevent losing it. A two or three minute reading will be sufficient to accurately check the temperature. The respiration rate—number of breaths taken per minute at rest—should average 16 but will vary with breeds and individuals. Horses should be checked when known to be normal to establish a standard. Watch the in and out motion of nostrils or rib cage for an accurately timed minute to get normal respiration rate. The normal pulse should be slightly more than twice the respiration rate—36 on the average. Pulse, or heartbeat, is determined by the throb of an artery, most conveniently felt on the inner side of the horse's jaw.

GENERAL MUSCLE PAIN AND INFLAMMATION

When a horse is worked hard, especially one that is not used to it, muscle pains, soreness, and spasms in the feet and legs may occur. The signs are an appearance of being "stove up," and may be a problem in young horses as well as older animals. However, it is more pronounced in aged horses. An aged horse taken from a stall or small pasture and ridden even moderately for a full day may be able to move only with difficulty the following day. Relief of this condition is normally brought about by rest, rub downs with horse liniments and in severe cases, use of corticosteroids or antiinflammatory products such as Arquel, Butazoladone, and Equiproxine. The most common preventive measure, however, is to anticipate when a horse will be needed heavily and use warm-up periods, gradually increasing the amount of exercise given a horse before it is requested to perform. This is similar to training for an Olympic event. Even though the event may only be a lengthy trail ride, the pre-event program will pay healthy dividends.

Inflammation is a term used frequently in this chapter and is now discussed in general terms to acquaint the horseman with a condition that affects virtually every part of the horse's body. Inflammation is merely a reaction to body injury, characterized by heat, swelling, sometimes discoloration, and disturbed function of muscles, nerves, etc. Inflammation is present whenever a sprain, strain, bump, twist, cut, puncture, or some other injury occurs to any part of the body. The reaction of the body is to send an extra supply of blood to the injured area to supply plenty of white blood cells which are responsible for removing contamination and debris caused by the injury.

This inflammation, then, is the body's natural protection. The white blood cells have many responsibilities, among them killing the infecting agents, preventing further spread of them, removing any toxic substances produced and promotion of healing.

The horseman may be able to hasten this natural healing process by cleaning the injury of contamination, thus creating the most advantageous situation for healing.

Another way of hastening the healing process is to intentionally use an agent that creates more damage sending more blood to the area. Blistering agents are used for this purpose as is the more severe practice used by veterinarians of "firing" (using a red hot needle to produce numerous punctures in the inflamed area). Although additional swelling will come about from hastening inflammation, the swelling is due to an increased blood supply, which may also hasten the healing process more quickly. Therefore, inflammation is a double-edged sword. It is bad because it produces swelling but it has been beneficial because it is part of the natural healing process. Perhaps this illustration will make the process of firing and blistering more understandable. Basically, it is a paradoxical method of making something worse so it can be made better. Nature's way of bringing this about is called inflammation.

MEDICAL EMERGENCIES

True medical emergencies require a veterinarian as soon as possible. Some situations that require immediate attention include colic, severe bleeding, deep wounds to the chest, deep wounds to the abdomen, eye injuries, and broken bones.

Although the handler must remain calm when an emergency occurs, and normally the horse should not be moved, no time should be lost in calling a veterinarian, and describing the wound and how it occurred.

In the case of a laceration, first-aid is of primary importance to control bleeding. However, horses rarely bleed to death from lower leg injuries, and even serious problems may be handled if the horse does not get excited. The average adult horse can lose up to one gallon of blood without serious consequences.

In the case of a bleeding injury, pressure should be applied with clean cloth, towel, diaper, quilted leg wrap, etc. Only slight pressure should be applied to slow the bleeding. A tourniquet is definitely not advised because of the risk of cutting off blood supply and creating gangrene in the horse. A steady, firm, even pressure is recommended.

The horse should be kept calm and quiet. The wound must be protected from further contamination but it is recommended that no disinfectant be used because it destroys tissue and retards healing. If a disinfectant is needed to destroy bacteria, the professional should determine proper application.

In the case of a deep puncture wound to the chest, with air being inhaled and exhaled through the hole, the horse will likely suffer a collapsed lung. The wound should be plugged with a clean cloth to stop the air from moving back and forth.

Occasionally, a deep wound to the abdomen, such as a stick accidentally penetrating the abdomen, will create emergency situations. The first inclination might be to remove the object but this is not recommended because this would allow the intestines to fall out through the hole. In the event a more severe wound has already occurred and the intestines are hanging out, wrap the horse with a clean bed sheet or hold the intestines in place with a clean towel. Keep the pressure applied to prevent further movement out of the body cavity until the veterinarian arrives.

Eye injuries are true emergencies and require that the horse be kept quiet and preferably be placed in a darkened stall. Don't touch the eye.

Broken bones are a significantly serious problem in horses as evidenced by the many "old west" movies in which the hero has to shoot his horse because it just stepped in a gopher hole. Broken bones are serious but some can be helped. First aid consists of preventing further injury. This is best done by not moving the animal, if possible, until the veterinarian arrives. Movement may create a compound fracture from one that was less serious. Movement of the horse to the barn could cause a break of the bone to penetrate the skin producing infection from dirt, gravel, and manure. After that happens, there is very little hope of recovery.

If a horse with a broken leg must be moved, the leg should be bandaged with a very thick, clean bandage by wrapping many layers of bandage and toweling on the leg until it is so thick, it looks ridiculous. Then, as the saying goes, "make it twice that thick." Leg injuries may even be splinted on top of that padding by use of a piece of plastic pipe cut lengthwise. The splint should run as far above the injury as possible.

In addition to the generalized discussion of detecting a sick animal and emergency first-aid medical treatment, it is helpful to horse lovers to have some specific knowledge of diseases and ailments in order to be better able to deal with the problem and prevent its reoccurrence.

RESPIRA-TORY DISEASES

The first signs of upper respiratory diseases include a nasal discharge (Fig. 6-1) that is initially thin but gradually becomes thicker. The general cause is thought to be a virus or bacteria.

Colds, Upper Respiratory Infection (URI), Distemper

For prevention of respiratory infections, the horse should not be subjected to variable extremes in temperature, and horses with obvious infections should be isolated from the herd.

The suggested treatment is to isolate the affected horse, consult a veterinarian if signs are severe, and possibly administer antibiotics such as penicillin or streptomycin.

Coughs

A hacking cough similar in sound to humans is also heard in horses. This condition may be caused by a variety of situations. Allergies, changes in food or temperature, even roundworm infestation causing a tickling sensation in the throat could precipitate the cough.

The horse should be kept in a comfortable, stable temperature, provided with shelter, fed dust-free feeds, and wormed regularly as preventive measures.

Usually a cough is not a serious sign of problems other than a simple respiratory malfunction similar to the human cold. A home remedy that will give the horse relief is a small dose of common cough syrup placed on the back of the tongue two or three times daily. If the con-

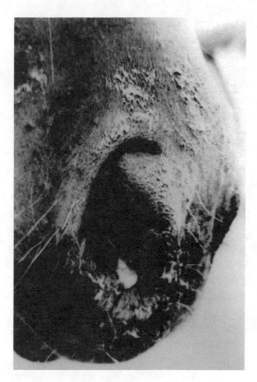

FIGURE 6-1. A nasal discharge may be the first symptom to appear in upper respiratory infections, colds, or distemper. (School of Veterinary Medicine, Texas A&M University)

dition persists more than 48 hours, professional help should be sought because the condition could be caused by worm infestations.

Equine Viral Rhinopneumonitis (EVR)

This condition draws its name from the severe deformation of nasal bone (rhinitis), and is accompanied by a cough, nasal discharge, and temperatures between 102 and 107 degrees Fahrenheit. Either constipation or diarrhea may be seen. Abortion by mares pregnant less than 4 months is often seen at the onset of the disease. If a mare so affected does not abort, the foal may be born weak, develop pneumonia, and die shortly after birth. The cause is a virus that may be carried through the air and water. This makes contamination of both hay and feed and water sources a severe problem. Horses, birds, dogs, man, and other animals may carry the virus and spread it without being affected themselves.

Adequate ventilation and proper sanitation of the stables are recommended as preventative measures. Although a vaccine is available for protection against the disease, a regular inoculation schedule, including booster shots, must be followed in order to maintain immunity.

Treatment is normally useless against this virus. Secondary infections created by the weakened condition, once recovery starts, may be through the use of penicillin and streptomycin. Rest, shelter, and comfortable temperature are supportive treatments.

Heaves (Broken Wind)

The reason a cough should be considered serious after 48 hours, as previously mentioned, is that if not treated, it could turn into the more serious condition of heaves. The characteristic sign is a heaving of the horse's flank twice, rather than once, as normal, during exhalation. This secondary reaction is caused by extra muscle effort from the abdomen. The cause is thought to be dusty food and is particularly causative if the horse inhales the dust just prior to work or other exertion. Excessively working a horse with a slight cough can further aggravate the condition. Another cause for this problem can be air pollution.

Once the disease is contracted, it is incurable. However, it can be controlled by keeping dust reduced to minimum in the feed and bedding. Molasses added to the feed or water sprinkled on feed and stable bedding will help. Antihistamines in the feed are also recommended.

Influenza

A high fever ranging from 102 to 106 degrees Fahrenheit and lasting 1 to 6 days is the chief sign of the onset of influenza. There may be nasal congestion, tear discharges, and coughing in the early stages. Foals can become very ill and even die. Normally, adult horses will recover within a week to 10 days. The cause is a virus infection. It is found in most countries throughout the world.

The only prevention is a rigorous sanitation schedule and isolation of infected animals. In cases where severe outbreaks occur, there is an effective vaccination program to prevent it. Only very young foals normally need treatment. Antibiotics administered throughout the course of the disease are recommended for foals. When temperatures remain normal for 24 to 48 hours and normal breathing is restored, treatment is normally discontinued. Adult hourses develop an immunity after having had the disease, but the immunity wears off within a couple of years and the infection may occur again.

Pneumonia

A rapid rise in temperature and dullness, with the highest part of the fever occurring during the early part of the disease, are signs of pneumonia. There is usually a discharge of mucus from the nose, a painful cough, and increased pulse and respiratory rate. Many agents may contribute to pneumonia, such as dust, but the chief causative agents are either a virus or bacteria. Damp quarters, exhaustion, or sudden weather changes most often bring on pneumonia.

Dry quarters and proper ventilation coupled with adequate feed are considered the best measures for preventing the problem.

An affected horse should be isolated from the herd, kept comfortable in well ventilated quarters, blanketed, and treated with antibiotics. A full dosage of penicillin, streptomycin, or a combination of the two should be given for at least 4 days until the body temperature returns to normal for at least 24 hours. Adequate water supply is also essential.

Roaring

Horses, particularly those doing heavy work, exhibit the clinical sign that gave roaring its name. A deep rumbling noise is made during exhalation. The primary cause is excessive working after a horse has had an attack of strangles. It is caused by a paralysis of the soft palate of the mouth, or paralysis of the larynx.

Although the condition is very difficult to treat, some veterinarians may use, in specific cases only, a hot iron (live firing) to the soft palate creating even greater inflammation. This firing technique is generally not used but is recommended in some cases in order to speed up the flow of blood to the affected area and, therefore, induce more rapid healing.

Strangles (Distemper)

The key sign of strangles is a swelling under the jaw, eventually creating an abscess. Often the abscess will erupt. Temperatures of infected horses may rise to 105 degrees Fahrenheit. They generally will produce a nasal discharge and appear listless. This is a disease of the lymph gland, normally affecting horses under 6 years of age. It is thought to be virus induced.

A highly contagious disease, horses diagnosed with it should be isolated from the herd and all gear and feeding utensils should be disinfected.

Very little can be done in the way of prevention but isolation is the key to preventing the spread to other animals. An infected horse should be kept warm, provided a laxative diet, and be placed in the care of a veterinarian. The disease usually lasts about 6 weeks requiring another 2 to 3 months for convalescence. A horse with strangles should be rested and returned to usual activities about 90 days after contracting the disease.

Whistling

A high-pitched noise coming from the throat of a horse that is heavily worked, particularly at running paces, is a chief clinical sign of this respiratory disease with the appropriate name. It is brought about by a rupture of one of the nerves of the larynx. This results in a paralysis of the vocal cord, creating a partial blockage and producing a whistle.

Although the condition is thought to be hereditary, and very little can be done about it, peculiarly, it does not normally occur in the smaller breeds of horses.

In the event whistling does occur, a veterinarian can perform a "tubing" operation to alleviate the restriction of air. An alternate operation allows for removal of a membrane behind the vocal cord that also reduces wind restriction.

REPRODUC-TIVE PROBLEMS

In order for reproductive efficiency in horses to be at its highest level, mares must have exercise, adequate nutrition, proper parasite control, and properly ventilated housing. The primary cause of a low foaling rate as compared to horses in the wild is a lack of proper sanitation due to acreage restrictions and a higher population. A combination of diseases and numerous other factors make a 50% foal crop seem ordinary. Strict control of sanitation, adequate grazing, exercise, and breeding during the natural mating time of horses (spring) can produce conception rates in captivity that may exceed 90%. However, even under the best circumstances, 60 to 80% is considered exceptionally good.

Abortions

Infections created by bacterial and viral invasions are the main cause of abortion in horses. For this reason, antiseptic measures are very important both at breeding time and during foaling. Approximately 40% of all causes of abortion are unknown but can probably be attributed to some form of improper sanitation. The reason for scrubbing the mare's and the stallion's genitals with soap and water and treating with a disinfectant is to prevent organisms from being introduced into the reproductive tract and thereby terminating pregnancy or preventing conception.

Certain types of organisms, such as streptococcal invasions, may cause abortion in mares even when sanitation procedures appear adequate. A retained placenta (afterbirth) or difficult birth may predispose the mare to streptococcal infections. About 20% of all abortions are caused by this organism. There is no vaccine available so the main method of defense is very strict sanitary conditions and careful observation during critical times such as foaling. Assistance when needed and prompt action may reduce considerably these influences.

One form of contagious equine abortion is caused by a bacterium called *Salmonella abortivo-equinus*. Abortion usually occurs about the fourth to eighth month because of invasion from this organism. Since it is contagious, a preventive measure is to bury the dead fetus and afterbirth, or burn them. Steam cleaning of barns and immediate disinfection should be carried out. Mares that have aborted should not be bred again until they are checked and found clean of the infection.

Although there is no treatment for abortions once they occur, the problem can be controlled best by eliminating carriers of the organisms in the herd. Some forms of abortion may be prevented by vaccination.

Ninety-seven percent of all abortions are caused by two organisms—Salmonella and Streptococci organisms. This figure should emphasize the importance of strict sanitation measures if reproductive efficiency and control of abortion are to remain high.

These sanitary measures might include quarantine areas, sterilization of equipment, restricting visitors from certain areas of the breeding farm, removal of bedding and manure, and steam cleaning of stalls and isolation wards. On a much smaller scale, the same strict sanitary conditions may be applied by burning all bedding and manure, steam cleaning the stall, checking the mare and applying the proper treatment according to the recommendations of a veterinarian, and a prevention of reinfection by common sense measures.

Abortions may also be caused by some drugs, deworming agents, poisonous plants, EVR (discussed on page 277), chemicals, or even moldy feed. It should be quite obvious to the concerned horse owner that specific recommendations for application to horses of both internal and external products should be followed closely if problems are to be prevented.

SYSTEMIC DISEASES, VIRAL AND BACTERIAL DISEASES

Azoturia (Monday Morning Disease)

This condition occurs most often after a horse has been rested over the weekend while continuing to consume a heavy ration of grain. This was most common in years past with hard working, well fed horses, especially during cold weather. The condition was formerly most prevalent in draft horses during the days of horse-drawn equipment. Grateful owners continued to feed their charges well throughout the weekend and when Monday morning came around, the animal exhibited signs of distress. The problem usually became noticeable during the first hour of exercise, often the first 15 minutes, when the horse began to sweat and appear stiff in the legs. This stiffness may affect front, back, or all four legs but most often affects the hind legs only. Horses so affected become stiff, try to remove pressure from their aching back legs, and eventually assume a "sitting dog" position. The horse later lies down and often the urinary tract is blocked. If urine is passed, it is discolored red, brown, or almost black. Although death occurs in severe cases, the horse usually remains down for 2 to 4 days after which recovery is possible. Those that do not go down or those whose front legs only are affected stand the chance of most rapid recovery.

Monday morning disease is caused by the system continuing a high metabolic rate creating an accumulation of lactic acid in the tissues and blood because of a lack of exercise to burn off the excessive lactic acid. This condition, although most often seen in hard working, heavy horses, is not uncommon in all horses that are used heavily, such as racing horses, cow horses, show horses, etc.

The key to controlling this problem is to reduce feed on the days that the horse is not being worked hard. If the horse is used heavily during the week but off on the weekends, a common procedure is to give a wet mash Saturday night and a light feeding on Sunday, then return to the full feed ration for heavy service during the week.

Owners should be cautioned that if a horse reacts in this way, with stiffness in the front or hind legs and azoturia is suspected, the horse should not be moved. The rider should dismount and leave the horse at that spot. Further movement severely aggravates the problem. A veterinarian should be consulted for treatment. Mild attacks, such as those that involve only the front legs, are often treated with a laxative of 2 to 4 liters of mineral oil to act as a purgative. In more severe cases, such as the sitting dog syndrome, tranquilizers may be needed to lessen the muscle tension. This is a very painful condition and veterinarians often also prescribe sedatives or anti-inflammatory substances.

Navel Ill

This condition occurs in newborn foals shortly after birth, most often in unsanitary conditions. Microorganisms (mainly Streptococcus) gain entrance through the umbilical cord. Newborn foals develop a high temperature and death can occur within 1 to 3 days after onset. Occasionally, infection of the navel occurs in foals that are 2 to 3 weeks or older; in this case the disease is less acute and results in stiffness in the joints and tender sheaths, and recovery is more rapid.

Once the condition is diagnosed as definite, treatment must start immediately because there is imminent danger of losing the foal. A common treatment is injectable penicillin-streptomycin, available in dosages of 1 to 2 grams of streptomycin in combination with pencillin. The dosage should be regulated according to streptomycin content rather than the penicillin portion. An injectable dose should be given every 12 hours for at least 3 days or longer.

The most effective way of combating navel ill, however, is to use preventive measures. This involves strict sanitation of the bedding area, if housed, and treatment of the umbilical cord immediately after birth with tincture of iodine. The umbilical cord should not be cut, as this often leads to contamination. Nature will normally take care of matters by causing the cord to break. Even though the foal may be on clean pasture, where normally navel ill would not be a problem, it is still a good idea to treat the stump with iodine and if it is fly season to use a repellent around the navel area.

Poll Evil or Fistula Withers

A running sore that breaks out from either the poll or the withers (Fig. 6-2) is the common sign of the infection referred to as poll evil or fistula withers. Although they occur in two different places, the condition is caused by the same organism (Brucella abortus) that infects a bursa (a saclike structure containing lubricating fluid to reduce friction).

The same organism produces Bang's disease in cattle, undulant fever in humans, and can be transmitted from horse to cattle, cattle to horses. Although the organism causes abortion in cattle, it "breaks out" in the form of running sores in horses (Fig. 6-2).

It is highly recommended that a veterinarian treat this condition because of its contagious nature. Severe cases may require surgery and treatment as an open wound. Less severe cases may respond to ice packs and anti-inflammatory agents. A vaccine (strain-19) has also proven effective in some cases.

Once an outbreak occurs, the key to preventing further infections is to maintain strict sanitary measures.

FIGURE 6-2. An advanced case of fistula withers. The condition is caused by the Brucella abortus organism, which can also affect the poll (poll evil). (School of Veterinary Medicine, Texas A & M University)

Sleeping Sickness (Equine Encephalomyelitis)

This condition, commonly called sleeping sickness, produces impaired vision and a drousy, lazy appearance (Fig. 6-3). First signs are usually a marked depression followed by a high temperature of 104 to 106 degrees Fahrenheit lasting for 24 to 48 hours. The horse will take on a dazed look, appear feverish, wander around, have reduced reflexes and coordination, will let the lower lip drop, yawn, may even

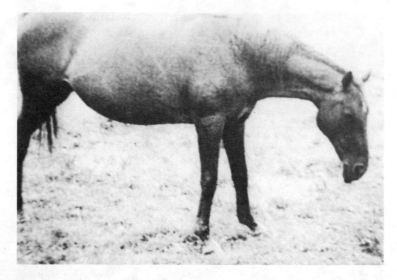

FIGURE 6-3. This horse is suffering from sleeping sickness. Note the dazed look, drooping lower lip. (School of Veterinary Medicine, Texas A & M University)

lie down and be unable to rise (Fig. 6-4). In some cases, the horse appears unable to hold its head up and may rest it on something solid or press the head against a wall. Inability to swallow is common and affected horses may appear to fall asleep while eating, food hanging out of the mouth (Fig. 6-5). Urination and defecation will usually be under strain. Advanced cases produce paralysis and death, occurring 2 to 4 days after the onset of fever.

A group of viruses may cause sleeping sickness and are normally carried by mosquitoes and birds. Even common domestic birds such as chickens, pidgeons, etc. act as hosts for the virus. Mosquitoes attack these birds and keep the condition spreading at an alarming rate. It is extremely difficult to control because of these insect–bird transfers. Mosquitoes that have attacked a bird carrying the virus will infect the horse by transmitting the virus directly to the bloodstream. Horses in pasture or wooded areas are more susceptible than those kept in stables.

Although there is no effective treatment for the condition once it appears, food, water, shade, and proper rest are recommended until nature can take its course. The disease in the United States is caused by an eastern or western-strain virus and a third type called VEE (Venezuelan Equine Encephalomyelitis). The eastern variety and VEE produces about 90% mortality, the western is less fatal at 20% to 50%. Vaccines are available to protect against all three strains but immunity

FIGURE 6-4. This mare, unable to rise, contracted VEE (Venezuelan Equine Encephalomyelitis), and later died from the disease. (School of Veterinary Medicine, Texas A & M University)

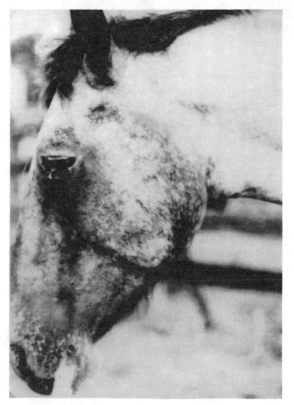

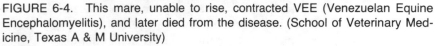

FIGURE 6-5. Horses affected with sleeping sickness often take on a drowsy appearance and may fall asleep even while eating. The foam produced in the mouth of this victim was caused by saliva secreted as the result of a mouthful of oats, which were unchewed because of a sudden desire to sleep. (School of Veterinary Medicine, Texas A & M University)

lasts only for one season. In areas where it has been a problem, vaccination is recommended annually and if possible, control of mosquitoes would appear the most worthwhile objective since outbreaks do not extend to stables where insect control is practiced.

Swamp Fever (Equine Infectious Anemia, EIA)

One of the chief characteristic signs of swamp fever is high fever (105 degrees Fahrenheit or more) and anemia. There is also depression, weakness, loss of appetite, and loss of weight. Horses develop high fever (usually intermittent but may be high and continuous), sweat, lie down, and appear lazy. Attacks often decrease in severity and the animal appears to have recovered. Actually, an affected horse never loses from the blood steam the virus that causes swamp fever and will remain a carrier of the organism although appearing in completely good health. Not all horses recover from the infection; mortality rates average 30% to 70%. A key sign in the disease is a reoccurrence of the swamp fever signs every week or two.

Mosquitoes are a chief cause of the transfer of the virus but it can also be mechanically transferred through the use of hypodermic needles or other unsterilized instruments.

Although there is no effective treatment, control of mosquitoes and flies in the area where outbreaks are known to occur and strict sanitary measures with surgical instruments and hypodermic needles are effective.

A veterinarian can perform a Coggins test to determine if an animal is a carrier. Any horse testing positive for the Coggins test should not be placed with other animals because of the danger of transfer of the virus to healthy animals through mosquitoes and other blood sucking insects.

Tetanus

One of the most dreaded diseases in the horse is tetanus, an infection caused by a bacterium (*Clostridium tetani*) that inhabits the soil in every part of the world. Invasion by this organism is most common through a deep puncture wound but can enter through the umbilical cord of foals as well to create a fatal condition unless treatment occurs rapidly. Even then, chances are poor for survival. Mortalities occur in 80% or more of the cases. Signs of the disease are often not noticed until the disease has progressed. Therefore, it is important to take preventive measures before an injury occurs or when an injury is first noted. Inoculation with a toxoid or antitoxin followed by annual booster injections are wise practices.

A horse affected with tetanus shows stiffness in the joints and a typical "saw horse stance," begins to move about as if it were walking on stilts, and the third eyelid flickers across the eye. This eyelid movement is one of the key signs for which veterinarians look. Coordination is also restricted, jaws eventually lock. For this reason, tetanus is often referred to as lock jaw.

Treatment definitely involves the advice and direction of a veterinarian. Usual treatment involves keeping the animal in a darkened stable and in a quiet area because even the clapping of the hands can produce a nervous reaction to the horse that often results in paralysis or "wild eyed" reactions. Tranquilizers and muscle relaxers are often used to relieve the tension created by the tetanus organism's reaction on nerves and muscles. Diet should be laxative, and plenty of water should be available.

Tying Up Syndrome (Myositis or Cording Up)

Horses afflicted with tying up syndrome begin breathing rapidly with expansion of the nostrils, heavy sweating, and a stiffness of movement. Advanced cases produce coffee-colored urine. This disorder has similar signs to azoturia but the chief difference is that the incidence of stiffness in tying up is not as severe. There may be some relation between the two diseases; the chief difference is that tying up occurs in horses that are worked every day, regardless of method of feeding and handling, whereas azoturia occurs on days when horses are rested without reduction of heavy grain diet.

Tying up is also less dangerous than azoturia. Horses commonly recover in an uneventful manner, whereas, azoturia can often be fatal.

Obviously, there is no way to prevent the disorder, but some work has indicated that vitamin E therapy has a beneficial effect as a form of treatment. The only known recommended method of treatment is to stable the horse, and if during the winter, apply a rub down and a blanket. Veterinarians may use sedatives and tranquilizers to reduce pain.

GASTROIN-TESTINAL PROBLEMS IN HORSES

Colic is not a specific disease but a disease complex, created in many ways. There are special types of colic but the primary cause of difficulty in all cases is a distention of the stomach or intestine which basically produces an abdominal pain.

Equine Colic

One type, called physical colic, which produces a blockage of the intestines, has numerous causes: bad teeth, compactions of lush green feeds, obstructions in the stomach brought about by foreign matter, grain compaction, strangulations of the intestine (twisting), and bloodworm infestations. All of these factors can produce distention, gas, and fluid accumulation, the signs associated with colic.

Another type of colic, called transient colic, is brought on by an inflammation of the intestines from parasites, microorganisms, poisons, or even spasms of the intestines resulting from such things as consumption of cold water when a horse is excessively hot, thunderstorms, and other factors that cause a horse to become excited.

Signs of colic include a gradual to sudden onset of pain which may be intermittent. Pain may cause depression and excessive sweating even when the horse is idle. The pulse may reach 80 to 100 beats per minute. Affected horses walk stiffly, kick toward the stomach, or bite at their flanks. They may assume a "sitting dog" position. Advanced stages may show very red mucous membranes around the mouth, later changing color to blue, indicating a restriction of oxygen supply from the blood. Temperature may increase, up to 102 to 103 degrees Fahrenheit. By placing one ear against the abdomen of the horse, you may hear a foaming or explosive gas noise. Respiration is usually very shallow or labored. A definite sign is to see the horse doing continuous rolls on its back. A healthy horse may lie down in the dust and roll a time or two but usually does not continue this at length. A horse affected by colic may rub the hairs off its back and head trying to get relief from the "tummy ache." If the cause of distention is not removed, death often occurs within 12 to 48 hours.

A most important factor in treatment is judging the severity of the attack. Mild colic can be relieved in an hour or so by simply walking the horse. In more severe cases, it could be fatal. Because of the intense pain, it is necessary to get relief right away in severe cases. A veterinarian should be called at first suspicion; the animal should be kept on its feet and walking until the veterinarian can get there. Do not allow it to lie on its back and roll as this can cause further twisting of the intestines and compound the problem. Treatment usually involves administration of injectable pain relievers and purging with mineral oil, a mild lubricant. Further treatment may be necessary depending on the cause of the obstruction. The pain may be brought on by a variety of disorders including "sand colic," which produces stretching of the intestinal tract and parasite blockage of the intestinal tract. Actually, 90% of colic cases are caused by parasitic infestations, especially strongyles (see Verminous Arteritis), reducing or blocking the flow of blood to segments of the intestines. Although colic should not be confused with founder (laminitis), an attack of colic can lead to the crippling disease of the feet (laminitis) to be discussed later.

Cantharis Poison (Blister Beetle or Spanish Beetle Poisoning)

The Spanish beetle, often called "blister beetle," which is very common in many parts of the southwest can produce severe pain and even death to a horse that ingests sufficient quantities of them. These poisonous insects often feed on alfalfa and may be baled with the hay. The dead beetle, eaten by the horse along with the hay, produces a toxic substance that can cause severe irritation to the mouth and intestinal tract. The horse will show signs of colic (previously discussed) but the pain is not relieved when treatment is applied. There is no effective treatment once the situation occurs.

The only preventive method is to control the beetles in the hay fields. Young colts are very susceptible to the beetles, and cantharis poison often occurs when colts follow the mother eating tender leaves that have been shaken out of alfalfa hay. The beetles are usually in the leaves, and the colts absorb an abnormally large amount because of the selectivity of feeding.

Choking

Gasping for air is a typical sign of choking and can be related to the same situation that occurs in humans. It may be a mild form of choke or a relatively severe case that could cause complete blockage and eventual death. It is not uncommon for horses to choke on ears of corn, apples, or fruit that a well meaning horse owner may offer to them. Most often, the blockage will pass due to the motion of the esophagus, but if the condition persists for 3 or 4 hours, a veterinarian should be consulted.

Although little can be done preventing a horse from choking on an ear of corn or similar morsel that he accidently comes upon, choking can be prevented when feeding a horse tidbits such as apples by simply splitting the apple with a knife so that there is no round surface that might completely block passage of air.

Verminous Arteritis, Mesenteric Arteritis, Bloodworm Colic

Strongyle (worm) infestations (Fig 6-6) produce an intestinal upset due to blockage and inflammation of the mesenteric arteries. This parasite, which migrates through the bloodstream, can accumulate to the point that complete blockage occurs, producing a rupture, and killing the animal. In other cases, it can create a colic-like syndrome (see colic).

The best prevention is to treat very young horses—at 4 to 6 months of age—with a deworming agent and continue this deworming program 3 to 5 times a year for the life of the horse. In the event a preventive program has not been established, treatment for the condition may include massive doses of thiabendazole or drugs recommended by a veterinarian. In any case, once the condition occurs, it should definitely be handled by a veterinarian because of the grave nature of the situation. The preventive program may easily be handled by the layman once proper supervision has been given by a veterinarian or other trained personnel.

Simple Diarrhea

Although it does not occur in horses as often as in cattle and other domestic animals, diarrhea does occur in horses, and is brought on by parasites, abrupt change of feed, engorgement by young foals with too much milk, and numerous bacterial and viral diseases.

Diarrhea is not a particularly dangerous situation and can usually be controlled by relatively simple means. Kaolin/Pectin-type products

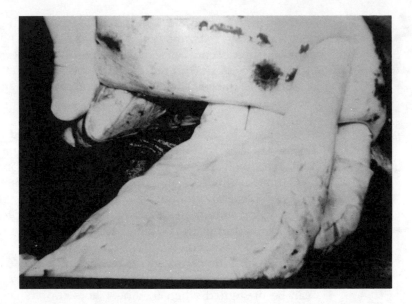

FIGURE 6-6. Surgery performed on this horse revealed an infestation of strongyles producing blockage of intestinal arteries and death of the animal. (School of Veterinary Medicine, Texas A&M University)

may be used as a mild attempt to bring the disorder under control. Usually this will work but if anything stronger is needed, a veterinarian should be consulted.

Colitis X (Acute Colitis)   This condition is a serious inflammation of the large intestine and often occurs in Quarter horses and racing animals. The signs are similar to simple diarrhea, but the condition is more sudden and profuse. The disease is usually secondary to stresses such as a respiratory disease outburst three to four weeks prior, very hard training for a race, or traveling over long, tiring distances. The culprit is rapid dehydration caused by watery diarrhea. This is followed by the production of toxins such as salmonella, E. Coli, and clostridium which creates a severe infection and inflammation as a result. The disease is so insidious that a horse may appear slick, fat, eat its evening ration, and be dead the next morning.

Treatment involves long-term, oral antibiotic therapy, anti-inflammatory drugs, intestinal protectants, and tremendous infusion of intravenous fluids. If the antibiotics can kill out the toxins, mainly salmonella, rehydration is effective, and adequate calories and nutrition can be maintained, then the animal has a chance to redevelop the immune system and survive.

Antiserum can be purchased to protect against acute colitis and there is now a salmonella vaccine to protect against the major toxin, but these are preventative measures only. A horse that is diagnosed with acute colitis must begin treatment immediately.

FOOT AND LEG PROBLEMS

The setting of the feet and legs is extremely important in the correct movement of the horse. Study Figures 5-3 and 5-4 to determine the ideal and commonly faulty setting of feet and legs. The best prevention of disorders is to avoid poorly set legs. However, in addition to poor conformation, accidents and infections may also produce an unsoundness of the feet and legs.

Although the occurrence of the following disorders is not restricted to animals that have poorly set feet and legs, their condition often predisposes the onset of a problem. Probably the greatest challenge to horse owners is problems that can affect the underpinning of their mounts. The various conditions that can occur and their point of occurrence is illustrated in Fig. 6-7. Study this illustration first to get a general idea of where the condition may occur. Once the location of

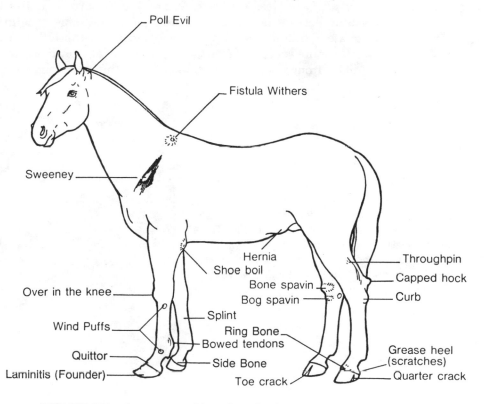

FIGURE 6-7. Anatomy and location of selected unsoundness in the horse.

the defect is noticed, then an in-depth study of a condition that affects that particular area of the horse may yield information on prevention and treatment.

Bowed Tendons (Tendinitis)

An inflammation of the tendon below the knee is generally referred to as bowed tendon or tendinitis (Fig. 6-8). The condition usually erupts when a horse is forced to work quickly without a proper warmup. The malady has been noted most often in the past in race horses, especially Thoroughbreds. It usually affects the inside of only one of the front legs, depending on which direction the horses race. Clockwise horses will have the inside of one leg affected, counterclockwise racers will produce a tendinitis condition on the inside of the opposite leg. In either case, a strained tendon produces swelling in which the horse elevates the heel to reduce pressure. The swelling is hot and painful. Heat around the inflammation may be detected by hand. The most obvious sign is visually comparing the size of one leg with the other. Since the condition normally affects only one leg, it is relatively easy to see. Some horses are prone to strain a tendon at frequent intervals, with less severe results. Others may strain the tendon and show serious lameness for up to a year. Some veterinarians have treated chronic cases by "firing," the use of the hot iron to create an even more severe infection which theoretically produces an acute condition from a chronic infection allowing the body to make a more rapid

FIGURE 6-8. A bowed tendon (tendinitis) most commonly affects only one of the front legs. The cause is usually strain produced by work without proper warmup. Lameness for up to a year is often the result. (School of Veterinary Medicine, Texas A & M University)

recovery. Some laymen have picked up this practice and use it with regularity but it is not recommended unless this rather questionable practice is supervised by a veterinarian. Surgical treatments are also utilized in some instances but in most cases, very little can be done other than complete rest; in some instances, a cast may be applied to the leg.

Although tendinitis is normally thought to be a genetic weakness, it can be caused in any horse when a severe strain is imposed on the legs without first properly warming up the horse. This is perhaps the chief reason horses are walked, galloped, and exercised at a steady pace before they are used in rodeo events, races, and other vigorous activities. The problem is strictly mechanical in nature and the key to prevention is a proper exercise program.

In the event the condition does occur even with the best of precautions, swelling and inflammation can be reduced by the application of cold packs, standing in cold water, and in some instances, the application of a plaster cast for 6 to 8 weeks. Although veterinarians may give injections of cortisone products to reduce the inflammation and swelling, the only real treatment is absolute rest by confinement. The horse owner will need a great deal of patience in this respect because the horse with a severe case of tendinitis will probably be out of commission for at least a year before it can be counted upon to function without the reoccurrence of tendinitis.

Bog Spavin

A bulge or swelling on the front inner side of the hock which has no apparent effect on the horse other than appearance is the first indication of bog spavin (Fig 6-9). Although the bulge is unsightly, heat is rarely felt and lameness seldom occurs with the onset of the swelling. Unless the bulge interferes with action, it does not create lameness.

The condition is thought to be inherited and most often occurs in horses that are straight-hocked. Fluid simply accumulates at the hock joint capsule causing the minor swelling. It is more often seen in young animals that are straight-hocked and worked excessively during early training periods. If signs do develop, the condition can be corrected, in many instances, through special shoes. After maturity, there is less likelihood of bog spavin occurring.

In most cases, no treatment is recommended, but if the condition is severe enough to cause an unsightly appearance, or on rare occasions when it does create lameness, a veterinarian should be consulted for treatment. Most horsemen simply ignore the condition unless it is extremely unsightly.

Bone Spavin

This is a condition that could easily be confused with bog spavin to the uninitiated. Unlike bog spavin, which is not serious, bone spavin

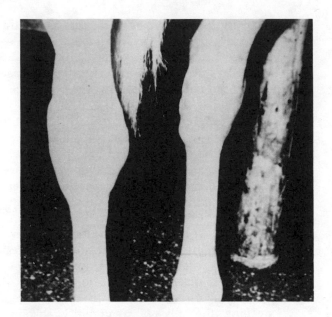

FIGURE 6-9. Bog Spavin is a bulge or swelling on the front inner side of the hock (leg on left). Although unsightly, it normally consists of an accumulation of fluid at the hock joint capsule, which usually does not cause lameness. It is thought to be inherited, seen most often in straight-hocked horses. (School of Veterinary Medicine, Texas A & M University)

involves the inflammation of bone in the hock joint (Fig. 6-10), an enlargement of the bone which can produce lameness. A typical sign is the dragging of a toe by the horse as an indication of lameness in the hind leg. In most instances, the lameness will appear to wear off after a warmup period but the hock, to the trained eye, may still appear stiff in some cases. If bone spavin is suspected, there is a very simple test to confirm suspicions. Pick the leg up for a few minutes before the horse is jogged and if the condition exists, lameness will show up in the first few steps. The test is quite accurate in older horses; younger horses may be more difficult to diagnose because the response is variable. Both legs should be tested as the condition can occur in one and not the other.

Several possibilities could create the problem, including faulty conformation, concussion caused by working on hard surfaces, and mineral deficiencies. Excessive work or exertion in the young horse is especially thought to be harmful. Mild exercise is recommended as a preventive measure, especially with young horses.

Although "firing" has been used in some instances, corrective shoeing to raise the heel and roll the toe is considered a more effective treatment.

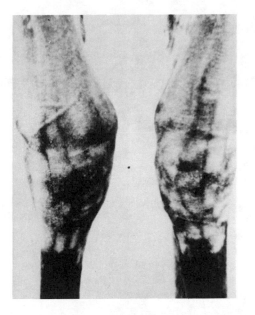

FIGURE 6-10. Bone spavin involves the inflammation of bone in the hock joint, an enlargement which can produce lameness. Rather than an accumulation of fluid as in bog spavin, bone spavin involves a serious disorder often producing lameness. Faulty conformation, pounding on hard pavement, or mineral deficiencies may cause the disorder. (School of Veterinary Medicine, Texas A & M University)

If all else fails, cunean tenectomy (corrective surgery), a procedure to remove the cunean tendon that runs across the bone and under the spavin, will remove the seat of pain. The condition does not go away but since there is no pain, there is no unsoundness. Cunean tenectomy may sound exotic but it is a most common treatment.

Curb

In many instances, curb is only a disfigurement but the horse may show lameness due to a swelling of the back leg directly below the hock (Fig. 6-11) and another enlargement about 3 to 4 inches below the point of the hock. There is obvious swelling, inflammation, and heat at these two spots.

The cause is strongly related to poor conformation with horses that have been stressed by strenuous exercise. The condition is brought on by a thickening of the plantar ligament. The condition normally does not occur in horses with good conformation unless it is from an injury such as a blow to the hock from kicking something solid. A horse with good leg conformation will often recover completely. Horses with poor conformation seldom recover. The best prevention in either case is to prevent injury. Warm up the horse properly before asking it to perform strenuous exercises.

Treatment of a horse with poor conformation is usually a waste of time and money. The condition will occur again and again without permanent recovery. Horses with good conformation will usually fully recover but may have a permanent blemish. Treatment consists of cold water to reduce swelling and pain in the early stages and possibly the

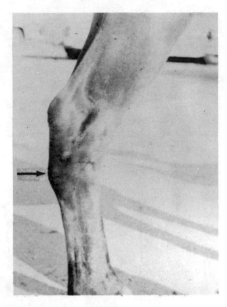

FIGURE 6-11. Curb is a blemish associated with poor leg conformation on horses that have been stressed by strenuous exercise. It may also be caused by a blow to the hock. (School of Veterinary Medicine, Texas A & M University)

use of corticosteroids to reduce inflammation. A complete rest is recommended until the blemish has adequately healed.

Capped Hock

The most obvious sign of this condition is an enlargement of the hock with swelling at the point of the hock. Capped hock may also be accompanied by curb. It is normally brought on by a direct injury such as kicking a solid object.

The injury produces swelling brought on by an accumulation of lubricating fluid from the bursa (the lubricating fluid of the hock) which protects the tendons from friction between bones. Cold water treatments, corticosteroids, and complete rest until recovery are recommended. Capped hock is usually not a serious condition and lameness does not occur but it may produce scar tissue and a permanent blemish.

Corns

Small, naturally occurring corns about the size of a quarter may be seen on either side of the frog, on the inner back side of the hoof (Fig. 6-12). There is often a discoloration, red or reddish-yellow, at the sites. Trimming the feet excessively, especially the front feet, can produce a chronic lameness and tenderness to the front feet. The problem is associated with excessive trimming of the hoof, neglected feet, improper or irregular shoeing, and long and irregular growth. These conditions may throw pressure on the feet, much like a tight pair of shoes would affect a human, creating the visual signs of obvious pain and tenderness. This tenderness may be tested with a hoof tester (Fig. 6-13) to verify the exact location of the discomfort.

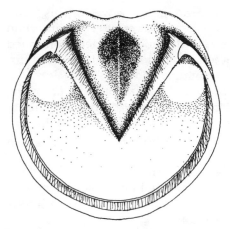

FIGURE 6-12. Corns, about the size of a quarter, on either side of the frog on the inner back side of the hoof, are the result of neglected feet, excessive trimming, improper shoeing, or other conditions that throw pressure on the feet. Corns are often discolored red or reddish-yellow.

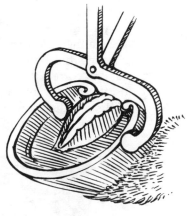

FIGURE 6-13. Hoof tester is used to detect pain-sensitive areas.

In many instances, the blacksmith can recognize and correct the problem by proper trimming and the use of special shoes such as a bar shoe to relieve pressure on the sole of the foot to allow healing. Later, a normal shoe may be returned to the affected feet. In the more severe cases, a veterinarian may have to drain the foot and apply the proper foot baths and antiseptic therapy.

Founder (see Laminitis)

Gravel

This condition is brought about by a crack first in the white line of the foot (see Figure 10-1). This may be caused by an injury, founder, or even a small stone or piece of gravel. Inflammation of the hoof is the result of invasion by microorganisms which work their way up into the foot breaking out in the only place where the foot has any elasticity to it—the heel. Excessively dry feet are prone to this disorder. Lameness usually occurs before the drainage is visible.

The proper draining of the infection, followed by a cleansing and soaking of the foot in Epsom salts, is recommended to further draw out infection. Other treatments include antiphlogistic pastes applied daily directly to the wound under a bandage for a week. This treatment should be continued once every 3 to 4 days after the infection has cleared up. The foot should be kept dry and treatment continued until completely healed. Tincture of iodine is often used to prevent further infection and a tetanus shot is recommended.

Perhaps the best treatment is to prevent the situation from occurring through adequate shoeing and attention to hooves, especially during the dry seasons of the year. Proper diet will also guard against the predisposition of the condition through founder prevention.

Grease Heel (Scratches)

Grease heel or scratches is a mangelike skin condition that affects the pasterns and fetlocks (Fig. 6-14). Poor sanitation measures, muddy lots, etc. are generally thought to be the chief causes although horses vary in their susceptibility to the condition.

Treatment consists of cleaning the skin with warm, soapy water and clipping the hair from the affected areas. The condition is relatively easy to correct through the use of astringents and antiseptic substances if attention is given to the problem quickly. Keeping the barns clean and stalls dry along with regular foot care and trimming are preventive measures that pay excellent dividends.

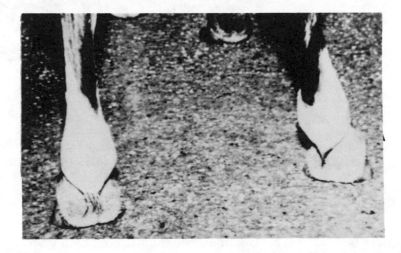

FIGURE 6-14. Grease heel (scratches) is a mange-like condition affecting pasterns and fetlocks. Note the rough scab-like infection caused, in this case, by unsanitary conditions in a muddy lot. (School of Veterinary Medicine, Texas A & M University)

Hoof Cracks

Although horses may have chips and small cracks in their hoof that are not serious, a vertical crack splitting from the coronet downward is

FIGURE 6-15. Hoof cracks are commonly caused by droughty conditions. Hoof dressings and proper shoeing may be necessary to prevent lameness. (School of Veterinary Medicine, Texas A & M University)

a serious, painful disorder. The more common cracks occur from the base of the foot running upward (Fig. 6-15). Several causes are brittle hooves, foot injuries, droughty conditions, and faulty conformation.

These cracks are generally not difficult to treat. Trimming of the hooves and proper shoeing to hold the foot together giving it time to heal is the recommended practice. In very dry sections of the country, it may be necessary to occasionally apply a hoof dressing to provide the necessary pliability to the hoof.

Laminitis (Founder)

Laminitis was given the name because it was thought to be an inflammation of the sensitive laminae of the foot.

The condition was described in France in the 1700s and named founder which means "send below." Research veterinarians have only recently discovered the complexity of the disease and identified it not as a disease of the foot but of the entire system, a systemic disorder. It involves the heart, blood vessels, lungs, kidneys, and endrocrine system. Lameness is only seen at the latter stages (Fig. 6-16). The French description of "send below" referred to the blood supply to the laminae of the hoof. For unknown reasons colic, metritis, or other disorders may result in high blood pressure "sending blood below," but

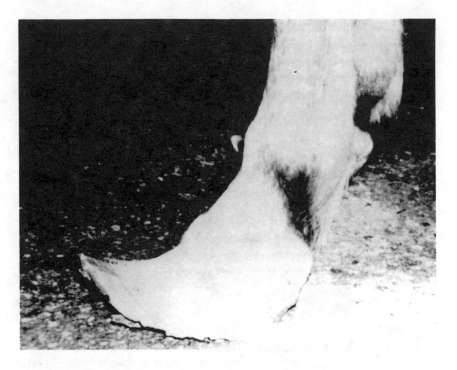

FIGURE 6-16. Founder is a serious disorder in horses producing excessive hoof growth and often permanent lameness. In some cases, the hoof may slough off. (School of Veterinary Medicine, Texas A & M University)

blood is shunted through a bypass thereby denying blood to a part of the foot. The effect is like a rope tightening to strangle the foot. The laminae between the hoof wall and coffin bone begins to die from lack of oxygen. Lameness usually starts at this point and progressively gets worse as the coffin bone rotates downward (Fig. 6-17) separating from the hoof wall and often penetrating the frog. The hoof may slough off. If the coffin bone rotates, the damage is irreparable.

Recent work indicates that it is actually a complex syndrome. Inflammation exists but not in the laminae. It is a general inflammation of the foot region, in which the blood supply is restricted to the laminar structures preventing a normal "cushioned gate." The feet often grow out in a long and grotesque manner.

The developmental phase (which lasts about 48 hours) of laminitis is an increase in the heart and pulse rate and an elevated temperature as high as 104 degrees Fahrenheit. Endocrine glands change hormonal output.

The acute stage starts with signs of lameness and lasts no longer

Foundered   Normal   Foundered

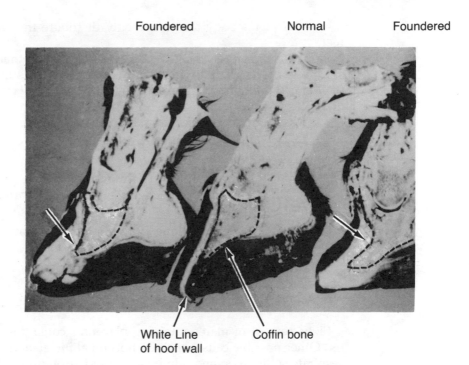

White Line   Coffin bone
of hoof wall

FIGURE 6-17. Founder (laminitis), a complex disorder affecting the feet, causes irreparable damage if the coffin bone rotates away from the hoof wall. Note normal alignment of coffin bone with hoof wall in center cross section compared to foundered specimens. (School of Veterinary Medicine, Texas A & M University)

than 48 hours. If the horse withstands this period, it seldom suffers permanent hoof damage.

The chronic stage occurs if and when the coffin bone rotates. Rotation usually occurs 6 to 12 hours after lameness is detected. If this happens, permanent unsoundness results, and the coffin bone and hoof cannot be rejoined.

In early stages, there exists an obviously painful lameness in the front feet, sometimes all four feet, followed by unusual growth of the hooves that must be trimmed often. Horses will often assume a stance that decreases the weight on the affected feet. Horses that have only the front feet affected, will stand with their hind feet well up under the body to remove as much weight as possible from the heel of the front feet. If all four feet are foundered, the horse may lie down for long periods and even refuse to get up. When standing, if all four feet are affected, the horse tries to pull both front and hind feet in closer to the center of his body to more evenly distribute the weight over the feet.

Laminitis or founder may be related to colic and other disorders but should not be confused with them. Laminitis is a result of some form of shock to the horse. There are five main causes of laminitis:

1. Road founder, caused by riding on hard surfaces
2. Grass founder, resulting from excessive consumption of lush green grass early in the spring
3. Grain founder (colic, the number one disease predisposing the horse to laminitis), caused by engorgement of rich carbohydrates such as corn or grain sorgum
4. Water founder, resulting from a large intake of very cold water when a horse is overheated
5. Metritis retained placenta, which creates a shock to the system of a mare that has just foaled and is suffering from infection from the retention of the afterbirth.

Sixty percent of mares retaining placentas come down with laminitis. Other possible causes include hormonal imbalances in mares, viral respiratory diseases, and administration of strong purgatives.

Treatment may include standing in mud puddles or cold water to reduce swelling of the blood vessels, or treatment by a veterinarian with hypodermic medications. In most cases, the damage is irremediable, and corrective shoeing and trimming of the feet is the only possible recourse.

Navicular Disease

A painful mechanical problem usually affecting the front feet is navicular disease. A tendon passes over the navicular bone, and some injuries such as pounding on hard pavement may cause this bone to change its shape and texture creating a painful sensation because of irritation to the tendon that runs over the rough surface. The deep flexer tendon of the foot is usually the chief tendon involved. The condition is not easily diagnosed but most horses will "point" with the affected foot when in the resting stage.

Although it is an inherited characteristic, it could be brought on by excessive pounding. In either case, the only treatment is to relieve the pressure of the tendon by using shoes with thinly rolled toes and thick heels. If this does not correct the situation, a veterinarian can denerve the tendon, completely eliminating the pain to the horse. There is some risk with this method because the horse may be prone to stumbling and a horse that is used for a child's mount or used in critical situations should not be used. However, the operation is safe and very successful and may add many years of effective use to the average recreation horse.

Quittor

The chief clinical sign of quittor is a chronic inflammation of the coronary band of the hoof which manifests itself in a deep seated running sore, usually on the front feet only. A puncture wound or other traumatic injury to the foot brings on the condition which reduces blood circulation in the foot. Inflammation must be reduced by drainage and antiseptics. Surgery has been used on occasions to remove infected material but has not been uniformly successful, sometimes resulting in hoof mutilation.

The most effective treatment appears to be opening the wound by surgical means to allow drainage and the application of a poultice to draw the infection from the foot. One such poultice is Denver Mud (Demco Co., Denver, Colorado). A mild antiseptic solution applied several times a day may also be beneficial in preventing further infection. The foot is usually bandaged to allow greater effectiveness of the poultice and to speed healing.

Ring Bone

Two types of ring bone may exist: a "low" ring bone affecting the coronet region and a "high" ring bone directly above the coronet. Although the high ring bone (Fig. 6-18) can be felt, the lower variety cannot be seen without an x-ray. In either case, the condition is an enlargement of the pastern bone resulting in a constant lameness. Finger pressure to the area will bring about a flinching reaction from the horse. It is usually caused by trauma such as a direct blow. Heat, swelling, and pain are the result creating the new bone growth. For unknown reasons, it is seldom seen in Thoroughbred horses but virtually all other breeds are susceptible to it.

The condition can also be brought about by pulling of the ligaments, so the hooves should not be allowed to grow too long, thus, saving the frog from the work of shock absorption to the feet. Proper shoeing will usually prevent the occurrence of the conditions that lead to ring bone and this is especially needed in clumsy horses because of their tendency to slap the ground or otherwise injure themselves.

Once ring bone occurs, the first step in treatment is complete rest. Cold packs may reduce the inflammation but more permanent relief is often found by "blistering" the area with an irritant which speeds up nature's reaction to heal. Cortisone may be used to reduce swelling and in some instances "firing" may be recommended. More severe cases may be handled by denerving the area. The same principle applies here that was previously discussed (denerving of the navicular bone).

FIGURE 6-18. Ring bone is an enlargement of bony growth of the pastern bone resulting in constant lameness. It is usually caused by a direct blow or pounding on hard surfaces. (School of Veterinary Medicine, Texas A & M University)

Shoe Boil

Shoe boil, also known as olecranon bursitis, or capped elbow, is a flabby swelling at the point of the elbow brought about by trauma (Fig. 6-19). It is similar to capped hock of the rear leg except the injury occurs to the elbow of the front leg. The most common cause of shoe boil is leaving a heavy heel when shoeing horses, the horse hitting himself with the shoe of the same foot on the same leg, stamping the feet to ward off flies, and improper bedding. Horses shod with the heel of the hoof left too long or those shod with elevated or weighted shoes most often produce the trauma necessary to produce shoe boil. The fact that the flabby condition is created by the shoe itself gives it the name.

In most instances, the condition is merely unsightly and does not often create lameness. The swelling may develop only after repeated trauma and even then may fluctuate in size.

The best method of prevention is to determine the exact cause of the trauma and then remove or reduce the incidence of that occurrence. Proper shoeing of horses or the use of a "doughnut" or bell boot (Fig. 6-20), a rubber device that fits around the ankle protecting the elbow from blows, can eliminate the problem if corrective shoeing does not do the job. A long standing injury or one that has become infected may need to be treated by a veterinarian. Long standing injuries composed of fibrous tissue may have to be surgically removed. Once the cause is removed, an injection of corticosteroid will often reduce the swelling and clear up the problem with only one treatment.

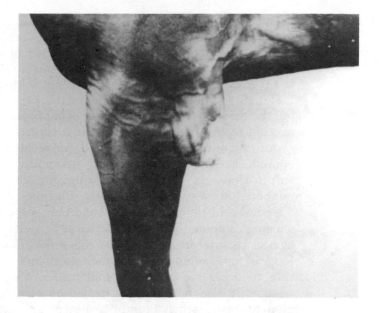

FIGURE 6-19.   Severe case of shoe boil (capped elbow) showing an excessive flabby swelling caused by trauma of the heel of the foot (or shoe) striking the elbow. (School of Veterinary Medicine, Texas A & M University)

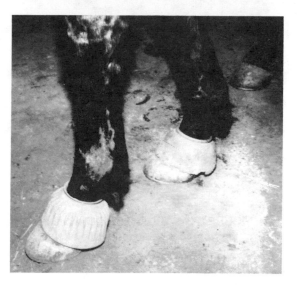

FIGURE 6-20.   A bell boot, a rubber device that slips over the front hoof, protects the horse from striking its own elbow with the shoe of the same foot on the same leg, thus guarding against shoe boil. This device also protects rear feet from injuring front pasterns by overstepping.

Side Bones   This condition usually occurs on either side of the front foot, seldom occurring in the hind feet. A build-up of bone (ossification) may occur on either side of the back part of the hoof just above the coronet (Fig. 6-21). In many instances, the ossification is so slight it cannot be seen. In other cases, it is more pronounced but seldom results in lameness.

Heredity probably plays a part in the predisposition to side bones but the most often suspected cause is improper shoeing, causing a contraction of the hoof at the heel, or a concussion to the foot brought about by pounding on pavement or an accidental injury. Interestingly enough, side bones are seen very frequently in mules but seldom result in lameness. On the other hand, for some strange reason, Thoroughbred horses seldom have this affliction.

Removal of the cause of the condition is the best treatment. Proper shoeing combined with the practice of "grooving" (cutting a small horizontal channel in the hoof to relieve the tension in one area of the foot) is most often recommended to relieve pressure from the hoof thus reducing the producing trauma. More serious cases which have resulted in lameness may be treated by blistering of the coronary region for faster relief. Prompt treatment and preventive measures are swift in returning the horse to normal.

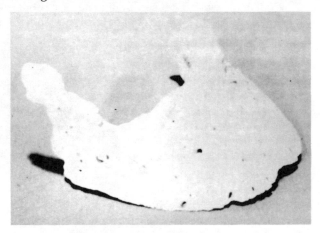

FIGURE 6-21.   Build-up of bone occurring just above the coronet on either side of the front foot is characteristic of *side bone*. The build-up may be pronounced as in this dramatic illustration but seldom results in lameness. (School of Veterinary Medicine, Texas A & M University)

Splints   The cannon bone, usually the inside of the front legs only, is the area most often affected by splints. The bony enlargement of the splint bones can be seen as well as felt and although the condition occurs frequently on the inside of front legs, it occurs infrequently on rear legs, and then confined to the outside of the rear cannon bones. This build up of bony growth is usually associated with horses under two years of age and brought on by hard training, poor nutrition, or faulty conformation. If the horse is not thoroughly warmed up, the trauma of slipping, running, falling, or jumping can induce the problem. As horses grow older, they are less prone to develop splints, 3- to 4-year old horses rarely being affected, and horses over 6 years of age almost never.

Boots or bandages are often worn by young horses to reduce the risk of splints. This is especially the case if excessively hard training is required of immature legs. Once the condition does occur, complete rest is recommended for at least 6 weeks. Blistering agents or "firing" may be recommended as a treatment. Cold treatment or injections of cortisone may also be recommended by veterinarians to speed recovery. Use of an antiphlogistic pack has been effective in reducing swelling. With rest and only walking exercise during the 6-week convalescence period, the condition is readily healed. The condition can be compared to "shin splints" which occur in young human athletes with regularity. In both cases, the leg disorders respond well to rest.

Stringhalt

This condition is more an aggravation than an unsoundness. The chief sign is an involuntary flexion upward of the hind legs (Fig. 6-22), most evident when backing a horse. The foot may be flexed so high that it actually hits the abdominal wall. The foot may just as violently descend to strike the ground. Stringhalt is considered a gross un-

FIGURE 6-22. Stringhalt is an involuntary flexion upward of the hind legs. The foot may just as violently descend to strike the ground. (School of Veterinary Medicine, Texas A & M University)

soundness but does not materially affect the ability of the horse to work.

The cause is thought to be a lesion of nerves leading to the hock or stifle. The condition can be corrected by surgical procedures to remove the tendon of the lateral digital flexor tendon. This will frequently relieve the tension, at least partially.

Sweeny

Atrophy (withering away) of the muscles in the slope of the shoulder, Sweeny (Fig. 6-23) is caused by paralysis of the suprascapular nerve usually due to a kick, collision, or sudden backward movement of the forelimb. The muscles at the forward point of the shoulder waste away causing a prominent appearance of the shoulder blade. In stepping foward on the affected limb, the shoulder may snap outward.

This is a nerve injury and although cold compresses and phenylbutazone during the first 24 hours after injury may help, there is no proven treatment. If the injury is temporary, recovery may be forthcoming within a couple of months. Observation and rest for 6 months or so is necessary to determine if the injury is permanent.

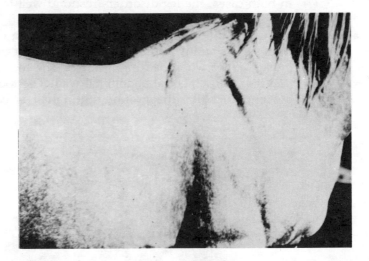

FIGURE 6-23. Sweeny is a withering away of the muscles in the slope of the shoulder. Note the depression just forward of the point of the shoulder. Atrophy of these muscles was brought about by a nerve injury from a collision. (School of Veterinary Medicine, Texas A & M University)

Thoroughpin

This condition may at first be confused with bog spavin. The main difference is that thoroughpin occurs as a "bulge," a puffy swelling in the web of the hock. It may be differentiated from bog spavin by simple palpation with the fingers. Pressure will cause it to move from one side of the leg to the other, whereas, bog spavin does not move. The condition is brought on by excessive strain, especially to the hocks of young, immature horses. Faulty conformation is the key predisposing factor.

Rest, treatment with liniments or massage, and cortisone injections may be required.

Thrush

Thrush is a condition brought about by poor sanitation and improper cleaning of the feet. It is most commonly found in the hind feet, the first sign being an offensive foot odor. It may also occur in the front feet, but not as often. In either case, the clinical signs are a degeneration of the frog of the foot (Fig. 6-24), black discharge, and an offensive odor.

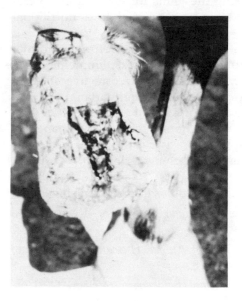

FIGURE 6-24. Clinical signs of thrush are a degeneration of the frog of the foot, black discharge, and an offensive odor. Thrush is most often caused by poor sanitation and improper footcare. (School of Veterinary Medicine, Texas A & M University)

The most important method of preventing the condition is to house horses in dry, clean stalls. It is most often associated with muddy, unsanitary lots. Proper trimming and hoof care will also reduce the incidence of thrush in those cases where muddy conditions cannot be avoided.

Treatment involves trimming away of the affected area, cleansing the foot and applying an antiseptic. Thrush remedies abound and are in use throughout the country. Copper sulfate used as a foot bath is among the most common treatments used. Others are iodine, formalin, creolin, carbolic acid, and numerous commercial preparations simply referred to as "thrush treatments," most of which contain some form of iodine. An alternate suitable thrush dressing may be made by mixing one part formalin with three parts water.

In mild cases, drying solutions like Kopertox in combination with a formalin solution may be applied directly to the frog area. Close observation should be made and if thrush affects the sensitive structures of the foot, tetanus antitoxin or toxoid should be given.

Wind Puffs (Wind Gall)

A small swelling just above the fetlock is the clinical sign of wind puffs. This small pocket of fluid accumulation arises from a strain within the joint. It is commonly seen in hard working horses, especially those that are ridden over rough terrain, or on hard pavement; race horses; etc. Just as human joggers create strain producing swollen ankles and knees, the horse similarly reacts by the secretion of excessive synovial fluid (fluid surrounding the joints for lubrication) to create the swelling. Another cause may be attributed to a nutritional deficiency.

In most instances, the condition is not serious and return to normal is swift with relatively simple treatments of cold packs, liniments, massage, or blistering agents. If lameness does occur, corrective shoeing with wedge heels may sometimes be helpful. Veterinarians may administer a corticosteroid intrasynovially or drain the joint capsule and apply an elastic support bandage. Young horses may need a change or adjustment of diet. If lameness appears, rest and the same treatment used for arthritis may be recommended by the veterinarian.

BIBLIOGRAPHY

Adams, O. R. *Lameness in Horses*. Philadelphia, PA: Lea & Febiger.

Blakely J., & Bade, D. *The Science of Animal Husbandry*. Reston, VA: Reston Publishing Co., 1979.

Blakely, J., & King, D. *The Brass Tacks of Animal Husbandry*. St. Louis, MO: Doane Agricultural Services, 1978.

Bradbury, P., & Werk, S. *Horse Nutrition Handbook*. Houston, TX: Cordovan Corp, 1974.

Equine Research Publications. *The Illustrated Veterinary Encyclopedia for Horsemen*, M. M. Vale, ed. Dallas, TX: Equine Research Publications, 1977.

Merck & Co., Inc. *The Merck Veterinary Manual*. Rahway, NJ, 1967.

Slahor, S. *The Laymen's Guide to Horse Health Care*. Houston, TX: Cordovan Corp, 1978.

Wagoner, D. M. *Veterinary Treatment and Medications for Horsemen*. Dallas, TX: Equine Research Publications, 1977.

7
Parasites

Most horsemen are vaguely aware of the term parasite and its meaning and relation to horses. External parasites such as flies, lice, mange, gnats, and other flying, creeping, crawling things are relatively easy to see. The most devastating forms of parasites however, are often not visible to the naked eye. There are at least 150 types of internal parasites that affect horses. Most of these are bacteria and protozoa, forms of "microscopic bugs" that affect the health of all living things. Others are internal worms, some of which at maturity can be a foot or more in length.

Parasitic organisms develop mostly in the alimentary tract, lungs, body cavity, and blood stream. Just as we desire to live in certain sections of the country because of preference to a style of living or environment, parasites prefer living in areas suitable to their needs, such as the stomach, liver, lungs, small or large intestines, etc. No matter where they are, they create damage to the horse and must simply be controlled, since elimination is virtually impossible.

PARASITE CONTROL

Before taking up specific organisms that influence the health and vigor of horses, preventive measures that guard against parasitic infections should be discussed. Prevention is always cheaper than treatment and cure.

A sanitation and health program is indispensable in controlling all forms of parasites. Although chemical dewormers are relied on heavily to maintain the health of horses, they should be used only in a supportive program of total health care. There may be instances—for example, with an ill horse or a pregnant mare—in which chemical treatment with dewormers is dangerous or impractical.

The first step in parasite control is to monitor the droppings of the horse to check for parasite eggs. Stool samples should be checked at 60 to 90 day intervals. At the first sign of parasite eggs, action should be taken and continued on a regular basis barring the previously mentioned exceptions.

An animal's ability to resist an attack of parasites is greatly affected by the nutritional level of the horse. Maintaining adequate levels of energy and the other essential elements previously discussed in Chapter 4 will assure the horse owner that the animal is in good condition to resist attacks to the fullest and build up as much natural resistance as possible.

Regardless of precautions under today's management system, it is impossible in most cases to rear horses in a parasite free environment. It is also recognized that dewormers used in the feed will not completely control parasite invasions and buildups. Although it may assist in keeping down infestations, the use of dewormers in the feed is not the most effective method. By far, the best approach is to "tube" a horse by passing a tube through the nose and directly into the stomach, bypassing any selectivity by poor or picky eaters. This tubing should not be done by amateurs because of the possibility of passing the tube into the lungs and giving the horse pneumonia.

A relatively convenient, simple, effective alternative to tubing is the use of paste or gel deworming agents, designed for application with a plastic syringe. The medicine adheres to the horse's mouth, thus reducing loss of medication. In addition, some paste dewormers are effective against early stages of botfly larvae in the mouth. A close approximation of the horse's weight must be known since doses are calculated accordingly. The disposable syringe is inserted in the interdental space between the teeth, passed to the back of the tongue, and the plunger depressed to release contents in the mouth. Chemical deworming agents administered only two times per year are now recognized as insufficient to control most parasites. Horses should be dewormed quarterly and the chemical treatment should be repeated 3 to 4 weeks after the initial dosage to assure expulsion of immature parasites that may have developed after the first deworming took place. Some establishments, in areas where parasites are extremely difficult to control, recommend deworming 6 to 12 times per year. The normal recommendation is to deworm early in the spring and repeat the treatment 3 weeks later, then repeat at 6 months from that date and again

3 weeks following. This procedure is followed in order to kill the adults as well as the immature stages of parasites. Since some parasites become drug resistant, it is recommended that 2 or 3 worming agents be used alternately to get the most effective control.

Some areas of the south especially have difficulty in controlling parasites because of the lack of freezing and thawing temperatures, which tend to serve as a natural control of parasites, larvae, and eggs. Northern latitudes produce less difficulty with parasites, especially during severe weather patterns.

As a horse grows older, it tends to develop some immunity to parasites, but all horses are susceptible to most parasites. The young horses, because of a lack of immunity buildup, are simply more affected by them.

The greatest factor in preventing parasite infestations, buildups, and reinoculations is a strict sanitation program. Stalls should be cleaned daily and if possible manure should be removed from stalls and kept in a pit that will allow the natural heat generated from it to destroy worm eggs. Keeping these manure piles away from young horses also helps reduce cross inoculation because foals have a tendency to pick around in manure and bedding thereby ingesting parasite eggs.

A good pasture management program will reduce or control parasitic attacks. These simple rules to follow will enable the average horseman to reduce parasitic infections to a minimum.

1.   Worm all horses simultaneously to reduce the possibility of reinfesting an animal that has been treated.

2.   If possible, do not mix horses of different age in the same pasture. As previously discussed, older horses are more immune to parasites but may be carriers of organisms that could be deadly to young horses.

3.   Plowing or harrowing of the pasture in the spring to allow the sunlight to sterilize worm eggs is advisable. Spreading of the manure or even shredding of pastures will help reduce most organisms as they do not grow and thrive in a dry, hot environment.

4.   Avoid grazing pastures extremely close to the ground because of the horse's ability to get its teeth next to the soil and picking up eggs of parasites.

5.   The parasite population may be reduced by a rotation pasture grazing system using two different species, such as cattle and horses. Different species do not normally carry the same parasites. A 60-to-90-day pasture rotation with horses following cattle is recommended.

TYPES OF PARASITES

INTERNAL
PARASITES

Ascarids or roundworms (Fig. 7-1) commonly affect very young horses that have not built up an immunity for resistance to them. Only rarely do they affect horses 4 to 5 years or older. The first signs in infected foals are usually a rough haircoat, pot belly, and slower growth. Colic and diarrhea may also be present. Because of the migra-

Ascarids
(Roundworms)

(a)

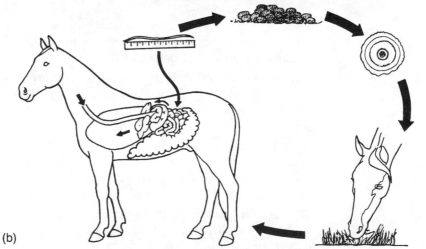

(b)

FIGURE 7-1. (a) Ascarids (roundworms) in the intestines of this young foal caused a rupture, peritonitis, and death. The life cycle (b) differs from strongyles in that damage is done in the liver and lungs. Larvae coughed up and swallowed mature in the stomach, produce eggs, and complete the cycle. (Shell Chemical Co., San Ramon, California)

tion of the larvae in the lungs, a dry hacking cough is also quite commonly present.

Ascarids are the largest of the parasites affecting horses, ranging from 5 to 15 inches in length and nearly a half inch in diameter at full growth.

The eggs of the roundworm are ingested via contaminated feed or water. The eggs hatch in the intestine and the larvae penetrate the intestinal wall migrating to the liver and lungs. Ascarids grow and develop in these organs creating a great deal of destruction before they invade the respiratory passage, creating the hacking cough previously mentioned. The larvae thus coughed up or swallowed return to the intestines, mature, and remain there. Adult worms may become so large and numerous that they cause partial obstruction, and colic in foals. A massing of the worms can create digestive disturbances or a rupture of the intestine, a frequent occurrence in foals, spilling poisonous wastes into the body cavity and creating peritonitis and death.

Ascarids are difficult to control because the adults remain in the intestinal cavity but produce eggs that pass out in the feces thereby contaminating pasture, feed, and water. A complete cycle from egg to mature adult takes only 3 months.

Treatment is relatively simple and effective. When foals are 8 weeks old, treatment with a chemical deworming agent should be initiated and repeated at 8-week intervals until foals are yearlings. A common deworming agent is piperazine given at the rate of 4 gm/100 lb. Table 7-1 lists other products that are equally effective.

Bots

Three major species of bots that exist in the United States are the *common bot*, the *nose bot*, and the *throat bot*. Although the life cycles of these species are similar, they are not identical. Since there is only slight variation, they will all be discussed together. Bots are caused by a fly that lives only about 2 weeks and in itself is not a parasite. However, this fly lays eggs on the hairs of the horse, especially about the neck, shoulder, and legs. In the case of the common bot, the eggs are layed on the hairs of the horse's legs (Fig. 7-2). The horse stimulates development in the eggs by warmth, moisture, and action of the horse's lips in instinctively trying to clean the eggs from its legs. This activates the egg to produce a larva that attaches in the mucosa of the mouth and tongue. This development takes only 2 to 3 days. The larva remains in the mouth for about 30 days and eventually migrates to the stomach, attaching itself to the lining of some part of the digestive system to feed off blood. Bots remain attached to the lining of the stomach for 8 to 10 months and may become so numerous that an autopsy reveals a sight similar to, and about the size of, pencil erasers lined up side by side (Fig. 7-3).

Table 7-1.
Common Deworming Agents and Their Effectiveness in Removing Horse Parasites

Wormer	Dose Level	Average Removal Expectancy (%)			
		Bots	Roundworms (Ascarids)	Strongyles (Bloodworms, palisade worms)	Pinworms
Dichlorvos[1]	1.6 gm/100 lb	80–100	95–100	70–100	90–100
Pyrantel[2]	.33 gm/100 lb	0	90–100	75–100	60–70
Thiabendazole[3]	2 gm/100 lb	0	10–30	90–100	90–100
Thiabendazole plus piperazine	2 + 2.5 gm/100 lb	0	95–100	95–100	30–40
Piperazine	4 gm/100 lb	0	95–100	10–60	50–70
Phenothiazine plus piperazine plus carbon disulfide	1.25 + 4 gm/100 lb	78–85	95–100	95–100	50–70
Phenothiazine plus piperazine	1.25 + 4 gm/100 lb	0	95–100	90–100	50–70
Piperazine plus carbon disulfide	4 gm/100 lb	78–85	95–100	40–60	40–60
Trichlorfon	1.8 gm/100 lb	90–100	95–100	0–10	90–100

Source: Blakely and King, *The Brass Tacks of Animal Health*, Doane Agricultural Service. 1978
Adapted from Gabby Hoeppner, D.V.M., *Horse and Horseman*, April 1977. Reprinted with permission.
Note: Trades names 1. Atvard, Shell Chemical Co.; 2. Banminth, Pfizer and Co.; 3. Thibenzole, Merck and Co.

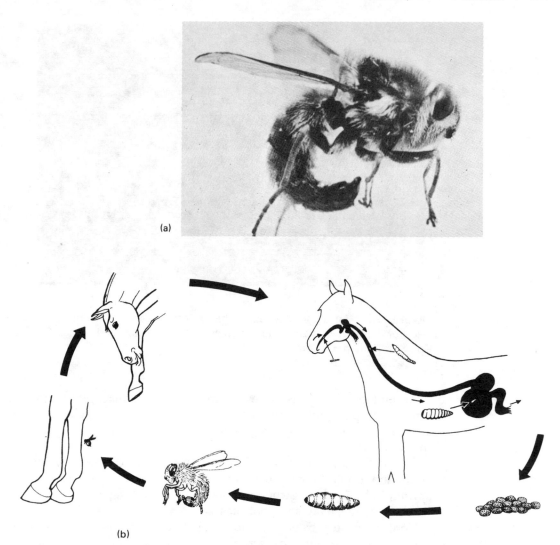

(a)

(b)

FIGURE 7-2.   The common bot fly (a) lays eggs in the spring on the leg hairs. Eggs are hatched by the stimulation of the horse's lips, producing larvae that migrate to the stomach where they attach and mature during the winter. Larvae are expelled with feces, pupate in the soil, and hatch out the following spring to produce another bot fly in the continuing cycle.

The nose and throat bots do not need stimulation by the moisture of the horse's mouth and the action of licking. They migrate directly to the mouth area without stimulation and develop in a similar manner. All three forms imbed themselves in the mucous linings of the mouth and eventually migrate to the stomach.

FIGURE 7-3. An autopsy revealed this severe infestation of bots, the larvae stage of the bot fly, attached to the lining of the stomach wall. (Shell Chemical Co., San Ramon, California)

About 8 or 10 months of development in the stomach is required before larvae pass out to pupate in the soil. About 4 weeks later, the adult bot fly hatches and begins to lay eggs again on legs, nose, and throat areas.

Bot flies are most active in most parts of the country during late summer and fall. In some parts of the southwest, they are active in the spring, subside during the summer, and appear again in the fall. A hard freeze inactivates the bot flies.

Control of the eggs is quite simple since they are visible to the naked eye. Proper grooming by scraping with a knife or curry comb and sponging with warm water is helpful to either remove the eggs or cause them to hatch when the larvae can be washed away 2 to 3 days later with another sponge bath.

The most effective method of control for bots is through the use of the chemical agent Trichlorfon (1.8 gm/100 lb.) used as a drench about 30 days after a frost has killed the flies. Table 7-1 gives other recommended chemical treatments.

Intestinal Threadworms

The small intestine of young foals under 6 months of age is the site of attachment by intestinal threadworms. They tend to disappear after the foal reaches 6 months of age. Although there is speculation that this infection may cause diarrhea, there is little definite research to support this theory.

The only known method of transmission is by the larvae being transmitted to the foal in the mare's milk.

Infections respond well to treatment with thiabendazole. A regular program of deworming is recommended as the best preventive. Table 7-1 gives recommended levels for the various chemical deworming agents.

Pinworms (Oxyuris)

Most commonly found in foals, pinworms may also be found in the mature horse. The main source of irritation is to the anal opening around the tail which produces an itching sensation. A "rattailed" appearance brought on by rubbing of the tail hairs against a fence or tree is the most common sign of pinworm presence.

Eggs of the pinworm are picked up in feed or water, mature in the intestines (Fig. 7-4), and migrate to the rectum and anus. Eggs are released around the anus and may pass out with the feces or may contaminate stable walls, trees, and fences due to horses rubbing their tails against these objects. It takes about 5 months from infection to maturity.

Pinworm infestations are normally not treated specifically. Treatment of other forms of parasitic infestations will normally take care of

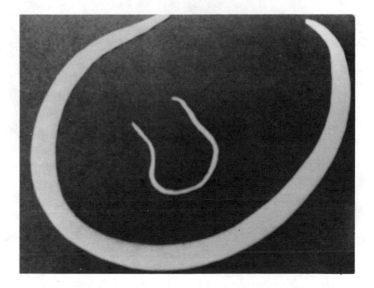

FIGURE 7-4. Pinworms (oxyuris) are whitish, may measure up to almost an inch in length, and can be seen in the feces of infested horses. The male (center) is much smaller than the female. (USDA)

these parasites as well; however, Table 7-1 gives specific recommendations for chemical agents effective on pinworms.

Stomach Worms

Gastric irritability, poor digestion, and colic may be brought on by an infestation of stomach worms. Location of this parasite is primarily in the stomach rather than the intestines, thus the name. The larvae from the stomach worm may also externally invade the skin through wounds, the eyes, and abrasions to create "summer sores," a lesion with pus pockets that is obviously infective in appearance.

Abscesses may be produced in the lungs and stomach as a result of invasion by the larvae. Visible signs may be limited to gastritis or digestive disturbances.

The house fly or stable fly (Fig. 7-5) serves as an intermediate host in spreading the stomach worm. Larvae are transferred from the fly to the lips of the horse. For this reason, a fly-free environment is necessary to reduce chances of stomach worm infestation. Stable hygiene and fly control is the best method of control but chemical wormers such as piperazine (Table 7-1) are also effective.

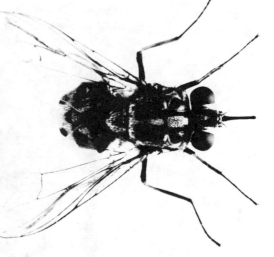

FIGURE 7-5. The stablefly, or common housefly, serves as an intermediate host in the spread of stomach worms and other parasites or diseases. (USDA)

Strongyles (Bloodworms— Palisade Worms)

Signs of strongyle attack include fever, lack of appetite, weakness, emaciation, depression, colic, constipation, diarrhea, and anemia. There may be other signs as well but the most characteristic sign is anemia caused by the "bloodworm" sucking blood. The large strongyle or bloodworm (Fig. 7-6) is the most dangerous of all internal parasites.

Two groups of strongyles, the large strongyles and the small stron-

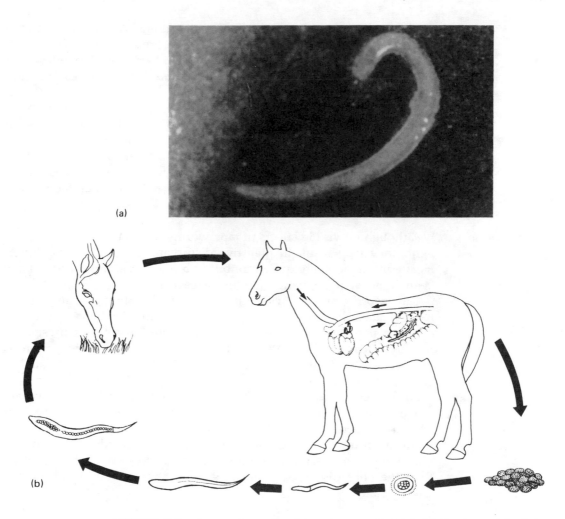

FIGURE 7-6. Large strongyles (a) are worms that inhabit the large intestine, and lay eggs that mature to larvae in the excreted manure. Larvae crawl up grass stems and are ingested by the horse to complete the cycle. Migration takes place through the stomach and circulatory system back to the large intestine where eggs are laid.

gyles, cause the heaviest damage. Eggs that pass out in the droppings develop in less than a week. This intestinal parasite is especially dangerous because it may lay as many as 5,000 eggs per day, any one of which could be picked up by a grazing animal and create a severe infestation. The larvae are swallowed, migrate to the digestive system, penetrate the intestine, and proceed through blood vessels creating damage to the arteries. The larvae may attack such essential organs as the heart, liver, and the abdominal cavity lining. Adults attach themselves to the intestines, suck blood, and produce eggs which are passed out in the feces and restart the cycle. Larvae are not effectively controlled by deworming agents until the adult stage when they appear in the intestine.

A recommended dewormer is Thiabendazole (2 gm/100 lbs. of body weight). This is a particularly effective dewormer because it is low on the scale of toxicity to the horse. Treatment should be repeated quarterly during the year for effective control. Thiabendazole is also effective for ascarids so these two internal parasites may be treated simultaneously with good results. Consult Table 7-1 for other recommendations.

Tape Worms   Although no visible effects of tape worms are seen if infestations are light, they may result in digestive disturbances and poor condition. Heavy infestations are quite rare but in a few cases, tape worms have been responsible for perforation of the caecum.

Tape worms are relatively rare in horses but they are mentioned here because they are most often brought to mind when the thought of internal parasites arises. The orbatid mite, sometimes present in pastures, is an intermediate host for tape worms. Two to four months of development in the mites are necessary before they are ingested to create tape worm infestations.

Fortunately, since tape worms are relatively rare in horses, we are not normally concerned with them and specific treatments have not been developed.

Although numerous equine parasites exist worldwide, only those of major importance have been discussed here. For the most part, other than the ones discussed in this chapter, they are found outside the United States.

EXTERNAL PARASITES   Fly, mosquito, lice, and mite control is best accomplished by destroying breeding sites for these external parasites. Rotting organic matter, manure, standing water, and poorly drained areas are a hot bed of activity for the breeding of external parasites. Stalls and stables should be kept clean of rotting matter and disinfected at periodic intervals.

A poor hair coat is usually the first sign of external parasitic problems, especially in the case of lice or mites. The neck, head, and flank are first signs of infestations but more severe outbreaks can affect the entire horse.

As previously discussed, it is necessary to control flies because of their ability to transmit intestinal parasites to the horse. Mosquitoes are known transmitters of sleeping sickness, and mites, as previously discussed, can be an intermediate host for tape worms.

Lice create injuries to the horse because of itching and scratching. Control of all external parasites can be greatly facilitated by cleaning up around the stable and farm. Numerous repellents are on the market that serve as a supplementary control program. A combination of these practices will pay large dividends.

Horseflies

A blood sucking insect, the horsefly is not only annoying to the horse but painful. They are known carriers of anthrax and probably transmit other diseases.

Horseflies vary in size from ½ inch to 1½ inches long. Eggs are layed on stones or vegetation around water and when hatched fall into the water and burrow into the mud. They pupate for about a year, emerging as an adult fly that can operate many miles away from their watery breeding grounds.

Repellents are not generally effective, especially against the smaller varieties. Preventive measures include destruction of their shallow water breeding grounds, when possible, by draining swamps, deepening the edges of ponds, etc.

FIGURE 7-7.　Horseflies are bloodsucking insects that not only annoy horses but are known carriers of anthrax and probably other diseases. (USDA)

Stableflies

More commonly known as houseflies (Fig. 7-5), the stablefly is an aggressive blood sucker that causes pain to both humans and animals. This blood sucking characteristic enables it to also transmit serious diseases.

Stableflies take their toll on an animal due to the worry it causes, especially when this annoyance is coupled with the loss of blood. They create a special problem when an animal is ill or suffering from an open wound.

Destruction of rotting matter such as manure, straw, leaves, etc. is the best method of control. Repellents are somewhat effective but traps such as electronic electrical "zappers" are recommended as a supplementary control measure. They are virtually impossible to eliminate but can be controlled to a very tolerable level.

Blowflies (Screw Worm Fly)

There are several kinds of blowflies scattered throughout the world but they have one common characteristic: they breed in open wounds. This has been a special problem in southern states in the United States and has brought about the screw worm eradication program which has been one of the most striking examples of fly control in North America. Through the release of irradiated males, the screw worm flies have been nearly bred out of existence. They are mentioned here because occasionally there are outbreaks of infestations. The wound infested by the blowfly produces maggots over the surface of the area. If not caught and treated in a short time, the animal can suffer irreparable harm or even die from blowfly maggot infestation.

If an outbreak is suspected or has been reported, a repellent such as pine oil will generally prevent the fly from depositing eggs if the treatment is continued at respectable intervals.

Gnats

A loss of weight and unsightly hair coat can be brought about by a severe infestation of gnats. They not only bite but suck blood and have been responsible for severe cases of weight loss, even death in certain instances. Gnats breed in streams and irrigation canals.

Gnat larvae can be controlled on the surface of the water where they breed, through aerial application of pesticides. Small scale control can be handled with available repellents applied directly to the animal.

Mosquitoes

At least 145 species of mosquitoes are known to exist in the United States. All of them develop in water and may transmit diseases (sleeping sickness for example) to both man and animal. The problem is so wide spread that usually the only effective form of control is community action by spraying known breeding grounds and repeating whenever necessary. Toxaphene, chlordane, heptachlor and other chemicals have proven effective in the past. Many areas along the coastal waters of the south have developed full-time personnel to operate a mosquito control service.

Ticks

Ticks (Fig. 7-8) are blood sucking parasites that not only transmit diseases but may be responsible for secondary infections. A favorite target

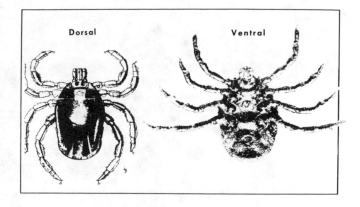

FIGURE 7-8. Ticks are blood sucking parasites that often attach themselves deep inside the bottom of the ear causing horses to shake their heads or resist bridling because of increased sensitivity. (USDA)

for ticks on the horse is inside the ear. Severe wounds made by this feeding insect can cause inflammation and severe disfigurement. One species of tick attaches itself deep inside the bottom of the ear, in some cases totally filling the cavity. Horses so affected will shake their heads and resist being bridled because of sensitivity to the ears. In some instances, when treatment is not forthcoming, the ears have been "broken" by the tick so that the ear is permanently disfigured. There have been numerous examples of this in the past. Such an affected horse is generally referred to as a "gotch eared" horse.

Control by dipping or spraying with toxaphene and lindane has proven effective. The treatment may have to be repeated at 4- to 6-week intervals during the "tick season." Treatment of the infested premises is also a recommended method of control.

Lice

Two primary species of lice, the common horse biting lice, and the horse sucking lice, affect horses. These tiny parasites (Fig. 7-9) are extremely small and difficult to see although they can be observed with the aid of close observation by parting the hair right down to the skin. Careful observation will detect movement of an almost transparent tiny parasite.

The effects of lice infestations are staggering. Irritation and the result of scratching produces loss of hair, nervousness, and restlessness in the animal.

Lice are most prevalent during the winter months, spring weather normally bringing about their inactivity. Infestation occurs as a result of spread from other infected animals. The premises can also become

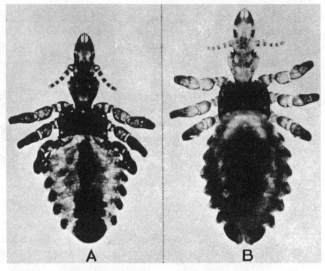

FIGURE 7-9. Lice are tiny but visible to the naked eye by parting the hair right down to the skin. Careful observation will detect movement of this whitish, almost transparent parasite. Two types infest horses—sucking lice, shown here, and biting lice. (USDA)

infested and sanitation measures may have to be taken for both animal and facilities.

Lice control is relatively easy. Shampooing the horse one day followed by application of a commercial spray or dusting powder will normally rid horses of the pest. Synergized pyrethrins used as a spray or rotenone dusting powder are common lice recommendations. Thorough coverage of the hair is necessary and the treatment may need to be repeated 2 weeks afterwards as a followup control method.

Fleas

Common dog fleas infest both man and horses. Although they are almost microscopic in size, they can cause great irritation to their host. The flea spends most of its adult life on the host, laying eggs on the animal or in its bedding. Larvae emerging from the eggs attach themselves to bedding particles and five days after emergence "hop on their horse" and continue to ride through its life cycle.

Fleas are relatively easy to detect if one rides often because they will invariably spread to humans bringing about their presence in a most dramatic way. If close contact with the horse is not maintained, flea infestations may be apparent from the horse's restlessness, and biting and rubbing itself to relieve the irritation.

Control of fleas can be combined with the control of lice. The previously recommended pyrethrins and rotenones also serve as a control measure of fleas. All bedding and facilities should be sprayed thoroughly before allowing a clean horse to inhabit a previously infested area.

Mange

A contagious skin disease commonly referred to as mange is caused by tiny mites (Fig. 7-10) that burrow into the skin of horses. The signs of infestation are the same as those commonly seen on dogs. There is a severe case of dermatitis in which the hair falls out; lesions appear, especially in the neck region; and skin thickens and forms crusts in severely affected areas.

Three principle mites attack horses, producing Sarcoptic Mange, Chorioptic Mange, and Psoroptic Mange. All are created by three different species of mange mites. Sarcoptic Mange is the most difficult of the three to control. However, usually all will respond to a lime sulphur solution normally recommended for their control.

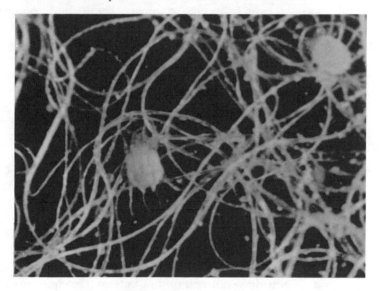

FIGURE 7-10.   The chorioptic mange mite can be seen only with the aid of a microscope. Mites burrow into the skin, producing dermatitis, hair loss, and thickened skin. (USDA)

MISCELLA-NEOUS EX-TERNAL DISORDERS

Warts are a virus-caused growth of epithelial tissue most often seen on the nose and lips but also are commonly found on the clitoris of the female and the penis of the male. Horses so affected are usually under 3 years of age, older horses apparently developing an immunity to them.

Warts

Normally, treatment is not recommended since the warts usually disappear anyway. Viruses are very difficult to control but some vaccines prepared from the horses' own tissues have been successful. Surgical removal is sometimes recommended for severe cases.

Since the cause is a virus, the best precaution, in the event warts show up in a stable, is to use separate grooming tools on affected horses and prevent social contact as much as possible. Nuzzling around on the same board fences, for instance, could spread the wart virus.

Allergies

Horses, like humans, may develop allergic reactions to pollen, feed, insect bites, drugs, etc. A very common allergic reaction in the warm season is Summer Itch, an intensely irritating skin rash brought on by a reaction, in some horses, to saliva from insect bites. Corticosteroids may give relief for 4 to 6 days but the best treatment is repellents or removal to an insect controlled environment.

Hives is another common allergy condition characterized by "bumps" appearing over the skin surface. Usually there is no itching. The cause may be attributed to reaction to pollen, stinging nettles, drugs, chemicals, insect bites, even unusual or high-protein feeds. Mild cases may disappear as the horse grows older and develops immunity. Treatment with antihistamines, adrenalin, and corticosteroids has proven beneficial in many cases. Usually one treatment is sufficient. Preventive measures should be used first, however, such as determining the cause and removing it.

Ringworms

Not a worm at all, but a fungus-caused infection, ringworm is characterized by round, scaley, or crusty patches on the skin that are hairless or have most of the hairs broken off. These circular lesions are contagious and easily spread but are fortunately easy to control.

Good grooming and nutrition are the best preventive measures. Treatment consists of topically applying iodine, glycerine, a captan wash, or Thiabendazole ointment daily for 1 to 2 weeks. If the condition does not respond, a veterinarian may prescribe an oral drug.

BIBLIOGRAPHY

Blakely, J., & King, D. *The Brass Tacks of Animal Health.* St. Louis, MO: Doane Agricultural Publications, 1978.

Wagoner, D. M. (ed.). *The Illustrated Veterinary Encyclopedia for Horsemen.* Dallas, TX: Equine Research Publications, 1977.

Wagoner, D. M. *Veterinary Treatments and Medications for Horsemen.* Dallas, TX: Equine Research Publications, 1977.

Weikel, B. (ed.). *How to Recognize Horse Health Problems.* Omaha, NB: Farnam Horse Library, 1972.

8
Sports

Horses have been used in sporting events as long as man has recorded history. Chariot and horse races were added to the Olympic games by the Greeks as early as 1450 B.C. Both horses and riders were trained to provide the utmost in daring deeds to please the spectators. Although equestrian sports have been modified since early beginnings, the basic component is still excitement for the amusement of the spectators. In other instances, the mere thrill of riding is the foundation of a sport. Although not all sports known to mankind will be covered in this chapter, concentration will be on the more popular and entertaining.

POLO

While stationed in Pakistan in 1854, Lieutenant Joseph F. Sherer "discovered" a stirring spectacle revolving around horses when he was invited by the Maharaja of Lahore to an exciting game. Amused at the excitement of the British officer, the Maharaja remarked that this "new" sport had been around for about 2,000 years.

Polo was probably founded in Tibet or Persia. The name polo possibly comes from the Tibetan word pulu, meaning a ball made of round root. Another possibility is the word palas, the Persian version of a ball made from a slow-burning wood. The Persians supposedly set the ball on fire to make it visible while following it during the course of night ceremonial games.

According to a Tibetan legend, the game actually started from a muskrat hunt held in the fall. Muskrats were pursued on horseback and chased until they dropped from exhaustion or succumbed from the hunters' clubs.

Originally, the game of polo was played with perhaps 50 to 100 men, ending in a free-for-all battle. Later, the mogul Akbar the Great (1542–1605), emperor and avid horseman, devised rules for regulated polo matches containing teams of 10 to 12 men.

The English, however, were quick to recognize an amazingly energetic sport and Lieutenant Sherer formed a team in 1859 to found the first organized club at Cachar, India. The first game was played before the public in 1863 sponsored by the newly organized Calcutta Polo Club. After that, it was taken up rapidly by English officers and spread just as rapidly to British civilians back in England.

Polo requires a completely different type of athlete in both man and horse. The rider must have complete control of his mount, a very light hand, uncanny ability with the mallet, and tactics or strategy gained through experience. Polo is a physically demanding sport: the player must hit the ball to a particular point while controlling the horse and fending off opposing players attempting to recover the ball, and play it in the opposite direction.

The horse must have great strength, durability, speed, and endurance. The bit for a polo pony is quite different from other bits, being hard and unyielding. This requires a light touch by the rider especially at the moment the player hits the ball. Horses used as polo mounts are usually quite large but out of tradition are referred to as polo ponies since the original Pakastani players used small ponies.

How to Play Polo

The polo field when located outdoors measures 160 yards long (200 if without boards) by 300 yards. Surrounding the level, grassy fields are safety zones. Goal posts measuring 10 feet high and 24 feet wide are located at either end of the field. Boards to keep the ball on the field measure 10 feet high. The glossy white ball measuring ¾ inch in diameter is made of solid willow root or an alternate hardwood. Indoor courts may be considerably smaller than the outdoor fields, utilizing wall stripes instead of goal posts, and a ball resembling a miniature soccer ball. Three players are on each team in the indoor version.

Outdoor teams consist of four men (Fig. 8-1). The best player, usually wearing the number one and called the captain (he is also the team coach), sets up shots for the man following him, who attempts to score. The fastest team member, usually number two, is also the most skillful at hitting the ball. Because of speed and fatigue, he has the largest string of horses. Number three is a defense position. Number four on the team guards the goal and back area as in soccer. Substitutions are not permitted except in case of injury.

Each player on a team is ranked according to his ability and will

FIGURE 8-1. Polo teams consist of four men. Players wear numbers signifying positions. The captain and team coach is #1, the most skillful player is #2, #3 plays a defensive position, and #4 guards the goal.

carry a handicap between zero and ten goals. The handicap represents their expected level of excellence. The combined total representing team handicaps for the two are compared and the weaker team receives the difference between the two figures. In addition to the usual riding gear, equipment may include a brimmed helmet, a mallet, and knee pads.

At the game's beginning, a coin is tossed to determine which goal each team will defend. The captains of each team face off in the center of the field backed by their number two men a few yards behind, followed by defense men. The number four men take winged positions behind their respective captains on the side of their own goal. Referees are positioned forward of the teams, at the edge of the field when starting the game. One referee tosses the ball between opposing teams to start the game and the two referees trot to positions where they can follow the play. The clock begins as soon as the ball is thrown to the ground by the referee. Judges are located one at either end of the field, staying outside the field itself, waving a white flag when a goal is scored.

The regulation polo match lasts 60 minutes, divided into eight "chukkers" (7½ minute periods), each chukker terminated by a referee blowing the whistle at the end of the time period. Indoor matches and amateur teams usually play only four chukkers. After each goal, the teams exchange sides and start over from the center of the field. If neither team scores, half time signals the changing of sides. The match is terminated with the ring of a bell. In the case of overtime, the first goal, similar to "sudden death playoff" terminates the game.

Since 1876, polo has been played in the United States. It was first introduced by James Gordon Bennett, publisher of the New York Herald. Chicago is the site for the governing body of the United States Polo Association.

FOX HUNTING

Fox hunting (Fig. 8-2) can be attributed to the Duke of Beaufort whose hounds lost their quarry one day in 1787 and raced off after a fox. The Duke followed across open country, hedges, around fields and soon discovered a new pleasure in this type of hunting. He soon decided to hunt foxes only.

The long rides over difficult country and the many jumps that were a part of the chase were soon discovered by the military as a good training ground for cavalry. Thus, the sport became not only a civilian endeavor but one used for military training as well.

Great Britain, Ireland, the United States, and France took up the sport in earnest. As more forests were cleared and foxes threatened crops and poultry, the justification became greater for the organization of fox hunting clubs. The Belvoir Hunt in 1730 is recognized as the first organized fox hunt. Perhaps one of the reasons for the attraction is best described by a historical writer: "Fox hunters who have all day long tried in vain to break their necks, join at night in a second attempt on their lives by drinking." In spite of its roudy beginnings, by the end of the century fox hunting had gained prestige as a serious sport. It spread to all those who could afford it, restricting itself mostly to aristocrats, and influenced the breeding of special horses known as hunters. In the beginning, these hunters were cold blooded horses but today most are Thoroughbred, superb athletes used in all types of jumping. A cross between the Cleveland Bay and the Thoroughbred makes for a very popular modern type jumper.

The organization of today's hunts revolves around a hunt committee and a master. The Master of Fox Hounds (MFH) takes charge of heading up the hunt. In addition to committee members, the master is aided by a huntsman, two whippers-in, grooms, and possibly an earth-stopper. The huntsman and one whipper-in is responsible for the hounds' conduct, care, training, feeding, etc. The other whipper-in has the responsibility of holding the pack together. The chief function of the earth-stopper is to plug the holes where a fox might take refuge.

The MFH is responsible for arranging all details of the hunt, order-

FIGURE 8-2. Fox hunting or running to the hounds is practiced both with live quarry and with a dragline, which merely leaves a scent.

ing the dogs, horses, and general equipment needed to produce the hunt. The MFH has complete charge of the organization. No member of the hunt passes the master except when ordered by the MFH to do so. Out of respect, the gentlemen of the hunt tip their hats in a salute to the MFH at the start. He is similarly thanked at the end of the day's sport.

The huntsman leads the pack at the start with the gentlemen riding to the side. The first whipper-in starts the fox and gives a cry of "hark halloa." When the hounds pick up the scent in full cry, the huntsmen signals with the call of "forrard away!" Once the hounds have "given tongue," hunters are free to ride where they wish except to cross the pack or ride through it.

The first whipper-in may ride with the group, generally opening gates and preventing the dogs from crossing posted land. The second whipper-in merely keeps the pack together.

According to age-old traditions, the MFH distributes trophies of the chase to the gentlemen, similar to the awarding of ears and tails at the bull fight. Novice huntsmen are often "baptized" with a drop of the quarry's blood when the MFH signs their forehead.

Although the sport has met with stiff opposition from humane societies in England and the United States, it continues to draw large numbers of participants. Weekly meetings attracting between 200 to 300 participants in England are not unusual. Fox hunting is conducted throughout 26 states in America with approximately 100 hunts recognized by the Masters of Fox Hounds Association. Virginia and Pennsylvania head the list of fox hunting states.

RODEO

Historians generally agree that the rodeo seems to have had no formal beginning. Origins are traced back to the southwestern United States and Mexico. Because of the long hours of loneliness that cowboys faced on roundups and trail drives they began to entertain themselves at the end of such events or at chance gatherings with skills they had acquired in their work. The inventive mind of the cowboy developed other sports just to be "showing off" or to prove themselves a more daring individual then the next. These gatherings apparently were such fun, combining skills, horsemanship, gambling, and drinking that they developed into a fixed event to be held at a fixed time and place. This often occurred at the end of the annual roundup on the open range. The word rodeo comes from the Spanish *rodear*, meaning "to go around," which itself was derived from an older Spanish word *rode*, meaning "a horse ring." The first "rings" used to enclose the arena were simply cowboys mounted in a circle. As the events became more sophisticated, a regular enclosure was added and the rodeo arena or "ring" was born.

There is speculation that the first public rodeo was held in Pecos, Texas on July 4, 1883. Cash prizes of $25 and $15 for first and second place were awarded for steer roping and bronc riding. According to some historians, the first rodeo charging admission was held at Prescott, Arizona, July 4, 1888. Events included riding and roping competitions. Other historians believe the first rodeo charging admission was held in Denver in 1887. However, most historians agree that the first rodeo, still in existence today, was held in Cheyenne, Wyoming in 1897 during the Cheyenne Frontier Days Celebration.

Today, the major league in rodeos are the Cheyenne Rodeo; the Roundup at Pendleton, Oregon; Houston Livestock Show and Rodeo in Texas; and the Salinas, California Rodeo. The largest of all rodeos, however, is the Calgary Stampede in Alberta, Canada. The most important winter rodeo is the World's Championship Rodeo held in Madison Square Garden, in New York City. The most important rodeo of all is the December National Finals held annually in Oklahoma City, for championship rider and roper titles.

As this sport began to develop, so did the organization to plan and execute these events. The Rodeo Association of America was formed in 1928 to promote harmony among producers. The group changed in 1946 to International Rodeo Association, and again in 1959 to International Rodeo Management, Inc.

The first association for participants was the Cowboy's Turtle Association, formed in 1936, to better working conditions for the participants. The word turtle comes from the old expression "turning turtle" meaning to be thrown on the back. The name was later changed to Rodeo Cowboys Association and more recently to Professional Rodeo Cowboys Association with headquarters in Colorado Springs, Colorado.

The modern rodeo centers around six major attractions today: bareback bronc riding, calf roping, saddle bronc riding, steer wrestling, barrel racing, and bull riding. Other events include steer riding, steer roping, team roping, goat tying, calf saddling, queen's contest, and breakaway roping. Trick horses and trick riding (Fig. 8-3) are two of the numerous horse acts that are used to fill in between major events. Top name entertainers and celebrities are also used as a drawing card for the general public, and, if they can ride at all, enter the arena with pride astride a prancing mount.

Participants in most rodeo events draw lots by chance to decide which stock they will work in the case of steer wrestling, calf roping, etc. In the riding events, chance also decides the mount, and contests are timed. Eight seconds constitutes a full-length regulation ride for bareback, saddle bronc, and bull riding. Participants are scored, based

FIGURE 8-3. Trick riding is a colorful event seen in rodeos as well as the circus.

on 100 for a perfect score, through a combination of points awarded to both the rider and mount. It is imperative, therefore, that the cowboy draw a good performing animal and perform well himself. An average score would be in the 60s, and an exceptional score in the 70s or 80s.

Bareback Bronc Riding

This event became official in the 1920s and is used as the leadoff event in most rodeos today. The rider has neither saddle nor rein, using only a 10-inch wide surcingle (bareback rigging) with a handhold to remain upright behind the withers. One hand must remain free and the rider uses spurs in "scratching" (raking the horse with spurs to score points).

Calf Roping

The mounted roper throws a loop over the calf's head and the horse comes to a sliding halt. It is the horse's duty to maintain back pressure and it is trained to do so. Dragging the calf more than three feet, however, draws a penalty of 20 seconds. The cowboy, upon dismounting, reaches the calf and throws it to the ground for tying. If the calf is not standing, he must make it regain its feet and then throw it to the ground. Any 3 feet are then tied with a "piggin string." The tie must hold for at least 5 seconds. A judge waves a flag in the event the tie does not hold and the time is disqualified. A roper is allowed to carry two ropes, but is not allowed two loops or chances with the same rope. Failure to catch the calf in one out of two tries disqualifies the participant.

Saddle Bronc Riding

The bronc rider is allowed a saddle and a braided rope rein tied to a halter. Wrapping the rein around the hand is not allowed. The rider is allowed the use of one hand, and is disqualified if his free hand touches the horse. Spurring or "scratching" (scoring by a raking action) is a part of point building. The cowboy is disqualified if he loses a stirrup or changes hands with the braided rope. If the horse fails to buck, the cowboy is entitled to a new horse.

Steer Wrestling

Often known as bulldogging, this event requires the steer wrestler (cowboy) to jump from the back of a horse onto the neck of the steer that enters the ring from a chute. The cowboy then wrestles the steer to the ground by the horns, sometimes using one foot to gain leverage in order to force the steer over. A "hazer" rides on the opposite side of the steer to keep it going in a straight line but remains on his horse. "Dogging" horses are specially trained and have a particular sense for this type of work.

Bull Riding

The rider is allowed one hand and only a rope around the animal's barrel. This rope is specially made and may be resined; the rider uses

FIGURE 8-4. Rodeo is a sport for young and old. Here three young contestants try their hand at calf saddling.

one glove, and a bell is added to the rope for weight to help the rope fall free after the ride. The rider is allowed to take a wrap with his rope in this event, which often leads to dangerous spills and thrills. Because of the wrap and the resin, the cowboy often gets "hung up in the rigging." Men on horseback are placed at strategic spots in the arena to offer assistance to the cowboy after he completes his ride, or to motivate the bull to return to the proper place. The clown, however, has the important job of distracting the dangerous bull until the cowboy can seek safety.

Barrel Racing   Mostly women and younger children participate in this event. The normal pattern is to place three barrels in the arena in a triangle position and the participants run a cloverleaf pattern against time. Barrels may be touched or moved slightly but not turned over. Knocking a barrel over draws a 5-second penalty. The participant with the fastest time is declared the winner.

GYMKHANA EVENTS   Fun and games for horsemen that also build skills is the basis for gymkhana events. Children and less experienced riders are often involved in these games, which include the following:

Balloon Race   In this event, balloons are tied to the ground in the center of the arena, numbering as many as there are members on a team. The first rider races toward the balloons and attempts to break one with a slender pointed stick. Upon reaching the end of the field, he passes his stick to another team member who repeats the process and so on until all the balloons have been broken. The first team to break all its balloons is declared the winner. There is a variation of this event called balloon scrimmage in which each rider carries a floating balloon and a stick. The object is to burst the balloon of the opponents without having your own balloon broken.

Potato Race or Potato-Picking Scramble

Small piles of potatoes are placed in the center of an arena. A whistle blows signifying 60 seconds of time allowed for the first go-round. The rider races to the center of the arena, dismounts, picks up his potato, remounts, and races back to the starting point. The participant drops his potato, while mounted, into the team bucket. If it fails to hit the bucket or remain inside it, the rider must dismount and drop the potato again from horseback. The whistle signifies the end of the 60-second time period and the beginning of the next participants. The team having the most potatoes in its bucket is declared the winner.

Paper Chase

This event is similar to the potato race except that small pieces of paper, cardboard boxes, even tin cans (an anti-litter campaign) are placed in the center of the arena. The first participant races to the center, pierces the object with a pointed stick without dismounting, and returns to the starting point to place the object in the team bucket without dismounting and without touching the object with the hand.

Knotted Cord Race

This is a race requiring two teams of three players or more on each team. The object is to divide up the team in equal numbers at opposite ends of the arena. Each team member is carrying a short length of cord or rope. On signal, the first rider from each team races to the opposite end, tying his rope to the rope of the number two member on the team. They then race to the opposite end where team member three unties the knot, reties his cord to team member number two and they, in turn, race to the opposite end to repeat the tying and untying. Since both teams are competing simultaneously, the first team to untie the last knot is declared the winner.

Egg or Racket Race

This is a relay race in which an egg is carried in a spoon at a walk, trot, or canter. The egg is relayed to a team member over a varying distance. Team members may not touch the egg with their hands. A tennis racket may be substituted for the spoon. The team completing the relay in the fastest time without dropping the egg is declared the winner.

Changing Horses Relay

This event takes on two types of contests. In the first type, four team members are placed at strategic points in the arena. Using one mount, number one races to number two, dismounts, number two mounts and races to number three, and so on. In the second type, four team members with four horses are placed at strategic points. Number one of each team races to each point, changing horses each time, using team mates to assist him at each point in remounting. As soon as the ones are finished, the twos, threes, and fours repeat the process. A variation of this race is the straight relay race in which a member rides a horse to the opposite end of the arena and dismounts, and a new rider mounts and races to the opposite end, and so on.

Trotting Race or Race at a Collected Gallop

Contestants race in pairs at a trot or collected gallop over a varying distance. If one breaks stride, a penalty is incurred. At the end of the point, the riders change horses and return to the starting point.

Outlaws and Pony Express Ride

A rider representing the pony express, escorted by two guards, attempts to transport a sack containing the miners' pay to the mine director. Two outlaws spring from a "robber's roost" to attack the pony express. The guards protect the rider by tagging the outlaws on the shoulder.

Treasure Hunt

Contestants first familiarize themselves with the terrain, which is previously marked by small flags. Envelopes are hidden near each flag. Contestants must dismount, find the envelope and read the contents, and follow the instructions in order to reach the treasure. The contestant reaching the treasure in the shortest period of time is declared the winner.

Musical Hats

Riders circle the field or arena at a prescribed gait to the tune of music. In the center of the arena are a number of poles containing hats. There is one less hat than contestants. At a signal, the contestants dash to the center of the arena, dismount, and grab a hat. The hatless horseman is eliminated. One or two hats are then removed and the process repeated until there are only two riders and one hat left. The winner is the participant who gets the hat.

Capture the Flag

This game requires two teams, and two different colored flags. For instance, a white flag is placed at one end of the field and a black flag at the other. Teams line up on either side of a line equally dividing the arena and attempt to capture the other team's flag. A tag on the shoulder by any horseman crossing the center line into enemy territory designates a prisoner of the opposing team. The team successfully capturing the enemy flag without being taken captive is declared the winner.

Six-Pole Race A slalom course containing six poles placed in the ground, or cemented in small cans, is used to provide a zig zag course for a racing contestant. Upon reaching the last pole, the contestant returns the way he came. The winner is the contestant with the fastest time.

Flag Race Each team consists of four members holding a different colored flag on a pole. The number one and number three team members are on one end; two and four are on opposite ends. The number one member races to the opposite end of the field and exchanges flags with number two who is racing back to exchange with number three, back again to exchange with number four, and returns to his original position to trade once again with number two, who repeats the course followed by number three and number four. The winner is declared when the number four team member crosses the finish line first with his exchanged flag.

Musical Chairs Similar to musical hats, chairs are placed in the center of the arena while contestants travel in a circle at a required gait. At the sound of a whistle or the cessation of music, riders dash to the center of the arena, dismount, and take a seat. One fewer chairs are in the center than riders. The standing rider is eliminated, a chair is removed, and the game continues. With two riders left, the first one to become seated in the remaining chair is declared the winner.

Other events in Gymkhana include racing and picking up a partner on the ground and swinging the partner up behind a mounted rider, saddling and bridling contests, racing with a full glass of water, bareback races, a shovel race in which a partner is dragged by a rope while sitting in the seat of a corn scoop, and many others.

THOROUGH-BRED RACING The cost of racing was of little concern to the originators of this sport. It was then and to some extent now is "the sport of kings." A very expensive sport, the financially endowed support it for the most part today.

King Charles II of England was responsible for the first major step in establishing racing practices. The English had been practicing some form of horse racing since the arrival of the Romans. The Romans probably picked it up from the Greeks, who recorded horse racing events as early as 642 B.C. in the Olympic games.

Although the owning of large numbers of race horses is strictly for the wealthy, there are numerous owners in the United States who own a few or perhaps just one race horse. Still, further enjoyment can be had by the masses through participation in the pride of ownership through the purchase of a pari-mutuel ticket on an animal. Thus, by a pooling of resources, the physical setting, natural beauty, and color and excitement of the race can be enjoyed by millions. The popularity of "the sport of kings" is undeniably enjoyed today by the common people. It may surprise many that more admission tickets were sold to horseraces than any other sporting event in the United States last year, including football, basketball, and baseball.

The practice of racing inside a circular track can be traced back to 1603 when King James I was King of England. Because the majority of his courtiers were Scottish noblemen, who were great lovers of horse racing, the King erected a circular fence to keep the enthusiastic spectators outside the limits of the race track in order that "one could better follow the progress of the race."

The term derby is used throughout the world in connection with Thoroughbred horse racing. The name stems from Edward Smith-Stanley, 12th Earl of Derby, who invited guests to a horse race in May 1780. Another racing enthusiast and friend, Sir Charles Bunbury, tossed a coin to decide whether the race would be called the Derby or the Bunbury. Derby won the toss but Bunbury's horse won the race. Subsequently, the mile track at Newmarket, England was named the Bunbury mile (a name used to this day), the Derby Race. The derby was imitated in Ireland, Scotland, and Britain's colonies and has spread throughout the world. In the United States, there is more than one derby. Derbies exist in California, Louisiana, Florida, New Jersey, Arkansas, Illinois, but the most famous is the Kentucky Derby started in Louisville in 1875.

The racecourses or "tracks" differ in surface, length, climate, etc. The most noticeable difference is the surface—dirt or turf (grass). Some horses run well on dirt but not on grass. Some run better on soft dirt, hard tracks, or even on wet, muddy, or sloppy tracks while others never do so. In the United States, trainers use special shoes or other devices to adjust for the type of course. The majority of race tracks in the United States and all the classics are run on dirt tracks. Forecasts are given the spectators concerning what to expect in the condition of the track. A sloppy track is flooded with water, a fast track is dry and even, a muddy track is a course soaked to the base. After a rain and the drying process continues on a track, it may be described as heavy, slow, good, and finally fast, once again.

The popularity of Thoroughbred racing (Fig. 8-5) has as its cornerstone the possibility of not only selecting a winner but winning money as a result of that selection. In the early days of racing this possibility was fraught with danger of losing the bets because of dishonest bookmakers who often ran off with the cash.

FIGURE 8-5. Thoroughbred racing has a higher payed attendance than football, basketball, or baseball.

Early participants found that by "pooling" their debts with a book-maker, they were able to participate in wagering in a style previously restricted to royalty. In 1864, Joseph Oller participated in such a pool, won, and was never paid. Because of this loss, he was inspired to secure the wagers of the average bettor. He developed the pari-mutuel betting system. The words themselves are taken from the French *mutuel* meaning mutual participation and *pari* meaning "to bet." This system differed from a pool in that bets could be as varied as possible.

In 1880 a New Zealand inventor named Ekberg, fascinated by Oller's system, developed a manually operated machine, the *totalisator*. This machine made possible the selling of tickets and computation of pay-offs quickly and accurately based on a fast, accurate talley system. The electric totalisator or "tote board" is a modernized version of Oller's original system which computes the odds prior to a race and the winners and payoffs immediately afterwards.

Another form of Thoroughbred racing is the Steeplechase (see Thoroughbred, Chapter 2). While flat racing concerns itself with fast races on an even track inside an enclosed predetermined length of course, the steeplechase is a grueling race crosscountry over numerous obstacles. Jumps over hedges, walls, fences, water ways, and every conceivable hardship produces a thrilling race for man and beast that is characterized by numerous spills and the potential for injury.

QUARTER HORSE RACING

Quarter horses, unlike their Thoroughbred counterparts, do not race over a varying distance. All races are one-quarter mile in length and the type of horse is considerably different, being more powerful and muscular and faster for a short distance, although some Thoroughbred blood is being infused into outstanding Quarter horse lines. The tracks are invariably dirt and subject to the same modifications by the environment as encountered in Thoroughbred racing. Presently, the richest purse in all of racing is for the American Futurity, held at Ruidosa Downs in New Mexico. (See Quarter horse, Chapter 2.)

HARNESS RACING

Since colonial days, Americans have been indulging their appetite for speed through harness racing events. The first type of horse racing in America revolved around trotters and pacers, since 1879 known as American Standardbreds.

Originally, trotters or pacers of the Norfolk Trotter or descendants thereof, were hooked to two-wheeled racing carts with room enough for only one driver. Trotters and pacers were also adapted to the family wagon or buggy and friendly contests invariably occurred on the road to town. These informal rivalries became known as "brushes." Today, brushing refers to a short dash at top speed, usually nearing the finish line.

Brushes became so numerous in New York about 1800 that complaints led to specific courses laid out for trotting races. Although the first tracks were merely a designated street in a town, tracks eventually developed so that spectators could watch these highly entertaining events.

As a rule, tracks were generally laid out in an oval pattern but one course in 1887 was in the shape of a kite. It was designed to permit a more appropriate angle on turns and increase speed for both trotters and pacers. The theory turned out to be fact and a ruling was made to the effect that all tracks and records made on such tracks be marked with a K to indicate the fact. Most harness tracks today are ½ mile in circumference; others are ⅝ mile; some a mile around. The difference in shape and length of tracks makes for different racing strategies.

Just as in pari-mutuel betting on Thoroughbreds, the same rules apply to harness racing. For a more detailed discussion on trotters, pacers, and description of events see Standardbred, Chapter 2.

EQUESTRIAN OLYMPIC SPORTS

The oldest international meet for horses is the Olympic games. Equestrian events are divided into three phases: the first, known as three-day eventing, is an equine marathon further divided into the Dressage Test, Cross-Country (speed, endurance, and steeplechase trials), and Show Jumping (Fig. 8-6). The second event is the Prix des

FIGURE 8-6.   There is keen competition in show jumping events, a part of international equestrian Olympic sports.

Nations, a competition of show jumping for teams and individuals; and the Grand Prix de Dressage, an event for teams and individuals.

In three-day eventing, the first day's activities are the dressage tests, held in a 60 × 20 meter regulation arena. Every contestant goes through a fixed set of movements that requires balance, obedience, manageability, and responsiveness to commands over the course in a specified time of 7½ minutes. Each movement is scored and penalties given for faults. The maximum score is 138 points.

The second day of three-day eventing includes endurance, speed tests, steeplechase, and the cross-country test, all completed without rest over a course 32,700 meters. The course may include swamp roads and rough, variable terrain which riders are allowed to survey the day before on foot. Contestants exceeding the time limit are eliminated. Extra points are earned for exceptional time over the steeplechase and the cross-country courses.

The third day of the three-day eventing includes show jumping over 12 obstacles, at a rate of 400 meters per minute on a 1,000 meter course. Although not a difficult course, it does require stamina and discipline from the horses, who have negotiated the grueling course two days previously.

The Prix des Nations is the last event of the Olympic games. Show jumping competition, 13 or 14 obstacles requiring 16 to 20 jumps at a specified height, including water jumps, make up the event. The course varies in length according to the stadium but should not exceed 1,100 meters.

In the past, Olympic equestrian games were sports for cavalry men—the military. Some nations, particularly Mexico, still field excellent military teams but for the most part, the games have switched to civilian participants.

HORSE SHOW CLASSES

Horses compete nationally in various sponsored or sanctioned horse shows basically in two areas: halter classes and performance classes. Halter classes are relatively simple events in which the horse itself is judged, mainly on physical characteristics. They are called halter classes because a handler merely brings the horse into an arena and shows it off to best advantage. Good conformation and correct way of traveling are important but this type of judgment goes no deeper than what the animal appears to be able to do based upon anatomical and genetic blessings. The real proof of the worth of a horse comes in performance classes, of which there are many.

A performance class refers to the athletic ability of a horse usually under a set series of circumstances. Not all performance classes will be covered in this chapter because of the variability from place to place and because horse shows place emphasis on different classes, depending upon local or association interests.

However, all equestrian sports come under the umbrella of the Fédération Equestre Internationale (FEI). The Olympic games and other international competitions draw their contestants from this world governing body. In the United States, the Association of American Horse Shows, Inc. (AHSA) is a member of the FEI and is the certifying agency for American equestrian athletes. The AHSA keeps records, licenses officials, handles disputes or discipline, awards prizes, and publishes the "Bible" of the horse show rules with its annual rule book.

There are many divisions of horse shows sanctioned by the AHSA. These include the various breed associations, from A to Z (Arabians to Welsh), dressage, equitation, gymkhana, hunters and jumpers, roadsters and western. Most breed associations have specific classes that apply only to their members, and other shows provide open shows for horses that may be of any breed or even non-registered.

For a complete, detailed outline, interested readers are referred to the official rules book of the AHSA or to the published rules in the program of local horse shows. Some of the more popular horse show classes follow.

HALTER CLASSES

Halter classes (Fig. 8-7) are extremely popular with every breed because this is the place where the breeders have an experienced judge view their entrants and compare them to the ideal type for the breed. Halter classes are judged on type, conformation, way of traveling,

FIGURE 8-7. Halter classes allow breeders to compete in conformation comparisons. (International Arabian Horse Association).

soundness, and other quality attributes. The halter classes cover various age groups such as weanlings, yearlings, fillies, mature stallions, mares, and geldings. There are also breeding classes which judge the progeny (offspring) of an outstanding dam or sire. For instance, two animals from the same dam are shown at halter as a *product of dam*, three animals by the same sire are shown as *get of sire*, and a sire with two offspring may be shown as *sire and get*.

EQUITATION DIVISION

As the name implies, equitation classes judge only the rider. Any horse that is suitable for riding and performing a class routine is acceptable for this event. The three divisions include the hunt, saddle, and stock seat class.

Hunt Seat Class

The rider uses an English hunt seat saddle, called a forward saddle, with knee rolls. Horses are required to perform at the walk, trot, canter, and hand gallop, and to execute specific figures, which may be over obstacles. Riders wear the traditional hunting dress—hunting cap and exposed, calf-length riding boots (Fig. 8-8).

Saddle Seat Class

A park saddle is used by competitors in this event. The horse is shown at a walk, trot, and canter while being put through the paces of an individual test. The rider (Fig. 8-9) wears the traditional costume seen in saddle seat competition—English Derby and riding pants that cover the leg (a pant loop slips under the shoe heel).

FIGURE 8-8. The Hunt Seat Class uses an English saddle with knee rolls. Note the traditional hunting attire.

FIGURE 8-9. The Saddle Seat Class uses a park saddle. Note the English Derby and riding pants, traditional attire for this event.

Stock Seat Class

This division of equitation requires a western style saddle to demonstrate the walk, trot, canter, and individual tests. The rider is dressed in western attire (Fig. 8-10).

FIGURE 8-10. The Stock Seat Class uses western saddle and attire.

WESTERN DIVISION

The western division is divided into stock horse classes, jacquima, trail, and pleasure classes.

Stock Horse Class

Stock horses are judged on rein, conformation, manners, and an individual test which may or may not include working cattle. If cattle are not worked, the stock horse goes through a routine pattern that involves figure eights, turns, stops, and back-ups. Riders are dressed in western attire and must carry a lariat or reata.

Jacquima

Similar to the stock horse class, the jacquima class (Fig. 8-11) differs in that horses may be shown that are up to five years old but must have never been shown with any head gear more advanced than a snaffle bit (no spade bits). Jacquima horses go through the same paces as the stock horses but are usually not required to work cattle. The main difference is that the jacquima horse is controlled with a hacka-more, the rider using both hands on the mecate (rein) of the hackamore.

Trail

Crossing bridges, backing through or around obstacles, riding through water or stepping over logs, mounting and dismounting are all part of the trail horse competition (Fig. 8-12). Horses are shown at the walk, trot, and lope in both directions of the ring. One requirement is that the horse allow the rider to open a gate, pass through it, and close it without dismounting. Although conformation is account-able for 20% of the score, the emphasis is on performance and manners.

FIGURE 8-11.   Jacquima, a stock horse category, involves horses up to 5 years of age. They are worked with a hackamore, although most often are not required to work cattle.

FIGURE 8-12.   Trail horse competition involves control and an even-tempered disposition.

Pleasure   This very popular class requires horses to be shown working both ways in an arena at the walk, trot, and lope. A reasonably loose rein must be maintained and horses are required to back in a straight line. Finalists may be required to do further ringwork because of the keen competition in this popular event.

JUMPER DIVISION   The jumper division is open to any horse regardless of breed, size, or sex. Horses are required to go over a series of jumps to demonstrate the abilities of all horses entered. Each course is carefully designed to suit the average training and capabilities of the entrants. A course that is so severe that no horse is able to negotiate all jumps without a fault is too severe. Jumpers are scored on penalty faults. A horse is penalized for disobedience, falling, knocking down any part of an obstacle, touching the obstacle, and exceeding a maximum time limit. The horse with the best score (the fewest faults) is declared the winner. Riders in this event wear the traditional hunting garb (Fig. 8-6) previously described in the hunting seat class. However, in this instance, it is the horse that is being judged rather than the rider.

HUNTER DIVISION   Hunters may be of either sex but divisions are usually divided into *breeding, conformation,* and *working* classes. In the first or second year of showing, regardless of class, a horse is known as green hunters, others as regular hunters.

Breeding classes are judged on quality, conformation, and suspected ability to produce other desirable hunter types.

Conformation classes, unlike halter classes previously described, emphasize performance as well as conformation.

Working hunters on the other hand, are judged mainly on performance and soundness. Both conformation and working hunters are exhibited over a course which includes simulated obstacles found in the hunting field. These include the stone wall, hedge, fence rail, white board fence or gate, chicken coop, and parallel bars with brush in the middle. Horses are scored in the manner previously described in which penalty faults are given for disobedience, etc.

SADDLE HORSE DIVISION   The American Saddle Horse with three-gaited and five-gaited entrants provide the competition for this event. All horses must be registered as American Saddlebreds and are required to be shown at the walk, trot, and canter for three-gaited horses; walk, trot, canter, slow gait, and rack for five-gaited horses. Horses are shown at all gaits moving in both directions of the ring. Finalists are required to exhibit further work at the discretion of the judge. Horses may be shown with any bridle and with a flat, English-type saddle. Riders (Fig. 8-13) wear informal attire during morning and afternoon classes, dark colored riding habit and derby or silk top hat for evening classes.

FIGURE 8-13. American Saddle horses compete in 3-gaited and 5-gaited contests.

ROADSTER DIVISION

Any breed is open to compete in the roadster division. The only requirements are that the horse be attractive, of good conformation, sound, and be well mannered to make the horse a safe harness animal in the ring. Horses are hitched to bike roadsters or road wagon roadsters. The bike roadster is the smaller of the two. Horses are shown at the walk, slow jog trot, fast trot (road gait), and full speed trot. Horses should show the flashy animation that characterizes the stylish appearance of a superior roadster. Exhibitors in bike classes wear matching cap and jacket, exhibiting the stable colors. A business suit and hat are worn by exhibitors in the road class (Fig. 8-14).

HEAVY HARNESS HORSE DIVISION (CARRIAGE HORSE, HACKNEY)

As the name implies, this category requires heavier leather than that used for the roadster or fine harness horse. This classification is of English origin (Fig. 8-15) because British drivers thought it was necessary to drive heavily in order to drive handsomely. Therefore, both harness and carriage are of stout design.

At one time, several breeds were used in heavy harness classes but currently only the Hackney is shown in this category. The Hackney is known as the leading heavy harness horse in the world. The AHSA refers to this classification as Hackney rather than heavy harness horse.

FINE HARNESS DIVISION

A fine horse in refined harness is the principle goal of fine harness horse driving. Grace, charm, and elegance are represented in this class, which is dominated by the American Saddle horse breed. (See

FIGURE 8-14. Any breed is open to compete in the Roadster division.

FIGURE 8-15. Heavy Harness Horseshow divisions use stout carriage and harness of English design.

American Saddle Horse for further descriptions.) These horses are shown at an animated walk and an animated park trot. American Saddle horses with long mane and tail draw a four-wheeled show wagon (topless) or with top drawn in the high stepping fine harness horse class (Fig. 8-16).

FIGURE 8-16. Fine Harness driving exhibits elegance, dominated by the American Saddle Horse breed.

BIBLIOGRA-PHY

Edwards, E. H. (ed.) *Encyclopedia of the Horse*. London: Octopus Books, 1977.

Evans, J. W. *The Horse*. San Francisco: Freeman, 1977.

Gianoli, L. *Horses and Horsemanship through the Ages*. New York: Crown, 1967.

Price, S. (ed.). *The Complete Horse Encyclopedia*. New York: Chartwell Books, 1976.

9
Tack

To the uninitiated, there is a mind-boggling variety of saddles, bridles, bits, martingales, girths, boots, and accessory items that make up the world of tack. The most common tack questions are What does this do? and, How does it work? This chapter was written to answer those questions, and more.

The bewildering variety of tack items can be condensed into the basic categories of saddles, communication devices (bits, bridles, spurs, accessories), and protective gear. The basic purpose for all tack is to maintain maximum control of the horse in the most demanding situations for which the horse is used and to provide a safe, comfortable seat for the rider. To understand why an item is needed is to understand how it works.

SADDLES

English or Flat Saddle

Although the saddle has many variations and trappings, the basic design has changed little since it was first invented. Historians conclude that the initial model probably originated in the Orient, most likely by the hordes of excellent horsemen that rode with Ghengis Khan and Atilla the Hun. In different periods of history, these fighting cavalrymen overran parts of what is now Continental Europe spreading destruction and leaving behind their innovative seats. Their saddles were designed for practicality and comfort. Legend has it that these horsemen placed a slab of raw meat under their saddles using it as a pad, to be later consumed as a part of their military ration. It would be difficult to find a better pad or a worse meal. Nevertheless, it may have given inspiration to types of saddle pads available today.

The general term for any saddle other than a western style, or stock saddle, is English, sometimes called Flat saddle. Although the English get credit for this seat, the development is in name only. This type of saddle was used for over 100 years by Italians, French, Germans, Poles, and Russians before the English built a reputation as saddle makers through exports of large quantities of leather goods. Their expertise in saddle making gave rise to the name English saddle.

The most popular English saddles today are of two types: the forward seat and the show saddle. (Fig. 9-1).

Forward seat The *forward seat* saddle was developed by the Italians, not the English, and was originally labeled dangerous by the "sit back" school of thinking. Nonetheless, the Italians prevailed, developing a saddle with a short stirrup, the rider inclined forward in the upper torso, stirrups hanging straight down, weight on the ball of the foot, inner calf, and thigh. It has become the accepted saddle for hunting, jumping, cross-country events, etc. The design is quite effective because it places the weight of the rider directly over the withers of the horse where it is more capable of carrying weight.

Show Saddle The *show saddle* is a different type of English seat, used primarily on Saddlebred and Walking horses. The seat is very flat as opposed to the forward seat type, the head is cut back, and the skirt is cut straight down from the head to lay directly behind the shoulder. It is designed to show off conformation and way of going in Saddlebreds and Walking horses. Originally it was designed for the same purpose to be used on a type of English horse known as a Show Hack. The style was adopted and slightly modified by the Americans.

Military Saddles

Military saddles (Fig. 9-2) are related to the English type of seat but have been modified for simplicity or for specialized purposes.

McClellen There is no saddle in the world that is comparable to the rugged, simple, standard military saddle that was used by the U.S. Cavalry from the Civil War to the end of World War II—the McClellen. It is interesting to note that the McClellen is designed quite similar to the first saddles ever developed in history, those from Korea and Tibet dating back to the fifteenth and sixteenth centuries A.D. The basic design was then and is now a tree covered with leather, stitched around the edges. Center-fire rigged (only one cinch and girth, centrally located), it was secured to the pommel and cantle with brass screws. A horse-hair cinch and hooded or iron English type stirrups completed the rig.

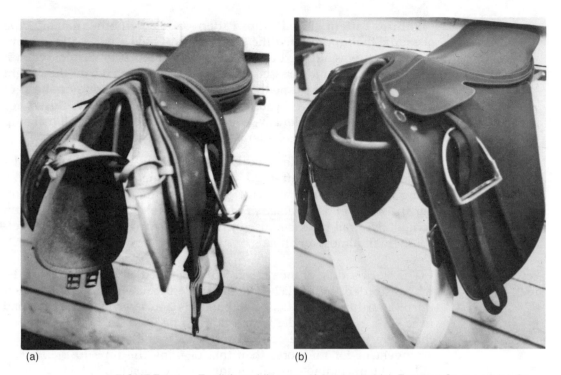

(a)   (b)

FIGURE 9-1.   English saddles are of two types: (a) Forward Seat and (b) Show
Saddle.

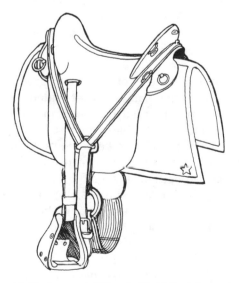

FIGURE 9-2.   The McClellen and Officer's Field Saddle or Semi-Military Saddle
have developed a reputation for ruggedness and adaptability.

Phillips Pattern The Phillips Pattern saddle is another military type of saddle that approached the forward seat English type saddle in appearance. It was adopted by the U.S. Army Equitation School when it was in operation and stressed a balanced seat, which meant the weight of the rider was carried neither behind the horse's action nor ahead of it. These saddles were beautifully designed and used by officers for show purposes. Occasionally, even today, saddle houses will make up a number of the Phillips Pattern saddles. They are quickly sold out.

Officer's Field Saddle The Officer's Field Saddle, unlike the McClellen, is patterned after the flat or hunting type English saddle, being much heavier. It is marketed today by many saddle houses under the name of *Semi-Military Saddle*. It has developed a reputation on competitive trail rides because of its comfort, ruggedness, and adaptability to fit almost any horse.

Western or Stock Saddle

The stock saddle of today (Fig. 9-3) originated among the Spaniards, who discarded the English type of saddle because it did not suit their purpose of herding cattle. The Spaniards and later the Mexicans had need for a rugged saddle with a horn to be used for holding animals that were roped on the open plains. This was a much more desirable arrangement for the horse than that of tying the rope to the horse's tail, a not uncommon idea in many parts of Spain or Latin America. Other accessories were added to the saddles such as tapederos or "toe fenders" used to protect the feet from cactus and brush.

The Mexican saddle was a single-rigged (only one girth) saddle with the girth attaching straight down from the root of the horn. The horn was big, flat, and round, often jokingly referred to as a "Mexican dinner plate." These saddles came into North America and were modified by two groups of settlers to produce the existing types of western, or stock type, saddles most widely used in the United States today. The Texans modified the Mexican saddle by adding a ring at the cantle to produce a double-rigged saddle. This was probably modified in this manner mostly to keep the cantle of the saddle level when roping large steers, horses, etc. Because of this "cowboy" activity, the horn was also modified to a half apple shaped horn making it easier to make a "dally," a couple of quick rounds of the loose end of the rope on the horn to hold the animal without permanently connecting a wild beast and a cowboy. Many a "greenhorn," accustomed to gentle stock, tied his rope to the horn and got a ton of crazed Longhorn trying to climb into the saddle with him. The dally offered at least one more option.

The Californians made the other modification to the basic Mexican or Texas saddle. They moved the rigging to just below the lowest point of the seat in a single ring, center fire saddle. The horn was made taller

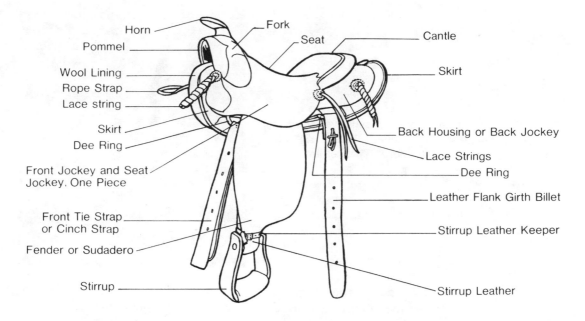

Horn

Pommel

Wool Lining

Rope Strap

Lace string

Skirt

Dee Ring

Front Jockey and Seat
Jockey, One Piece

Front Tie Strap
or Cinch Strap

Fender or Sudadero

Stirrup

Fork

Seat

Cantle

Skirt

Back Housing or Back Jockey

Lace Strings

Dee Ring

Leather Flank Girth Billet

Stirrup Leather Keeper

Stirrup Leather

FIGURE 9-3.   Western stock saddles originated among the Spaniards. They may be single or doubled rigged and come in a wide variety of styles.

and thinner. Skirts, tapederos, and fancy dressings were added and continue to last in today's styles.

The Texans and Californians each still hold influence over roughly half of the United States. Most all saddles and bridles east of the Rocky Mountains were influenced by the Texans. Everything west of the Rocky Mountains conforms to the fancy, flashy style made popular by the Californians.

RESTRAINTS, CONTROLS, AIDS

If the horse could reason at all, it would soon discover that it has the mechanical advantage over man in every way. Because the horse has such a great advantage in height, weight, and strength, it must be made to think that man can control it by some extremely powerful method. Man has developed this power over horses by the simple application of pressure to sensitive areas on the horse's body. Most of the devices designed by man have been made to apply pressure to seven sensitive points about the horse's head. These points should be well understood, then the myriad of bridles, bits, and other paraphernalia will be better understood.

Fig. 9-4 illustrates the seven pressure points on the horse's head used by man to control the horse.

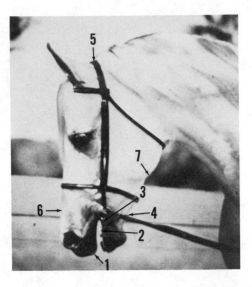

FIGURE 9-4. Pressure points of sensitivity used to control the horse are (1) tongue, (2) bars, (3) lips, (4) curb groove, (5) poll, (6) nose, (7) lower jaw.

1. Tongue. The tongue is the first basic point of pressure. Regardless of the mouth piece used on a bridle, the tongue will receive a certain amount of pressure.

2. Bars. The bars are also an essential control point. The bars are those portions of the jaw bones lying inside the mouth and between the front and back teeth. This "gap" is thinly covered with flesh and very sensitive.

3. Lips. The lips are an excellent control area, thinly covered with skin and very sensitive, especially at the corners of the mouth. When snaffle bits are used, often rubber or leather bit guards are used to prevent minor irritations or injuries.

4. Curb groove. The curb groove located on the underside of the horse's head where the curb strap fits is another sensitive area because of a thinly fleshed bony part of the jaw. Contrary to what amateurs may think, the curb strap is not just something to hold the bit in place. It is a control device itself.

5. Poll. The poll or top of the head is the fifth control point and comes into play when the halter or gag bit (discussed later) is used.

6. Nose. The nose is a sixth point of control, being very sensitive because it too is a thinly fleshed bony structure. The hackamore and some types of curb bit headstalls are effective because of pressure applied to the nose.

7. Lower jaw. The lower jaw is the seventh point of control. At a point on either side of the jaw directly below the eyes is a very sensitive, thinly fleshed area that is the principle control for the rawhide bosal (discussed later). Bosals are made of very stiff material which when pulled apply pressure to this sensitive area.

The question might arise, Why not select only one of these sensitive pressure points and simplify all of the control methods? The reason for the variety of head gear in use is that not all horses are uniformly sensitive to the same area. Therefore, one might have to experiment before finding the type of device that will effectively control the mount in question. Also, as a horse grows older, it often becomes calloused to pressure on a certain area. By experimenting, the horseman can discover the proper type of equipment for each horse. The purpose should always be to obtain maximum control with minimum discomfort to the horse.

Bridles, Cavessons, Reins

The bridle has changed little since it was originally invented. Basically, it is a device to hold the bit in place in the horse's mouth.

Headstalls of leather, rope, or webbing are simple devices used to hold the bit or to restrain or control the horse.

Reins are made of the same type of material as headstalls and merely used as a communicating device from the hand of the horseman to the pressure points previously discussed.

English type bridles are made of leather and differ from the western style bridles because of their simplicity, adjustments, and use for which they were designed.

In the English bridle field, there are several variations of types. The *Continental type* differs slightly from the *English headstall.* Two billets and a throatlatch on the crown, and two bridle cheeks identify the English headstall; the Continental style is similar but has no adjustment on the cheeks. Continental cheeks are cut from a solid strap, with a buckle sewn in at the poll position. The Continental bridle is used mostly in Europe. The English bridle, as it is called, is more commonly used in the United States (Fig. 9-5).

The saddle horse group uses a very narrow-width bridle with comparable reins and a wide and showy browband. It is sometimes used with a cavesson.

The hunter group uses a heavier-built bridle, wider cheeks, and reins. The reins are often laced or braided to give a more secure grip in foul weather. The flashy bridle fronts are not favored by the hunter group either in the ring or the field.

Sliphead (Fig. 9-5) is another variation of the English bridle, actually a simple strap, or bridle cheek, attached to a snaffle (bradoon) bit which is adjusted under the headstall and used with a Weymouth or

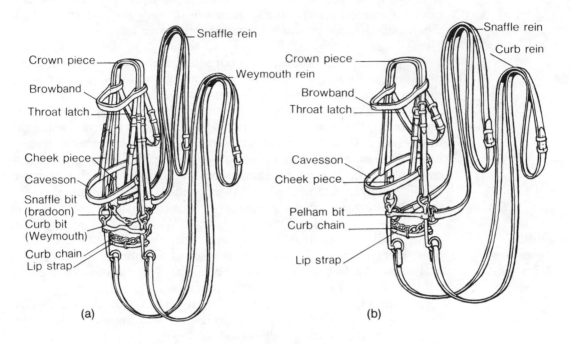

Snaffle rein

Crown piece
Browband
Throat latch

Weymouth rein

Cheek piece
Cavesson
Snaffle bit
(bradoon)
Curb bit
(Weymouth)
Curb chain
Lip strap

(a)

Snaffle rein
Curb rein

Crown piece
Browband
Throat latch

Cavesson
Cheek piece

Pelham bit
Curb chain

Lip strap

(b)

FIGURE 9-5. English bridles or headstalls are of two basic types: (a) the Weymouth bridle and (b) the Pelham.

full bridle. This allows for a double set of reins with two types of bits used simultaneously in the mouth of the horse.

The *Weymouth bridle* (Fig. 9-5), and Weymouth curb bit, is used in English riding, quite often used in combination with a snaffle (Bradoon) bit. The Weymouth used alone can be rigged for single rein use. When a sliphead and snaffle (bradoon) bit are added, it can be very effective as a double-rein bridle, also referred to as a *bit and bradoon.*

The *Cavesson* (Fig. 9-5) is basically a noseband with two independent cheek-pieces adjusted to ride about two fingers width above the bit. It is used primarily with young horses and its action is felt only when the horse opens its mouth to try to avoid action from the bit. A type of cavesson uses a sheepskin-covered, very prominent, rolled nosepiece called a "shadow roll." This limits the field of vision to reduce "spooking" at objects and shadows. Shadow roll cavessons are especially commonly used on harness race horses and some jumpers.

Round-sewn bridles are handmade bridles that have become very popular because of the influence of German saddlery manufacturers, who are producing a very attractive bridle, which is also very expensive because of the hand labor involved. There is no advantage over flat leather bridles, the only difference being eye appeal.

Longeing cavesson is used to make the horse perform at the end of a rope or long leather line. This is referred to as longeing, also called "the gyp line" at racetracks. Although the horse can be longed off of a bridle or halter, most professionals prefer the longeing cavesson. This is a headstall device much like a bridle, but the bridle cheeks split at the bottom and buckle to a hinged set of metal plates adjustable to fit the horse's nose. Three rings, one at the front in the center of the nosepiece, and one on either side are attached to these plates. The inside of the noseband is heavily padded to protect the horse. The longe line may be attached in the center or on either side of the longeing cavesson to provide a variety of training exercises or controls.

Gag bridle is most in demand by the jumper people and was also adopted by cutting horse and reining enthusiasts. The idea was borrowed from polo gear, which has many variations of the gag bridle. Basically, small pullies allow the bit to be drawn up into the horse's mouth while pressure is simultaneously applied at the poll when pulling on the reins. Some gag bridles are used alone, other types used in conjunction with another bit with an extra pair of reins attached to the gag bit. The horse is ridden with the regular rein unless stronger control is needed, then the gag rein is pulled, exerting pressure in both the mouth and at the poll.

Draw reins is a tack item borrowed from the polo players. Draw reins are reins of any width that are double the normal length. A loop is sewn into the end of the reins, wide enough to allow the girth to pass through. Reins are then adjusted on either side of the horse at the girth and the free end is passed through the snaffle bit and each rein is returned over the horse's neck where they are connected together with a buckle. Draw reins are used with a snaffle bit but provide powerful leverage for stronger control.

Both the gag bridle and the draw reins can be harmful to the horse in the hands of an unskillful rider. If these devices are used, much care should be taken to prevent injury to the horse.

Race bridle, also called a running horse bridle, is made (the American form) of doubled or lined and stitched leather. It consists of a slip type headstall with a throatlatch. The reins are unique, always finished with rubber hand parts. This allows a firmer grip and more control. Hunters and jumpers also use reins with rubber hand parts.

Although there are literally hundreds of variations of bits, there are actually only two types that have ever been used—the snaffle and the curb bit. All bits in use today are simply some modification of these two control devices.

Snaffle (bradoon) bit (Fig. 9-5), called a bradoon bit in England, is a simple device developed by the Greeks. Action of the snaffle is on the tongue and corners of the mouth. Most snaffle bits are jointed in the middle with an O-ring or Dee-ring fashioned at the end for attachment to the reins. Some are not jointed in the middle, being merely a straight bar, twisted wire, or some other variation with rings at the end. At any rate, the snaffle is a very mild bit and is most often used in training young horses, especially east of the Rocky Mountains where the English form of training and ideas prevail. The snaffle is invariably followed, after training, by the curb bit.

West of the Rocky Mountains, the Spanish ideas of training are followed and the snaffle bit is seldom used, horsemen preferring to use the Bosal or hackamore, graduating the horse directly to the spade (curb) bit.

The *curb* bit (Fig. 9-5) is a type of bit used by both Western and English riders. The design of bit varies depending on the use of mouthpieces, straps, and chains. Most curb bits have a fixed mouthpiece with cheek pieces welded, bolted, or riveted to rigidly apply pressure through the leverage or increased length of the cheek pieces. This is a much more effective method of control because the curb bit exerts pressure on the mouth, the curb groove, poll, and depending upon the design and use of accessories, the tongue and the sensitive nose. Thus, the curb bit exerts pressure on three to five of the sensitive control points previously discussed. One interesting version is the "loose jaw" form of curb which is jointed in the middle like a snaffle bit but has riveted or welded shanks corresponding to the normal curb bit. This type originated with the old Spanish bit masters and provided a less severe control on younger horses.

The Western style bit has many mouthpieces, the most famous of which is the spade bit. There are thousands of variations of mouthpieces. Some versions use a "cricket," a small revolving roller, usually made of copper. Copper promotes salivation in the horse's mouth which in itself is a protective device lubricating the mouth and protecting against tugs from the reins.

The *Pelham bit* (Fig. 9-5) is a British curb consisting of double rings for attaching dual reins. This bit can also be used with single reins by the attachment of a bit converter, a leather strap that simply forms one Dee-circle between the two rings allowing attachment of a single rein. It is used in park or pleasure riding and in hunting.

The *Weymouth bit* (Fig. 9-5) is a curb bit of English design with a single ring for a single set of reins. The Weymouth bit is often used along with a snaffle or bradoon bit, as the English call it, to provide for a double set of reins with two bits in the horse's mouth. This combination can be "made up" by applying a sliphead first followed by a Weymouth bit attached to a headstall. The *Weymouth* or *full bridle* (Fig. 9-5) is a headstall designed to accommodate dual reins and both curb and bradoon mouthpieces. The bradoon is used for mild control, the Weymouth for more leverage and force when needed.

In the case of both snaffle and curb bits, the mouthpieces may vary considerably. Numerous variations have been found effective under conditions for horses depending on their age, use, etc. They are illustrated in Fig. 9-6 and 9-7.

Straps and chains add to accessory items for the bit. The strap is simply a leather device, rope, or other suitable material, that holds the bit in place in the horse's mouth and also exerts pressure at one of the sensitive control points.

Chains are also used on bits, similar to the strap, but are more effective because of the harsher surface to which pressure is applied by the bit and reins. Two types of chains are used, a single link chain which has the harshest effect, and a double link chain which provides more surface area and less discomfort to the horse (Fig. 9-8). Whether a strap, chain, or some combination is used, the long coarse hairs from the back of the chin and curb groove of the horse should be removed to make the most comfortable control zone. The key to control of any type is to provide the mildest form of control that will work on the particular mount being ridden or driven.

Fake bit or mechanical hackamore (Fig. 9-9) combines some of the ideas from the curb bit, and the hackamore (to be discussed later in this chapter). Simply stated, it is a headstall or cavesson with a "fake" curb bit ending at the point where a curb bit passes through the mouth. The fake bit or mechanical hackamore rides much higher on the nose, however, and has no mouthpiece. The leverage from the shank allows for great pressure to be applied on the nose and the strap which encircles the curb groove under the jaw. Severity varies with the nosepiece selected on the mechanical hackamore. A flat leather strap or a sheepskin-covered nosepiece applies very mild pressure while a braided rawhide nosepiece, or one with a spring steel core, applies more harsh control methods.

Halters (headcollars) are devices designed to control the horse when it is not wearing a bridle. Halters, or headcollars (English term), are made of various styles of web, rope, leather, or other material fashioned to adjust to the horse's head. The leather halter is probably the most popular. A universal type of leather halter is the Newmarket pattern, a double leather halter, usually three-row stitched with a round throatlatch and a double buckle crown.

On the other end of the scale are halters made of a single length of rope threaded through special hardware making them adjustable to the horse. A nosepiece is the only separate part in this type of halter.

Although the fake bit, or *hackamore bit*, previously described, is a

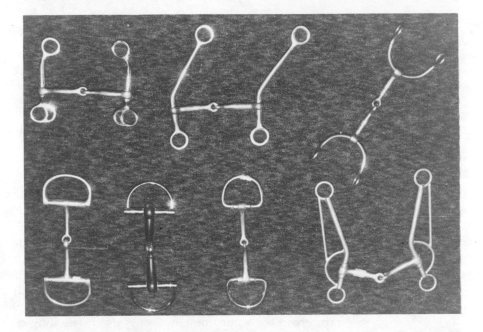

FIGURE 9-6. Snaffle bits come in a variety of styles, some with O-rings, and others with Dee-rings, even shanks. All, however, share the common mouthpiece.

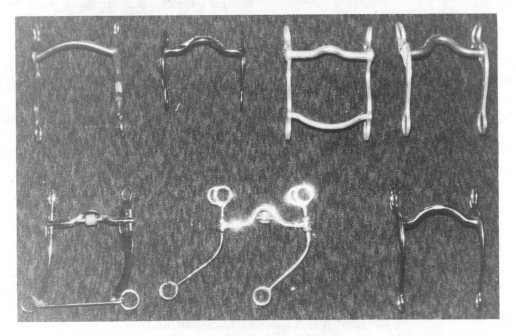

FIGURE 9-7. Curb bits vary according to length of shank and type of mouthpiece. Note the two bits in the bottom lower left row with copper rollers to stimulate salivation.

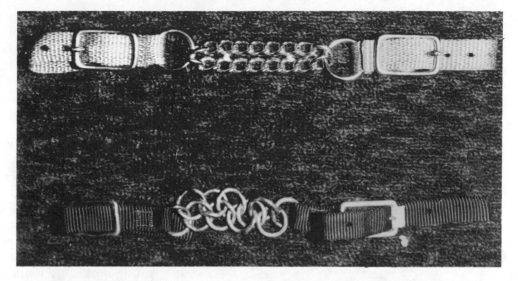

FIGURE 9-8. Curb chains, single link (left) or double link (right), act as controls because of pressure applied by the belt and reins.

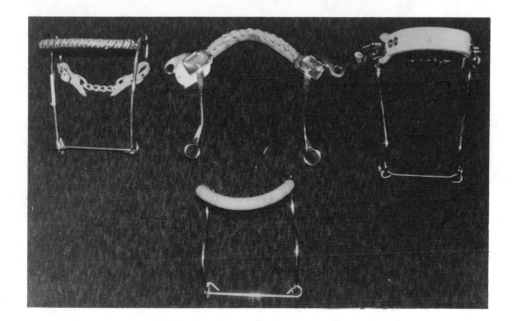

FIGURE 9-9. The fake bit or mechanical hackamore combines ideas from curb bit and hackamore control without the use of a bit. It is used most often in training young horses.

type of hackamore, the basic design goes back to the rawhide *bosal* used for centuries by Spanish horsemen. The term hackamore comes from the Spanish word *jaquima* (which sounded like "hackamore" to Anglo ears), a type of Spanish noseband giving control through pressure on the nose and jaws alone. Proper size and shape of the bosal is essential in control. They are made very stiff in order to provide pressure at the proper sensitive points. Basically, a bosal curves around the horse's nose, and joins under the jaw in a heel knot. This is a plaited rawhide arrangement, often held by a leather headstall in a very simple arrangement. A browband may be added. Bosals or hackamores (Fig. 9-10) are used on young horses when training for later acceptance of the spade bit (curb). Attached to the heel knot are *mecate* reins (a Spanish word meaning rope) woven of thick horsehair. The bosal is allowed to slide down at the heel knot and pressure on the reins brings the back side of the stiff rawhide bosal into contact with the thinly covered jawbones, which are quite sensitive. It also applies pressure to the nose. In this manner, young horses are trained to ride without having to adjust to the bit at the same time.

Western style bridles (Fig. 9-11) are used on stock type horses. These

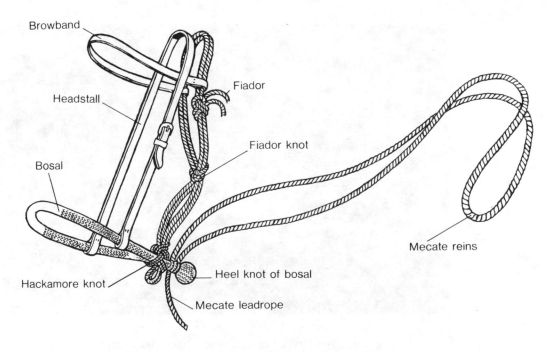

FIGURE 9-10. The hackamore is widely used in the Southwest on young horses when training for later acceptance of the curb bit.

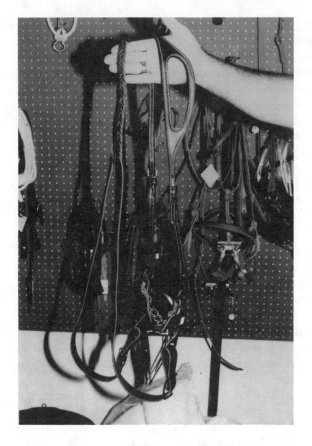

FIGURE 9-11.   Western style bridles come in a variety of styles. Most use some form of the curb bit as in this split-ear bridle.

bridles can be constructed of braided leather, doubled and stitched leather, rope, rawhide, plaited, buckstitched, trimmed with silver, one-ear style, two-ear style, with or without throatlatch, and browband. Most Western bridles use some form of the curb bit but the variety and combination of bridle, bit, and reins is endless.

There are two basic patterns from which all western bridles have evolved. The Texas-style originally developed from the Mexican forms which grew out of Spanish influence. Texas-style bridles normally have a browband, throatlatch, and noseband. Reins are always split, that is, not joined at the ends with a buckle or other means. Texas horses were originally taught to be "ground tied" and dropping of one rein to the ground signified that the horse was anchored to that spot. Texas-style bridles have migrated through the center of the United States and eastward of the Rockies.

The California-style bridles caught on east of the Rocky Mountains. It too was influenced by the Mexicans and Spaniards but the styles adopted were mostly of braided rawhide, braided horsehair, or flat leather with ornate decorations. California-style reins are joined in the center, fitted with a *romal* (an apparatus used to join the reins as well as serve as a quirt-like "popper"). California-style enthusiasts preferred to use hobbles rather than teach their horses to ground tie.

Martingales or *tiedowns* are devices used to restrain or hold the horse's head down. The English refer to the term martingale whereas the Western term is tiedown.

The *standing martingale* is a device that consists of a strap with a loop at each end, and containing a collar or yoke that goes around the horse's neck. One end of the loop allows for the girth to pass through it. The other end of the loop is normally a buckle-adjustable loop for attachment to the cavesson. The yoke or neckstrap is also adjustable by a buckle. The standing martingale simply limits the height to which a horse can elevate its head. It is used in training some horses and restraining others who may have bad habits of throwing the head up or holding it too high.

Running or *ring martingale* (Fig. 9-12) consists of a strap with a sewn-in loop for attachment to the girth but the opposite end splits to form a "Y" to which two rings are sewn. The reins are run through each fork of the ring to control the horse's head elevation by rein action. The running martingale also has a neck yoke or strap with an adjustable buckle. Running or ring martingales are widely used by hunters and jumpers.

The *hunting breastplate* is an accessory item that fits in the martingale category. The hunting breastplate does not limit the horse's head elevation but has as its chief function holding the saddle forward on the withers. One looped end of the strap attaches to the girth and goes between the front legs where the strap forks at the base of the neck to join again at the withers where O-rings and billets attach to the pommel of the saddle. Hunting breastplates are used on English saddles.

Breast collar is a Western term for a hunting breastplate. The variations are endless and usually heavier, more elaborately decorated, but they serve the same purpose, to hold the saddle forward on the withers. Western styles are often hand-carved, curved, tooled leather or buck-stitched. Others may be made of braided mohair or nylon. Almost all are brightly colored or decorated. Still, it serves the same purpose as the hunting breastplate, holding the saddle forward on the withers.

The *chambon* (Fig. 9-13) is a device widely used in Europe but very little in the United States. This is a training device, never used with a mounted rider, to make the horse keep its head down and mechanically force the hind legs farther under its center of gravity. Basically, it consists of a bridle with a snaffle bit. Just beneath the browband on either side of the head, a gag runner (ring that acts as a pully) is attached and two straps are adjusted to run from the girth through each

FIGURE 9-12. The Running or Ring Martingale is widely used by hunters and jumpers. The horse's head elevation is controlled by rein action.

FIGURE 9-13. The Chambon, never used with rider, is a training device to keep the horse's head down. It is used mostly in Europe. (From *Know All About Tack*, G. Dulaney, Farnam Horse Library, Omaha, 1972)

pulley and snapped back to the snaffle bit to complete the chambon. Raising the head above a preset position automatically activates the gag and trains the horse to keeps its head down.

A variation of the chambon, called the "brain chain," is used by cutting horse trainers. The device has a gag runner situated on either side of the bridle just below the browband. A chain running across and just below the browband is attached to two straps that pass through the gag runner and are adjusted to fit the girth holding the head in the proper position. The tension applied when the horse tries to raise its head exerts pressure on the chain across the forehead encouraging the horse to keep its head low. Again, this is a training device and must be used only in the hands of experts, even then, not while the horse is being ridden because a spirited horse could hurt itself and the rider.

ACCESSORIES

Although there are hundreds of accessory items, we shall concentrate on the major accessories of protective devices (boots), girths, stirrups, and spurs.

Protective Boots

The Standardbred Trotters or Pacers have the greatest need and variety of protective boots. They use everything from shin, tendon, elbow, ankle, knee, and fore and hind leg protectors made of leather, plastic, felt, rubber, and some combinations of each. The running horse does not use such a wide variety of protective devices, relying more on elastic bandages. However, some Quarter boots, especially for the Saddlebred horse and the Tennessee Walker are used to increase their action. These boots are lead-weighted, while other breeds use them mainly as a protective device to prevent injury.

Jumpers especially wear a rubber bell boot to protect the heel and coronet from injury by the hind feet. Of course, if a horse has a tendency to "scar up" an ankle or other area, protective boots are available for that purpose.

The stock horse most often wears a skid boot, placed on the hind legs. These are quite often seen on top roping horses because of their excessive use and quick, sliding stops necessary for competition on the rodeo circuit. This is simply a device to protect the fetlocks from abrasion.

Girths

Western style girths are called *cinchas*, and are much more standardized in shape and size than English girths. The typical western girth is made of braided cord, rope, mohair, nylon, or some combination thereof (Fig. 9-14).

English or flat saddle type girths (Fig. 9-14) are much more varied. A baghide leather girth, with or without elastic, is the standard English type girth. Elastic may be placed at both ends of the girth giving

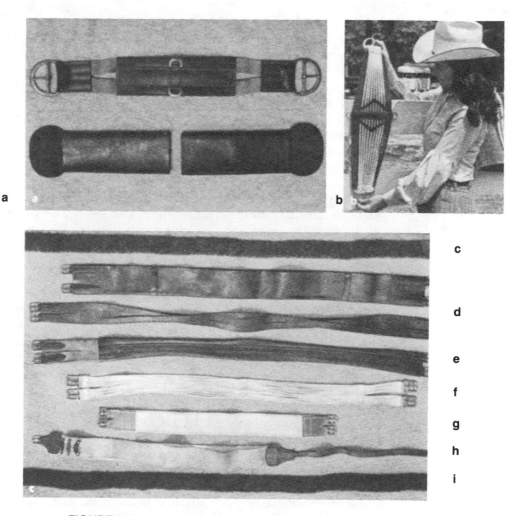

FIGURE 9-14. A wide variety of girths are used to secure the saddle: (a) elastic type with slip-over protectors, (b) cincha or western cinch, (c) Fitzwilliams girth, (d) Balding girth, (e) shaped girth with elastic, (f) nylon string girth, (g) elastic web girth, (h) race girth, (i) overgirth. (From *Know All About Tack*, G. Dulaney, Farnam Horse Library, Omaha, 1972)

the horse more breathing room while maintaining adequate tension on the saddle.

The *balding girth* is an invention of the polo enthusiast. Basically, it is a leather strap slit lengthwise into three equal parts, almost to each end. The straps are crossed over in the center and sewn in such a way as to provide a girth that is relatively wide in the center but narrow behind the elbows of the horse. A leather shield slips over this and is padded and stitched. The purpose of the balding girth is to prevent pinching behind the elbow.

The *web*, also known as *union web girth*, is made of woven linen and wool.

Jockeys use a type of girth that is different from any other arrangement. The universally used material is elastic web. It is basically two layers of elastic web with a buckle at each end. Also used is an *over-girth*, made of the same material, but long enough to go completely around the horse over the top of the saddle. This arrangement is also used by jumper riders, especially in international competition.

Stirrups

English or flat saddle type stirrups are made of metal and vary considerably according to the tread, weight, and style. The variations are small and to the untrained eye, all English type stirrups may look the same, but there are many differences, depending on preferences and regional tastes.

The Western style stirrup is basically a wooden stirrup covered with leather. They range from very narrow, rounded bronc riding styles that decrease the danger of a rider hanging a foot if thrown, to very broad stirrups, with or without tapaderos (toe fenders), adornments, etc.

The roping horse saddle may be equipped with a functional, common wooden stirrup covered with a small piece of leather for a secure footing.

The California stirrups may be covered with hand-tooled tapaderos with silver trappings.

The Peruvian stirrup (see Peruvian Paso, Chapter 2) on the other hand, is used not only to house the foot but also as a weapon to be used in case of ambush by banditos.

Spurs

The first spur was a thorn attached to the heel. Although many advancements have been made from that early invention, the principle is still the same. The purpose is to urge the horse to increase its effort.

English spurs tend to be very small and blunt, with a minimum of show. Western spurs, on the other hand, are flashy, mostly with rowels, that revolve and jingle. They range from very plain to richly ornate. Western spurs are still subconsciously used as a status symbol, especially in the Western states. This is not unusual since the knights of old wore gold spurs, pages wore silver spurs, and peasants used simple iron spurs. Thus, a rider could be ranked by social order merely by a glance at his footwear.

BIBLIOGRA-PHY

Dulaney, G. *Know All About Tack*. Omaha, NB: Farnam Horse Library, 1972.

Edwards, E. H. (ed.). *Encyclopedia of the Horse.* London: Octopus Books, 1977.

Ensminger, M. E. *Tack, Tack, Tack.* Clovis, CA: Pegus Co., 1960.

Gianoli, L. *Horses and Horsemanship through the Ages.* New York: Crown, 1967.

Price, S. (ed.). *The Complete Horse Encyclopedia.* New York: Chartwell, 1976.

10
Horseshoes and Horseshoeing

The first step in understanding horseshoes and the process of shoeing is to be familiar with the anatomy and terminology of the foot. Figure 10-1 illustrates the parts of a horse's foot. After becoming familiar with this nomenclature, it is much easier for horse owners and farriers (blacksmith, horseshoer) to communicate.

Although horse owners seldom shoe their own horses, they should be familiar with the processes involved in order to make proper decisions concerning shoe selection or corrective shoeing. In most instances, shoes will not be needed for corrective purposes, merely for protection. In either case, the owner should be aware of options and make a decision based upon the materials available. Just as a financial consultant can only recommend where to place investments, the ultimate decision lies with the owner.

Horse owners should be familiar with what constitutes a proper stance, motions, or faulty motions, and ways of improving them through trimming and shoeing.

The owner should also be familiar with horseshoeing tools (Fig. 10-2) and how to use them, be able to recognize good or faulty shoeing, be familiar with various types of shoes, and be able to give emergency assistance in the event a shoe is torn off, etc.

The principle of shoeing is simply to hold a protective plate against the hoof fastened by a few nails driven into the insensitive part of the hoof. The key to shoeing is to thoroughly understand the separation between sensitive and insensitive parts. A closer study of Fig. 10-1 at

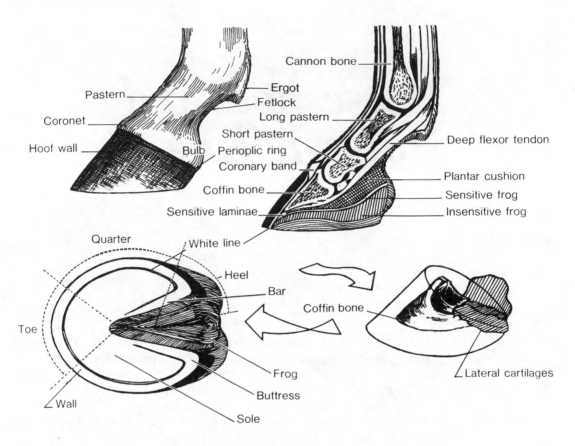

FIGURE 10-1. Parts of the pastern and foot.

this point will be an invaluable aid in completely understanding the discussion to follow.

PARTS OF THE HOOF

The hoof of a horse is divided into two basic parts. The outside part is a thick, hard wall of horn, the same substance of which hair is made. In the center is a soft, sensitive area known as the *frog*. The horny *wall* serves as a protective device for the foot, the wearing surface, which extends itself from the outer shell inward to the rear forming the *bar*. The *bar* extends forward toward the center of the foot. The V-shaped *frog* in the middle of the *sole* has several important functions. This is the shock absorber of the foot, transmitting pressure to more flexible structures. It also serves as a pump to the heart, increasing blood circulation from the lower limbs. In addition, it gives traction to the otherwise hard surface of the foot.

On the external portion of the hoof where the *horn* meets the hair of

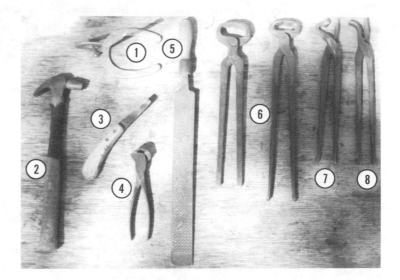

FIGURE 10-2. Some basic tools used in horse shoeing: (1) hoof leveler; (2) lightweight shoeing hammer; (3) "J" knife; (4) nippers; (5) rasp; (6) nippers; (7) gooseneck clinchers; (8) alligator clinchers.

the leg, the *perioplic ring* is an important feature. This is the seat of *periople* production, a varnish-like substance covering the outer surface of the wall preventing it from drying out, sealing moisture in the hoof. Moisture, amounting to one-fourth of the weight of the foot, is extremely important in providing elasticity to the normal foot.

Other features of the hoof include the *commissures*, the deep grooves found on either side of the *frog* which give elasticity to the foot. If the commissures are not kept clean, thrush often results. The horny *sole* is a thick plate about ⅜ of an inch growing out from the fleshy sole at the bottom of the foot, which protects the foot from injury from the bottom. This horny sole is convex in shape and does not carry much weight. Weight rests on the wall and frog area, the horny sole merely protecting the soft area from rocks, etc. The *bars* have evolved in such a way as to support the foot and maintain an open heel. This might be thought of as internal reinforcement and a natural drainage system allowing the horse to operate in mud or hard surface.

The hoof grows downward and forward at the rate of about ⅜ inch per month. This growth necessitates trimming of the horse's feet whether shoes are used or not. Wild horses wear their hooves off from rocky or sandy terrain. Domestic horses must have their feet trimmed if they are shod. Feet are trimmed and shoes are normally reset at 6-week intervals.

**REASONS
FOR
SHOEING**

Basically, only two sound reasons exist for shoeing a horse: protection from some form of abuse or correction of a fault.

Protection for the foot is of the utmost importance when a horse is being worked on rocky ground, hard surface, abrasive ranges, icy surfaces, race tracks, etc. This protection may vary from a light weight race shoe weighing only a few ounces up to the huge scotch-bottom shoes used on draft horses in shows and pulling contests that weigh several pounds. The key elements, however, are protection and traction. Selection of the style, size, and weight of the shoe will depend upon the use to which the horse is put.

Corrective shoeing, much like corrective footwear in humans, is used to improve or alleviate a condition that interferes with the horse's movement or function. Trimming to reposition the angle of the foot and application of shoes to create a new improved placement of the foot may be in order. Some common faults that can be corrected by trimming and proper shoeing are the conditions of splayfoot (toes turned out, heels turned in), pigeon-toed (toes in, heels out), quarter crack (see Chapter 6), navicular disease (see Chapter 6), cocked ankles (a forward bend to the fetlocks, especially the hind feet) forging (toe of hind feet striking bottom center of front feet), and contracted heels (shriveling up of the heel due to dry feet). Many gaited saddle horses and harness racing horses may have their gaits modified or improved through the use of proper shoeing. In some instances, pacers and trotters have been known to fail to pace or trot until properly aided with the right kind of shoes.

**PRINCIPLES
OF SHOEING**

Reduced to its simplest terms, horseshoeing is merely holding a shoe fitted to the bottom of the foot and nailing it in place. If done properly, the horse feels no pain whatsoever and is much better off for the addition of the protective plate. If done improperly, the horse can be crippled. Therefore, it is extremely important to understand the correct method of shoeing, the tools involved, and the types of shoes available for conditions under which the horse would be best used. The *white line* (Fig. 10-1) that runs the arch of the foot about an inch and a half from the edge of the wall is an important landmark. This line separates the dead horn of the hoof with the living interior. A nail driven into the area outside this white line will not cause pain. A nail that curves inside the line or is driven directly inside the white line is said to hit the "quick" or be driven "too green." That creates pain, produces sensitivity, and may cause the more serious condition of blood poisoning. The farrier, therefore, has 1½ inches to work with in order to firmly secure the selected shoe to the bottom of the foot.

There are two ways to shoe horses—*hot shoeing* (Fig. 10-3), requiring

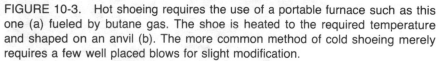

(a)

(b)

FIGURE 10-3.   Hot shoeing requires the use of a portable furnace such as this one (a) fueled by butane gas. The shoe is heated to the required temperature and shaped on an anvil (b). The more common method of cold shoeing merely requires a few well placed blows for slight modification.

shaping and molding on an anvil, most commonly used in corrective shoeing; and *cold shoeing*, the more common protective manner of horse shoeing. Although hot shoeing should be left to the seasoned experts, anyone can learn cold shoeing within a short period of time. Horseshoeing schools or seminars are conducted throughout the nation to teach this art.

Once the selection of shoe (to be discussed later) has been made, the tools are relatively simple. Basically, a rasp, file, cutting nippers, a special horseshoeing "J" knife, and a lightweight horseshoeing hammer are all that will normally be needed. Clinchers (also called alligator or gooseneck pinchers) may also come in handy, and clinch cutters for removing shoes are good to have available.

The first step is to thoroughly clean the foot. This is done with a special hoof cleaning knife shaped like an elongated "J" (Fig. 10-4). A hoof pick may also be needed to pick out mud, manure, and other debris.

(a)

(b)

FIGURE 10-4. The first step in shoeing is to remove the old shoe with an old pair of nippers (a), and if preparing the foot for the first time, to clean the foot of debris and dead tissue (b).

The most common position to use in working on a horse is to bring the foot upward and hold it between the knees. This frees both hands for the work. If an assistant is used, both handlers should be on the same side so the horse will not feel trapped. It is also helpful to lean into the horse, otherwise, it has a tendency to lean into the handler creating unnecessary weight and stress on the farrier.

After the hoof is thoroughly cleaned, the nippers are used to clip the horny wall back to within an inch or so of the white line (Fig. 10-5). A large rasp is then used to level the foot (Fig. 10-6), making sure that the angle of the foot is not repositioned, which would create stress or tension on the tendons and produce lameness. There are hoof levelers on the market to assure that the proper angle is maintained but most horseshoers simply use the eye and good judgment. Once the hoof has been flattened out to meet flush with the new shoe, the shoe is

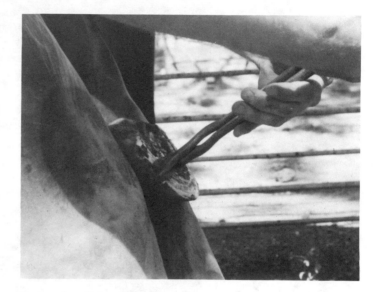

FIGURE 10-5. Nippers are used to clip the horny wall back to within an inch or so of the white line.

FIGURE 10-6. A rasp is used to level the horny base of the foot at the proper angle.

(a)

(b)

FIGURE 10-7. Applying a hoof leveler (a) to the newly rasped foot is a recommended practice to determine that the proper angle is maintained so as not to create unnecessary strain on tendons.

matched to the hoof (Fig. 10-8); never match the foot to the shoe. In cold shoeing, the selected plate will probably require only a swing or two of the hammer to make it properly fit the rasped surface of the foot.

Horseshoes are made with prepunched holes. The last holes are

FIGURE 10-8.   The shoe is always matched to the foot, never the foot to the shoe.

only slightly to the rear of the center of the foot, allowing for expansion of the heel over the surface of the horseshoe wings at the rear. This expansion may amount to $\frac{1}{16}$ inch on each side of the foot and is very necessary if proper elasticity of the feet is to be maintained.

Shoeing nails (Fig. 10-9) are actually small chisels bevelled on only one side. This produces a nail that will curve in the same direction as the bevel of the nail. With the shoe properly fitted in place, a couple of nails are driven in the prepunched holes and grooves in such a way that the nail curves just outside the white line and if properly driven with the lightweight hammer, will exit the wall of the hoof. The protruding points are wrung off with the claws of the hammer. Six to eight nails are usually required to properly secure a shoe. This nailing requires the most skill and is the most dangerous part of shoeing for both man and beast. With the nail protruding from the side of the horny wall, it is easy to visualize a startled animal creating havoc by a properly placed kick with a small sharp chisel attached to its powerful foot. Both man and horse have been severely lacerated when proper precautions have not been taken to prevent excitement at this point. The farrier's leather apron is a protective device to prevent even minor injuries due to even an unintentional movement.

After all nails are set (Fig. 10-10) and the points wrung off (Fig. 10-11), a rasp is usually used to cut a small groove directly below the broken end of each nail. A blunt metal edge or the side of the rasp is

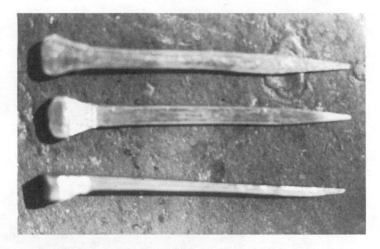

FIGURE 10-9. Horseshoe nails are small chisels with a bevel on only one side. The nail curves in the same direction of the bevel.

FIGURE 10-10. Nails are set by the hammer, using a set of nippers or other blunt tool as a backup.

FIGURE 10-11. Protruding horseshoe nails may be wrung off with the claws of the hammer or nipped as shown here.

used to serve as an instrument that is tapped a couple of times with the hammer, curling the broken end of the nail into the hoof wall. A set of "gooseneck" clinchers or "alligator pinchers" (Fig. 10-12) may be used to complete the curl back toward the shoe and prevent exposure. The job is smoothed up with a smooth metal file to remove any rough edges (Fig. 10-13). It is important not to overdo this smoothing and file off the entire hoof because this may cause the hoof to loose its natural moisture, dry out, and produce cracks or contracted heels.

Another fine point to remember is that a horse should never be allowed to put its foot down at its own leisure. The foot should be "placed" on the ground so that the mastery of the handler over the animal is psychologically assured in the mind of the horse. This makes future cleaning, reshoeing, or inspection of the foot much easier.

Another interesting point is that some horses like to "nibble" at the rear end of the handler. A bandana dangling from the rear pocket of farriers is often seen for this reason. The horse has something to nibble at that is far less sensitive than human anatomy.

KINDS OF SHOES

Kinds of shoes vary depending on whether the horse is used for riding, draft purposes, racing, or some other sport. The kind of shoe depends on the position of the horse's legs, the shape of the feet, the services demanded of it, and the surface over which it will be working.

The shoes used on the front feet are slightly different from those on the hind feet. The front feet are more rounded at the toe and quar-

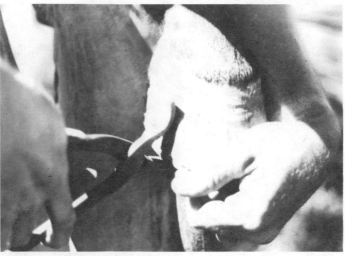

FIGURE 10-12. Alligator clinchers are used to clinch the broken end of exposed nails.

FIGURE 10-13. A smooth metal file removes any rough edges from the completed job.

ters, the hind feet more pointed. The hind feet are also commonly more narrow at the heels. Thus, shoes are divided into front shoes and rear shoes.

A variety of shoes exist that have specific functions. For the most part, the variety involves protrusions of some type that have been added to the surface of the shoe to aid in traction or provide weight for the specific purpose of improving a gait, etc. These protrusions are referred to as nubs, bars, calks, or some generic term denoting a style.

A wide variety of shoes is available. Some of the names are nub, rim, swedged, rolled toe, scooped, calk, bar, dubbed, square toe.

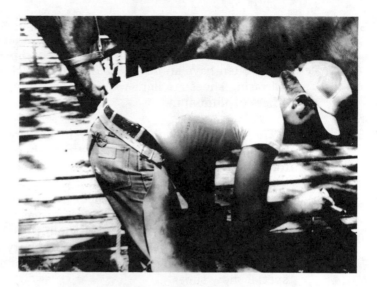

FIGURE 10-14. Some horses like to nibble at the posterior of the farrier. Note the bandana extending from the farrier's back pocket. Some claim this serves as an effective distraction.

Trotter and Pacer Shoes

A wider variety of shoes is available for this category than for any other. Among harness racers, the weight and style of shoe may be changed quite often. Improvement of action or corrections of a fault are the most common reasons for selecting shoes for trotters and pacers. When in training, a colt's shoes may be removed, and his feet leveled and dressed every ten days or so. The size, shape, and weight of shoes may be changed from time to time to correspond to the racing conditions or the state of development for the horse. Calk shoes, bar shoes, nub shoes, and pacing shoes are some of the common generic forms used by trotters and pacers.

Saddle Horse Shoes

Shoes for three-gaited and five-gaited horses are quite simple in design. A relatively plain, light, short, snuggly fitted shoe is used.

The hoof surface of the shoe must be wide enough to support the hoof wall, cover the white line, and a portion of the sole. Wings of the front shoe must be wide enough to give support, yet snug enough so that the hind feet does not catch them and tear them off. The outer bevel of the shoe lends a fine neat finished appearance of workmanship. Some saddle horse shoes may have additional weight in the width of the shoe (front) to produce a longer stride. Weights in the web of rear shoes help to break or lift the knees, adding height to the stride.

Racing Shoes   Light racing plates are used on Thoroughbreds and Quarter horses simply to protect the hoof wall and give a solid footing on the track surface. Front shoes usually have a toe clip to help secure it; hind shoes often have an inner and/or outer toe clip for the same purpose. All racing shoes are light weight (3 or 4 ounces), some made of iron, others of aluminum.

Draft Shoes   The most commonly seen shoe in the draft horse category is the Scotch-bottom. Both the front and rear shoes are beveled at an angle that extends the wall of the hoof beyond the rim of the shoe continuing the slope of the hoof wall to the ground. This makes a draft horse's foot appear even larger. Toe clips, front and rear, are used to secure the Scotch-bottom plates in place. Ordinary plates are usually used, prior to the shoeing with Scotch-bottom plates. This permits sufficient growth of the hoof wall so that when ordinary plates are removed, the blacksmith will have enough hoof to trim and shape them to fit the special show shoes.

RUBBER PADS   Because parade horses, draft animals, and specialized performance animals often perform on slippery material such as pavement, rubber pads may be used to give the horse's feet a safe grip. This involves a rubber pad, sufficiently wide enough to cover the frog and buttresses of the hoof, cemented to a leather sole. Used with a 7- to 10-ounce short shoe, about one-third of the thickness of a rubber pad projects below the ground surface of the shoe giving the horse protection as well as a firm grip on slippery surfaces. These pads are normally used only on the front feet and may also be used to relieve sore feet and sore heels, corns, or bruised soles.

POINTS TO REMEMBER   Horse owners should realize that any kind of covering on the feet is unnatural for the horse. If they have sound feet with hoof walls that will stand up properly under natural conditions, their feet may simply be trimmed regularly at 10-day intervals and shoes may not be required.

However, horses used frequently and under modern conditions, will often need to have the hoof protected or have assistance for good traction. Shoes may be the answer to improve the way of going of show horses, or to prevent wear and tear on the hoof.

The horse owner should be aware that the hoof continues to grow even though shod, at about the rate of ⅓ inch per month. Unshod hooves grow faster than shod hooves. At any rate, the shoes should be removed, feet trimmed, releveled, and reshod at 6-week intervals. The same shoes may be used, simply reset.

Although most owners do not shoe their own horses, a working knowledge of the principles involved is essential for the horse owner to cope with a thrown shoe or for emergency repairs. For instance, a loose shoe may simply need to be removed until a farrier can correct the condition before tendons are sprained and foot injury results.

A horse owner who decides to become his own farrier should receive instructions from a master farrier or one of the established farrier schools that teach the proper execution of the art.

Although the material contained in this chapter is not intended to provide a self-study course, it should serve as an introduction to the more serious student.

Several key points cannot be overemphasized, even for the more experienced farrier. The shoe should always be shaped and fitted to the foot, not the foot to the shoe. This is very important to maintain the natural size and shape of the foot except when otherwise dictated by an expert. Expansion of the heel is of utmost importance. Nails should never be driven too far to the rear because this natural elasticity would be restricted. Horseshoes are made in such a way as to allow this natural expansion. Contraction of the heels may result if nails are driven too far to the rear. The hoof wall should not be rasped, especially above the clinches. This removes the periople, a natural layer of moisture to keep the hoof wall pliable. Destruction of the periople can lead to dryness, contracted heels, and pinching of sensitive tissues leading to lameness. Commercial hoof dressings are available to treat dry hooves.

BIBLIOGRAPHY

Ensminger, M. E. *Tack, Tack, Tack.* Clovis, CA: Pegus, 1960.

Kays, J. M. *The Horse.* New York: Arco, 1977.

Urshel, W., Jr. *The Western Horseman,* "Shoeing Basics," October, 1978.

11
Breaking and Training

A prerequisite to harnessing equine power is patience and understanding of the horse. A kind and gentle disposition in a trainer will result in the same type of finished product in the horse. The methods discussed in this chapter are only a few of the ways to accomplish the task and they are humane. Most every horse owner will realize when the methods employed are resulting in progress or the horse is not responding. Intuition will surely give a hint to any sensible horseman as to whether he should continue with his own training and experimentation or put the horse in the hands of a more experienced trainer.

While a qualified horseman can no doubt turn out a superb product, there is no greater thrill to the individual horseman than to rely upon his own techniques and skills in accomplishing the goal of training his own mount to meet his own specifications.

The information contained in this chapter will be divided into the logical sequences of *ground work* (haltering, leading, bridling, saddling, bitting, head set, driving); *mounting; preliminary riding;* and *reining.*

In addition, finishing the training of the horse will cover the fundamentals of *head set, collection, lightness,* and *side passes.*

BREAKING AND GENTLING

Contrary to the layman's popular belief, horses are not broken by the old west method of roping a horse, holding it down, throwing on a saddle, bucking for a few vigorous rounds in a corral, and then riding off pleasantly into the sunset. Although exhibitions are common that show the skill of some exceptionally talented trainers who can take a completely unbroken horse and be riding it within the hour, the process is very premeditated involving a great deal of effort and concentration on the part of the trainer. In most cases, it may take 6 weeks to green break a young horse, the trainee often spending a year in hackamore, 6 months in snaffle, 6 months on grazing bits, and another year in a spade bit before the training can be considered complete. This is merely one example of the progressive steps in training a horse. However, the average time remains fairly constant. The trainer usually has to spend about 3 years in developing a top-notch mount. The owner of the trainee may eventually praise or curse the trainer, depending on the quality of the product.

Although training methods vary, two major schools have evolved: the California style of training, using the hackamore, and the Texas style of training using snaffles and bits. In either case, however, breaking and gentling methods, as with most other methods, can be divided into the basics of ground work, mounting, preliminary riding and reining.

Ground Work   The average age at which a horse should begin training varies from a few days to 4 years of age. This is a judgment call in most cases, with some of the small or light-legged horses being 3 or 4 years old before they enter training. Big-boned horses may be started as early as 2 or 2½. Thoroughbreds may be racing at 2 years of age or less.

The first step, which can begin even earlier than 2 years, and in most instances should, is to teach a horse to accept a halter and remain tied without fighting it. Some trainers claim that a foal can be "imprinted" with the fearless acceptance of a halter and taught to lead just hours after birth. When haltered at a later date, the youngster unconsciously "remembers" this training and responds with good discipline in short order.

A web-type halter and a large, soft lead rope are important tools. Remember to go slow so that the horse learns the lesson perfectly before being asked to go on to the next one. A young horse should be observed closely when teaching it to remain halter-tied to a post. It is important to tie the colt to a post or fence that will not break. If the rope, halter, or post ever gives, especially in very early training, the horse will be very likely to remember this and try to break away again and again. The rope should not be long enough so that it could get tangled and the knot should be the type in which a quick jerk on the loose end will release the rope in the event the young horse gets excited and needs a quick but controlled release. The lead end should be tied about withers high to guard against the colt getting a leg over the rope and creating panic (Fig. 11-1). Snaps are not recommended on halter or lead rope at this stage because of the possibility of one breaking and "spoiling" a horse early in halter tying sessions.

FIGURE 11-1. In halter-breaking the young colt, the lead rope should be tied short and about withers-high to prevent entanglement of a foot.

If a horse has been previously spoiled and has developed the habit of breaking bridle reins, etc., one technique to retrain and rehabilitate the horse is to tie it with unbreakable halter and rope in a dirt arena, wet down the area with a garden hose to produce a muddy under-footing (the slicker the better), and leave the horse or sack it out (see Fig. 11-2) for a couple of hours at a time. The horse will soon discover it is easier to stand tied than exhaust itself in ineffective, uncomfortable activity.

After the horse has learned respect for the halter and realizes it cannot get away and becomes gentle enough to remain tied to a spot for an hour or so at a time, the horse should be taught to lead and backup. Initial response will be greater if the horse is not pulled directly ahead to make it lead but rather maneuvered by turning the head to one side. Soon the horse will respond to a slight tug. Some trainers prefer snubbing the halter rope to the saddle horn of another horse. Not only is more pressure applied but the company of another horse is incentive to move with that companion.

Another method of teaching the horse to lead, using gentle pressure, is to pass a loop over the horse's nose and slide it down to just above the nostrils. By pulling forward gently on the rope, the loop cuts off air passage and the horse will instinctively step forward to breathe better. It soon learns that a step forward will loosen the pressure on the rope and will lead with a very loose rein.

Backing may be taught at this stage and is recommended by some trainers, although others prefer to use the driving method (discussed later) to put a reverse on a horse. In teaching the horse to back from a halter, the process is relatively simple but patience is required. The trainer stands to the side of the horse with one hand on the back side of the halter and gently tugs with tremors against the halter while tapping the chest with a stiff-type quirt or bat. This tapping should be light enough to make a little noise but cause no pain. The tapping, therefore, merely becomes a nuisance and the horse backs away from it. As soon as this happens, the horse may be rewarded with a few kind words and gentle pats on the neck. Throughout these training procedures, it is recommended that the trainer speak softly to the horse and reward it frequently but only with affection. Feeding sugar cubes or other tidbits is definitely not recommended, except in the case of show animals. This tends to spoil a horse, and is seldom recommended by any trainer. Speaking to a horse has great advantage, not only because the words may be meaningful, but because the tone of voice can be sensed by an animal and, therefore, communication made.

The next step is a fairly well accepted method and used quite frequently among western horse trainers. The method is usually referred to as *sacking out* (Fig. 11-2) and refers to the early use of a burlap sack or similar substance to use as a harmless device to rub, touch or slap the horse on the various parts of its body. Sacking out involves tying the horse to a fence strong enough that it cannot break, solid enough to not get feet or legs hung, and high enough that it cannot attempt to jump. A strong halter and rope should be used for this, never a hackamore or bridle. When the horse is thoroughly secured, the *sack* (saddle blanket, old bedspread, slicker, etc.) can be used to begin the gentling process. The horse should be allowed to smell the sack first and become thoroughly familiar with the object that will be touching its body. Then the trainer slowly rubs the sack along the horse's neck, forearm, and withers, and gradually increases the severity of slapping and increasing the scope of his coverage. Starting on the upper part of the young horse's body makes it less likely to "spook." The sack is gradually worked around under the belly between the legs, nearly everywhere but the eyes and nose. The horse should be worked only 10 to 15 minutes in this manner every day until it becomes so accustomed to the sacking that the trainer can make the wildest motions and slappings anywhere on the horse's body without causing the least concern on the part of the horse. This teaches the horse to be calm and to accept the fact that man is not going to attack even though he may

FIGURE 11-2. Sacking out a horse with one foot tied up. Note that a soft rope yoke is tied around the neck with a knot that will not slip. The horse may also be sacked without a foot tied, and halter breakers may be retrained by sacking out on mud or purposely wetted ground.

pounce around like a wild animal. Some trainers even throw old paper boxes under the horse and wave slickers in their faces without the horse even tightening the rope. *Sacking out* is a preliminary step to putting on the saddle and may be repeated again prior to *mounting* and *riding*.

If the horse is particularly wild or the temperamental type that may kick, one hind leg may be tied up (Fig. 11-2) prior to sacking to insure that no harm will come to the horse or trainer. Using a thick, soft cotton rope, a loop is tied around the horse's neck so that it is open and loose and has a knot that will not slip. This forms a rope yoke to which can be tied another large, soft rope with 15 or 20 feet of line. The loose end of the rope is worked between the horse's hind legs by standing well clear of the kicking range of the horse and then the rope slowly brought around to encircle the foot, passing the loose end back through the neck piece. By gently pulling on this rope, the hind foot can be brought forward enough so that the horse finds itself with its weight on three feet. The horse cannot kick in this way and soon finds that it is immobilized and accepts its fate. The handler still should use caution, because with a loose loop, the horse could still easily kick free. Some trainers take an additional wrap around the foot to prevent this from happening. Precaution must be taken to have a very large, soft rope so as not to burn the foot. With one foot tied up, the wildest horse can be sacked out quite thoroughly. Some trainers even tie up a foot when *mounting* the horse for the first time.

The horse is now ready to be taught a few voice signals, especially "whoa." In this case, a longeing cavesson, or better yet, a hackamore, is very effective. The horse is encouraged to travel in a circle on a longe line (except for roping horse trainees where longeing is not recommended at all), motivated by a buggy whip used to pop the ground behind him. A young horse can be encouraged to travel in a small circle at first and with the trainer gradually letting out more line. After the horse has been taught to walk at a steady pace in a circle, the voice command "whoa" can be given at the same instant a flip of the rope causes a slight jerk back on the hackamore. This puts pressure on the sensitive part of the nose and the horse will soon get the idea to stop at the combination of voice command and backward pressure on the hackamore. Some trainers get the same effect using a snaffle bit instead of a hackamore. In this case, it probably should be a rubber-covered snaffle. The process is repeated at the trot and canter until the horse has mastered the stop or "whoa" command. Work the horse in a circle both ways.

The next logical step after the horse has been taught to respond to "whoa" and respects the halter, hackamore, or longe line is *bridling* and *saddling*. This may be as early as the third day of training although some colts may require several more days of sacking and longe line training. If the snaffle bit is used instead of the hackamore, some trainers claim the saddling can take place at the same time because the horse will be so busy thinking about this new device in its mouth that it will pay little attention to the saddle. If a hackamore is used, the horse will have only the saddle to think about. If a snaffle bit is to be used, hobbles may be used or one foot tied up as previously mentioned before the bit is eased into the mouth. The head should remain untied although a loose rope around the neck may be helpful. Using the thumb and forefinger on either side of the jaw will usually open the mouth wide enough to accept the bit. The other hand can hold the top of the headstall near the poll and guide the bit into the horse's mouth while pulling the headstall over the ears.

Once the colt has become accustomed to the bridle, the saddle blanket and saddle may be put on. Because of the sacking procedure, the colt should offer no resistance to the blanket. When putting the saddle on, the offside stirrup and cinch should be folded back over the seat of the saddle to prevent the iron cinch ring from accidentally injuring the horse by flopping over and striking an elbow, etc. Walk to the offside and pull the stirrup and cinch down in the proper position keeping one hand on the horse's shoulder in the event it should jump. This is a protective stance that would merely knock the trainer away from the horse in the event it gets excited. Move back to the left side at this point, and pat the horse on the belly while retrieving the cinch. The saddle should be snugged up slightly, but not tightly. Young horses often learn to protect themselves from early tightening by taking a deep breath creating a condition known among some horsemen as "cinch bound." After the horse is saddled, the stirrups should be moved around by hand so that the horse becomes aware that they are there. Because of the broad lateral vision of the horse, it can see rearward quite well and this merely accustoms the young horse to the presence of the strange new device on its back. At this point, if a leg has been tied, it should be released and the horse allowed to walk around, riderless, with the saddle on its back. A preliminary *head set* can be worked on at this point.

Head set refers to the carriage of the horse's head. It should be neither too high nor too low. Judgment of the proper position becomes critical and is learned only through experience but most can visualize proper head carriage. A high headed horse would make it difficult for a roper to see the calf; therefore, early training would try to correct this carriage to a lower position through proper enforcement.

A very low carriage of the head is undesirable because the horse may not see some objects that would be in its path. Therefore, the trainer can use the reins to the snaffle or hackamore as a preliminary head set by tying them to three positions on the saddle—the cinch, the Dee-rings on the saddle, and the horn. (Fig. 11-3). In most instances, the reins would be attached to either side of the cinch in order to pull the head down somewhat since most horses will have a tendency to hold the head a little high. If the horse needs to have the head raised, the reins may be attached to the Dee rings or in the case of an abnormally low natural head set, they may be attached to the horn. Now the horse is merely turned loose in a corral and allowed to walk around or worry with the bit and saddle for 30 minutes to an hour. (Some trainers use a device known as a *bitting rig* to put a head set on a horse but the saddle method works as well as any, especially with nonprofessional trainers who may not have access to such a device.) This process is repeated for 4 or 5 days, shortening the reins until they are short enough to maintain the head of the colt perpendicular to the ground. A rubber strip or stethoscope tube about 12 inches long may be used to tie into the three previously described spots to maintain some pressure on the reins but allow for give in the event the colt throws its head. This is an unnatural position and the head set is very tiring to the horse so it should not be continued for more than 10 to 15 minutes.

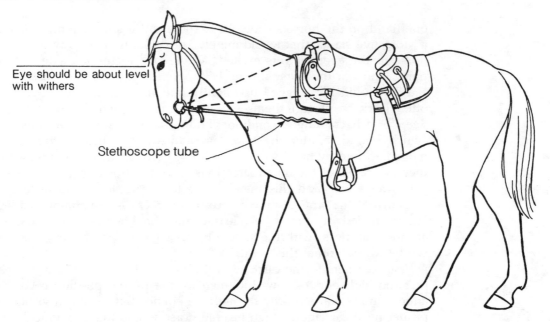

Eye should be about level
with withers

Stethoscope tube

FIGURE 11-3. Preliminary head set can be initiated by tying reins to three points on the saddle. Rubber stethoscope tube allows for some give to prevent mouth injury yet maintains pressure.

It should be mentioned that the head set (Fig. 11-3) is not just for looks, it is a very functional training period. In the old days, a head set was put on a horse in order to make it more responsive to the bit, more agile and maneuverable for warfare. Today the head set is necessary in order for the horse to make quick, responsive moves for roping, cutting, working, etc. Man has known for centuries, at least in superior horse training countries, that a flexing of the head at the poll was a necessary part of training a superior mount.

Although a great deal of time and effort has been invested up to this point, the colt still has more ground work to do before mounting. Although some trainers skip this procedure because they have no experience with driving, it is recommended and certainly could do no harm. *Driving* merely reinforces what the colt has learned up to this point but provides a margin of safety for the rider to put some rein training on the horse before mounting. Driving consists of using two 20- to 30-foot lines with a heavy-duty snap in each end. The snap is attached to a halter, not the snaffle bit, and one line is run through the stirrup of either side of the saddle. The stirrups are further tied with a soft cotton rope under the belly of the horse so that they will not flop around. The result is similar to plough lines on work horses with the trainer standing well behind the horse, controlling it with the lines (Fig. 11-4). A hackamore may also be used in driving with some modification for snapping the lines to the fiador (a matter of tying a few small, strong ropes in the proper place). The colt can be started on lines by the third day after learning to wear the saddle.

With the trainer well back out of kicking distance from the horse, he urges the horse to move foward by a slight jiggling of the lines on either side of the horse. The trainer may in this case need an assistant at the horse's head to get it started but it will soon learn the procedure and move forward at the command of the trainer. The horse is then guided with the lines and turned in a corral to put a rough rein on the horse. Some trainers continue this driving process to the point where the horse can work off of it as a longe line allowing the trainer to stand in the center and not get as much exercise as the horse. The horse is also trained to stop with the driving lines by back pressure and the voice command of "whoa." Some trainers also prefer to wait until this point before teaching a horse to back, using the lines and driving technique for 90% of the training to teach a horse to back up. The second day of driving can start the colt on turns.

After 2 or 3 days of driving, the colt is ready for advancement past

FIGURE 11-4.   With stirrups tied together under the belly of the horse, lines are run from the halter or hackamore, never a bridle, through stirrups for driving. An assistant may be needed to lead rope initially.

the walk into the trot either as previously described or in the longe line fashion.

Several important lessons are learned through the use of driving by the colt. He learns to respond to commands that come from behind him, the natural position of the rider later on. He gets used to the movement of lines and stirrups along his side, which stimulates the position of the rider's legs. The pull of the lines through the stirrup are rather low, thus reinforcing some flexing at the poll, previously discussed as a desirable training technique. Additionally, the horse has gained more experience at voice command stops at the walk, trot, and lope.

Mounting

Mounting can be the most dangerous part of horse training but if the discussed ground work has been thoroughly done, the danger is greatly reduced. Still, some trainers prefer to mount a horse that has one hind foot tied up, as previously described. A few key points about mounting the horse are to go very slow and never mount the horse until it is standing completely still. This may require some patience but will pay off in handsome dividends with a mount that is properly trained to allow the rider to mount without moving. The first day, the rider may merely mount and dismount, usually from both sides, sit for a few moments, pat the horse on the neck, and shift the weight around, but make no attempt at going further. If the foot is tied up at this point, it would be impossible to ride anyway. If the horse appears a little nervous, it should be sacked very thoroughly before mounting.

The second day the horse can be mounted again for 10 to 15 minutes and this time sacked from the saddle until it pays no attention to the sacking.

Preliminary Riding

On the day of the first ride, which should be the third day in most instances, the horse should be warmed up first by driving or running on a longe line for 10 minutes or so to remove the edge from the start of the day's activity. It would also be advisable to have another gentle horse and rider to accompany the colt on the first ride. If it is the nervous type, a halter may be left on the horse with the lead rope snubbed up to the saddle horn of the gentle horse. Within a day or so, the trainer can tell if the horse can be ridden with safety without being accompanied by another horse. After some gentle persuasion in the walk only, it is time to teach the horse to trot and eventually to lope. Usually, a young horse will not want to move this fast and it may be necessary to tap him with a quirt, switch, or bat. It is best to use a very stiff whip and use it only as a gentle tap directly over the tail head of the horse. Slapping the horse on either side of the tail may result in a tail switching, an undesirable habit. If the switch is needed, the first cue should be a voice command for moving ahead such as "get up," then a squeeze or kick with your legs, and finally a tap with the switch. A few such lessons usually result in a horse responding to voice and leg commands, and the tapping on the buttocks can be discontinued. The process is repeated again and again over a period of several days and gradually increased to exercise the horse in the walk, trot, and lope in the manner just described. Training is largely a matter of repetition, reinforcement, and reward. Add exercises at variable speeds and the process has been completed.

Another essential function for the horse is to back while mounted. If the previous training has included some backing on the ground, this will be much easier for the horse to grasp. The horse should already know the cue to back up but the weight of the rider in the saddle throws additional weight on the rear legs of the horse, which are much more difficult for it to move than the front ones. It is much easier for the horse to back up if the rider shifts his weight by leaning forward in the saddle while pulling back on the reins and giving the voice command "back." These three cues are the key to backing a horse while mounted.

Reining

An old saying among horsemen is "when you start riding a horse, if you just ride him straight down the road, you're wasting your time." This adage has come about because of the belief that rein training is so important in the production of a quality horse. It must begin very early and be reinforced in the early stages if the finishing touches are to be later applied. There are several methods to teach a horse to *rein*; this is only one of them.

First, place goggles over the horse's eyes to protect it from accidental damage to those sensitive organs. Tap the horse on the side of the neck with a loose rein or a switch while pulling on the opposite rein. If the horse is to be turned to the right, the left side of the neck or cheek will be tapped while pulling with the right rein. A tap on the right side of the neck and a pull on the left rein causes the horse to turn in the opposite direction. Soon the horse begins to associate the tapping or touching sensation with the need to turn, and *neck reining* may gradually replace the tapping. Neck reining means holding both reins in one hand and merely moving the hand in the direction that is desired for the horse to turn. A right turn would bring the left rein against the neck of the horse and the touching of the rein against the neck or cheek replaces the early tapping signal from the switch. Hours of practice are needed riding the horse in circles and figure eights in order to "put a rein on a horse."

At this point, the horse is considered to be "green broke" and is ready for the finishing stages of its training. It should be, by now, gentle, reliable, and willing to respond to commands.

FINISHING   A horse is safe to ride and considered broken when it is gentle enough not to try any unforeseen moves and to respond to the basic commands of starting, stopping, turning, and moving backwards. A finished horse is one that has been trained for a specific purpose such as roping, cutting, rodeo work, etc. Nearly all finished horses will share similar characteristics in training that lend themselves to a specific use. In general, certain performance characteristics such as the correct carriage of the head, ability to move at a collected gait, a light response to all cues and commands, and movement forward, backward, and sideways are basic areas that will be discussed in the finishing touches to a well-trained horse.

In the heyday of the horse, the old Spanish Dons of California sent their sons back to Spain to study horsemanship for a year or two. So important was the well trained mount that advanced horsemanship required a couple of years to learn. These techniques were brought back in the 1800s to California and Texas and have spread since that time throughout the world where western horsemanship is taught. Both the Texans and the Californians generally used the hackamore for green breaking a horse in order to teach it basic manners without danger of damaging its mouth. A spade bit was later used in combination with a hackamore, the hackamore gradually becoming less important and eventually removed altogether. These methods are still in use today.

The English method, later adopted by many Texans, utilizes the snaffle bit in place of the hackamore but did not gain popularity until after the turn of this century. Regardless of whether a snaffle bit or hackamore is used to initially break a horse, the horse should be at least 3 years old, well developed, and willing to work before starting on the finishing trials. The ideal age for finishing is 4 to 5 years of age.

Neck reining is extremely important in Western or English type horses because it is often necessary for the rider to have one hand free to swing a rope, etc. If the horse has been taught to yield only to plough reining, then the neck reining technique must be practiced until the horse responds to a very light touch.

If the horse has been broken with a hackamore, a change to the curb bit may result in head throwing, open mouths, etc. The California method to prevent this involved not only the use of tie downs or martingales but a combination of the hackamore and curb bit together with two sets of reins. After six months to a year, the hackamore is removed and the horse is ridden only with a snaffle, gradually replacing it with a curb bit. The English method uses double reins on a Pelham or Weymouth, a combination of snaffle and curb bit previously described.

The four basic categories to keep in mind for a finishing horse are a correct *head set*, mild *collection*, *lightness*, and movement forward, backward, and *sideways*. Although there are many other characteristics that would signify an extremely well trained, finished horse, these four characteristics make up the basic expectations for any horse that might fall under the category of broke, well-trained, finished.

Head Set

The set of the head involves both flexion at the poll and the height at which the head is carried. A horse that carries the head too high will have problems with balance and seeing the ground. This would be undesirable for a trail horse because it couldn't see where it was going or for a roping horse because the rider couldn't see the calf. A good guideline to follow in setting the head is to train a horse to carry the head so that the *eye is level with the withers* (Fig. 11-3). Of course, this will vary from breed to breed and will not apply to some breeds that have been bred to carry their head high such as the Arabians, Morgans, Tennessee Walking horses, etc. On the other end of the scale, Quarter horses have been bred to carry their head somewhat lower than normal. Using judgment, however, the horse owner can determine for himself the level at which the horse should carry its head and train it accordingly.

Training the horse to flex at the poll and carry the head at the right position has always been a very important function. Ancient warriors and even recent cavalrymen knew the importance of a horse that would flex at the poll, making it more responsive to the rein and other cues for movement. No horseman wanted to go into battle riding a stiff-necked, cold-jawed, inattentive horse, especially if he were facing well-mounted, well-trained enemy cavalry.

Teaching of flexion and setting the head is mainly a matter of holding the reins in the right position. A horse with a natural, high head carriage will need to have the reins held low; a horse with a low carriage will need to have the reins held high. High headed horses may also necessitate the use of running or German martingales to lower it sufficiently. Force should never be applied in teaching flexion and head set, rather the reins should be run under the little finger up through the hand to the index finger with the thumb applied to the top of the reins, much as one would hold a bottle with the thumb pointing straight up. Slight tremors with the reins give clues to the horse as to what it must do. Some trainers also use a heavy bit, the extra weight encouraging the horse to carry its head in the proper position. This produces flexion merely because the horse will tire from holding the extra weight out in front if it does not flex at the poll. By lowering the head, the weight of the bit is transferred from the mouth through the headstall to the poll creating a more comfortable effect and producing the desired flexion.

Collection

Collection means keeping the hind legs of the horse up under the body as it moves, working off the hind legs. Western horses are taught only a mild form of collection; highly trained English dressage horses are taught much more. Dressage horses doing the *piaffe* actually trot or lope in place without moving forward. This is an extreme example of collection. Cutting horses are an intermediate example of collection. The horse pivots off the hind feet sometimes appearing to dance lightly on the front feet in performing the cutting chores while working with cattle.

The teaching of collection is basically urging the horse forward using voice or leg cues or both while slowing it down with rein pressure. Collection at the trot is desirable before progressing to the lope. When the rider uses voice and leg squeezes, the horse is urged into an extended trot. The reins are then pulled back lightly while the rider continues to squeeze with the calf of the legs and urges the horse on by voice commands, such as clucking. The horse will usually slow and drop into a walk, at which time the hands are released to extend the horse into a trot. The process is repeated until a slow collected trot is developed, usually requiring a week or longer to learn.

Lightness

The term lightness refers to quick response to very light cues from hands, legs, and shifting of weight. Most all riders unconsciously give the horse these slight clues. Although a rider may not realize it, he unconsciously sits back in the saddle when he is ready to stop, will shift weight slightly to the stirrup in which he is dismounting, etc. The horse soon learns to respond to these cues almost as if it were reading the mind of the rider if it has been taught to pay close attention. Horses that do not develop lightness are usually those that have an incorrect head carriage or those that have developed hard mouths, either one of which can be traced back to improper use of hands during breaking and finishing. To avoid these problems and to develop lightness, most trainers develop a light touch and patiently train their horses to respond to the visual, auditory, and sensory cues given during the exercise of reining, stopping, and lateral movements. One key point that some trainers look for to determine if the horse is really paying close attention to him is to watch the ears. A horse that has one ear forward and one ear back is using one of the ears to listen for cues from the rider. Because of the lateral monocular vision of the horse, it can also see the rider quite well and will be looking forward with one eye as well as backward with the other at the same time. A horse with droopy ears will usually not be paying attention at all and a horse with both ears forward and erect is paying too much attention to something in front of it. Lightness is a matter of teaching a horse to pay attention and then giving it proper cues and expecting performance in response to those cues.

Side Passes

Movement forward and backward is commonly expected of horses but movements to the side are often overlooked. This is not the case with finished horses, however. The sideways movement of the entire body or of only the forehand or rearhand has practical use in closing gates while mounted, positioning a roping horse or steer wrestling horse, and numerous other uses.

By now, it should be commonly understood and observed that the hands, legs, weight, and voice can easily control the forward and backward movement of the horse. These same forces are used to cause the movement of the horse in *side passes*. Leg pressure can cause the horse to move sideways as well as forward and this is a key point to understand and a proper place to begin. In teaching the horse to move to the side, many trainers begin their lateral movement training sessions from the ground. The trainer stands on one side of the horse, pulls one rein so that the head is pulled toward the trainer, stands in the normal mounting position, and then applies pressure with a thumb, hand, or fist to the side of the horse. When the horse moves the rearhand in response to this pressure, he is rewarded by a pat on the neck and the process is repeated. The trainer then moves to the other side, pulling the head slightly to one side with the rein and applying pressure as previously done. Soon the horse gets the idea that it is to move the rear end in response to pressure to one side and a slight tug on the rein. Once the lesson has been learned from the ground, it can be repeated from the saddle with leg pressure replacing the hand (Fig. 11-5). Some horses may require spurs or a switch to learn this movement. Once the horse responds, however, the trainer should go back to only leg pressure to maintain the light response previously described.

Once the horse responds to proper leg pressure by moving the rearhand to one side, the horse can be exercised in moving the rearhand and forehand separately to gradually produce lateral movement. Once the trainer is satisfied with this progress, then training can begin for the *side pass* (Fig. 11-5) and *two-track* (Fig. 11-6). The horse is positioned motionless facing a fence to prevent forward movement in side pass training and left leg pressure is used to move the hind quarter to the right. By holding left leg pressure and pulling the right rein, the horse will continue to side pass down the fence line. The process is repeated several times in each direction.

The two-track is taught to the horse by facing the fence at a 45-

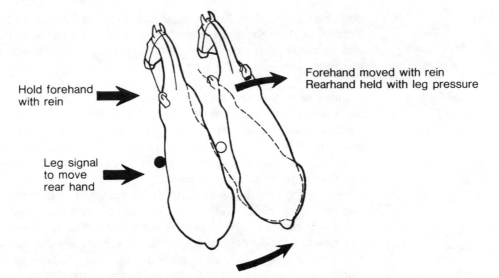

Hold forehand
with rein

Forehand moved with rein
Rearhand held with leg pressure

Leg signal
to move
rear hand

FIGURE 11-5. Movement sideways is communicated to the horse through use of the leg to move or hold the rearhand and rein pressure to move or hold the forehand.

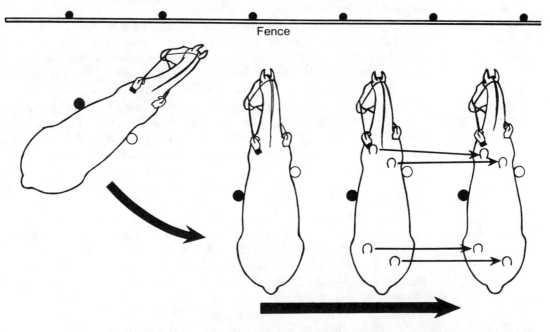

Fence

FIGURE 11-6. Two-tracking is accomplished by approaching a fence at a 45-degree angle, applying leg and rein pressure on the same side, and maintaining correct pressure for the desired two-track movement. Opposite leg and rein are used for two-track movement to the left.

degree angle in a moving position. For example, the trainer uses the left leg to strongly push the hind quarters away from the fence, also located on the left, and uses the left leading rein to bend the head toward the same side this time as the leg pressure. This produces a horse that is capable of facing one direction and traveling almost 90 degrees to the right or left. The movement is repeated in both directions during training until the horse has learned to respond to the two-track movement.

At this point, the horse is considered finished for the general characteristics of a well-trained average horse. Advanced training sessions can teach the horse pivots, off-sets, rollbacks, lead changes, and numerous other advanced movements. However, any horse that has reached this point is considered well educated, safe, gentle, and dependable. Just as with man, the education process never stops, depending upon the use for which the education is needed.

BIBLIOGRA-PHY

Henry, P. *Pat Henry's Instructions for Breaking-Training Horses.* Pat Henry, 1945.

Miller, R. W. *Western Horse Behavior and Training.* Garden City, NY: Doubleday, 1975.

Thiffault, M., & Lewis, J. *Western Horse and Horseman's Digest.* Northfield, IL: Digest Books, 1975.

12
Psychology

Contrary to popular belief, horses are not empowered with intellect and a great sense of reasoning; they are basically creatures of instinct. Understanding a horse's limited mental power yet respecting its amazing powers of instinctual behavior are the keys to controlling this magnificent beast. Although it is not a relevant point, the horse's brain is quite small in relation to its body mass. In general terms, the brain of a horse is only slightly larger than the brain of a common turtle. Since it is recognized that there is some correlation between size of brain and intellect, it stands to reason that the horse is not an intellectual giant. The horse has survived, however, through the years, and in many instances is quite superior to man because of instincts that have not failed him.

The horse has herd instincts as well as individual instincts and both of these can be exploited by man. Never a very aggressive animal, the horse relies on well developed flight mechanisms to preserve the species. Horses have instinctually felt safer in a herd and this instinct has been exploited in various ways, such as the sport of racing, which is a simulation of a herd fleeing from danger. Jumpers are also exploited in this way because horses prefer to remain with the herd and the jumping of fences and other barriers is more easily facilitated if the horse feels it is remaining with the herd in fox hunts, etc.

The natural instinct to remain in a herd can be subdued by training and still take advantage of those individual instincts. To produce jumpers that will perform alone in a show-jumping arena, man has learned to take advantage of the "gravitational pull" of the collecting ring. An individual horse will leave the "herd," jumping progressively more difficult barriers, until it returns over the highest or most difficult obstacles back to the collecting ring, representing the herd.

In the wild, a dominant stallion controlled and disciplined members of the herd. Their social system depended upon the acceptance of this dominance. It was not that the stallion was so bright compared to the rest of the herd, but that he exhibited strength and leadership qualities through survival instincts to best preserve the lives of all the animals in the herd. Fortunately, horses have instinctively learned to accept the dominance of man in place of the stallion. The extent of man's dominion over the horse depends upon his understanding of the psychology of the horse. If an individual is to train a horse, he must first understand the horse's basic fears handed down through generations of instinctual behavior. Then he must understand how a horse thinks, sees, hears, smells, feels, and communicates with others of his species. Great teachers are those who understand the minds of their students. Great horse trainers are those who understand the mind of the horse.

INSTINCTS   Nature has a way of protecting all her species. It is best described as "survival of the fittest." Those animals that do not adapt to changing climates, predators, and other changes simply die out because of stupidity, stubbornness, or inability to cope in some way with the changing environment. For example, animals that are too slow are often caught and killed by predators. Those that survive are possibly the more swift of the species. Since only the swift are left to mate with the swift, they produce offspring which have inherited their qualities of speed; thus contributing to improvement of the speed of the existing species and bringing about preservation and continuation of this type of animal. Although many other factors also molded the horse, the chief reason for the development of horses today has been escape from danger. Instincts that served the horse well over the past thousands of years are ingrained in the genes of equines. These instincts are not reactions of a wild, stupid beast but genetic reflections of nature's wisdom. Understanding the horse's basic fear of being caught and killed is the key to overcoming these fears and training the horse to accept dominion of man. The slow horse became a meal for a cat; so did the dumb, injured, trapped, careless. As centuries passed, the survival instincts became fixed in the genes. Run when threatened. Run when a twig snaps. Run when a movement is glimpsed in the grass. Every foal is born with these wild, blind instincts to this day and must be trained to overcome the strong desire to flee from what it perceives as danger.

The most amazing thing is the adaptability of the horse to do every-thing man asks, violating every natural instinct to do otherwise. Horses carry flapping flags and riders with flowing robes, allow bugles to be blown from their backs and firearms to be discharged, march in parades with fireworks going off overhead. They will tolerate a charge from an enraged fighting bull, jump from cliffs, enter a dark, vibrating trailer, swim rivers, jump over 6-foot barriers, and even allow a dead cougar to be strapped to their back—all contrary to their natural instincts.

There are three mental factors of the horse's mind that allow this adaptability: (1) the horse's natural timidity, (2) ability to completely disregard instincts when assured through training that it will not be harmed, and (3) willingness to accept domination.

Self-Protective Behavior

Although a horse is seldom in danger from predators today, trainers must constantly reflect back to the historical behavior of the horse in the wild to capitalize on its modern behavior. In the wild, horses had only two ways of reacting to predators: fight or flight. Since the horse's natural inclination is not to fight except when cornered, which was a rare occasion, the horse depended almost totally upon flight for self-preservation. As the horse progressed and moved out of protective cover onto the plains, it became more and more dependent upon speed to flee from predators. Confinement or restraint in any fashion to the wild horse usually meant death. For this reason, horses have a basic fear of being caught, roped, placed in a stall, haltered, and having their feet tied. They fear weight placed on their back because this represented a vulnerable spot in which cougars or other prehistoric predators could attack and be safe from the flying hooves of the horse, its chief mechanism of defense. Even after thousands of years of do-mestication, the horse still sees any method of restraint or something jumping on its back as a predator.

Horses are stimulated to buck by nerves in their back and by their vision. If a horse does buck and is obviously looking back, this is a very dangerous situation because the horse may continue to watch the rider on its back and run into something directly in front of it. This may seem peculiar until the vision range of the horse is fully under-stood (to be discussed later).

Old time horse trainers used to say that if a horse didn't buck, it would never make a good mount. This is partially true because if a horse didn't have enough intellect to try to buck a rider off its back, it probably could not survive in the wild and would be a dunce com-pared to others. This is not true today because training methods have progressed to the point where the mind of the horse is better under-stood and the emphasis is on overcoming its natural fears, accepting the dominance of man, putting trust in him, and never bucking at all in most instances.

Another form of self-protective behavior has given rise to an unusual condition in horses, the ability to founder on completely natural feed-stuffs. Lush green grass, especially those that produce seedheads such as rye grass, can produce founder in horses because of their ingestive behavior. Horses in the wild tended to eat constantly as do their descendants because of the natural instinct to keep the digestive tract full of feed in the event of a lengthy chase by predators. With modern forms of concentrated feeds, this self-protective behavior, if not controlled by denying access, may become self-destructive due to founder or colic. Beginners often feel sorry for their horses because they seem to beg constantly for feed. Understanding the horse's natural instincts will better guide the hand that feeds the horse. Horses are very much like children. There's an old saying, "Give a pig and a child everything they want and you will get a good pig and a bad child." The same is true in the case of the horse; compassion must be mixed with knowledge if true understanding is to result.

Another form of ingestive behavior in newborn foals appears harmful but is normally beneficial and a throwback to wild horse instincts. Newborn foals often nibble on the feces (manure) of other horses. On the surface, this appears both distasteful and harmful but may have good long-range benefits. Wild horses nibbled on the feces of more mature animals as nature's way of inoculating the digestive system with microorganisms that are helpful in aiding the digestion of the grasses which the newborn foal will eventually have to digest. As previously discussed in Chapter 4, the digestive system of the horse relies heavily on microorganisms in the cecum to aid in digestion, although it would appear that spread of parasites could result in this nibbling. Apparently this is not the case because parasite eggs must go through about 2 weeks of incubation in the ground before they can be infective. Foals usually will nibble on feces that are only a day or two old.

Two unusual drinking habits have evolved with the horse that are peculiar to this species. First, the horse is one of the few domestic animals that will derive its water needs directly from eating snow. Cattle and most other domestic animals will not take in water this way and many actually die of thirst after being caught in blizzards. Second, the horse can drink with the nostrils completely submerged beneath the water without drowning because water ingested in this way will go to the stomach rather than the lungs. Both of these peculiarities appear to be self-protective behavior patterns instilled in horses to survive the winter months away from open water and to be able to fill their water needs very quickly in the event predators are hanging around the water hole.

Finally, self-protective behavior in horses has led to sexual or reproductive modifications that coincide with foaling during the spring time so that newborn foals will be dropped when there is a plentiful feed supply. Researchers have discovered that mares react to lengthening periods of sunlight triggering the estrous cycle so that foaling occurs in nature's most productive period of time. By artificially lengthening light in the stalls or barns during the winter months, man has experimented with producing foals earlier and earlier during the year. Just as chickens are induced to lay eggs year-round through artificial light stimulation, it appears that horses are capable of being stimulated in the same way. Since man is able to feed these artificially induced foals at any time of the year, it will be interesting to see if further future biological changes are the result of man's interference in this area.

Forms of Communication

Horses communicate with one another and with humans in the same way. Forms of communication basically involve voice signals and body language.

First, let's consider the voice signals. A *snort* is a warning sound used in the wild to express impending danger. By rapidly expelling air through the nostrils, the snort serves as a warning to other members of the herd. A trainer hearing this sound should be patient enough to let the horse investigate the source of his fear, sniff it, and receive assurance from the trainer that it will not hurt him.

A *neigh* or *whinny* is a cry of distress from the horse. It is a loud piercing sound quite commonly heard in western movies and on television shows when a horse cries across the plains for its mates. Apparently, wild horses answered this call as a self-preservation method of returning individuals to the herd. Domesticated horses normally do not answer a whinny but the horse owner should be alert for this distress call in the event the horse is truly in need. However, it most often is a cry of loneliness, concern, fear, or anxiety.

A *nicker* is a pleasant sound often heard when owners enter the barn at feeding time. Learning to read this pleasant greeting is helpful in recognizing when a horse finds other pleasurable pursuits.

The *squeal* is a vocal expression of anger and is occasionally heard in rodeos by extremely active bucking horses. It is also heard when horses are fighting. Astute trainers keep an ear open for these kinds of sounds to ward off trouble before it progresses.

The *mating call* is given only by stallions and is extremely loud, shrill, and unforgettable. Stallions often give this call when they see a horse, think they see a horse, or think they hear one. It was a challenge of warning to other stallions among wild horses but considered purely a mating call today.

The *rolling snort* is a pleasant sound made when horses are truly enjoying themselves, for instance, when they are turned out to pasture for the first few days of a new grazing season. The sound is similar to a human blowing air through loosely closed lips.

Mare sounds are a form of communication between the mare and her newborn foal. Mare sounds are best described as soft nickers that vary in length and intensity to reassure her foal that it is safe from danger.

All these voice communications have practical significance to the trainer and handler of horses. For instance, a horse that is in danger may give a distress call and need assistance, a stallion that gives a mating call may have seen or heard strange horses nearby, a loud whinny may indicate an unnatural separation of one horse from the herd requiring assistance from man. Sounds of anger may indicate fights that need to be broken up.

There is a great deal of body language in communication between horses and other horses, and between horses and man. The ears are one of the most prominent visual signals, a mirror of the mind reflecting thoughts and attitudes. The ears of a horse are closely correlated with its vision. A horse wishes to hear everything it can see and vice versa. As will be more fully discussed later, the horse is able to focus each eye in different directions separately to watch two different events. The ears are correlated with the eyes. A horse with both ears forward is straining to see with all its might an object, real or imagined, in front of it. A horse with one ear forward and one ear back is focusing the eyes in two different directions, one forward and one backward. However, a horse with both ears layed back tight against the head is expressing anger. Race horses and cutting horses often do this to express determination. A horse expresses fear through the eyes and ears, ears standing forward and erect, eyes open wide and dilated. The head will be high and eyes will appear to be concentrating hard. On the other hand, a relaxed horse will have the ears slightly turned to the side or to the back.

By watching the ears of a horse, the trainer or handler is given some practical clues as to what to expect when approaching or handling the horse. The proper action can then be taken with fewer surprises to the handler.

The movement of the tail is also a key visual signal. A frisky horse on a cold morning often develops what horsemen refer to as a *kink* in the tail (a slight "s" shape contour unnoticeable to the amateur). This is often accompanied by a hump in the back of the horse and an uncomfortable landing for a rider that has been unexpectedly ejected from his seat. A horse with a kink in the tail should be mounted with care and caution.

A horse communicates a desire for recreation by holding the tail high. This indicates a feeling of good health and a spirit of playfulness.

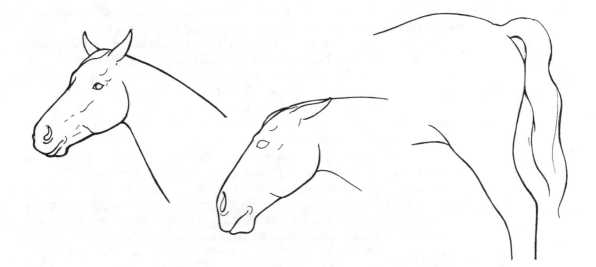

FIGURE 12-1.   Body language can be expressed through ears, tail, and other parts easily observed. (a) One ear forward and one cocked back indicates that the horse is looking forward with one eye and backward with the other. (b) Ears laid back mean anger or determination. (c) A kink in the tail can mean a rough ride on a bucking horse for the unsuspecting rider.

This kind of horse may also require a little extra exercise to drain off a bit of the excess energy before mounting. This will not be necessary on a well finished horse but green horses may need to be longed for a few minutes.

The tail can also indicate the horse's fear. When the tail is tucked tightly between the legs like a frightened dog, it is an indication either of fear or submission, such as is given after a fight with another horse.

Tail switching, a continuous movement of the tail from side to side, is an indication of aggravation or frustration from some source, perhaps spurs or a switch. The horse that's switching its tail could be telling the owner that he's using these accessory items excessively. A more extreme form of irritation is tail wringing in which the horse is communicating extreme irritation or exhaustion.

The mouth and lips give visual clues if horse trainers know how to read them. A horse will lift the upper lip to express dislike for certain feeds or medications. This can occur when feed is moldy or when medication is placed in the feed. It is also a sign given occasionally when a horse has colic. By raising the lip, the horse is expressing mild discomfort or pain in the digestive system and may be giving its owner an early warning signal. This should not be confused with the stallion's habit of raising the upper lip in order to detect the odor of a mare that is in estrus. The female apparently produces an odor that is detectable when stallions raise the upper lip in this manner.

Young horses communicate with older animals by approaching strangers with their head extended while rapidly opening and closing their mouth and lips. In some way, this indicates immaturity to older animals and signals them to be tolerant of their young intruders.

The eyes and nostrils are also forms of communication, normally expressing fear or anxiety. A frightened horse will open the eye lids wide in what has come to be known as a "wild eyed" appearance. The nostrils will also flare open widely indicating that his system is ready to inhale large quantities of air to make the body prepared for flight.

A key point in pleasant communicating, horse to horse, or man to horse, is massaging, petting, or rubbing the *withers*. Social partners that have a strong affection for one another are often seen in a herd standing with their head drooped over each other's back. With chin or teeth, the withers are gently massaged to the delight of the massagee. Taking a clue from this natural sensitivity, man can communicate his desire to become friends and reinforce approval of behavior. For instance, if a horse allows man to approach or even comes to him, it is a natural inclination of man to reward the horse by petting him on the face, lips, neck, poll or ears—all instinctively fearful areas for the horse. A human being would be apprehensive too if a horse thrust a

FIGURE 12-2.   Contrary to popular opinion, the key to effective communication with horses is not a pat on the neck or head but closer to the withers. Here two social partners from a herd massage each other's withers with jaw, lips, or teeth to communicate acceptance and favor.

front foot in his face, no matter how gently. The key then is to remember that to the mind of the horse, the most pleasant sensation of touch communication is around the withers. Leave the head alone, the horse will appreciate it. Few people realize the importance of this simple discovery but all animals have a "hot spot" to communicate approval and acceptance. In the case of the dog, it is the flank (again not the head), contrary to popular belief. With the horse, it is the *withers*. This should come as no surprise. When man wins great approval, where do people slap him, on the face or neck? No, on the back which corresponds to the horse's withers.

Sense of Hearing

In prehistoric times, the sense of hearing was very important to the horse when it lived in swampy areas because it depended upon hearing as well as seeing and smelling predators. When the horse progressed to the plains areas, the sense of hearing, no doubt, became less acute but was still needed because horses had to occasionally pass through timbered areas that could conceal predators from sight. The sense of hearing evolved many millions of years ago as a protective device for the horse and has existed for all those years in excellent condition.

Today, the sense of hearing serves the horse well because trainers can give it soft voice commands which are readily received and responded to if the proper training has reinforced the commands. Voice commands for walk, trot, lope, whoa, and start are just a few of the cues which the horse understands. Another practical use for the sense of hearing in the horse is utilized by hunting guides who have learned to rely on the more sensitive hearing of their mounts to detect game. The horse hears antelope, deer, elk, etc. in timbered areas long before man can pick up these sounds. By watching the horse's ears, which point toward the game, guides have been able to detect individuals or herds long before they could be seen.

Sense of Vision

The eyes of the horse are totally unlike ours. Humans have binocular vision, the coordination of both eyes focused on a single spot to give sight as well as depth perception. Horses use binocular vision, too, but more commonly used is monocular vision, the ability to focus one eye independently of the other. Monocular vision enables the horse to focus one eye forward and one eye backward so that it may watch in two directions simultaneously. The eyes set laterally on the sides of the head. By making a slight turn of the neck, the horse can see behind itself, commanding a full view of the surrounding terrain.

The horse can see in front, to the side, and behind all at the same time but it does have a few blind spots. Without turning the head, it is limited to a field of vision of about 300 degrees. The horse does not see directly in front, especially close to the face, and it does not see

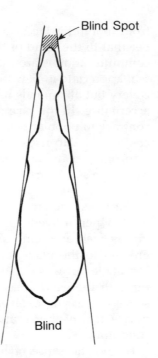

Blind Spot

Clear   Blind   Clear

FIGURE 12-3. Vision is remarkable in the horse. Except for a small area directly in front of the nose and an area directly behind, equines have a full view of surrounding terrain. A slight turn of the neck will even bring this into view because of the horse's optical equipment which allows simultaneous forward and backward vision.

directly behind, about the width of its body. Both these blind spots are problems for man and horse. For instance, imagine a situation in which a horse is being ridden through a pasture and comes upon a covey of quail, completely camouflaged to man and animal until the horse is right upon them. Then the quail fly in their characteristic manner directly under the nose of the horse appearing to explode, because of lack of depth perception. This is an understandable situation because man is often similarly deceived. However, in other situations, say, for example, when a piece of paper suddenly flies up in front of the horse, this doesn't concern the man but the horse sees it as a similar "explosion."

The blind spot behind the horse has dangerous consequences. If someone happens to walk up directly behind a horse while it is resting, sleeping, or concentrating on something else, it may appear to the horse that something has suddenly jumped out unseen upon its rear quarters. For this reason, experienced horsemen always talk to a horse when going around behind it. It is also a good idea to keep one hand on the rump even with gentle horses.

Since the horse practices mostly monocular vision, it has difficulty in seeing depth as humans do. For this reason, it often sees a shadow on the road as a deep hole, the darkness of the inside of a trailer or barn as a huge cave, or the flapping of a piece of paper on a fence several hundred feet away as being directly in front of it. Knowledge of a horse's vision should give the rider and trainer more patience and understanding with the horse when approaching these kinds of situations.

Some horses have greater ability at judging distance than others. This is perhaps because of a difference in the set of the eyes. Some jumpers that must rely on more binocular vision in order to judge heights and distances have eyes that are noticeably set further to the front. This could give a greater ability to utilize binocular vision and thus explain why some horses are better jumpers than others.

Because the retina of the horse's eye is flattened rather than curved as in humans, it frequently sees things out of focus. To bring them into focus, it must raise or lower its head. A practical application of this principle is to let the horse have its head when it is investigating an object which it obviously fears, such as a flapping piece of paper in the trail.

Horses also do not see well above eye level because of a special system within its eye which absorbs light rays. Therefore, a horse working in a stable or barn with a low ceiling may panic when something touches the top of its head because it cannot see the object. In the old days of the plantation south, this characteristic was early discovered in the tobacco barns. Horses that pulled sleds of tobacco in the curing sheds often felt something touch the poll, reared up, and injured themselves. The mule, having a more docile temperament, reacted in the opposite manner by calmly lowering its head when something touched it and soon replaced the horse.

Understanding how a horse sees and why it reacts because of what it sees is of significant practical importance to the trainer. A horse cannot be jerked, spanked, or forced into doing something that its vision indicates is dangerous until it sees the object in the proper light and proper focus, and until it has overcome its original fears by the assurance of the handler. Building a bond of confidence between the handler and the horse starts with understanding the way the horse sees things, not the way it appears to man.

Although there is some dispute over whether horses see color, there is evidence they they see some shades of color and can recognize differences in them because of experiments that have been conducted with different colored discs, which when nuzzled by the horse, produce a reward of feed.

Although this discussion may seem to indicate that the horse has poor vision, it is only poor in some circumstances. In others, it is keenly superior to man's. Perhaps the most obvious example of this is seen in circus horses that work at liberty, responding only to slight visual cues given by their trainers. Probably the most unusual example of vision was exhibited by a horse called Clever Hans, a horse owned by a German showman during the early 1900s. Clever Hans was supposed to be able to tell time, count, multiply, divide, and give all sorts of correct answers to mathematical problems by pawing out the answer with his front feet. The horse used one leg for tens and the other leg for tapping out the numbers one through nine. No visible cues could be seen from the trainer but the horse always gave the correct answer. Scientists who were determined to find out how the cues were being given studied both horse and trainer for many, many hours. The mystery was finally solved when the trainer was detected giving signals to the horse through tiny pulsations of a vein in the neck. As the trainer calculated the answer, he cued the horse as to the proper response by tiny vein pulsations which were clearly visible and understandable to the horse.

In a few ways, the horse's eyesight is inferior to man's, namely in depth perception and focusing ability. In many other instances, it is far superior to man. A horse can see the flicker of a leaf long before the leaf itself is visible to man. And because of a structure in the eye—the tapetum lucidum—which glows in the dark, horses have night vision that cannot be humanly matched. Many hunters have been spirited safely down treacherous mountain trails in total darkness by trusting the eyesight and "horse sense" of their mounts. By "giving the horse its head," and hanging on to the saddle horn, riders speak with awe about the ability of equines to sense their way through inky blackness. What most do not know is that this sensory ability is attributable more to the soft glow of the tapetum lucidum than anything else. Knowledge of this structure can lessen fears and build confidence in riders faced with similar situations.

Sense of Smell

Modern horses use the sense of smell mostly as a form of identification for other horses as well as humans. They apparently have a very acute memory for odors and can detect old equine friends from odor, as well as human friends. There is some evidence that indicate that horses can detect fear in humans due to a change in hormonal output, sweat glands, etc. This could explain why some horses are harder to manage by inexperienced or frightened riders.

Stallions use the sense of smell to detect mares that are in heat, often many hundreds of yards away. A practical application for the sense of smell is to let a horse sniff an object that has frightened it by sight alone. Allowing the horse to investigate with both the eyes and the nose may, and usually does, calm the fears of the horse.

Sense of Touch   One of the areas of the horse which is very sensitive to touch is the frog. By feeling with the frog of the foot, horses have been known to detect tremors, shifting in the earth, softness of the ground, changes in terrain, and other conditions which could affect the safety of both horse and rider. The frog is an organ of the horse that feels by touching the ground.

The sense of touch also plays an important part in training horses. Horses are particularly sensitive to being touched about the head, especially the eyes and ears. Abused horses often refuse to let man touch their ears. In this case, it may be necessary to use a bridle with a buckle so that this area can be avoided. Great care must be taken to convince the green horse that the trainer will not injure the horse by handling these vulnerable areas.

We touch the horse in many ways during training, through the mouth, nose, poll, neck, ribs, and withers (previously discussed under communication in this chapter). The two areas used most to control a horse, the mouth and ribs, lack the nerve endings that other parts of the horse have. This means that the initial response comes from pain rather than light pressure. If patience and understanding is not shown the horse during the early training methods and an impatient handler forces a horse to respond through inducing pain at these areas, the result is often a hard mouth and dead ribs.

Just as the withers are a key positive point of communication, the flank is a negative area. The horse is very sensitive about this spot because it is the most vulnerable, having no skeletal protection against attack. The flanks should be touched very gently and then only when necessary.

A light touch is important in cueing the horse to respond to lightness, previously discussed in the breaking and training chapter.

We touch the horse with our hands through the reins to the mouth, nose, and poll, depending on the type of headgear being used. We touch the horse in the ribs through leg pressure or spurs to give further cues. We touch the horse on the withers through the shifts in weight. Proper development of these cues can result in a response to sense of touch so sensitive that it is almost impossible to detect a rider giving cues to the horse. This is the great practical application of the sense of touch.

Sleeping and Resting   The horse has a very unusual skeletal system that allows it to lock the legs and sleep in a standing position. The healthy horse almost never lies down for any length of time. Although foals may be seen sunning themselves broadside during early spring and warm summer days, mature horses sleep and rest in a standing position. Most often the horse is on three legs during rest or sleep position. Unless there is an injury to the front feet, the three legs always involve two front legs and one rear leg in the locked position. One hind leg cocked up is a typical resting or sleeping position for the horse. In addition, the horse will usually allow the neck, head, ears, and eyes to droop. The eyes do not have to close for the horse to sleep soundly. The practical application of this observation is to never approach a horse with any sudden movements because although it may appear to be awake, it could be sound asleep and this sudden encroachment on its territory could result in injury to horse or man or both.

MEMORY

Although the horse is not a mental giant by comparison to other domestic animals, it does have one of the most remarkable memories in all the animal kingdom. Once a horse is trained, it never forgets the basic lessons learned. There are numerous examples of old circus or trick horses that have been put out to pasture and retired for 10 or 15 years or more. The horses can be caught and immediately returned to their old routines with a minimum of encouragement.

Unfortunately, the horse not only remembers good training but never forgets bad experiences either. This is why it is so important to halter break a horse, for instance, without ever letting it break away. Once this happens, the horse never forgets that it was successful in resisting man's attempt to control it and may become incurable. If a young horse should become entangled in a rope and is allowed to fight and kick until it releases itself, it will remember this experience the rest of its life and will continue to react in a similar way under similar circumstances unless retrained.

One system of utilizing this instinctive memory is halter breaking foals when they are only a few days old. It only takes a few minutes but trainers claim that the horse is thus "imprinted" with the knowledge of man's control over it and never forgets this lesson, which is merely reinforced at later halter breaking sessions.

The elephant is considered to have one of the most remarkable memories but horses are a close parallel according to animal behavior specialists. One dramatic example involving the memory of elephants might reinforce the importance of the same practical application of memory to horses. Baby elephants are trained to remain tied to a stake by an iron clamp around one leg. The clamp has sharp teeth and when the baby elephants try to break free, the iron chain and stake hold it fast by producing pain in the leg. The elephant remembers this lesson the rest of its life and soon may be held to a simple wooden stake driven in the ground attached to a small string tied to the leg. Many elephants were thus staked out by a circus in Florida. A fire broke out which consumed the building in which the elephants were housed. Forty per cent of the herd of elephants died in the fire because they refused to break the tiny string fastening their leg to the stake. The other sixty per cent that escaped had to be destroyed because they could never again be contained by any method, so great was their strength, so profound was their memory of their circumstance. Horses, like elephants, may never respond once the bonds of memory are shattered by experiences which allow the horse to remember that it has superior strength over its handler.

OVERCOM-ING FEARS

The horse has developed over many thousands of years because of instincts that have served it well in preserving the species. Most of these instincts involve suspicion, fear, or caution. Overcoming these fears is the role of the trainer in breaking, gentling, and finishing horses for their required chores.

Flight Reactions

Because of the countless prehistoric experiences of being hunted by predators such as mountain lions, the horse's natural reaction to any kind of sudden movement is to run. This is an instinctual reaction to anything the horse sees, hears, smells, or feels that pertains to possible danger. These flight reactions must be controlled by assuring the horse through training and communication that its fears are unfounded and nothing will happen that will threaten its existence. All horses are capable of running and spooking. They even sleep standing with their eyes open which makes for a decided advantage for a quick escape. This is why we fold lead ropes in our hands rather than wrapping them around the hand to invite being dragged accidently. A good horseman always ties a horse high and short to prevent a sudden bolting reaction resulting in a leg becoming entangled in a low dangling rope. Because of the great memory of the horse, previously discussed, it is also important to use unbreakable equipment, especially in the early training period, to enforce the idea that the horse cannot escape man's domination no matter how hard it tries. Understanding the horse's natural flight reaction instincts may perhaps enable a trainer to develop more patience with the green horse.

Habituation

Horses, like humans, are creatures of habit. To change these habits to a more manageable pattern, it is necessary to train, or retrain, a horse using the process of habituation. By repeatedly subjecting a horse to a potentially frightening situtaion, it eventually develops the habit of disregarding an event that does not bring it pain or discomfort. For example, parade horses have a fear of a flapping flag in the initial exposure to such an experience. With patience, the trainer gradually changes the habitual pattern of the horse so that it completely ignores the flapping. Another example is the process of "sacking out" a young horse. The green horse is terrified by this flapping object that is touching its body and making such horrible, unnatural sounds and movements. The horse soon learns, however, that this new experience is not going to harm him and if halter, ropes, and other restraining devices function well, the horse understands that it cannot get away from this aggravation. The habit of being frightened suddenly is changed to one of complete acceptance and the horse is said to be "broke to the sack" through habituation. Later, even though the horse's original instincts were to become frightened and run away from the sack, it ignores even more frightening experiences such as large pieces of paper blowing between its legs, or even large cardboard boxes.

This process works well if no actual pain is inflicted on the horse. However, it works in reverse if a fencepost should break, the horse should get entangled in a rope, the halter breaks, or any kind of painful stimuli occur during the sacking process. This merely reinforces the horse's original instinctual fears and causes it to react in a similar manner again. The fear becomes justified in its mind and it may react this way for the rest of its life unless it is retrained through positive rather than negative habituation.

The ideal habituation process is to instill in the horse the idea that it can be touched by a human on any part of its body including the eyes, ears, nose, feet, genitalia, flanks, or other vulnerable spots without the least bit of fear that it will be harmed. The horse must also be made to understand that it does not have the right to touch a human in any fashion. It must not bite, kick, or nudge without receiving immediate unpleasant feedback as a result. Thus, the ideal horse must be trained through habituation to be touched but not to touch. The result is a gentle, trustworthy, well-trained dependable mount.

Comforting Sound Stimuli

Horses and humans are capable of communication, one with the other through a simple system of comforting sounds. The sounds the horse makes have already been discussed. The sounds the human makes are equally important and comforting. Most all sounds should be of a rhythmical nature. Many horsemen have used rhythmical stimuli for years in working with animals but may not have consciously been aware of what they were doing. The jingling of a halter before applying it is one such stimulus, light quivering on the reins while rhythmically saying "whoa boy, whoa boy, whoa boy," over and over is another example. Old time trail drivers used to sing and whistle to the cattle, a system that works equally well on horses. Some veterinarians are especially adept with the use of rhythmical sound stimuli, using clucking and hissing sounds to a rhythmical cadence that corresponds to actions of the fingers. For instance, in tubing a horse for worms, the veterinarian can make a rhythmical squeezing of the thumb and forefingers on the nose of the horse while simultaneously coordinating the rhythm with a hissing sound. By gradually working the fingers around to the nose, most horses, if they are not spoiled, will appear to hypnotically accept these comforting sound and touch stimuli, and then the fingers in the nose can be replaced with a tube, so long as the horse is not injured in this process or feels any pain. If it does react by throwing up its head and pulling away, a lip chain can be used which the horse soon learns is pain inducing and much less pleasant than the fingers or tube in the nose. By gradually conditioning with the nose chain and working back to the fingers and hissing sound, the horse can be habituated and comforted with sounds that it associates with nonpainful experiences.

It is customary among groomsmen to talk softly to horses while currying them. It is a common sound to hear the rhythmical chant of "easy, easy, easy" among those who are gifted at calming horses through the artful use of sound stimuli.

Understanding the Horse's Mind

One of the basic psychological principles in handling horses is to be aware that the horse reasons between choices just as we do. It may want to flee from an aggravating situation but it will invariably choose the "lesser of two evils" when subjected to a choice between a painful experience and a frightening but nonpainful experience.

For example, most horses initially refuse to cross a stream or go into water while being ridden. Spurs and a quirt can be skillfully applied at this point and the horse soon discovers that in order to escape a painful stimuli, it can go into the water to avoid this experience. However, some unskillful riders will continue to use the whip and spurs even though the horse has done what it was supposed to do. This can be totally confusing to the horse because no matter what it does, it cannot escape the painful stimuli. If the spurs and whip are stopped as soon as the horse enters the water, it learns that in order to escape the stimuli, it simply goes into the water. Repeated exposures to this experience reinforce the exact course of action in the horse's mind. The same holds true for loading in a trailer, going into a darkened barn, etc.

One of the most irritating experiences working with horses is encountering a horse that will not let the potential rider catch it, even in a small enclosure. Some horses develop a habit of turning the rear end to the human and soon learn that human contact is avoided as long as possible when this position is maintained. One way to correct this is to use a long buggy whip, enclose the horse in a safe, escape-proof enclosure so that no pain will be inflicted other than that given by the human, and every time it turns the rear end the wrong way, the back of the legs are stung by flicks of the whip. Sooner or later, the horse understands that this is a painful position and will turn toward the human. When this happens, the trainer uses a pleasant sound stimulus of clucking, talking, hissing, or whistling, slowly approaches and rewards the horse by petting the withers. The horse soon learns the lesson that it must always face a human, or some painful experience may result. A properly trained horse can be caught even in a pasture once it is trained in this manner.

DOMINANCE   Many people do not understand that the chief motivational factor behind discipline in a horse is dominance. In the wild, a dominant stallion takes charge and the more submissive followers gladly do his bidding. Even among the mares, younger stallions, or geldings, there is a pecking order of dominance. This makes for a regimented social order based on the need for a horse to be dominated in order to be controlled.

Except for the unusual outlaw, a super dominant individual, horses want to be dominated. When horsemen speak of kind horses, willing horses, honest horses, they are referring to horses that are submissive to man's dominance. A submissive trainer becomes dominated by the horse and training is soon in jeopardy. Through habituation, such a horse discovers that it can do whatever it wants to and if the trainer tries to force it to do otherwise, the horse becomes difficult to manage. However, once the horse becomes thoroughly convinced that man is the substitute domination represented by the wild stallion, the vast majority of horses fall into the submissive instinctual pattern of accepting this guidance and leadership without question.

Gaining Command   Among wild horses, the stallion or the dominant mare whipped the herd into shape through brute strength, aggressive communication by squeals, with ears layed back, eyes dilated, and through biting and kicking. Although this may seem like rough treatment, man must not imitate the horse's aggressiveness with cruelty or unnecessary physical abuse. We can, however, communicate our dominance to the horse in such a way as to gain complete command.

Old-time horsemen knew horse psychology well and used it effectively. One method the old timers used to gain command quickly was to rope a horse, catch its feet, and throw it to the ground with the feet remaining tied so that it was in a completely helpless position. With all four feet tied, the wild horse was in the most terrifying of positions because this meant complete helplessness and death according to its instincts. The horsemen then proceeded to crawl over the horse rubbing, patting, sacking it out until there was absolutely no fear left in the horse. Psychologically this conveyed to the horse that man had complete mastery over it and had gained complete command. Since nothing terrible happened at this point, the horse learned a lesson that it never forgot—man is dominant and no matter how terrifying the experience, it will not be hurt if it follows orders.

Other methods of gaining command of the horse involve such simple aides as a halter and lead chain, hobbles, and a longe line and cavesson. All these methods deprive a horse of its ability to flee, establishing the dominance of man and gaining command through habituation.

Taming the Outlaw

A spoiled horse or one that has gone bad, turned outlaw, is no job for an amateur, but the psychology of eventual submission is interesting to study. The techniques may also work on less difficult cases and give trainers some additional insight into the mind of the horse.

One method used quite frequently by trainers and veterinarians is to immobilize a horse through the use of a one-leg hobble. This consists of a leather strap (soft cotton rope, leather belt, or English stirrup leather may be substituted) to pull one leg up and immobilize it so that the knee cannot be straightened out.

An unruly horse can be haltered with a lead rope, have a one-leg hobble applied, then simply turn the horse loose inside a corral. It will probably hop away and fight furiously for a few minutes. Shortly thereafter, fatigue sets in and the horse starts to shake and sweat. The trainer quietly approaches the horse, catches the lead rope, and releases the one-leg hobble. After a few minutes rest, the hobble is applied again if the horse is still unruly and the process continued until the horse shows signs of submission. A most common body language sign of submission is for the horse to lower its head against the chest of the man and stand dejectedly. To the mind of the horse, man has some tremendous power over him that he cannot understand. Psychologically, this renders him helpless to do man's bidding.

John Rarey, from Ohio, who lived from 1827 to 1866, is credited with developing the one-leg hobble which has also since been known as Rarey's strap. Rarey also apparently had other powers with horses that some have claimed approached hypnotic but the Rarey strap, which was his belt in the beginning, was a key element in the power he held over unruly horses. Working with wild horses on Texas ranges, he gained a notable reputation in the late 1800s and his fame even spread to Europe. He became so well known that he was asked for a command performance by the Queen of England. One of his most startling examples involved a Thoroughbred English horse named Cruiser. The horse had turned outlaw and kicked two grooms to death. Although Cruiser was valued as a breeding animal, he could not be handled by

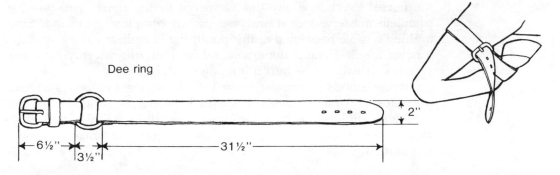

Dee ring

6½" 3½" 31½" 2"

FIGURE 12-4. The one-leg hobble or Rarey strap is used to go around the pastern and forearm bringing about almost complete immobilization and a magical power of man's domination in the mind of the horse.

man in any manner. On a bet of approximately $500, John Rarey accepted the owner's challenge to tame him, entered the stall where Cruiser was contained, in some manner gained the confidence of the horse to apply his strap, and within three hours was riding the outlaw stallion and handling him in a routine manner. The outlaw was tamed through this strange psychological power and later other people were also able to handle the stallion without problems.

John Rarey became famous throughout the United States and Europe for his unusual abilities in taming outlaws. Some writers speculate that he also had the rare gift of communicating with animals in such a way as to hypnotize them. Hypnotism in animals may sound far fetched but most people who have worked with animals for any length of time have seen it demonstrated very easily in chickens. A chicken can be layed on its back and stroked comfortingly for a few moments and then quietly left alone and it appears to lay motionless as if hypnotized for some period of time. Through the use of the Rarey strap, petting, softly comforting, John Rarey apparently developed a technique that did the same thing with horses. Although Rarey probably didn't understand the psychological implications of what he was doing, he did stumble upon a technique that worked exceedingly well. It is interesting to note that the key to his success was to never raise his voice in anger, and to never use force on a horse other than to immobilize the one leg. The horse expended all energy fighting itself and the only reassuring sounds it heard came from the man who apparently could cause these magical powers to be enforced but did it in a nonthreatening way.

An even more unexplainable case history is that of Jack Healy, 1870–1932, from Helena, Montana. Healy specialized in driving horses without lines, even wild range horses that had never been hooked to a hitch. His method, according to eye witness accounts, merely consisted of talking to horses and looking them in the eye. He became well known in this country and performed exhibition shows in many parts of the United States. One of his favorite tricks was to approach a team of horses, unknown to him, being driven by another man, and by merely looking them in the eye caused them to be completely immobilized. No matter what the owner did, the horses would not move until Healy released them from his power. Although he never divulged his secrets, psychologists explain that the most likely possibility was a strange gift that a few horsemen possess, to be able to communicate with animals in such a way as to create a hypnotic state. This is not apparently something that can be learned, it is a gift. Perhaps this dramatic example can serve as partial explanation for why some trainers are able to produce magical results with horses, even outlaws, where others have failed.

Self-Punishment Philosophy

To be properly trained, a horse must receive reward or punishment immediately upon doing the right or wrong thing. If the horse does what the rider wants it to do, the praise and petting should commence immediately. Everyone has seen how well this works with dogs and the results are often dramatically given with wags of the tail and an obviously happy expression. Although the horse does not show these outward signs of affection, it must feel the same way when it does something right.

When the horse does something wrong, the punishment must come immediately also. It does no good to wait until the horse has returned to the barn to "teach it a lesson." By then, there is no association whatsoever with having done something wrong and being punished for it. The horse must be made to think that the wrong action creates a self-inflicted pain. Self-punishment is the strongest deterrent to inappropriate behavior. A few examples will better illustrate the philosophy and wisdom of this immediate retaliation.

Occasionally, a colt will turn the hind end toward approaching people and kick or threaten to kick. By using a buggy whip to sting the hind end immediately upon this type of behavior, without saying a word, the colt soon gets the message that every time it turns the hind end toward a person, it stings itself. It is important for the trainer to remain calm, as motionless as possible and utter no sound whatsoever so as to create a stronger association that the horse is creating its own punishment. The colt will soon get the idea and give up the bad habit to form a good one. Every time it is approached by a human, it turns the head toward that human and, just as the horse thought, the stinging of the rear end stops and the association with humans becomes much more pleasant.

Horses, young and old, occasionally develop bad tempers and will try to bite or nip people. When this is done, an immediate thumping or stinging of the nose, again accompanied by no sound, creates an impression in the horse's mind that every time it tries to bite a human, its nose gets stung. Since there are no war cries or sounds of attack coming from the human, the horse thinks it must be self-inflicting this punishment. A few lessons are all that are needed.

A final example involves the irritating habit of cow kicking—a horse reaching out with a hind foot and kicking to the side when a rider stands in the mounting position or thereabouts. By haltering a horse and standing in the usual place, the horse is actually encouraged to kick. However, by standing a little further to the front out of reach of the kick the trainer delivers a swift kick of his own with the side of the foot (never the toe) to the flank of the horse. This is a vulnerable communication spot previously discussed, to which the horse feels very insecure. Again, with the trainer remaining silent and calm, the horse is kicked in the flank mildly every time it offers to cow kick. The association soon becomes one of "every time I try to cow kick a human, I miss and kick myself."

Training horses is a bit like working with children. If the trainer can learn how a horse thinks and can communicate with it on a level that it understands, the result is a well-disciplined, well-mannered, gentle, honest, willing horse. Horses require discipline, respond to love and understanding, and will give every ounce of energy in their possession when properly motivated and skillfully trained. This training and motivation comes through the art of understanding the horse psychologically to gain its confidence.

The horse is one of the few animals in the world that will literally work or run itself to death for its owner. Many instances in history record the gallant deeds of horses who carried their riders on missions of mercy or daring to give the supreme sacrifice by dropping dead in their tracks while still striving to please their master. No animal in the history of mankind can match their achievements in this respect. Perhaps that is why the horse has been so revered and so honored around the world with statues of gallant humans mounted astride gallant horses. When the horse fails man, it is usually man's fault.

BIBLIOGRA- PHY

Miller, R. M. "Horse Psychology," *The Western Horseman*, Jan., Feb., & March 1970 issues.

Miller, R. W. *Western Horse Behavior and Training*. Garden City, NY: Doubleday, 1975.

Williamson, M. *Applied Horse Psychology*. Houston, TX: Cordovan Corp., 1977.

Appendix

Breed Associations and Other Information Sources

1. International American **Albino** (American Creme and American White Horse) Association
   Rt. 1, Box 20
   Naper, NE 68755-2020

2. The **American Horse** Council
   1700 K Street, NW
   Washington, DC 20006
   202 / 296-4031

3. **American Indian** Horse Registry, Inc.
   Rt. 3, Box 64
   Lockhart, TX 78644-9713
   512 / 398-6642

4. **American Walking** Pony Association
   P.O. Box 5282
   Macon, GA 31208
   912 / 743-2321

5. International **Andalusian** and Lusitano Horse Association
   4089 Ironworks Pike
   Lexington, KY 40511

6. **Appaloosa** Horse Club, Inc.
   5070 Hwy 8 West
   P.O. Box 8403
   Moscow, ID 83843
   208 / 882-5578

7. **Arabian** Horse Registration Association
   12000 Zuni Street
   Westminster, CO 80234-2300
   303 / 450-4748

8. American **Bashir** Curly Registry
   P.O. Box 246
   Ely, NV 89301-0246

9. American **Buckskin** Registry Association, Inc.
   P.O. Box 3850
   Redding, CA 96049-3850

10. **Colorado Ranger** Horse Association
    c/o Laurel Kosior
    RD #1, Box 1290
    Wampum, PA 16157
    412 / 535-4841

11. American **Connemara** Pony Society
    Rt. 2, P.O. Box 577
    Winchester, VA 22601

12. National **Cutting Horse** Association
    4704 Hwy 377 South
    Fort Worth, TX 76116
    817 / 244-6188

13. American **Donkey** and Mule Society, Miniature Donkey
    Registry of the United States
    2901 N. Elm
    Denton, TX 76201
    817 / 382-6845

14. **Galiceno** Horse Breeders Association
    Box 219
    Godley, TX 76044-0219

15. **Gotland** Horse Registry USA
    2633 E. La Palma Avenue, #120
    Anaheim, CA 92806-2353

16. **Jockey** Club, The Executive Offices
40 E. 52nd Street
New York, NY 10022-5911
212 / 371-5970
Fax 212 / 371-6123

17. **Kentucky** Horse Park
4089 Ironworks Pike
Lexington, KY 40511
606 / 233-4303 (general information)
606 / 259-4231 (museum)

18. United States **Lipizzan** Registry
13351 Chula Road
Amelia, VA 23002

19. American **Miniature** Horse Association, Inc.
5601 South IH 35W
Alvarado, TX 76009
817 / 783-5600
Fax 817 / 783-6403

20. **Missouri** Foxtrotting Horse Breed Association, Inc.
P.O. Box 1027
Ava, MO 65608-1027
417 / 683-2468
Fax 416 / 683-6144

21. International **Morab** Breeders Associations
S101 W34628 Hwy. 99
Eagle, WI 53119
414 / 594-3667

22. American **Morgan** Horse Association
P.O. Box 960
Shelburne, VT 05482-0960
802 / 985-4944

23. Southwest Spanish **Mustang** Association, Inc.
P.O. Box 48
Finley, OK 74543

23. **Norwegian Fjord** Association of North America
24570 W. Chardon Road
Grayslake, IL 60030
708 / 546-7881

25. American **Paint** Horse Association
P.O. Box 961023
Fort Worth, TX 76161-0023
817 / 439-3400

26. **Palomino** Horse Association, Inc., The
15253 E. Skelly Drive
Tulsa, OK 74116-2637
918 / 438-1234
Fax 918 / 438-1232

27. American **Part-Blooded** Horse Registry
4120 S.E. River Drive
Portland, OR 97267-6899

28. **Paso Fino** Horse Association, The
101 North Collins Street
Plant City, FL 33566-3311
813 / 719-7777

29. **Percheron** Horse Association of America
P.O. Box 141
Fredericktown, OH 43019
614 / 694-3602

30. American Association of Owners and Breeders of
Peruvian Paso Horses
P.O. Box 30723
Oakland, CA 94604
510 / 895-2720

31. **Pinto** Horse Association of America, Inc.
1900 Samuels Ave.
Fort Worth, TX 76107-1141
817 / 336-7842

32. **Pony of the Americas** Club, Inc.
5240 Elmwood Avenue
Indianapolis, IN 46203-5990
317 / 788-0107

33. American **Quarter Horse** Association
1600 Quarter Horse Drive
Amarillo, TX 79104
806 / 376-4888

34. **Racking Horse** Breeders Association of America
Rt. 2, Box 72-A

Decatur, AL 35603
205 / 353-7225

35. American **Saddlebred** Horse Association
4093 Ironworks Pike
Lexington, KY 40511-8434
606 / 259-2742
Fax 606 / 259-1628

36. Half **Saddlebred** Registry of America, The
319 South Sixth Street
Coshocton, OH 43812-2119
614 / 622-1012
Fax 614 / 622-8305

37. American **Shetland** Pony Club
6748 N. Froshwook Parkway
Peoria, IL 61615-2402

38. **Spanish-Barb** Breeders Association
188 Springridge Road
Terry, MS 39170
601 / 372-8801

39. **Standardbred**
The United States Trotting Association
750 Michigan Avenue
Columbus, OH 43215-1191
614 / 224-2291

40. American **Suffolk** Horse Association
4240 Goehring Road
Ledbetter, TX 78946-9707
409 / 249-5795

41. American **Tarpan** Stud Book Association
1658 Coleman Avenue
Macon, GA 31201-6602
912 / 741-2062

42. American **Trakehner** Association
1520 West Church Street
Newark, OH 43055
614 / 344-1111

43. **Welsh** Pony and Cob Society of America
P.O. Box 2977
Winchester, VA 22604
540 / 667-6195

Index